Not Your Mother's®

MAKE-AHEAD AND FREEZE

Cookbook

REVISED AND EXPANDED EDITION

Jessica Fisher

Contents

Introduction ■ 4

THIS IS *NOT* YOUR MOTHER'S MAKE-AHEAD AND FREEZE COOKBOOK ■ 4

QUICK-START GUIDE ■ 7

THE BASICS OF FREEZER COOKING ■ 8

COOKING PLANS TO FIT YOUR NEEDS ■ 25

CREATING YOUR OWN COOKING PLAN ■ 65

1
WHERE'S THE BEEF?
72

2
WINNING CHICKEN DINNERS
110

3
THE CATCH OF THE DAY
150

4
SIZZLING PORK AND SAUSAGE
160

5
MEATLESS MARVELS
188

6

SOUP'S ON

———

220

7

PERFECT PIZZAS

———

248

8

BREAKFASTS FOR CHAMPIONS

———

266

9

BREADS, MUFFINS, SCONES, ROLLS, AND THEN SOME

———

298

10

DESSERTS WHEN YOU CRAVE THEM

———

336

Acknowledgments ▪ 369

About the Author ▪ 370

Index ▪ 371

Introduction

This is *Not* Your Mother's Make-Ahead and Freeze Cookbook

Dinnertime. The word can evoke memories of lively voices, cozy suppers, and candlelight; images of forks chasing the last morsels of this or that on the plate; flavors blending in a happy symphony; satisfied hearts and tummies. Contentment.

But the notion of dinnertime can also bring to mind that frantic feeling when you come home tired, the dog is barking, the phone is ringing, and the entire household is clamoring, "What's for dinner?"

They don't call it the witching hour for nothing.

You grope for an answer. Fast food? TV dinners? Canned soup? These are all quick fixes, but at what cost? All have excess sodium and additives, dubiously sourced ingredients, and questionable taste. What can you do to make mealtimes more enjoyable without resorting to less-than-best menu options? How can you make contentment, not stress, the norm at dinnertime?

Turn to your freezer—what Alton Brown calls "the most potent food-preservation device ever devised." That precious appliance can save your bacon when it comes to putting healthy, wholesome meals on the table in record time.

I've been preparing make-ahead and freeze meals for over 20 years now, since I was a young high-school teacher with no one to feed but my husband and myself. Today I cook for a small army of eight: me, my husband, and our six children, of every age and size. While I have my fair share of "Calgon, take me away" moments, mealtimes are usually pleasurable at our house. I have my freezer to thank for that.

Good eating has always been part of our family culture, from enjoying upscale Santa Barbara restaurants during our dating years to laughing as our first-born, at 10 months, devoured peach salsa from a spoon to grilling pizzas today on the backyard barbecue for a pack of famished children. For us, mealtimes are an event.

And while I love to cook, as a work-at-home mom, I also like to enjoy time with my family. Or by myself! Making many meals ahead of time allows me to have the best of all worlds, including some time to put my feet up. I regularly spend focused time in the kitchen, cooking up a storm and stashing the results away in the freezer for later use. The outcome? Perfect homemade convenience foods that serve us well, without undue stress.

In as little as an hour a week, you, too, can stock your freezer with make-ahead meals and meal components that are tasty, filling, healthy, and budget-friendly.

But don't worry: These are not your mother's —or your grandmother's—frozen casseroles. Drawing on modern technology and a global food market full of diverse ingredients, the recipes that follow feature a wide variety of flavor profiles and cooking methods. They appeal to modern taste buds, and they can all be prepared in bulk to help you save time in the kitchen. These meals will put the lively conversation and cozy suppers back into your dinnertimes.

THE CASE FOR MAKE-AHEAD AND FREEZE MEALS

Home cooks lead busy lives. Students, single parents, stay-at-home moms, work-at-home parents, working professionals, retired folks— all are looking for delicious meals that are easy and affordable. They crave tasty meals, but due to lack of planning, lack of knowledge, or simply a lack of cooking mojo, they settle for less than the best. Deep down, lots of folks feel there must be a better and easier way to eat well. Many of our mothers practiced cook-and-freeze methods. Whether they engaged in a once-a-month marathon kitchen session or

spent a harvest season preserving the surplus vegetables and fruits on hand, the cooks who came before us were known to stash meals and meal components away in the deep freeze.

Unfortunately, many of those dishes were forgotten in deep storage and developed a serious case of frostbite. Or, worse, they weren't all that tasty to begin with. If you remember the heavy, starch-laden casseroles of yesteryear, you might think you want to pass on homemade frozen entrées.

But times, technology, and tastes have all changed. And a freezer packed with ready-to-go breakfasts, lunches, and dinners can be a boon to any home cook. Taking a different approach to food preparation and storage could change your kitchen, your mealtimes, and your life.

Many of today's home cooks either are intimidated by the prospect of cooking many meals at once or simply don't know where to start in freezing foods for later enjoyment. Some have never even heard of "freezer cooking." Others may enjoy cooking but lack the time and energy to spend hours in the kitchen, especially after a full day of work.

But freezer cooking can provide a handy solution to dinner dilemmas. Imagine enjoying inexpensive, healthy, tasty meals any night of the week. Picture your freezer stocked with several weeks' worth of easy, versatile dinners that please any palate, young or old. Consider preparing a multitude of meals in just a few hours without breaking a sweat. Or the bank.

I started my cook-and-freeze adventure the traditional way, spending 8 to 24 hours shopping, chopping, and hopping about my kitchen, trying to get 30 meals ready to freeze at once. Twenty-one years ago, I was in the final stages

of pregnancy, awaiting my first child and preparing to quit my job as a high-school teacher. My friend Jessika and I had read *Once a Month Cooking*, the grandmother of all freezer cookbooks, and we decided to give it a go. My pregnant, swollen feet weren't too sure about the project, but it all seemed worth it when I ended up with 40 meals stashed in the freezer for the coming month and beyond.

The practice has proved to be a winner time and again.

Over the years, as my family has grown from one little baby to six active children, I have needed the convenience of premade meals all the more. But, I'm not as spry as I once was. I've been pressed to find the time and energy it takes to cook massive amounts of food in just a day or two. I've needed to

find ways to fill my freezer without spending an inordinate amount of time doing it. Typical shortcuts like canned soups and sauces can't compete with my desire to feed my family less-processed, healthier foods. I want it all.

I've sought simpler ways to fill the freezer, like doing triple-batch cooking to make three lasagnas instead of one on a weeknight and mini cooking sessions wherein I create a range of meals built around one main ingredient. I've challenged myself to find the most efficient methods for cooking ahead of time.

After years of freezer cooking the traditional way, I've realized that it can be more streamlined, that I can have home-cooked meals ready and waiting, and that I don't have to spend days in the effort to pull it off—unless I want to. Instead, I have found ways to condense my cooking tasks and develop bulk cooking plans that I can pull off in about five hours, sometimes an afternoon when I putter in the kitchen, sipping wine and watching BBC miniseries with my daughters.

We live in an age of instant gratification. While hard work is still important, ours is a fast-paced society. But good home cooking still has a place in it. Through careful planning and making use of modern technologies, I'm now able to prepare 20 to 30 breakfasts, lunches, or dinners in a matter of hours.

Donna Reed, it's time to meet Jane Jetson. While we may not have home vending machines producing food to order the way the Jetsons did, we can have tasty, healthy meals at the ready without an inordinate amount of work.

Efficient freezer cooking is the wave of the future—and it's definitely not your mother's frozen dinner.

Quick-Start Guide

INSTRUCTIONS FOR BIG-BATCH COOKING

Every four to six weeks, I take time out of my schedule to prepare several meals for the freezer. It's a little gift to myself, to make dinnertime easier in the weeks ahead. I might spend an hour or two cooking on a lazy afternoon, or I might wake up with the sun on a weekend day and cook all morning. It really depends on what our household needs at any given moment and what I feel like doing that day.

The one constant is the time that it saves me throughout the month as I go to the freezer for a pan of enchiladas or pop some homemade scones into the oven in a matter of seconds. My family avoids the drive-through, and we eat exceptionally well with minimal last-minute work.

On a recent Saturday afternoon, I was sorely tempted to "run for the border"—or at least the closest taco stand. After thinking through my options, I headed for my kitchen instead. I pulled a container of taco meat and a pan of enchiladas from the freezer. While those reheated in the microwave, I chopped lettuce, shredded cheese, and laid out tubs of sour cream and salsa. Within five minutes, I had assembled a complete taco bar and fed my family a feast that certainly beat anything the local taco joint had to offer. And it was thanks to make-ahead meals in my freezer.

Some folks might thumb their noses at cook-and-freeze meals. Perhaps they've had bad experiences; maybe they're haunted by a memory or two of Mom's Mystery Meat Casserole. However, those are relics of the past! I am a self-proclaimed food snob, yet after finding and developing recipes that really work for my family, I've found bulk cooking to be a happy compromise between a busy life, a tight budget, and a desire for good, home-cooked food.

Perhaps you've heard or read about this freezer-cooking thing. That it's a bit overwhelming, and you just don't have the time to figure it all out. It sounds complicated; it involves lots of charts; it takes too much time. Or maybe you're just so eager to get started that you don't want to spend time reading.

It's easier than you think! Big-batch cooking is as simple as preparing a double batch of tonight's dinner and freezing half for another night. It only takes a few minutes longer to make that second helping, but the rewards are huge: There's no extra cleanup or prep work when you serve that meal in a few weeks' time!

If you want to put away 8 to 12 meals at one time, here's a quick-start guide to cooking, freezing, and enjoying homemade meals in the weeks ahead.

1. Copy or print out a Freezer Cooking Master Plan (page 69).

2. Choose one protein, such as chicken, to cook for this round. Write that in the first square under "Main Ingredient/Protein." (Next time, you can make different kinds of dishes, but we're doing baby steps here.)

3. List your four favorite chicken recipes in the next column. Check out the chicken chapter, which starts on page 110, for inspiration.

4. Create a Grocery List in column three, based on the recipes you chose. You're going to prepare double or triple batches of each

of these items, so adjust your Grocery List accordingly. Check your pantry to see what you have and what you will need to buy.

5. Go shopping. Before you leave, make sure there's enough room in the fridge to store all the perishables. Do a quick clean-out if needed.

6. Prior to your freezer-cooking session, prep all your vegetables and any other ingredients that might need chopping, slicing, and dicing.

7. Let the freezer cooking begin! Prepare each recipe in assembly-line fashion. Don't forget that you're doubling or tripling recipes. For each of the four recipes, lay out two or three baking dishes to fill and put them together quickly and efficiently. Then continue with the next recipe.

8. Wrap, label, and freeze as you go. Make sure that food cools to room temperature before freezing. To enable quicker freezing and a better result, completely chill the food in the refrigerator before placing it in the freezer.

9. By the time you're done, you should have 8 to 12 dinners ready to go for the coming weeks. If you choose four simple recipes, you'll be done in a few hours. And you'll be amazed at how much time you just bought yourself.

The Basics of Freezer Cooking

When convenience-food items and home refrigeration units started to come on the scene in the first part of the twentieth century, they offered a welcome respite from all the hard work it took to put food on the table. Home cooks have always welcomed convenience, from store-bought sliced bread (1920s) to a complete frozen entrée (1940s). We are no different from our predecessors in wanting shortcuts to get us to dinnertime faster and more economically. However, modern-day convenience items are no longer "the best thing since sliced bread." They can take a huge bite out of one's budget, and they usually aren't the healthiest food choices around.

There is a better way.

Make your favorite foods ahead of time to store in the freezer for the perfect, customized convenience meals. Not only will you save time and money by cooking in bulk, you'll also be able to feed your family exactly what you want to feed them instead of settling for second best.

CHILL OUT: WHAT CAN YOU FREEZE?

The short answer: a lot. The variety of foods that can be partially or completely prepped ahead of time is vast. Many of your favorite meals or meal components can be made weeks in advance and stored in the freezer, enabling you to have the home-cooked meals you crave any night of the week. You will be surprised at the choices available to you.

Just be sure to chill all items in the refrigerator prior to stashing them in the freezer. This will help them freeze quickly and avoid freezer burn.

Complete Main Dishes

- **Meatloaf.** I like to mix and form the loaf, and then wrap and freeze it prior to baking. It tastes fresher than a loaf that's been cooked and then frozen.

- **Meatballs.** Use the same meat mix you use for meatloaves. Form the balls, bake them in the oven, and then freeze family size portions in freezer bags. Later you can turn them into simple spaghetti and meatballs with Easy Slow Cooker Red Sauce (page 217) or try the variations such as Swedish Meatballs with Dill (page 94), Barbecue Sauce for Meatballs (page 106), and *Boules de Picolat* (page 108).

- **Hamburger patties.** Quick-freeze the uncooked patties on a baking sheet lined with plastic wrap. Once the patties are frozen, place them in a freezer bag. When you're ready to serve them, the burgers can be placed on the grill without thawing, making for quick cookouts. Alternatively, bundle the patties in dinner-size packs, separating each one by a bit of deli waxed paper and wrapping the entire bundle securely in plastic wrap.

- **Marinated meat and poultry.** Place the uncooked meats along with the marinade in a freezer bag or freezer-safe container. Freeze the marinade and meat. The meat will marinate as it thaws later in the refrigerator. Cook as you normally would.

- **Casseroles, lasagnas, and enchiladas.** Assemble several pans at once to freeze for later baking.

- **Burritos.** Prepare the burritos and seal them in freezer bags. Thaw and heat them in the microwave or crisp them on a stovetop griddle. Burritos can also be heated directly from the freezer; no need to thaw.

- **Tamales.** Leave the steamed tamales in their cornhusk wrappings. Seal them in a freezer bag. Resteam them right before serving (no need to thaw).

- **Taquitos.** Quick-freeze assembled taquitos on baking sheets, and then seal them in a freezer bag. When ready to serve, bake them without thawing.

- **Stews, soups, and chili.** Freeze these dishes in freezer-safe containers. Consider freezing individual portions in small containers for quick lunches and snacks.

MEAL COMPONENTS AND BASIC INGREDIENTS

Meal components are simply parts of meals that are precooked or premixed in order to help you get a head start on dinner. Precooking and freezing a few meal components can save you valuable minutes in the kitchen. Seasoned ground beef, tomato sauce, marinades, sliced meats for stir-fries, cooked proteins to add to salads and sandwiches, compound butters, baking mixes, and spice blends are all homemade convenience items that you can prepare in bulk and store in the freezer for later use.

- **Seasoned ground beef.** Cool the cooked meat and store in a freezer bag or freezer-safe container. Incorporate this later into tacos, chili, casseroles, nachos, burritos, and more.

- **Meat and chicken precut for stir-fries.** Trim and slice the meat and seal it in a freezer bag or freezer-safe container, with or without a marinade. Thaw in the refrigerator before using in your favorite recipes.

- **Cooked chicken.** Cook chicken in the slow cooker or oven or poach it on the stovetop (pages 111, 112, and 113). Chop or shred the cooked chicken and seal it in a freezer bag to use later in chicken salads, soft tacos, burritos, Asian dishes, soups, sandwich fillings, and more.

- **Carnitas and shredded beef or pork.** Place cooked meat in freezer bags or freezer-safe containers. Use it in tacos, burritos, nachos, soups, and barbecue sandwiches.

- **Pasta sauce.** Cook up a big batch of sauce, with or without meat, and store it in whatever size freezer-safe containers you like.

- **Cooked beans.** Prepare a big batch of dried beans and store them in 2-cup portions in freezer bags or freezer-safe containers. Canned beans are cheap, but home-cooked beans are cheaper!

- **Pizza dough, sauce, and toppings.** As soon as you've allowed the dough to rise for a short time, seal the dough ball(s) in freezer bags and freeze. The pizza sauce and toppings can be packaged in freezer bags or freezer-safe containers. Put together a kit so you can pull just one package out of the freezer when you're planning pizza for dinner.

- **Club warehouse purchases.** Bulk packs of cheeses, meats, and breads can be repackaged for storage in the freezer, helping you make the most of the bulk savings. Shredded cheeses like mozzarella, cheddar, Monterey Jack, and Parmesan freeze well, as do some softer cheeses, such as goat cheese.

Crumbled cheeses, including Gorgonzola, blue, and feta, also hold up well when frozen. **Note:** Block cheese will crumble after freezing, making it difficult to slice. Shred cheese in advance of freezing if you buy the block variety.

- **Surplus produce.** If you belong to a produce co-op or CSA, you may find yourself inundated with fresh produce at times. While enjoying it fresh from the farm is divine, letting it go to waste because you can't eat it fast enough is not. Diced or sliced bell peppers and onions, berries, and chopped or whole bananas can all be frozen without much extra preparation; freeze them on trays so that they won't stick together and then seal them in freezer bags. Other vegetables, like green beans and snap peas, can easily be blanched, cooled, and frozen for later use.

- **Dinner kits.** Grocery stores sell meal kits, packages of ingredients to put together before serving. Why not make your own? Consider preparing "dinner kits" for easy-to-assemble meals such as tacos, sloppy Joes, burritos, or pizza. Cook and season meat or beans. Steam a pot of rice. Portion out the cheese. Package each of these components in meal-size portions and place all the bags for a certain meal in one larger bag. Label the bag and freeze it for later use. Transfer the bag to the refrigerator the day before serving, and the work is practically done for you come dinnertime.

- **Baking mixes and other baked goods.** If you love to bake but find yourself pressed for time, assemble your own baking mixes. When you have your dry ingredients already measured and mixed, pancakes, muffins, waffles, biscuits, brownies, and quick breads can be ready in a flash. Preformed frozen scones and biscuits bake quickly, making for a delicious morning treat. Whole-Grain Cinnamon Rolls (page 324) and Chocolate Butterhorn Rolls (page 329) can be pulled from the freezer to thaw in the refrigerator overnight, providing you with freshly baked breads for breakfast or brunch the next day.

WHAT CAN'T YOU FREEZE?

There are a few things that are better left unfrozen. Here's my short list:

- **White potatoes.** Don't think you can chop up a bunch of uncooked potatoes and freeze them for later use. They generally discolor and lose texture. The best way to freeze white potatoes successfully is to cook them first, as for Potatoes Stuffed with Caramelized Onions and Dubliner Cheese (page 206) or Cream Cheese Mashed Potatoes (page 86).

- **Recipes containing mayonnaise.** This category includes dips, chicken salads, casseroles with mayo, and so on. The mayonnaise tends to separate, and the texture and flavor of the dish suffer.

- **Lettuce, greens, and other vegetables to use raw.** Lettuce and other salad greens should not be frozen. Most other vegetables can be frozen if they are to be cooked later, but otherwise, it's Sog City, baby.

- **Block cheeses and sliced cheeses.** These do not generally freeze well—they crumble upon defrosting—but shredded cheese can be frozen successfully. Very soft cheeses like Brie and Camembert should not be frozen.

FROZEN ASSETS: APPROACHES TO FREEZER COOKING

In the 1990s, once-a-month cooking hit the scene. It is a method of cooking 30 meals in a day or two and freezing them for later use. And it works! I started using this technique years ago and have found it to be a great way to save time, money, and brain power. I save time when I use the assembly-line method; I save money by buying and cooking in bulk; and I save brain power by not having to think too much about what's for dinner. I can go to the freezer and grab a pan of enchiladas or a bag of taquitos for a quick dinner, thereby avoiding the fast-food trap.

Today there are a myriad of ways to approach make-and-freeze cooking in addition to the all-day cooking party:

Double (or Triple) Duty

This is perhaps the easiest and most painless way to fill your freezer. Simply double or triple tonight's dinner and freeze the extra. Do this for several nights, and your freezer will be stocked with a variety of meals. All the recipes in this book can be easily doubled or tripled, making it simple to create a freezer stash quickly.

This is my favorite strategy during busy seasons.

Short but Sweet

Mini sessions are short cooking sessions focused on preparing several meals around a certain protein or key ingredient. You might do this once a week or do several mini sessions over the course of several days. Either way, over time you will have built a massive stockpile of

▶ Taking Freezer Meals on the Road

My family and I love to eat! Good eating is definitely part of our family culture. We're not afraid to spend money on dining out, as long as we get what we pay for. Unfortunately, we've had a few too many overpriced, tasteless restaurant meals or scrambled to find someplace that could accommodate my daughter's food allergies. It makes vacation eating a little challenging: Eating out in unfamiliar places can be difficult to navigate if you don't know which restaurants are worthy of your patronage.

Whether we are going for a week in the mountains or a weekend at Grandma's house, we generally want to rest, relax, and eat well in our leisure time. Freezer meals help make that happen—and save us from those overpriced restaurant disappointments.

If you are heading out on vacation, packing several meals in the cooler will serve you well.

- You will know what you're eating. This is particularly helpful if you have folks with special diets or food aversions in your group.

- You can save money. By packing meals for a recent three-day ski trip, our family easily saved $200. We ate like kings with food we knew we liked, and we kept a lot of change in our wallets. With the money you save, you can splurge on other things. On that same three-day trip, we were able to upgrade our accommodations, which included a complete gourmet kitchen. You could also apply your savings toward a couple of restaurant meals for other nights.

- If you're visiting family or friends, bringing a meal or two to share takes the burden off your host and helps you all enjoy the visit a little more. Bonus: You'll be invited back!

- You can eat on your schedule. Packing snacks and meals allows you to eat when you're hungry. If your kids wake long before the hotel breakfast—or Grandma—is ready, you can easily serve them some Milk and Honey Granola (page 267) or Breakfast Sliders (page 296) without disrupting the flow of those around you.

Some things to remember when taking meals on the road:

- Don't bring more than you can store or eat at your destination. You don't want to pack stuff only to waste it due to insufficient refrigeration, cooking facilities, or mouths to feed. Make sure that you will have a refrigerator/freezer and at least a microwave in your condo, cabin, or hotel.

- Bring meals that are easy to prepare. Casseroles and soups are great for traveling since they reheat easily. The fact that they are virtually one-dish dinners also helps.

- Frozen meals can go camping, too! Chicken burritos and stuffed potatoescan be reheated over a hot fire. Pasta and red sauce are easy to cook on the camp stove. And of course, marinated or spice-rubbed meats and fish will cook well on the grill. You can pack a feast for camping and have very little work to do once you reach your destination.

meals in your freezer. Grab an hour or two and do some assembly-line cooking!

Pro tip: Next time you see a killer sale on your favorite cut of meat, stock up and prep it for the freezer right away. It's a double win—at the checkout counter and at the dinner table.

Cook for a Month

In the early days of freezer cooking, cooks spent several days shopping, chopping, and hopping around the kitchen, cooking up a month's worth of meals, many of them casseroles. Today's lifestyles don't always afford such lengthy cooking sessions. With careful planning, however, three to five hours of efficient cooking time *can* result in a month's worth of meals and meal components without a lot of fuss. There are several cooking plans in this book that will help you prepare 20-plus meals in less than a day.

Make a Day of It

While you know I favor short and sweet cooking sessions, rest easy; there's no rule that says you can't spend a day in the kitchen if you'd like to! The method you choose depends on your inclination and the time you have available. There's no "right" way to do it, except the way that works for YOU this month.

The cooking plans that begin on page 25 will walk you through every step. Or you can build your own plan following the suggestions in a later section (page 65). And if you're someone who just wants to get cooking, consult the Quick-Start Guide (page 7) and get to work.

KEEP YOUR COOL: PROPER FREEZING TECHNIQUES

Freezing preserves food because it inhibits the action of microorganisms that would otherwise lead to spoilage. Food stored in the freezer shouldn't go "bad," as the enzyme action is effectively halted while the food is frozen. As long as you start with fresh food in the first place and the food stays frozen for the entire storage time, you shouldn't have to worry about spoilage of frozen foods. In fact, the USDA says that "frozen foods remain safe indefinitely," provided they are stored at 0°F (-18°C). However, taste and texture can be adversely affected depending on how a food is packaged and frozen and how long it is kept in cold storage.

Additionally, it can be difficult to keep a home freezer at a steady 0°F (-18°C) because typically the door is opened fairly frequently. It's a good idea to serve foods within a reasonable amount of time to ensure the best taste and texture. A general rule of thumb is not to store items longer than two to three months in the freezer compartment of a refrigerator or six months in a dedicated deep freezer.

Often, folks worry that their frozen foods will have a funny taste or develop unsightly ice crystals. These problems are easily prevented if food is cooled, packaged, and stored correctly. An understanding of the freezing process can help you maximize and preserve your food's quality.

The colder the food is before it hits the freezer, the faster it will freeze. Quick freezing keeps ice crystals small, leading to better quality control, less cell damage, and less loss of moisture upon thawing. Large ice crystals, formed during slow freezing, can hurt the texture of the food, causing it to lose moisture and resulting in dry, tasteless food. Therefore, chilling a dish in the refrigerator before freezing it is always a good idea.

Your goal is to have food taste as good or better on the other side of freezing. (And yes, some flavors do improve upon freezing.)

Warm food releases moisture or steam into the air. If you cover the food before it has had a chance to cool, the steam will condense on the inside of the lid. Warm food placed in the freezer will take longer to freeze, and upon freezing, it will have lots of large unsightly ice crystals.

One approach, which I recommend, is to allow hot foods to cool slightly, uncovered, at room temperature, before refrigerating them. While hot foods can be refrigerated safely, your refrigerator will have to work harder to cool them. Once a food has cooled slightly at room temperature, you can chill it thoroughly in the refrigerator before freezing it. Keep in mind that perishable food should never stand at room temperature longer than two hours.

Frozen food should stay at 0°F (-18°C) or colder. A freezer thermometer is essential to keeping your food fresh. A freezer alarm is even better. An inexpensive gadget, a freezer alarm will alert you when the freezer's temperature rises to an unsafe temperature. There is almost nothing more discouraging to a cook than finding a freezer full of food thawing and spoiling due to a power outage, blown fuse, or a freezer door inadvertently left slightly open. Installing a freezer alarm can save your bacon—and your ice cream sandwiches, too.

THAT'S A WRAP: A VARIETY OF PACKAGING METHODS

There are several methods for packaging food for the freezer. What you use will depend on the storage space you have available and the foods you are preparing to freeze.

Using zip-top freezer bags

Zip-top freezer bags are great for storing meats, baked goods, and other items that hold their own shape. You can save space by putting soups, stews, or beans in these as well—but there is a possibility of leakage. Always thaw a zip-top freezer bag full of food on a tray in the refrigerator to catch any drips.

One of the benefits of zip-top bags is that they can be laid flat, frozen, and then lined up like books on a shelf or stacked like pancakes. They provide a great way to store a lot of food in a small amount of space. You can reuse bags that you've used for baked goods and baking mixes; simply store the empty bags in the freezer until next time. Never reuse bags that have held raw meat, poultry, or seafood.

When using zip-top freezer bags, be sure to remove as much air as possible from the bag before sealing it. You can easily use a straw to suck out the air from bags holding fruits, vegetables, or baked goods. Seal the bag almost completely, squeezing out as much air as you can with your hands. Then insert a plastic drinking straw into a small gap in the seal. Suck out any remaining air, pinching the bag's seal and the straw closed as the plastic encloses itself around the food. Remove the straw and seal the bag quickly to prevent air from reentering the bag. While this may seem like an odd method, it is quite effective in removing excess air from the bags. Do not use this technique with uncooked meats or seafood, to avoid contact with bacteria.

There are also commercial freezer bags with valves available, but they are rather expensive compared to the handy duo of freezer bag and drinking straw.

Quick freezing or *open freezing* is the practice of individually freezing items like scones, berries, or burgers on trays and then transferring them to freezer bags or closed containers for longer-term freezing. When foods are frozen this way, it isn't necessary to thaw the entire package to use just a few items. You can simply remove the number of items you plan to serve while leaving the rest in the freezer. Freezer bags are ideal for storing these quick-frozen items.

Using plastic containers with lids

Reusable/disposable plastic containers with lids are wonderful for storing foods like sauces, soups, and stews. These are leak-proof, making them ideal at thawing time and quick for reheating. Since slightly frozen foods will pop out easily from the container into the stockpot for stovetop reheating, you won't need to wait for them to thaw completely.

This type of container doesn't last forever; the plastic tends to etch, stain, or wear down over time, but they are a nice, inexpensive option. They also lend themselves to gifting food items easily and not worrying about getting the containers back.

Using aluminum baking pans

You may recognize aluminum baking pans from that frozen lasagna you bought in the freezer section that time. Caterers use disposable steam pans at buffet events. They come in a variety of sizes and strengths and are available at discount stores, food service shops, and even party stores. My favorites come in a variety of colors with aluminum lids.

Disposable aluminum baking pans are very convenient, especially if you know you'll be giving meals as gifts or taking them to potluck dinners. The brands that come with sturdy aluminum lids are the ones to buy; they make wrapping up your freezer meals especially quick and easy and add extra stability for stacking in the freezer. While disposables are not everyone's favorite, they are certainly convenient.

Using glass or metal baking dishes

Glass or metal baking dishes are the longest lasting of the freezer-friendly packaging choices. If you have a large supply, they are your best bet. If you have a limited supply, you might not want to have all your pans sitting in the freezer when you decide to bake an impromptu cake.

I keep multiples of many sizes of these pans as they are my favorite vessels to store mashed potatoes, enchiladas, and other meals that I want to pop straight into the oven. Some glass bakeware comes with plastic lids for storage, reducing the need for foil or other wrappings. These are wonderful options, as they are completely reusable and stack beautifully in the freezer.

Using fancy sealing machines

Vacuum-sealing machines that encase your food in airtight plastic are also available. These are said to protect extremely well against freezer burn. I have one and loved using it that first month I got it. After that, however, it proved

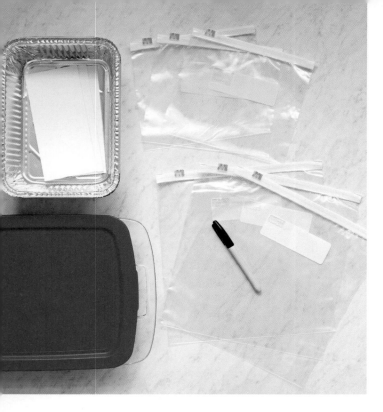

Although I do currently own a large deep
freezer, that hasn't always been the case. I
know from years of personal experience that
you don't need a dedicated freezer to make
freezer cooking work for you. In fact, when
I started practicing this mode of cooking, I
owned the smallest refrigerator known to man.
It was only one step up from a dorm fridge,
but it regularly held the makings of a dozen
or more meals at a time.

Here are some suggestions for making it
work with whatever freezer you have:

- Start with a mostly empty freezer. You
won't be able to store several weeks' worth
of meals in it if it already holds multiple
containers of ice cream, loaves of bread, and
packages of hamburger. Consider "eating
down the freezer" prior to a big cooking
session so that you can reduce what is
already there. Hold off on buying a lot of
other frozen foods until you know how much
space you will need for homemade dinners.
Remember, since you're going to be making
your own convenience foods, you won't need
the store-bought versions anyway.

- If you already have a stockpile of frozen
meats and poultry, use them as the building
blocks of your make-ahead and freeze meals.
Uncooked meat can be thawed, cooked,
and refrozen without loss of taste or texture.
Good recipes to try would be Best-Ever
Chicken Pot Pie (page 127) or Oven-Baked
Beef Taquitos (page 76). You won't need
much extra space for these meals; you're
simply going to take the frozen hamburger
or chicken out, thaw it, cook it up, give it

to be bulky to store and a pain to haul in from
the garage whenever I needed it. Additionally,
these machines are costly to purchase, as are
the special plastic bags they require. A vacuum
sealer generally works best for food items that
hold their shape, such as steaks or loaves of
bread. They cannot be easily used for liquids.

Using common sense
(a.k.a. labeling your meals)

However you package your foods, be sure
to label them with the date, the name of the
contents, and the cooking or reheating instructions, if applicable. It's easy to forget once
something's been in cold storage for a while.
Some foods change color when frozen, making
it difficult to determine what they are. The last
thing you want to do is confuse mushroom
gravy with chocolate fudge sauce.

▶ Good Labeling

Accurate labeling is key to enjoying your frozen meals to the fullest. Be sure to include the following:

1. Date, so that you can eat the food within 2 to 3 months, ideally.
2. Recipe name: no mystery meat!
3. Baking/serving instructions, so that you don't have to hunt down the recipe in order to figure out how to serve the meal.

a makeover, and put it back where it was, transformed from a frozen raw ingredient into a homemade, frozen convenience food.

- Use freezer bags. Zip-top freezer bags, designed for cold temperatures and durability, can hold many kinds of frozen foods. These are especially useful for meats in marinades, taco fillings, pizza dough, and some thicker stews and chilis. As you cool, label, and freeze the food in these bags, seal them and lay them flat in your freezer. Once they are frozen, you will be able to stand them on end and line them up like books on a shelf, making the best use of your storage space. Make sure that you remove as much excess air as possible before sealing the bag in order to avoid freezer burn.

- Use similarly shaped plastic containers. For liquids, like pasta sauce, use containers that are all the same shape and size. These will stack well and make the best use of your space. Square containers fill space more efficiently than round ones.

- Organize like with like. If you have three 9 × 13-inch (23 × 33 cm) pans, stack those on top of each other. Stash all your sauce containers in one spot. Line up all your freezer bags like books on a shelf. Not only will those meals be easier to find, you'll also make the most of your space.

- Consider freezing meal components. Casseroles are big and bulky. Your average refrigerator-freezer can only hold so much, but if you use meal components as a preferred dinnertime shortcut, you can make the most of it, stashing a vast quantity of meats, vegetables, grains, and other building blocks in a small amount of space.

BREAKING THE ICE: PROPER THAWING

What about thawing? Some foods, like unbaked pies, don't need to be thawed prior to baking and serving. Soups and chilis can be thawed and reheated in a pot on the stove. Frozen burritos can be baked or microwaved directly from the freezer.

But other foods, like lasagna, meats, and casseroles, do best when completely defrosted prior to cooking. This should be done in the refrigerator, not on the counter, so that the thawing food does not reach unsafe temperatures. Place zip-top freezer bags and foil-wrapped packages on a tray to catch drips before stowing them in the refrigerator. A slow thaw also allows the food to reabsorb some of the moisture it lost when it was frozen.

You'll have a better-tasting meal if it's had adequate time to thaw, so plan ahead and pull out two or three meals at a time to defrost in the refrigerator. Some will thaw more quickly than others. If you have a variety of items thawing in the refrigerator, you'll have some options come dinnertime.

CASH FOR YOUR CACHE: FREEZER COOKING CAN SAVE YOU MONEY

One of the most tangible benefits of freezer cooking is that it can save you money. Here's how:

- **You can buy in bulk.** Ever shake your head in wonder at folks who shop at warehouse clubs and come home with ginormous packages of food? Large families like mine go quickly through a bulk pack of chicken breasts or a 5-pound (2270 g) bag of shredded cheese, items that can often be a terrific bargain. But smaller households may have a harder time using up those huge packages. With freezer cooking, you can easily reap the cost savings from that bulk package. Divide a 5-pound (2270 g) bag of cheese into smaller meal-size bags for tacos, burritos, or pizzas. Divvy up the bulk pack of chicken breasts into zip-top freezer bags, add a marinade to each bag for good measure, and you're halfway to dinnertime.

- **You can avoid processed foods.** Processed foods have one major thing going for them—convenience. They help us save time and get us from hungry to fed in short order. But there's a cost involved, and processed foods aren't always the best tasting or healthiest choices. By putting a few hours of work into cooking and freezing foods prepared from scratch, you can avoid the junk.

- **You can limit your takeout.** Although I love to have someone else do the cooking, I know that eating too many restaurant meals isn't good for our health or our pocketbooks. Having a stash of freezer meals on hand helps us avoid takeout and keeps some extra cash in our pockets.

- **You can go grocery shopping less often.** Since I do big shopping trips to do big cooking, I go grocery shopping less frequently. Frequent shopping can lead to impulse buys, so staying out of the store saves me money by helping me avoid those unnecessary purchases.

HOW TO SWING THE DEAL

Although your overall monthly grocery bill will probably be lower when you switch to freezer cooking, it can initially be difficult to fund a bulk cooking session. Currently I feed my family of eight on less than $1,300/month, the amount the USDA allots as "frugal" for a group of our size, sex, and ages, in part because I practice big-batch cooking and making good use of my deep freeze. However, if I'm cooking in bulk, I'm also paying in bulk. That one grocery bill for a month's worth of meals can seem daunting. There are several ways that you can swing economical batch cooking, even on a fixed budget.

- **Use what you have on hand.** Don't make recipes that call for ingredients that might not fit your budget during this pay period. Instead, scan your fridge, freezer, and pantry for what's already on the shelves and build your menu plan from there.

- **Compare prices at different stores.** Keep track of the prices on things that you buy on a regular basis and note which stores have the best prices. You may be surprised that there's a vast price difference between Store A and Store B.

- **Practice stockpiling.** Buy ingredients you use frequently in larger quantities when they are on sale, rather than paying full price later when you need them. If you make this a regular practice, you'll find that you can keep a fuller pantry. Provided you don't buy more than you will use in a reasonable length of time, this is wise investing. If my local store has a great price on chuck roast one week, I will probably buy several packages and store them in the freezer until my next bulk cooking session, when I will turn them into Beef Stew with Eggplant and Carrots (page 242), Mexican Beef Tortas (page 77), and Beef and Barley Soup with Dill (page 233). Good sale prices tend to repeat every six weeks. This kind of stockpiling works for all ingredients except some fresh produce items or other foods that have a short shelf life.

- **Straddle the sales.** Find out the beginning and ending dates of your local grocery stores' sales. Build your menus around the sale items from two consecutive weeks. Usually, you can get an ad for the new sale the night before it starts, sometimes sooner. Just check your junk mail or ask at your store. If you don't mind going shopping on back-to-back days, you can take advantage of two weeks' worth of sales in one week. Some stores even offer double-ad days, where they overlap the two weeks' sales for one day. Shop the week you plan to cook to maximize the ingredients' freshness.

- **Cook enough meals or meal components to last longer than one month.** If you find a great deal on a main ingredient, buy enough for two months of meals. For instance, at the beginning of one month, I can make enough Easy Slow Cooker Red Sauce (page 217) to last us six to eight weeks. With proper packaging and storage, I know it will be fresh tasting for even longer. Not only does this provide us with a little more variety in our menus for both months, it also helps me offset my costs because I cooked a sale-priced item in greater quantity.

- **Make in-season recipes.** It just makes sense to cook what is in season and on sale. Roasted Vegetable Quiche (page 208) and Easy Stovetop Ratatouille (page 200) are ideal for the summer harvest season. Sales on boneless chicken breasts are also abundant during the summer months. November and December are ideal months to prepare turkey recipes. A few birds will make several batches of enchiladas, tamales, and a turkey version of Chicken Divan with Cheddar Crust (page 131). In winter, chuck roast is often a butcher's special; use it to make stews, chilis, and ragus.

- **Build your freezer meals to feature items that you can reliably get for a good price.** Meat can be expensive, but eggs, beans, rice, and pasta are almost always good deals. You can easily make many meals based on these ingredients. Spinach and Feta Manicotti with Lemon and Oregano (page 214), Green Chile Rice Casserole (page 197), and Red Lentil Dal (page 203) are not only meatless, they're also built on economical ingredients.

MEAL PLANNING: DINNERTIME AND BEYOND

Most home managers know that having a meal plan is key to a smoothly running household. If you know what the dinner plan is, you can avoid the fast-food drive-through on the way home from soccer practice. The kids won't be crying for something to eat while you stare dazedly into the cupboards. And you can put the lively voices and candlelight back into dinnertime.

Having a freezer stocked with homemade meals facilitates meal planning. You can scan the freezer contents at the beginning of the week and decide what to serve, working around the week's activities.

But freezer meals can go beyond just dinnertime. Ginger-Coconut Scones (page 316) make a delicious breakfast. Freezer Breakfast Smoothies (page 287) are quick on-the-go snacks. Foods like Chipotle Chicken and Onion Wraps (page 138) and Cheesy Butternut Squash Soup with Herbs (page 226) are great packed into a lunch box and reheated at work or school. You can work freezer cooking into good eating all day long.

These make-ahead meals can go on vacation with you, help a friend who's just had a baby, or comfort the neighbors who've just lost a loved one. Stocking your freezer does more than just provide dinner: It can improve the quality of your life, your budget, and your friendships.

KEYS TO EFFICIENCY

Efficiency in bulk cooking combines the best of all worlds. You can get home-cooked food the way you want it. You have convenience on the nights you need it. You conserve valuable resources (like money, utilities, and packaging) by buying and cooking in bulk. And you don't have to spend an inordinate amount of time stocking the freezer if you use some time-saving techniques.

Here are the keys to efficient freezer cooking:

- Cooking in bulk

- Planning your meals around common ingredients and core proteins

- Making good use of the tools and technology (that is, small appliances) at your fingertips

- Using the assembly-line method to prepare several batches of a recipe at one time

Cooking in Bulk

If you cooked 30 different meals in one day, you'd have a month's worth of dinners in the freezer, but you would not have saved any time and you would be utterly exhausted. Efficient freezer cooking relies on cooking in bulk and making several "copies" of the same thing. It won't save you time unless you prepare double or triple batches of the recipes you've chosen.

You may be concerned that you will get bored with your meal choices over the month's

▶ How Freezer Cooking Helps Me

My dad was born and raised on a farm in Minnesota, and his parents grew most—if not all—of what they ate. I remember stories of my grandmother and my aunts working long days in their hot farmhouse kitchen, putting up jars and jars of preserves and pickles, freezing the summer's produce, and preparing big batches of food to get them through the winter months. Not only was it part of the agrarian society they lived in, it was also necessary in order to put food on the table.

Times have changed. While we may have a wider variety of foods and healthier eating options today, many of the old ways are worth holding on to. My grandma had it right when she cooked ahead. Bulk cooking is a great way to eat well and save money. And there are lots of ways to tweak bulk cooking to fit your lifestyle.

Here's what readers of my blog, Life as Mom, had to say about it, in response to these questions: How does freezer cooking help you? How does it help your family eat better? How do you make it work for your life?

"Freezer cooking helps me in the mornings. We are always rushed to get going out the door, so I keep the freezer stocked with our favorites so I don't have to tell the kids, 'I don't have time.' Pancakes, waffles, and muffins are popular freezer items around here. I make time for freezer cooking by making larger batches. For instance, instead of making 'just enough' waffles for breakfast on a Saturday morning, I will triple the recipe and save the extras in the freezer."

   —Katie K., mom of four

"Freezer cooking helps me make sure my family is eating well, even though I'm juggling working full time, mothering two kids under three, and spending time with my husband. On nights when I get home just in time for dinner, knowing that the freezer is well stocked helps me avoid the temptation of grabbing fast food or expensive takeout on the way home. And if I have to miss dinner for a meeting, I can leave instructions for my husband so that he and the kids still eat real food. (Left to their own devices, it'd be frozen pizza for sure!)"

   —Kate S., mom of three

"I cook with whole and fresh foods in large quantities. For example, I prefer making my own bread dough in five minutes and using it for a multitude of breakfast, snack, lunch, and dinner items. I can use natural and organic ingredients without breaking the bank. My family is eating food without preservatives or additives and with whole-food ingredients we can pronounce."

   —Jackie B., mom of four

time. But if you surveyed your eating habits over the past month, you'd probably find that you had several meals more than once during that period. People do that.

And if you include meal components in your cooking plan, you'll find that a few variations can really change up your suppers. A triple batch of seasoned taco meat can go into tacos one night, fill Mexican-style omelets another night, and top off Six-Layer Nachos (page 195) on a third night. That triple batch doesn't seem so boring after all, does it? You can mix and match meal components to create a huge variety of meals.

Common Ingredients

One of the best ways to save time during a bulk cooking session is to combine common ingredients in different ways. The humble chicken breast can be transformed into Tandoori Chicken (page 119), Not Your Mother's Chicken Noodle Soup (page 223), Creamy Chicken Enchiladas (page 129), and Best-Ever Chicken Pot Pie (page 127). All four meals vary in flavor, but they come from the same starting point.

Using common ingredients can also help you take advantage of grocery-store sales. If you find ground beef or steaks on special, then stock up, prepare those items in different ways, and stash the meals in the freezer for later. You'll eat well for a few bucks instead of having to pay full price when you have a hankering for a certain food—when it's not on sale.

Tools to Help You

Efficiency is the goal in freezer cooking, not only on serving day but during your cooking session as well. There are a number of tools that can make quick work of your cooking tasks or even take them off your hands completely, so that you can work on other recipes in your meal plan.

You probably already have basic cookery tools at your disposal, but the following are especially suited to making your bulk cooking sessions more efficient. If there's something on this list you don't own, consider borrowing from a friend for your next cooking session or investing in the item if you have the space to store it.

SLOW COOKERS

The slow cooker is a home cook's best friend. Who else simmers a stew for you while you turn your attention to other tasks? Using one or two large slow cookers during your cooking session will not only result in several prepared meals, it will also free up valuable stovetop real estate for other dishes.

LARGE STOCKPOTS

While the slow cooker works on a stew, the stockpot on your stove can be busy with soup or red sauce. It is also helpful for browning large batches of ground beef. Having one or even two large stockpots is helpful when cooking up a storm.

BREAD MACHINE

The bread machine is an efficient kitchen servant that can work wonders. In less than 2 hours, it can prepare dough for 4 pizzas or 32 rolls. Since yeast dough freezes best without long rising times, you can instead run your bread machine through more than one mixing cycle in a short amount of time.

▶ Keep a Freezer Inventory

After you spend good time and money planning, shopping, and cooking, you want to make sure that you enjoy those frozen assets in a timely manner. Frozen food, properly stored at 0°F (−18°C), will keep indefinitely. But eventually, texture and taste can break down under cold storage.

A good rule of thumb is to consume your frozen meals within two to three months. Good labeling is key, so that you know when you made a certain dish and what that dish is. No mystery meat allowed!

Depending on what kind of freezer storage you are using, you may want to keep track of your freezer meals by posting a list of some kind in a prominent spot. If you cross off the items as you use them and add to the list as you add to your freezer inventory, you should always have a good idea of what meals are available to you. There are even smartphone apps to help you track what you've got!

STAND MIXER

A stand mixer is ideal for mashing large batches of potatoes or mixing up mega batches of cookie dough. It can also knead bread dough and whip up a cheesecake in a matter of minutes. A stand mixer can reduce your prep time tremendously.

FOOD PROCESSOR

A food processor is a whiz at shredding cheeses and chopping vegetables quickly, helping you get your food from the grocery bag to the freezer in the shortest time possible. It's also great for blending sauces and soups.

IMMERSION BLENDER

An immersion, or stick, blender can quickly puree a smoothie or soup—no need to transfer the mixture to a blender or food processor. It also reduces the number of items to wash, getting you out of the kitchen even faster.

A Home-Kitchen Assembly Line

Henry Ford probably never dreamed that his assembly-line practices of sequential organization and minimal worker motion would help out a home cook a century later. Ford realized that creating many of the same items in succession saves time and money because the worker is simply repeating a motion many times over instead of starting from scratch each time. The same holds true for bulk cooking.

Assembling a lasagna from start to finish might take 30 minutes. But assembling four lasagnas does not take two hours. Mass production takes less time than making several single items one after another.

By creating a sequence in food prep and having all your ingredients within arm's reach, you can prepare bulk batches of any number of recipes and decrease the effort and time that it takes.

Batch cooking can free you up to have your cake and eat it, too. You can enjoy home-cooked meals any night of the week without

a lot of fuss. You don't need to spend a lot of time in the kitchen in order to fill your freezer and make things easier for yourself in the days and weeks ahead. A little efficiency goes a long way.

WORK IT—FOR *YOU*

Freezer cooking can work for any household, budget, or size of freezer. Explore the different modes of packaging, purchasing, and preparation until you find the ones you like the best. With proper planning and equipment, you can easily prepare delicious meals at home, on a budget, and in accord with your own dietary preferences. Make-ahead-and-freeze cooking can enable you to have home-cooked meals whenever you want them, without the marathon cooking sessions of yesteryear.

Cooking Plans to Fit Your Needs

It's certainly true that you can run through the grocery store, pile your cart high, rush home, cook up a storm, and stash your results in the freezer, without following any particular plan. I've done this kind of spontaneous cooking myself.

However, it may take longer than you think. You may find yourself missing key ingredients. And you may discover that a 15-pound (6800 g) turkey cannot be cooked on a sheet pan when you've misplaced your roasting pan. Ask me how I know.

Truth be told, it's always better to have a plan. Whether you are traveling across the country, looking toward retirement, or simply filling your freezer with homemade convenience foods, a plan will serve you well. It will ensure that you have everything you need, and it will also help you use your time in the most efficient manner. Freezer cooking is all about saving time so that you can enjoy the rest of your life—as well as your mealtimes.

The following plans produce 10 to 30 meals each. In determining the number of meals each plan makes, I've used the recipe yields as my guideline; exactly how many meals each plan produces will depend on the portion sizes you prefer and the extent to which you supplement your meals with side dishes. The plans will walk you through the shopping, cooking, and freezing phases of bulk cooking. Consult the section entitled "Creating Your Own Cooking Plan," page 65, for tips on how to develop your own plan and adapt your personal favorite recipes for freezing.

These plans range in duration from one hour to all day. If you have only an hour or two to cook, make the most of it and get a head start on 10 meals and meal components to help you get through the next couple of weeks without a lot of fuss. If you've got a free day to spend in the kitchen, then stock that freezer up with homemade convenience to feed you and your family throughout the month!

The time frames suggested assume that you have already purchased the groceries listed, own or can borrow all the appliances needed, and have completed your Prep List.

The Grocery Lists include the specific amounts needed for each plan in parentheses after the item in question. Where there are additional shortcuts to take, those are noted as well. In some cases, certain ingredients in a given recipe are not in the meal plan, because those ingredients aren't added until the day the dish is served. For example, in the Everything Plan III, I haven't listed the salmon that goes into the fish chowder, because you freeze the chowder base without the fish.

Read the recipes carefully to make sure you've got whatever ingredients are needed to finish the dish when you serve it, and read each cooking plan and each recipe involved prior to shopping. That way, you'll have a view of where you're headed in terms of finished meals and know what tasks are in store.

A note about flours: Whole-wheat pastry flour may be difficult to find. Most health food grocery stores will carry it, as does Amazon. Feel free to use regular, all-purpose flour instead of the whole-wheat pastry flour. A note about oils: Use whatever oil you like for baking. The oils specified are those that I used for recipe testing. Feel free to use your preferred baking oil.

- Breakfast Plan I (2 hours or less)
- Breakfast Plan II (3 to 4 hours)
- Cozy Winter Breakfast Plan (4 hours)
- Meatless Plan I (2 hours or less)
- Meatless Plan II (3 to 4 hours)
- Beef Plan (2 hours or less)
- Poultry and Seafood Plan (2 hours or less)
- Meat and Poultry Plan (3 to 4 hours)
- Holiday Baking Plan (4 to 6 hours)
- Protein Power Cooking Plan (4 to 6 hours)
- Everything Plan I (1 day)
- Everything Plan II (1 day)
- Everything Plan III (1 day)

BREAKFAST PLAN I: 2 HOURS OR LESS

10-plus meals serving at least 4 people

Individual Greek Egg Casseroles, page 209, 8 servings
Better Instant Oatmeal Packets, page 274, 24 packets
Bulk-Batch Pancake mix, page 275, 2 batches
Cinnamon Banana Bread, page 306, 3 dozen mini breads
Mix-and-Match Muffin mix, page 309, 2 batches

Grocery List

FRESH PRODUCE:

☐ Bananas (6)

DAIRY:

☐ Eggs (19)

☐ Crumbled feta cheese (2⅔ cups [400 g])

☐ Milk (1 quart [1 L])

☐ Half-and-half (1½ cups [355 ml])

FROZEN:

☐ Frozen chopped spinach (two 9-ounce [252 g] packages)

CANNED/BOTTLED/DRY GOODS:

☐ Unbleached all-purpose flour (12 cups [1440 g])

☐ Whole-wheat pastry flour (7 cups [840 g])

☐ Quick-cooking rolled oats (6 cups [480 g])

☐ Granulated sugar (2½ cups [500 g])

☐ Light or dark brown sugar (2¾ cups [620 g])

☐ Raisins, dried cranberries, or dried blueberries (optional; 1½ cups [225 g])

☐ Vegetable oil (¾ cup [180 ml])

☐ Instant dry milk powder (optional; ½ cup [60 g])

☐ Baking powder (5 tablespoons plus 2 teaspoons [46 g])

☐ Baking soda (4½ teaspoons [14 g])

SEASONINGS:

☐ Ground cinnamon (1½ teaspoons)

☐ Salt and freshly ground black pepper

BAKERY:

☐ Italian bread (1 large loaf, for 8 cups [400 g] bread cubes)

TO SAVE MORE TIME, PURCHASE:

☐ Cubed bread in the bakery department

** On the day of serving the pancakes and muffins, you will also need the wet ingredients as specified in the recipe. Please consult the recipe so that you have these items on hand.

Packaging

☐ 24 snack-size zip-top bags, labeled Instant Oatmeal (if you prefer not to label each bag, simply collect them all in a large, labeled canister to store in the pantry or freezer)

☐ 4 quart-size (1 L) zip-top freezer bags, labeled Pancake Mix (2) and Mix-and-Match Muffin Mix (2)

☐ 3 gallon-size (4 L) zip-top freezer bags, labeled Cinnamon Banana Breads

☐ Eight 2-cup (450 g) ramekins with lids, labeled Greek Egg Casseroles

Gadgets and Small Appliances

- Three 12-cup muffin pans and papers for lining

Prep List

1. Assemble the storage containers and ingredients.

2. Thaw the spinach.

3. Cube the bread.

Cooking Plan

1. Preheat the oven to 350°F (180°C or gas mark 4). Prepare a batch of cinnamon banana bread, pour the batter into the lined muffin tins, and put them in the oven.

2. Assemble the Greek egg casseroles. Cover and place in freezer. [EGG CASSEROLES DONE]

3. Prepare the instant oatmeal packets. [OATMEAL PACKETS DONE]

4. When the timer for the banana breads rings, remove the breads from the oven and allow them to cool on a rack.

5. Assemble all the baking-mix ingredients and prepare two batches each of pancake and muffin mixes. [PANCAKE MIXES AND MUFFIN MIXES DONE]

6. Clean up while you wait for the banana breads to finish cooling.

7. Package the cooled breads in zip-top freezer bags and store the bags in the freezer. [BANANA BREADS DONE]

8. Finish up by wiping down the counters. Put away any remaining ingredients.

BREAKFAST PLAN II: 3 TO 4 HOURS

18-plus meals serving at least 4 people

Cranberry-Orange Granola, page 269, 1 batch
Better Instant Oatmeal Packets, page 274, 24 packets
Lemon-and-Honey Flax Waffle mix, page 278, 2 batches
Buttered French Toast Casserole with Almonds and Ginger, page 284, 2 batches
Savory Ham and Swiss Clafouti, page 293, 2 batches
Lemon-Blueberry Scones, page 313, 2 batches
Whole-Grain Cinnamon Rolls, page 324, 1 batch

Grocery List
FRESH PRODUCE:

☐ **Lemons (2)**
☐ **Orange (1)**

☐ **Parsley (2 tablespoons chopped)**

DAIRY:

- ☐ Butter (about 1½ pounds [680 g])
- ☐ Milk (2 cups [470 ml])
- ☐ Buttermilk (1 quart [1 L])
- ☐ Eggs (12)
- ☐ Half-and-half (5 cups [1175 ml])
- ☐ Swiss cheese (8 ounces [224 g]; 2 cups shredded)

FROZEN:

- ☐ Frozen blueberries (3 cups [450 g])

MEAT:

- ☐ Ham (1 pound [454 g])

CANNED/BOTTLED/DRY GOODS:

- ☐ Unbleached all-purpose flour (14 cups [1680 g])
- ☐ Whole-wheat pastry flour (12 cups [1440 g])
- ☐ Quick-cooking rolled oats (6½ cups [520 g])
- ☐ Old-fashioned rolled oats (5 cups [400 g])
- ☐ Whole-wheat flour (1 cup [120 g])
- ☐ Granulated sugar (2¾ cups [550 g])
- ☐ Light or dark brown sugar (2½ cups [563 g])
- ☐ Dried fruit, such as raisins, dried cranberries, or dried blueberries (optional; 1½ cups [225 g])
- ☐ Instant dried milk powder (optional; 1 cup [120 g])
- ☐ Nuts of your choice (1 cup [150 g] chopped)
- ☐ Baking powder (½ cup plus 2 tablespoons [76 g])
- ☐ Baking soda (2 teaspoons)
- ☐ Vegetable oil (½ cup [120 ml])
- ☐ Raisins: dark, golden, or a combination (½ cup [75 g])
- ☐ Sliced almonds (¼ cup [50 g])
- ☐ Dried cranberries (½ cup [38 g])
- ☐ Crystallized ginger (¼ cup [20 g] chopped)
- ☐ Active dry yeast (3¾ teaspoons [15 g])
- ☐ Vanilla extract (2½ teaspoons [12 ml])
- ☐ Dijon mustard (2 teaspoons)

SEASONINGS:

- ☐ Salt and freshly ground black pepper
- ☐ Ground cinnamon (2 tablespoons [14 g])
- ☐ Dried parsley flakes (2 teaspoons), if not using fresh herb

BAKERY:

- ☐ Italian or brioche bread (2 large loaves)

TO SAVE MORE TIME, PURCHASE:

- ☐ Diced ham
- ☐ Shredded cheese
- ☐ Chopped nuts

** On the day of serving the waffles and scones, you will also need the wet ingredients as specified in the recipe. Please consult the recipe so that you have these items on hand.

Packaging

☐ 24 snack-size zip-top bags, labeled Instant Oatmeal (if you prefer not to label each bag, simply collect them all in a large, labeled canister to store in the pantry)

☐ 7 gallon-size (4 L) zip-top freezer bags, labeled Lemon-Blueberry Scones (2), Cranberry-Orange Granola (1), Whole-Grain Cinnamon Rolls (2), Lemon-and-Honey Flax Waffle Mix (2)

☐ Two 9 × 13-inch (23 × 33 cm) pans with lids or heavy-duty aluminum foil to cover, labeled French Toast Casserole

☐ Two 8-inch (20.3 cm) pie or cake pans with lids or heavy-duty aluminum foil to cover, labeled Ham and Swiss Clafouti

Gadgets and Small Appliances

- Bread machine
- Food processor
- Several baking sheets that will fit in your freezer

Prep List

1. Assemble the storage containers and ingredients.

2. Slice the bread into 1½-inch (3.8 cm) slices.

3. Dice the ham.

4. Shred the cheese.

5. Zest the lemons and orange.

6. Chop the parsley, if using fresh.

Cooking Plan

1. Preheat the oven to 300°F (150°C or gas mark 2). Begin the cinnamon roll dough in the bread machine. Allow the kneading cycle to run, scraping down the sides so that all the ingredients are incorporated.

2. Mix up the granola and start it baking in the oven.

3. Check the cinnamon roll dough and make sure that all the ingredients are incorporated and that the dough ball is formed. Allow the machine to finish the dough cycle.

4. Mix up one batch of scones, form them, and freeze them on trays.

5. Stir the granola.

6. Make the second batch of scones, form them, and freeze them on trays. (20 min.)

7. Check the granola.

8. In assembly-line fashion, prepare the instant oatmeal packets. [OATMEAL PACKETS DONE]

9. Mix up the ham and Swiss clafoutis. Wrap and freeze. [CLAFOUTIS DONE]

10. The granola should be done. If so, remove it from the oven and allow it to cool.

11. The scones should be firm. Remove the scones from the freezer and transfer them to zip-top freezer bags. Return them to the freezer immediately. [SCONES DONE]

12. Form the cinnamon rolls. Freeze on trays.

13. Assemble the French toast casseroles. Wrap and freeze. [FRENCH TOAST CASSEROLES DONE]

14. Assemble the waffle mix in two zip-top freezer bags. Store in the freezer. [WAFFLE MIXES DONE]

15. Place the cooled granola into the labeled gallon-size zip-top freezer bags. [GRANOLA DONE]

16. Remove the cinnamon rolls from the freezer and transfer them to the labeled zip-top freezer bags. Return the bags to the freezer immediately. [CINNAMON ROLLS DONE]

17. Clean up the workspace. Wipe down the counters.

COZY WINTER BREAKFAST PLAN: 4 HOURS

The recipes in this plan cover a range of quick breads, oatmeal dishes, cereals, and other baked goods.

Spiced Pumpkin Flax Bread, page 303, 1 batch
Wholesome Energy Bars, page 333, 24 bars
Better Instant Oatmeal Packets, page 274, 40 packets
Bulk-Batch Pancake mix, page 275, 4 batches
Lemon-and-Honey Flax Waffle mix, page 278, 2 batches
Cranberry-Orange Granola, page 269, 2 batches
Breakfast Cookies, page 286, 1 batch
Raspberry Baked Oatmeal, page 270, 2 batches

Grocery List

FRESH PRODUCE:

☐ **Oranges for zesting (4)**

☐ **Raspberries (can use frozen) (4 cups [600 g])**

DAIRY:

☐ **Eggs (6)**

☐ **Butter (approx. 2 sticks [225 g])**

☐ **Milk (3 cups [705 ml])**

☐ **Plain yogurt (1 cup [225 g])**

CANNED/BOTTLED/DRY GOODS:

☐ **Unbleached all-purpose flour (19 cups [2280 g])**

☐ **Old-fashioned rolled oats (16 cups [1280 g])**

☐ **Whole-wheat pastry flour (13½ cups [1620 g])**

☐ **Quick oats (12 cups [960 g])**

☐ **Dried fruit (6¼ cups [938 g] total; the recipes call for 2¾ cups [412 g] dried cranberries,**

½ cup [75 g] golden raisins, ½ cup [75 g] dark raisins, AND approximately 2½ cups [375 g] dried cranberries OR raisins, but you can use all cranberries, all raisins, or a combo)

☐ **Brown sugar (4½ cups [1013 g])**

☐ **Granulated sugar (3 cups [600 g])**

- ☐ Nuts (2¼ cups 338 g])
- ☐ Whole-wheat flour (2 cups [240 g])
- ☐ Dry milk powder (approx. 2 cups [240 g])
- ☐ Pumpkin puree (15-ounce [420 g] can)
- ☐ Applesauce (1 cup [245 g])
- ☐ Oat flour (1 cup [120 g])
- ☐ Honey (approx. 1 cup [320 g])
- ☐ Raw sunflower seeds (¾ cup [108 g])
- ☐ Flaxseed meal (¾ cup [84 g])
- ☐ Cornmeal (½ cup [70 g])

- ☐ Chocolate chips (¼ cup [45 g])
- ☐ Pumpkin seeds (¼ cup [35 g])
- ☐ Light olive oil
- ☐ Coconut oil
- ☐ Vegetable and/or canola oil
- ☐ Baking soda
- ☐ Baking powder (at least 1 cup [120 g])
- ☐ Salt
- ☐ Vanilla extract
- ☐ Yeast (2 packets)

SPICES:

- ☐ Ground cinnamon
- ☐ Ground ginger

- ☐ Ground nutmeg

** On the day of serving the pancakes and waffles, you will also need the wet ingredients as specified in the recipe. Please consult the recipe so that you have these items on hand.

Packaging

- ☐ Plastic wrap
- ☐ Waxed paper or parchment
- ☐ 11 gallon-size (4 L) zip-top freezer bags, labeled Spiced Pumpkin Flax Bread (1), Bulk-Batch Pancake Mix (4), Lemon-and-Honey-Flax Waffle Mix (2), Cranberry-Orange Granola, (2) Wholesome Energy Bars (1), Breakfast Cookies (1)

- ☐ Two 9 × 13-inch (23 × 33 cm) baking dishes with lids, labeled Raspberry Baked Oatmeal
- ☐ 40 snack-sized zip-top bags for Better Instant Oatmeal Packets and a canister or container to hold them

Special Equipment

- Bread machine, if possible
- Stand mixer or hand mixer
- 2 bread loaf pans

- Several rimmed sheet pans
- Cooling racks

Prep List

1. Print labels and cooking plans.

2. Soften butter.

3. Zest oranges.

Cooking Plan

Note: One of the tricks to saving time during a large baking plan like this is to make sure you maximize every action. Heat the oven once and keep it baking. The steps with an asterisk (*) indicate that you will be using the oven. If you are quicker or slower with any of the steps and find that you have an empty oven, skip to the next * so that you can maximize that energy. Then go back to the step that you finished previously.

1. Mix up pumpkin bread and bake.

2. Start dough for Wholesome Energy Bars in the bread machine or mixer. Do not double the recipe. Mix each batch separately and place dough in greased bowls to rise. Set a timer for 90 minutes. After timer rings, form bars and allow to rise. Then continue with the Cooking Plan at whatever step you left off on.

3. Mix granola and wait for oven.

4. Pumpkin bread should be done. Pull the loaves from the oven to cool on rack for 10 minutes. Remove from pans and allow to cool completely.

5. Bake granola.

6. Assemble Instant Oatmeal Packets. [INSTANT OATMEAL PACKETS DONE]

7. Make pancake and waffle mixes. Freeze. [PANCAKE AND WAFFLE MIXES DONE]

8. Energy bar dough should be ready. Form bars and allow to rise. Bake when granola is done.

9. Mix Raspberry Baked Oatmeal and freeze. [RASPBERRY BAKED OATMEAL DONE]

10. Mix breakfast cookie dough and form cookies on trays.

11. Once energy bars are done, remove from oven and cool on wire racks.

12. Bake breakfast cookies.

13. Once all baking recipes are complete and have had a sufficient chance to cool, wrap well and freeze. [PUMPKIN BREAD, GRANOLA, ENERGY BARS, BREAKFAST COOKIES DONE]

14. Clean up the workspace. Wipe down the counters.

MEATLESS PLAN I: 2 HOURS OR LESS

10-plus meals serving at least 4 people

Jamie's Spice Mix, page 98, 1 batch
Pepper Jack and Chile Burritos, page 197, 1 batch
Easy Stovetop Ratatouille, page 200, 1 batch
Sun-Dried Tomato Pesto, page 218, 1 batch
Basic Pizza Dough, page 249, 1 batch
Tomato and Herb Pizza Sauce, page 251, 1 batch
Easy-Peasy Cheesy Pizza kit, page 253, 4 kits
Parmesan Herb Blend, page 255, 2 batches

Grocery List

FRESH PRODUCE:

- ☐ Onion (1 medium, for 1 cup [160 g] chopped)
- ☐ Garlic (1 head, for 2 tablespoons plus 2 teaspoons [27 g] chopped)
- ☐ Red bell pepper (1)
- ☐ Green bell pepper (1)
- ☐ Zucchini (1 medium)
- ☐ Yellow squash (1 medium)
- ☐ Eggplant (1 medium)
- ☐ Mushrooms (4 ounces [112 g])
- ☐ Lemon (1)
- ☐ Basil (about ½ cup plus 2 tablespoons [45 g] chopped)
- ☐ Parsley (about 2 tablespoons chopped)

DAIRY:

- ☐ Parmesan cheese (12 ounces [336 g]; 3 cups finely shredded)
- ☐ Mozzarella cheese (12 ounces [336 g]; 3 cups shredded)
- ☐ Monterey Jack cheese (12 ounces [336 g]; 3 cups shredded)
- ☐ Pepper Jack cheese (8 ounces [224 g]; 2 cups shredded)

CANNED/BOTTLED/DRY GOODS:

- ☐ Petite diced tomatoes (one 28-ounce [784 g] can plus two 14.5-ounce [406 g] cans)
- ☐ Unbleached all-purpose flour (4½ cups [540 g])
- ☐ Refried beans (two 15-ounce [420 g] cans)
- ☐ Sun-dried tomatoes (16 ounces [454 g]; 2 cups)
- ☐ Olive oil (1½ cups [355 ml])
- ☐ Pine nuts or walnuts (¾ cup [110 g])
- ☐ Tomato paste (one 6-ounce [168 g] can)
- ☐ Chopped green chiles (one 4-ounce [112 g] can)
- ☐ Honey (2 tablespoons [40 g])
- ☐ Active dry yeast (1 tablespoon [12 g])

SEASONINGS:

- ☐ Dried basil (3 tablespoons), if not using fresh herb
- ☐ Kosher salt, fine sea salt, and freshly ground black pepper
- ☐ Garlic powder (2 tablespoons plus 2 teaspoons [24 g])
- ☐ Onion powder (2 tablespoons [14 g])
- ☐ Paprika (1½ tablespoons)
- ☐ Dried oregano (1 tablespoon plus 1 teaspoon)
- ☐ Dried parsley flakes (2 teaspoons), if not using fresh herb
- ☐ Herbes de Provence (1½ teaspoons)
- ☐ Celery seeds (1 teaspoon)
- ☐ Crushed red pepper flakes (½ teaspoon)
- ☐ Dried thyme (½ teaspoon)
- ☐ Cayenne pepper (½ teaspoon)

BAKERY:

- ☐ Burrito-size flour tortillas (12)

TO SAVE MORE TIME, PURCHASE:

- ☐ Chopped onions
- ☐ Chopped garlic
- ☐ Sliced mushrooms
- ☐ Shredded cheese

Packaging

- ☐ 4 snack-size zip-top freezer bags, labeled Parmesan Herb Blend for Pizzas
- ☐ 6 sandwich-size zip-top bags, labeled Pizza Dough (4), Jamie's Spice Mix (1), Parmesan Herb Blend (1)
- ☐ 14 pint-size (470 ml) zip-top freezer bags, labeled Pizza Sauce (9), Sun-Dried-Tomato Pesto (5)
- ☐ 4 quart-size (1 L) zip-top freezer bags, labeled Pizza Cheese
- ☐ 6 gallon-size (4 L) zip-top freezer bags, labeled Pizza Kit (4), Pepper Jack and Chile Burritos (2)
- ☐ Two 5-cup (1175 ml) plastic containers with lids, labeled Ratatouille

Gadgets and Small Appliances

- Bread machine
- Food processor
- Immersion blender

Prep List

1. Assemble the storage containers and ingredients.

2. Chop the onions and garlic.

3. Chop the herbs.

4. Shred the cheeses if they are not already shredded.

5. Chop the vegetables for the Easy Stovetop Ratatouille.

6. Zest the lemon.

Cooking Plan

1. Start the pizza dough in the bread machine.

2. Prepare the pizza sauce on the stove.

3. Check the pizza dough to make sure that all the ingredients have been incorporated into the dough ball. Scrape the sides of the dough pan, if necessary. Once the kneading cycle is over, set the timer for 30 minutes.

4. Prepare two batches of the Parmesan herb blend. Place 1 cup (100 g) in the sandwich bag labeled Parmesan Herb Blend. Divide the remainder between the 4 snack-size bags labeled Parmesan Herb Blend for pizza. Put one of the 4 bags in each of the gallon-size pizza kit bags. [PARMESAN HERB BLEND DONE]

5. Start the ratatouille on the stove.

6. Finish up the pizza sauce. Portion and cool the pizza sauce. Each of 9 bags should have ½ cup (118 ml) sauce. Chill the sauce in the refrigerator before freezing. [PIZZA SAUCE DONE]

7. Portion the pizza cheese: ¾ cup (90 g) Monterey Jack cheese and ½ cup (90 g) mozzarella cheese in each pizza cheese bag. Place one bag of cheese in each large pizza kit bag.

8. The pizza dough hits the 30-minute mark. Divide the dough into four portions and place in sandwich-size bags. Add one dough ball to each large pizza kit and place the kits in the freezer immediately. [PIZZA DOUGH AND KITS DONE]

9. Make the sun-dried tomato pesto. Portion the pesto into the 5 marked bags. Freeze. [SUN-DRIED TOMATO PESTO DONE]

10. Prepare a batch of Jamie's spice mix. Bag and freeze. [JAMIE'S SPICE MIX DONE]

11. The ratatouille is done. Portion and cool the ratatouille. Chill the containers in the refrigerator before freezing. [RATATOUILLE DONE]

12. Prepare the burrito filling. Assemble the burritos. Bag and freeze the burritos. [BURRITOS DONE]

13. Wipe down the counters. Put away the herbs, spices, and other ingredients. Once the pizza sauce is chilled, add one container to each pizza kit bag already in the freezer. The remaining bags of pizza sauce can be frozen and used for other pizzas or on pasta, as well as for dipping sauce for garlic bread. Transfer the containers of ratatouille to the freezer once they are chilled.

MEATLESS PLAN II: 3 TO 4 HOURS

15-plus meals serving at least 4 people

Quick and Easy Cheese Enchiladas, page 190, 1 batch
Green Chile Rice Casserole, page 197, 2 batches
Tahini Vegetable Patties, page 204, 2 batches
Broccoli Gratin with Tarragon and Buttered Bread Crumbs, page 207, 2 batches
Tomato Sauce with Oregano and Kalamata Olives, page 215, 1 batch
Black Bean Soup with Jalapeño, page 234, 1 batch
Homemade Cream of Celery Soup for Cooking, page 238, 4 batches
Oatmeal–Chocolate Chip Pancake mix, page 276, 2 batches
Spiced Whole-Grain Waffle mix, page 280, 2 batches

Grocery List

FRESH PRODUCE:

☐ **Broccoli florets (3 pounds [1362 g])**
☐ **Onions (3 medium, for 2½ cups [400 g] chopped)**
☐ **Celery (3 ribs, for 1½ cups [180 g] chopped)**
☐ **Carrots (3, for 1 cup [110 g] shredded)**
☐ **Red bell pepper (1, for 1 cup [150 g] chopped)**
☐ **Zucchini (1, for 1 cup [120 g] shredded)**
☐ **Russet potato (1 medium, for 1 cup [110 g] shredded)**
☐ **Jalapeño peppers (2, for about ⅓ cup [45 g] chopped)**
☐ **Garlic (4 to 6 cloves)**
☐ **Scallions (1 bunch, for ¼ cup [25 g] sliced)**
☐ **Orange (1)**
☐ **Lemon (1)**

DAIRY:

- ☐ Milk (1 quart [1 L])
- ☐ Sour cream or plain Greek yogurt (4 cups [1 L])
- ☐ Cheddar cheese (2½ pounds [1135 g]; 10 cups shredded)
- ☐ Parmesan cheese (1 ounce [28 g]; 1¼ cups finely shredded)
- ☐ Eggs (4)
- ☐ Butter (1¼ cups [295 g])

CANNED/BOTTLED/DRY GOODS:

- ☐ Unbleached all-purpose flour (10 cups [1200 g])
- ☐ Whole-wheat pastry flour (6 cups [720 g])
- ☐ Oat flour (2 cups [240 g])
- ☐ Brown rice (2 cups [380 g], to yield 6 cups [990 g] cooked)
- ☐ Quick-cooking rolled oats (1½ cups [120 g])
- ☐ Chopped green chiles (two 4-ounce [112 g] cans)
- ☐ Light or dark brown sugar (1 cup [225 g])
- ☐ Mini chocolate chips (1 cup [175 g])
- ☐ Baking powder (½ cup plus 2 tablespoons [76 g])
- ☐ Cornmeal (½ cup [70 g])
- ☐ White wine (¼ cup [60 ml])
- ☐ Baking soda (2 teaspoons)
- ☐ Petite diced tomatoes (two 14.5-ounce [406 g] cans or one 28-ounce [784 g] can)
- ☐ Black beans (four 15-ounce [420 g] cans)
- ☐ Reduced-sodium vegetable broth (6 cups [1410 ml]; 48 ounces [1410 ml])
- ☐ Garbanzo beans (two 15-ounce [420 g] cans)
- ☐ Tomato sauce (one 15-ounce [420 g] can)
- ☐ Enchilada sauce (one 28-ounce [784 g] can)
- ☐ Sliced black olives (one 2.25-ounce [65 g] can)
- ☐ Kalamata olives (⅓ cup [35 g] chopped)
- ☐ Tahini (¼ cup [80 g])
- ☐ Vegetable oil
- ☐ Olive oil (5 tablespoons [75 ml])

SEASONINGS:

- ☐ Bay leaf (1)
- ☐ Kosher salt, fine sea salt, and freshly ground black pepper
- ☐ Dried oregano (1 tablespoon)
- ☐ Ground cinnamon (1 tablespoon)
- ☐ Ground nutmeg (2 teaspoons)
- ☐ Ground ginger (2 teaspoons)
- ☐ Ground cumin (1 teaspoon)
- ☐ Dried tarragon (1 teaspoon)
- ☐ Onion powder (1 teaspoon)
- ☐ Paprika (½ teaspoon)

BAKERY:

- ☐ Corn tortillas (24)
- ☐ Fresh bread crumbs (5½ cups [275 g]; about 1 loaf of French bread)

TO SAVE MORE TIME, PURCHASE:

- ☐ Broccoli florets in ready-to-steam packaging
- ☐ Chopped garlic
- ☐ Shredded cheese
- ☐ Fresh bread crumbs

Packaging

☐ Two 5-cup (1175 ml) containers labeled Black Bean Soup with Jalapeño

☐ Five 2-cup (470 ml) containers labeled Tomato Sauce with Oregano and Kalamata Olives (3), Cream of Celery Soup (2)

☐ Two 3-quart (3 L) baking dishes with lids or heavy-duty aluminum foil to cover, labeled Green Chile Rice Casserole

☐ Two quart-size (1 L) zip-top freezer bags, labeled Tahini Vegetable Patties

☐ 4 gallon-size (4 L) zip-top freezer bags, labeled Spiced Waffle Mix (2), Oatmeal–Chocolate Chip Pancake Mix (2)

☐ Four 9 × 13-inch (23 × 33 cm) pans with lids or heavy-duty aluminum foil to cover, labeled Cheese Enchiladas (2), Broccoli Gratin (2)

☐ Plastic wrap

☐ Waxed paper

Gadgets and Small Appliances

- Food processor
- Slow cooker
- Rice cooker
- Immersion blender
- At least two large stockpots

Prep List

1. Assemble the storage containers and ingredients.

2. Chop the onions, pepper, celery, garlic, jalapeño, and scallions.

3. Shred the zucchini and carrot (shred the potato just before adding it to the soup).

4. Cook the rice and allow it to cool.

5. Cut the broccoli into florets if not purchased that way.

6. Make the bread crumbs in the blender or food processor.

7. Shred the cheese.

8. Zest the orange.

9. Juice the lemon.

Cooking Plan

1. Start the black bean soup, using canned black beans.

2. Prepare four batches of the cream of celery soup. Allow it to cool.

3. Prepare a double batch of the tahini veggie patties. Wrap and freeze. [VEGGIE PATTIES DONE]

4. Steam the broccoli. Assemble two batches of the broccoli gratin. Allow the casseroles to cool

at room temperature. Chill them in the refrigerator before freezing. [BROCCOLI GRATINS DONE]

5. You should have 4 cups (940 ml) of the cream of celery soup left. Package this soup in 2-cup (470 ml) portions in plastic containers with lids and chill in the refrigerator before freezing. [CREAM OF CELERY SOUP DONE]

6. Wash out the pot and start the tomato sauce.

7. Assemble two batches of the green chile rice. Chill in the refrigerator before freezing. [GREEN CHILE RICE DONE]

8. Portion the black bean soup. Cool at room temperature. Chill the containers in the refrigerator before freezing. [BLACK BEAN SOUP DONE]

9. Fry the tortillas for the enchiladas. Assemble the enchiladas. Chill in the refrigerator before freezing. [CHEESE ENCHILADAS DONE]

10. Prepare pancake and waffle mixes assembly-line style. Divide among labeled bags. [PANCAKE MIXES AND WAFFLE MIXES DONE]

11. Portion the tomato sauce. Cool at room temperature. Chill the containers in the refrigerator before freezing. [TOMATO SAUCE DONE]

12. Clean up the workspace. Wipe down the counters. Once the items in the refrigerator have chilled for several hours, transfer them to the freezer.

BEEF PLAN: 2 HOURS OR LESS

10-plus meals serving at least 4 people

Chipotle-Rubbed Tri-Tip, page 80, 2 batches
Seasoned taco meat, 2 pounds (908 g)
Chipotle Taco Seasoning Mix, page 98, 1 batch
Soy-Balsamic Burgers, page 102, 2 batches
Herbed Meatballs (with meatloaf variation), page 106, 1 batch
Easy Make-Ahead Garlic Bread, page 335, 2 batches

Grocery List

FRESH PRODUCE:
- [ ] Onion (1 medium, for 1 cup [160 g] chopped)
- [ ] Garlic (7 cloves)
- [ ] Basil (5 tablespoons chopped)
- [ ] Parsley (½ cup plus 1 tablespoon [34 g] chopped)

DAIRY:
- [ ] Eggs (6)
- [ ] Butter (1 cup [225 g])

MEAT:
- [ ] Ground beef (10 pounds [4540 g])
- [ ] Tri-tip roasts (2 roasts, 2 pounds [908 g] each)

CANNED/BOTTLED/DRY GOODS:
- [ ] Balsamic vinegar (2 tablespoons [30 ml])
- [ ] Soy sauce (2 tablespoons [30 ml])

SEASONINGS:

☐ Dried parsley flakes (3 tablespoons), if not using fresh herb

☐ Ground chipotle chile powder (2 tablespoons plus 2 teaspoons [16 g])

☐ Kosher salt, fine sea salt, and freshly ground black pepper

☐ Onion flakes (2 tablespoons)

☐ Garlic powder (1 tablespoon plus 2 teaspoons)

☐ Dried basil (about 2 tablespoons), if not using fresh herb

☐ Ground cumin (1 tablespoon)

☐ Dried oregano (1 tablespoon)

☐ Dried thyme (1 teaspoon)

BAKERY:

☐ Fresh bread crumbs (3 cups [150 g], or about 9 slices of bread)

☐ French or Italian bread (2 large loaves)

TO SAVE MORE TIME, PURCHASE:

☐ Chopped onions

☐ Chopped garlic

☐ Fresh bread crumbs

Packaging

☐ 2 snack-size zip-top bags, labeled Chipotle Rub

☐ 1 pint-size (470 ml) zip-top freezer bag, labeled Chipotle Taco Seasoning

☐ 4 quart-size (1 L) zip-top freezer bags, labeled Beef Taco Meat (2), Meatballs (2)

☐ 5 gallon-size (4 L) zip-top freezer bags, labeled Tri-tip (2), Soy-Balsamic Burgers (2), Meatloaf (1)

☐ Heavy-duty aluminum foil

☐ Waxed paper

☐ Plastic wrap

Gadgets and Small Appliances

▪ Food processor

▪ Cookie scoop, quick release

▪ Food scale

Prep List

1. Assemble the storage containers and ingredients.

2. Make the bread crumbs in the blender or food processor.

3. Chop the herbs.

4. Chop the onion.

5. Chop the garlic.

6. Soften the butter.

Cooking Plan

1. Preheat the oven to 350°F (180°C or gas mark 4). In a large mixing bowl, prepare the meatball mixture. Using a quick-release cookie scoop, form half the prepared mixture into meatballs, arrange them on the prepared baking sheets, and place them in the oven.

2. Divide the remaining meatball mixture in half. Form each portion into a meatloaf. Wrap each loaf in aluminum foil, label, and bag. Two loaves should fit in 1 bag, but you can bag them separately if you prefer. Place in the freezer. [MEATLOAVES DONE]

3. Start cooking 2 pounds (908 g) of ground beef, to make the seasoned taco meat, in a large skillet on the stovetop.

4. Prepare the chipotle taco seasoning mix (single batch) and the chipotle rub for the tri-tip (two batches) at the same time, since they share common ingredients. Pack the chipotle rub into two snack-size bags and seal. The taco seasoning can go in the pint-size bag.

5. Stir 2 to 4 tablespoons (16 to 32 g) of the taco seasoning mix into the ground beef on the stove once it has started to brown; store the remainder of the taco seasoning mix for another cooking session. Clean up and put away the spices while the taco meat cooks; leave the thyme, balsamic, parsley, soy sauce, and black pepper out for the hamburgers. Portion the cooked meat into two quart-size zip-top bags and allow it to cool to room temperature. Chill the cooked meat in the refrigerator before freezing. [SEASONED TACO MEAT DONE]

6. The meatballs should be done cooking. Remove them from the oven and loosen them from the foil, if they're sticking. Allow them to cool to room temperature and then bag them. Chill the meatballs in the refrigerator before storing in the freezer. [MEATBALLS DONE]

7. Package each tri-tip and its snack-size bag of chipotle rub together in a labeled freezer bag. Freeze. [TRI-TIPS DONE]

8. In a large mixing bowl, prepare the soy-balsamic burgers, using the remaining 4 pounds (1816 g) of ground beef. Form the mixture into 16 patties. Stack the patties in groups of 4, separating them with waxed paper. Wrap with plastic wrap and place the bundles in the labeled freezer bags. Freeze. [HAMBURGERS DONE]

9. Prepare the garlic bread, wrap in foil, and freeze. [GARLIC BREAD DONE]

10. Clean up the workspace. Wipe down the counters. Once the items in the refrigerator have chilled for several hours, transfer them to the freezer.

10-plus meals serving at least 4 people

Seasoned turkey taco meat, 2 pounds (908 g)
Basic Taco Seasoning Mix, page 97, 1 batch
Tandoori Chicken, page 119, 2 batches
Spicy Taco Lasagna, page 142, 2 batches
Turkey Burgers with Scallions, page 143, 2 batches
Mahi Mahi with Almond-Lime Butter, page 152, 2 batches

Grocery List

FRESH PRODUCE:

☐ Lemon (1)
☐ Limes (2)
☐ Scallions (½ to 1 bunch, for ½ cup [50 g] chopped)

☐ Ginger (1-inch [2.5 cm] piece for 2 teaspoons chopped)
☐ Dill (1 tablespoon chopped)
☐ Garlic (2 cloves)

DAIRY:

☐ Pepper Jack cheese (1 pound [454 g]; 4 cups shredded)
☐ Cheddar cheese (1 pound [454 g]; 4 cups shredded)

☐ Cream cheese (two 8-ounce [225 g] packages)
☐ Plain yogurt or buttermilk (1½ cups [355 ml])
☐ Butter (1 cup [225 g])

MEAT/POULTRY/SEAFOOD:

☐ Chicken pieces, such as boneless, skinless chicken breast (8 to 12 pieces)
☐ Ground turkey (6½ pounds [2951 g])

☐ Mahi mahi or other fish fillets (8 fillets, 5 to 8 ounces [140 to 224 g] each)

CANNED/BOTTLED/DRY GOODS:

☐ Olive oil (2 tablespoons [30 ml])
☐ Sherry (2 tablespoons [30 ml])
☐ Favorite purchased pasta sauce, or homemade (6 cups [1410 ml]; 48 ounces [1410 ml])

☐ Favorite purchased salsa, or Easy Homemade Salsa, page 77 (16 ounces [454 g])
☐ Reduced-sodium chicken broth (2 cups [470 ml])
☐ Lasagna noodles (12 to 16)
☐ Sliced almonds (½ cup [50 g])

SEASONINGS:

- ☐ Chili powder (½ cup [24 g] plus 1 teaspoon)
- ☐ Kosher salt, fine sea salt, and freshly ground black pepper
- ☐ Onion flakes (2 tablespoons)
- ☐ Dried oregano (2 tablespoons)
- ☐ Garlic powder (1 tablespoon)
- ☐ Paprika (2 teaspoons)
- ☐ Curry powder (2 teaspoons)
- ☐ Dried dill (1 teaspoon), if not using fresh herb

BAKERY:

- ☐ Fresh bread crumbs (1 cup [50 g], or about 3 slices of bread)

TO SAVE MORE TIME, PURCHASE:

- ☐ Chopped ginger and garlic
- ☐ Shredded cheese
- ☐ Fresh bread crumbs

Packaging

- ☐ 2 quart-size (1 L) zip-top freezer bags, labeled Seasoned Turkey Taco Meat
- ☐ 6 gallon-size (4 L) zip-top freezer bags, labeled Tandoori Chicken (2), Mahi Mahi with Almond-Lime Butter (2), Turkey Burgers with Scallions (2)
- ☐ Two 9 × 13-inch (23 × 33 cm) pans with lids or heavy-duty aluminum foil to cover, labeled Spicy Taco Lasagna
- ☐ 1 pint-size (470 ml) zip-top freezer bag, labeled Taco Seasoning Mix
- ☐ Freezer paper for wrapping fish, if not already wrapped
- ☐ Plastic wrap
- ☐ Waxed paper

Gadgets and Small Appliances

- ▪ Food processor

Prep List

1. Assemble the storage containers and ingredients.

2. Make the bread crumbs in the blender or food processor. Toast the almonds.

3. Soften the butter.

4. Chop the scallions.

5. Shred the cheeses for the lasagna.

6. Juice the lemons.

7. Chop the garlic and ginger.

8. Zest the lime.

Cooking Plan

1. Mix up a batch of taco seasoning mix.

2. Brown 4 pounds (1816 g) of the ground turkey and season it with 1 to 2 tablespoons of the taco seasoning mix. Reserve the remaining seasoning mix for another time. It can be stored in the labeled bag in the pantry or in the freezer for longer keeping.

3. Portion out half of the cooked taco meat and set it aside to use in the lasagna. Divide the remaining taco meat between the labeled zip-top freezer bags. Allow the meat to cool to room temperature and then chill it in the refrigerator before freezing. [SEASONED TACO MEAT DONE]

4. Assemble the spicy taco lasagna. Chill and freeze. [LASAGNA DONE]

5. Using the remaining 2½ pounds (1135 g) of ground turkey, make the turkey burgers. Wrap and freeze. [TURKEY BURGERS DONE]

6. Prepare the almond-lime butter. Assemble the mahi mahi kits as directed in the recipe. Freeze. [MAHI MAHI DONE]

7. Prepare two batches of the tandoori chicken. Pack into labeled bags and freeze. [TANDOORI CHICKEN DONE]

8. Clean up the workspace. Wipe down the counters. Once the items in the refrigerator have chilled for several hours, transfer them to the freezer.

MEAT AND POULTRY PLAN: 3 TO 4 HOURS

28 meals serving at least 4 people

Not Your Convenience Store's Frozen Burritos, page 96, 4 batches
Taco kit, using ground turkey, page 97, 2 kits, using 2 pounds (908 g) meat
Basic Taco Seasoning Mix, page 97, 2 batches
Outside-In Cheeseburgers, page 105, 2 batches
Herbed Meatballs, page 106, 1 batch
Spicy Taco Lasagna, page 142, 2 batches
Southwest Seasoned Pork Chops, page 162, 2 batches
Easy Slow Cooker Red Sauce, page 217, 1 batch
Basic pizza kits, page 252; 1 batch dough, page 249, to make kits for 4 pizzas
Eggs Florentine Casserole, page 292, 2 batches

Grocery List

FRESH PRODUCE:

☐ **Onions (6 medium, for 6 cups [960 g] chopped)**
☐ **1 head garlic**
☐ **Basil (about ½ cup [30 g] chopped)**
☐ **Parsley (about ½ cup [30 g] chopped)**
☐ **Dill (1 tablespoon chopped)**

DAIRY:

- ☐ Cheddar cheese (a little over 4 pounds [1816 g]; 17 cups shredded)
- ☐ Mozzarella cheese (1½ pounds [680 g]; 6 cups shredded)
- ☐ Pepper Jack or Monterey Jack cheese (1 pound [454 g]; 4 cups shredded)
- ☐ Swiss cheese (1 pound [454 g]; 4 cups shredded)
- ☐ Feta cheese (4 cups [600 g] crumbled)
- ☐ Cottage cheese (2 pints [450 g])
- ☐ Cream cheese (two 8-ounce [225 g] packages)
- ☐ Eggs (2 dozen)

MEAT:

- ☐ Ground beef (12 pounds [5448 g])
- ☐ Ground turkey (4 pounds [1816 g])
- ☐ Pork chops (8 chops, ½ inch [1.3 cm] thick)

FROZEN:

- ☐ Frozen chopped spinach (two 10-ounce [280 g] packages)

CANNED/BOTTLED/DRY GOODS:

- ☐ Refried beans or cooked pinto beans (12 cups, 96 ounces [2688 g], about seven 15-ounce [420 g] cans)
- ☐ Enchilada sauce (32 ounces [940 ml])
- ☐ Reduced-sodium chicken broth (2 cups [470 ml])
- ☐ Diced green chiles (four 4-ounce [112 g] cans)
- ☐ Favorite purchased salsa, or Easy Homemade Salsa, page 77 (16 ounces [454 g])
- ☐ Lasagna noodles (12 to 16 noodles)
- ☐ Crushed tomatoes (four 28-ounce [784 g] cans)
- ☐ Unbleached all-purpose flour (4½ cups [540 g])
- ☐ Vegetable oil (½ cup [120 ml])
- ☐ Olive oil (½ cup [120 ml])
- ☐ Red wine vinegar (½ cup [120 ml])
- ☐ Honey or granulated sugar (2 tablespoons [40 or 24 g])
- ☐ Active dry yeast (1 tablespoon [12 g])

SEASONINGS:

- ☐ Chile powder (½ cup [48 g])
- ☐ Dried basil (3 tablespoons), if not using fresh herb
- ☐ Dried parsley flakes (about 3 tablespoons), if not using fresh herb
- ☐ Kosher salt, fine sea salt, and freshly ground black pepper
- ☐ Dried oregano (¼ cup)
- ☐ Garlic powder (2 tablespoons [14 g])
- ☐ Onion flakes (¼ cup [4 g])
- ☐ Dried dill (1 teaspoon), if not using fresh herb
- ☐ Crushed red pepper flakes (½ teaspoon)

BAKERY:

- ☐ Soft taco-size flour tortillas (two 12-count packages)
- ☐ Burrito-size flour tortillas (48)
- ☐ Fresh bread crumbs (3 cups [150 g], or about 9 slices of bread)

TO SAVE MORE TIME, PURCHASE:

☐ Chopped garlic
☐ Chopped onions

☐ Shredded cheese
☐ Fresh bread crumbs

Packaging

☐ 4 sandwich-size bags, labeled Pizza Dough
☐ 1 pint-size (470 ml) freezer bag, labeled Taco Seasoning Mix
☐ 12 quart-size (1 L) zip-top freezer bags, labeled Seasoned Turkey Taco Meat (2), Taco Cheese if not prepackaged in 2-cup (470 ml) portions (2), Meatballs (4), Pizza Cheese (4)
☐ 18 gallon-size (4 L) zip-top freezer bags, labeled Turkey Taco Kit (2), Burritos (8), Southwest Pork Chops (2), Pizza Kit (4), Outside-In Cheeseburgers (2)

☐ Four 9 × 13-inch (23 × 33 cm) pans with lids or heavy-duty aluminum foil for covering, labeled Eggs Florentine (2), Taco Lasagna (2)
☐ Three or four 2-cup (470 ml) plastic containers with lids, labeled Red Sauce
☐ Four ½-cup (120 ml) plastic containers with lids for Red Sauce for pizza kits
☐ Heavy-duty aluminum foil

Gadgets and Small Appliances

▪ Food processor

▪ Bread machine

Prep List

1. Assemble the storage containers and ingredients.

2. Make the bread crumbs in the food processor or blender.

3. Chop the onions and garlic.

4. Chop the herbs.

5. Make the salsa, if using homemade.

6. Shred the cheese.

7. Thaw the spinach.

Cooking Plan

1. Start cooking the red sauce on the stovetop. It will simmer for 2 hours.

2. Begin the pizza dough in the bread machine. After it's been mixing for a few minutes, make sure all the ingredients are incorporated by scraping the sides of the bread pan with a rubber scraper. Allow the kneading cycle to run.

3. Meanwhile, season and form the cheeseburgers, using 4 pounds (1816 g) of the ground beef. Lay the patties on a tray or trays and freeze.

4. Once the bread machine is done kneading the dough, set the timer for a 30-minute rise.

5. Mix up two batches of taco seasoning mix.

6. Brown 4 pounds (1816 g) of the ground beef in a large skillet or pot. Season it with the taco seasoning mix to taste, using 1 to 2 tablespoons per pound (454 g). Drain and transfer the meat to a large bowl. Allow the meat to cool. Wash the pot.

7. The pizza dough is done with the first rise. Turn the dough out onto a lightly oiled surface. Divide the dough ball into 4 sections. Form each section into a tight ball and place in a labeled sandwich-size bag. Place 1 dough ball into each pizza kit bag and place in the freezer immediately. The dough will continue to rise, so move quickly.

8. Portion the mozzarella cheese into the 4 bags labeled Pizza Cheese, 1½ cups (180 g) of cheese per bag. Slip the bags into the pizza kit bags in the freezer.

9. Assemble the burritos with the 4 pounds (1816 g) of cooled cooked beef. Place 6 in each labeled freezer bag. Seal the bags, removing as much air as possible before sealing. Place the bags in the freezer. [BURRITOS DONE]

10. Cook the ground turkey in a large pot. Season the meat with the remaining taco seasoning mix according to taste. Remove half of the meat to a large mixing bowl for the lasagna. Spoon the remaining meat into the two bags labeled Taco Meat. Allow the meat to cool slightly on the counter and then chill it in the refrigerator.

11. Remove 6 cups (1410 ml) of the red sauce to prepare the spicy taco lasagna. Cool the lasagna, cover, and chill in the refrigerator. [LASAGNA DONE]

12. Preheat the oven to 350°F (180°C or gas mark 4). Use the remaining 4 pounds (1816 g) of ground beef to prepare the meatballs. Place the meatballs on a foil-lined rimmed baking sheet and place in the oven.

13. Divide 2 cups (470 ml) of the red sauce among the four ½-cup (120 ml) plastic containers. These will be added to the pizza kits. Allow the sauce to cool slightly before securing the lids.

Chill the sauce in the refrigerator. [PIZZA KITS DONE]

14. Portion the remaining red sauce into the labeled 2-cup (470 ml) containers. [RED SAUCE DONE]

15. Remove the cheeseburgers from the trays in the freezer and place them in the labeled bags. Seal the bags and return the burgers to freezer. [BURGERS DONE]

16. Portion the remaining cheddar cheese into bags labeled Taco Cheese. Place one cheese bag in each taco kit bag. Add a chilled bag of taco meat and a package of taco-size tortillas to each bag. [TACO KITS DONE]

17. When the meatballs are done, remove from the oven and allow to cool.

18. Assemble the egg casseroles. Wrap and freeze. [EGG CASSEROLES DONE]

19. Prepare the marinade for the pork chops and divide it between the labeled bags. Add the chops to the bags, putting 4 pork chops in each bag. Seal the bags and freeze. [PORK CHOPS DONE]

20. Package the meatballs in the labeled freezer bags. Chill the meatballs in the refrigerator before freezing. [MEATBALLS DONE]

21. Package any remaining taco seasoning mix in the labeled bag and store in the pantry or freezer for later use.

22. Clean up the workspace. Wipe down the counters. Once the items in the refrigerator have chilled for several hours, transfer the packages to the freezer.

HOLIDAY BAKING PLAN (4 TO 6 HOURS)

This is a full day of baking that should yield nine types of cookies, three loaves of bread, 18 cinnamon rolls, at least a dozen scones, a cheesecake, two muffin mixes, and a partridge in a pear tree.

Whole-Grain Cinnamon Rolls, page 324, 1 batch
Pretzel Berry Cheesecake, page 356, 1 batch
Ginger-Coconut Scones, page 316, 1 batch
Mix-and-Match Muffin mixes, page 309, 2 batches
Vanilla Cranberry Bread, page 307, 1 batch
Sugar and Spice Cookies, page 337, 1 batch
Lemon Whole-Wheat Spritz Cookies, page 341, 1 batch
Gingerbread Crinkles, page 342, 1 batch
Chocolate-Almond Biscotti, page 343, 1 batch
White Chocolate–Walnut Jumbles, page 339, 1 batch
Chocolate-Toffee Cookies, page 344, 1 batch
Chocolate Minty Melts, page 345, 1 batch
Double Chocolate Magic Bars, page 348, 1 batch
Kahlúa Brownies, page 347, 1 batch

Grocery List

FRESH PRODUCE:

☐ **Lemons (2)**

☐ **Cranberries (3 cups [450 g])**

DAIRY:

☐ **Eggs (22)**

☐ **Butter (4¾ pounds [2157 g])**

☐ **Cream cheese (two 8-ounce [225 g] packages)**

☐ **Milk (3 cups [705 ml])**

☐ **Plain yogurt (1 cup [225 g])**

☐ **Whipping cream (¾ cup [180 ml])**

CANNED/BOTTLED/DRY GOODS:

☐ **Unbleached, all-purpose flour (29 cups, about 8 pounds [3632 g])**

☐ **Granulated sugar (11 cups, about 6 pounds [2724 g])**

☐ **Whole-wheat pastry flour (9 cups, about 3 pounds [1362 g])**

☐ **Dark brown sugar (6 cups, about 3 pounds [1362 g])**

☐ **Unsweetened, shredded coconut (2 cups [170 g]) (Check the organic section of your store. If it's unavailable in your area, simply use sweetened. The end result will simply be a little more sweet than otherwise.)**

☐ **Chocolate chips (2½ cups [438 g])**

☐ **Whole-wheat flour (2 cups [240 g])**

☐ **Sweetened condensed milk (one 14-ounce [392 g] can)**

- ☐ Light coconut milk (12 ounces [355 ml])
- ☐ White chocolate chips (12 ounces [340 g])
- ☐ Cocoa powder (1⅓ cups [150 g])
- ☐ Whole almonds (1 cup [140 g])
- ☐ Toffee bits (1 cup [240 g])
- ☐ Walnuts (1 cup [135 g] chopped)
- ☐ Mini chocolate chips (¾ cup [130 g])
- ☐ Pecans (½ cup [65 g] chopped)
- ☐ Quick oats (½ cup [40 g])
- ☐ Berry jam (½ cup [115 g])
- ☐ Kahlúa (¼ cup [60 ml])
- ☐ Crystallized ginger (¼ cup [25 g])
- ☐ Oreo cookie crumbs (1½ cups [165 g])
- ☐ Hershey Kisses, preferably mint-flavored (42)

- ☐ Molasses (2 tablespoons [40 g])
- ☐ Pretzels (10-ounce [280 g] bag; there will be extra left over)
- ☐ Baking powder
- ☐ Baking soda
- ☐ Salt
- ☐ Vegetable oil
- ☐ Cream of tartar
- ☐ Yeast
- ☐ Extracts: vanilla, lemon, peppermint, and almond
- ☐ Ground decaf coffee
- ☐ Colored sugar or sprinkles
- ☐ Powdered sugar
- ☐ Demerara or turbinado sugar

SPICES:

- ☐ Ground cinnamon
- ☐ Ground ginger

- ☐ Ground nutmeg
- ☐ Ground cloves

** On the day of serving the muffins, you will also need the wet ingredients as specified in the recipe. Please consult the recipe so that you have these items on hand.

Packaging

- ☐ Aluminum foil
- ☐ Plastic wrap
- ☐ Waxed paper or parchment
- ☐ 6 gallon-size (4 L) zip-top freezer bags, labeled Muffin Mixes (2), Vanilla Cranberry Bread (2), Ginger-Coconut Scones (2)

- ☐ Three 8-inch (20.3 cm) pie plates or two 9 × 13-inch (23 × 33 cm) baking dishes, labeled Whole Grain Cinnamon Rolls
- ☐ Plastic containers with lids for baked cookies or extra zip-top freezer bags for cookie dough

Prep List

1. Soften cream cheese and butter.

2. Zest lemon.

3. Chop pecans and walnuts.

4. Wash cranberries.

5. Toast almonds.

6. Crush Oreos.

7. Crush pretzels.

8. Warm jam.

Special Equipment

- Food processor
- Stand mixer or hand mixer
- Three bread pans
- Springform baking pan
- Several cookie sheets
- Cookie press

Cooking Plan

1. Start cinnamon roll dough in the bread machine or mixer. Allow to rise.

2. * Prepare pretzel crust for cheesecake, bake, and cool on a rack.

3. Prepare scones and quick freeze.

4. Prepare cheesecake and bake. Be sure to set the timer. When the timer rings, place the cake on a rack and cool completely.

5. Assemble muffin mixes in marked bags. Use either flour you have for the whole wheat specified in the recipe. The difference is minimal. [MIX-AND-MATCH MUFFIN MIXES DONE]

6. Cinnamon roll dough should be done. Form rolls. Instead of freezing them flat on a cookie sheet, place them in the marked pans, 6 per pie plate or 9 per 9 × 13-inch (23 × 33 cm) pan. Cover, label, and freeze. [CINNAMON ROLLS DONE]

7. Remove scones from the freezer, package in marked bags, and freeze. [GINGER-COCONUT SCONES DONE]

8. Prepare cranberry breads and bake. When the timer rings, place the breads on a rack to cool for 10 minutes. Remove from the pans and allow breads to cool completely on the rack.

9. Begin making cookie doughs: Sugar Cookie, Lemon Whole-Wheat Spritz, and Gingerbread Crinkles. As each dough is complete, wrap in plastic wrap and chill.

10. Wash cookie bowl.

11. If cheesecake is cooled to room temperature, chill it in the refrigerator.

12. * Make biscotti and bake logs. Set the timer. When the timer rings, come back to this recipe to slice the logs and do the double bakes. Then continue with the steps until the timer rings again, when you will turn the cookies and continue baking them. When they are done with the final baking, cool on a rack.

13. Wash biscotti bowl.

14. Cranberry breads should be cooled by now. Wrap in plastic wrap and place in marked freezer bags. Freeze. [VANILLA CRANBERRY BREADS DONE]

15. Make chocolate cookie doughs in this order: White Chocolate Walnut Jumbles, Chocolate Toffee, Minty Melts. As each dough is complete, wrap in plastic wrap and chill. (There's no need to wash the bowl in between batches if you are making them in quick succession.)

16. Wash the bowl.

17. Make Magic Bars, bake, and cool on rack.

18. Make Kahlúa Brownies, bake, and cool on rack.

19. You should now have three types of cookies already baked (biscotti, magic bars, and brownies) and six types of dough chilling in the refrigerator. Determine which of the remaining doughs you will bake at this time. You can bake all the cookies, cool on racks, and then freeze in airtight containers, according to recipe directions. Or you can freeze the doughs to be baked later. Form the dough into a disk or log, wrap tightly with plastic wrap, and slip into a freezer bag for added protection. Store in the freezer. When ready to use, thaw the dough in the refrigerator prior to baking. [LEMON WHOLE-WHEAT SPRITZ, CHOCOLATE-TOFFEE COOKIES, CHOCOLATE MINTY MELTS, SUGAR AND SPICE COOKIES, GINGERBREAD CRINKLES, WHITE CHOCOLATE–WALNUT JUMBLES DONE]

20. Cut and wrap the Magic Bars and the Kahlúa Brownies. Freeze. [MAGIC BARS AND KAHLÚA BROWNIES DONE]

21. Wrap the biscotti in an airtight container and freeze. [BISCOTTI DONE]

22. Wrap the cheesecake in layers of plastic wrap and freeze. [PRETZEL BERRY CHEESECAKE DONE]

23. Clean up the workspace. Wipe down the counters.

PROTEIN POWER COOKING PLAN (4 TO 6 HOURS)

16 meals serving at least 4 people

Spicy Southwest Chicken, page 118, 2 batches
Grilled Tilapia or Shrimp Tacos, page 155, 2 batches
Herbed Pork Sausage Patties, page 182, 2 batches
Tarragon and Lemon Rubbed Fish, page 154, 2 batches
Our Favorite Irish Stew, page 240, 2 batches
Quick and Easy Texas Chili, page 244, 2 batches
Chili and Sausage Oven Frittata, page 294, 2 batches
Salsa Verde Chicken, page 124, 2 batches

Grocery List

FRESH PRODUCE:

- ☐ **Onions (5 medium)**
- ☐ **Garlic (14 cloves)**
- ☐ **Jalapeño pepper (1)**
- ☐ **Baby carrots (4 cups [480 g])**
- ☐ **Potatoes (8 medium)**
- ☐ **Tomatoes (2 medium)**

- ☐ **Cilantro (1 bunch)**
- ☐ **Lemon (1, for zest)**
- ☐ **Limes (3)**
- ☐ **Fresh parsley (if not using dried)**
- ☐ **Fresh dill (if not using dried)**

DAIRY:

- ☐ **Monterey Jack cheese (1½ cups [180 g] shredded)**
- ☐ **Eggs (12)**

- ☐ **Unsalted butter (4 tablespoons [56 g])**

MEAT AND POULTRY:

- ☐ Chuck roast, cut into cubes (4 pounds [1816 g])
- ☐ Ground beef or ground turkey (5 pounds [2270 g])
- ☐ Boneless, skinless chicken breasts (8 to 10)
- ☐ Chicken tenders (4 to 6 pounds [1816 to 2724 g])
- ☐ Salmon fillets or steaks (8 fillets, 5 to 8 ounces [140 to 225 g] each)
- ☐ Tilapia or medium-size shrimp (62/80 count) (2 pounds [908 g])
- ☐ Sweet Italian sausage (8 ounces [224 g])
- ☐ Lean ground pork (2 pounds [908 g])

CANNED/BOTTLED/DRY GOODS:

- ☐ Salsa verde (1 cup [235 ml])
- ☐ Diced green chiles (two 4-ounce [112 g] cans)
- ☐ Tomato sauce (two 15-ounce [420 g] cans)
- ☐ Beef broth (1 cup [235 ml])
- ☐ Soy sauce (½ cup [120 ml])
- ☐ Olive oil
- ☐ Vegetable oil
- ☐ All-purpose flour (about ⅔ cup [80 g])

SEASONINGS:

- ☐ Bay leaves
- ☐ Cayenne pepper
- ☐ Chili powder
- ☐ Cumin
- ☐ Ground ginger
- ☐ Dry mustard
- ☐ Paprika
- ☐ Sesame seeds
- ☐ Dried dill (if not using fresh)
- ☐ Dried oregano
- ☐ Dried parsley (if not using fresh)
- ☐ Dried tarragon
- ☐ Dried thyme
- ☐ Garlic powder
- ☐ Onion powder
- ☐ Rubbed sage
- ☐ Kosher salt
- ☐ Ground black pepper

Packaging

- ☐ Aluminum foil
- ☐ Waxed paper
- ☐ Plastic wrap
- ☐ Freezer paper to wrap seafood
- ☐ 6 gallon-size (4 L) zip-top freezer bag labeled Tarragon and Lemon Rubbed Fish (2), Grilled Tilapia or Shrimp Tacos (2), Herbed Pork Sausage Patties (2), Spicy Southwest Chicken (2), Salsa Verde Chicken (2)
- ☐ 2 snack-size zip-top bags labeled Tarragon and Lemon Spice Rub (2), Grilled Tilapia or Shrimp Taco Spices (2)
- ☐ Large plastic containers in meal-size portions labeled Texas Chili (2), Irish Stew (2)
- ☐ 2 deep-dish 9-inch (23 cm) pie pans with foil labeled Chile and Sausage Oven Frittata (2)

Special Equipment

- Two 5-quart (5 L) slow cookers
- Two 9-inch (23 cm) deep-dish pie pans
- Food processor or blender

Prep List

1. Chop onions.

2. Coarsely chop tomato, jalapeño, and cilantro for Spicy Southwest Chicken. Reserve 2 table-spoons chopped cilantro for frittata.

3. Cook sausage for frittata.

4. Zest lemon.

Cooking Plan

1. Start Irish Stew in slow cookers.

2. Cook Quick and Easy Texas Chili in pot on stove. Portion into meal-size containers. Cool. Refrigerate before freezing. [QUICK AND EASY TEXAS CHILI DONE]

3. Assemble sausage patties. Form. Pack, label, and freeze. [HERBED PORK SAUSAGE PATTIES DONE]

4. Make spice mixes for Tarragon and Lemon Rubbed Fish and Grilled Tilapia Tacos. Assemble kits. Pack, label, and freeze. [TARRAGON AND LEMON RUBBED FISH and GRILLED TILAPIA OR SHRIMP TACOS DONE]

5. Make marinades for chicken. Distribute marinades and chicken pieces into labeled bags. Pack, label, and freeze. [SPICY SOUTHWEST CHICKEN and SALSA VERDE CHICKEN DONE]

6. Assemble the frittatas. Place on a level space in the freezer. Once frozen, wrap well and return to the freezer. [CHILI AND SAUSAGE OVEN FRITTATA DONE]

7. Clean up the kitchen space.

8. When stew is done, portion into meal-size containers. Cool. Refrigerate before freezing. [OUR FAVORITE IRISH STEW DONE]

EVERYTHING PLAN I: 1 DAY

25-plus meals serving at least 4 people

Beefy Mushroom Gravy, page 87, 4 batches
Vegetable Bolognese, page 90, 2 batches
Jamie's Spice Mix, page 98, 1 batch
Sweet and Spicy Joes, page 99, 2 batches
Swedish Meatballs with Dill, page 94, 1 batch
Simply Poached Chicken, page 113, 2 batches
Spicy Southwest Chicken, page 118, 2 batches
Spicy Dijon Chicken, page 119, 2 batches
Garlicky Italian Chicken Breasts, page 121, 2 batches

Garlic Butter Chicken with Lemon Sauce, page 133, 2 batches
Crumb-Topped Cod Fillets, page 154, 2 batches
Tarragon-and-Lemon-Rubbed Fish, page 154, 2 batches
Shrimp Tacos, page 155, 2 batches
Potatoes Stuffed with Caramelized Onions and Dubliner Cheese, page 206, 1 batch

Grocery List

FRESH PRODUCE:

- ☐ Onions (5 or 6 medium, for about 5½ cups [880 g] chopped)
- ☐ 8 baking potatoes
- ☐ Red bell peppers (2)
- ☐ Carrots (2)
- ☐ Eggplants (2 medium)
- ☐ Zucchini (2)
- ☐ Tomatoes (2 medium)
- ☐ Mushrooms (8 ounces [225 g])

- ☐ Garlic (3 heads)
- ☐ Jalapeño pepper (1)
- ☐ Lime (1)
- ☐ Lemons (3)
- ☐ Parsley (1 bunch chopped)
- ☐ Basil (about ½ cup [45 g] chopped)
- ☐ Dill (about ½ cup [16 g] chopped)
- ☐ Cilantro (1 bunch)

MEAT:

- ☐ Ground beef (9 pounds [4086 g])
- ☐ Chicken pieces for marinating (24 to 36 pieces)
- ☐ Boneless, skinless chicken breasts (8)
- ☐ Boneless, skinless chicken tenders (4 pounds [1816 g])

- ☐ Medium-size shrimp, peeled and deveined (2 pounds [908 g])
- ☐ Cod fillets (8 fillets, 5 to 8 ounces [140 to 224 g] each)
- ☐ Fish fillets, such as salmon (8 fillets, 5 to 8 ounces [140 to 224 g] each)
- ☐ Ground pork (1 pound [454 g])

DAIRY:

- ☐ Eggs (6)
- ☐ Butter (about 1½ pounds [680 g])

- ☐ Dubliner cheese (4 ounces [112 g]; 1 cup [120 g] shredded)
- ☐ Sour cream (8 ounces [225 g])

CANNED/BOTTLED/DRY GOODS:

- ☐ Tomato sauce (six 15-ounce [420 g] cans)
- ☐ Reduced-sodium beef broth (64 ounces [1880 ml])
- ☐ Petite diced tomatoes (two 14.5-ounce [406 g] cans)
- ☐ Vegetable oil (½ cup [120 ml])

- ☐ Olive oil (about 2 cups [470 ml])
- ☐ Panko bread crumbs (1 cup [50 g])
- ☐ Unbleached all-purpose flour (1 cup [120 g])
- ☐ Red wine vinegar (¾ cup [180 ml])
- ☐ Dijon mustard (⅔ cup [116 g])
- ☐ Red wine (½ cup [120 ml]), optional

- ☐ White wine or sherry (½ cup [120 ml])
- ☐ Soy sauce (½ cup [120 ml])
- ☐ Light or dark brown sugar (2 tablespoons [24 g])
- ☐ Granulated sugar (2 pinches)

SEASONINGS:

- ☐ Dried parsley flakes (about ⅓ cup), if not using fresh herb
- ☐ Kosher salt, fine sea salt, and freshly ground pepper
- ☐ Paprika (about ¼ cup [24 g])
- ☐ Dried basil (about ¼ cup), if not using fresh herb
- ☐ Onion powder (2 tablespoons)
- ☐ Dried dill (2 to 3 tablespoons), if not using fresh herb
- ☐ Garlic powder (3 tablespoons plus 1 teaspoon [23 g])

- ☐ Dried oregano (1 tablespoon plus 1 teaspoon)
- ☐ Cayenne pepper (1 tablespoon)
- ☐ Sesame seeds (1 tablespoon)
- ☐ Celery seeds (2 teaspoons)
- ☐ Dried tarragon (2 teaspoons)
- ☐ Dried thyme (2 teaspoons)
- ☐ Ground ginger (1 teaspoon)
- ☐ Ground allspice (¼ teaspoon)
- ☐ Bay leaves (4)
- ☐ Peppercorns (8)

BAKERY:

- ☐ Fresh bread crumbs (6 cups [300 g], or about 18 slices of bread)

TO SAVE MORE TIME, PURCHASE:

- ☐ Shredded cheeses
- ☐ Chopped onion
- ☐ Chopped garlic
- ☐ Fresh bread crumbs

Packaging

- ☐ 6 snack-size zip-top bags, labeled Shrimp Taco Spice (2), Crumb Topping for Fish (2), Tarragon-Lemon Rub (2), Jamie's Spice Mix (1)
- ☐ 5 pint-size (470 ml) zip-top freezer bags, labeled Gravy for Swedish Meatballs (4), Jaime's Spice Mix (1)
- ☐ 6 quart-size (1 L) zip-top freezer bags, labeled Swedish Meatballs (4), Poached Chicken (2)
- ☐ 14 gallon-size (4 L) zip-top freezer bags, labeled Stuffed Potatoes with Caramelized Onions and Dubliner Cheese (2), Spicy Southwest Chicken (2), Dijon Chicken (2), Garlicky Italian Chicken (2), Shrimp Taco Kit (2), Crumb-Topped Cod Kit (2), Tarragon-Lemon Fish (2)
- ☐ Two 9 × 13-inch (23 × 33 cm) pans with lids or heavy-duty aluminum foil to cover, labeled Garlic Butter Chicken with Lemon Sauce
- ☐ 7 quart-size (1 L) plastic containers with lids, labeled Vegetable Bolognese (3) and Sweet and Spicy Joes (4)
- ☐ Plastic wrap

Gadgets and Small Appliances

- ▪ Food processor and/or blender
- ▪ At least 2 large stockpots

Prep List

1. Assemble the storage containers and ingredients.

2. Shred the cheese.

3. Chop the onion and garlic.

4. Chop the herbs.

5. Make the bread crumbs in the blender or food processor.

6. Soften the butter.

7. Make the garlic butter for the stuffed chicken.

8. Bake the baking potatoes.

9. Chop the mushrooms, carrots, red bell peppers, and zucchini.

10. Core and halve the tomatoes.

11. Peel and chop the eggplants.

12. Halve the chicken breasts for stuffing.

Cooking Plan

1. Make an 8-cup (1880 ml) batch of the beefy mushroom gravy. Add 2 tablespoons (2 g) of the fresh dill. Place 4 pint-size (470 ml) bags marked Gravy for Swedish Meatballs inside a bowl, so that the bags are stabilized to hold liquids. Divide the gravy among the pint-size bags. Allow the bags to cool to room temperature and then chill the bags in the refrigerator before freezing them.

2. Wash the pot.

3. Mix one batch of Jamie's spice mix, placing it in the labeled pint-size (470 ml) bag.

4. Brown 4 pounds (1816 g) of meat for the sweet and spicy Joes. Add the remaining ingredients to the stockpot and allow the mixture to simmer.

5. Start cooking the Bolognese in a second pot, using 2 pounds (908 g) of the ground beef.

6. Prepare the stuffed baked potatoes. Cool, wrap, place in labeled bags, and chill in refrigerator. [STUFFED POTATOES DONE]

7. Portion out the sweet and spicy Joes in the labeled containers. Allow to cool on the counter before covering the containers and chilling them in the refrigerator. [SWEET AND SPICY JOES DONE]

8. Preheat the oven to 350°F (180°C or gas mark 4). Prepare the meatballs using the remaining 3 pounds (1362 g) of ground beef and the ground pork. Place the meatballs on a foil-lined rimmed baking sheet and place them in the oven.

9. Start poaching the 4 pounds (1816 g) of chicken tenders. Be sure to set a timer, according to the recipe instructions.

10. Portion out the Bolognese in the labeled containers. Allow it to cool on the counter before covering the containers and chilling them in the refrigerator. [BOLOGNESE DONE]

11. The meatballs should be done. Remove them from the oven. Loosen the meatballs from the aluminum foil, if they are sticking. Allow them to cool.

12. Wash the pots.

13. Prepare the garlic butter chicken breasts, using the 8 boneless chicken breasts. Wrap and freeze. [GARLIC BUTTER CHICKEN DONE]

14. Portion the meatballs into the labeled bags. Allow them to cool on the counter before chilling them in the refrigerator. [MEATBALLS DONE]

15. Prepare the marinades for the spicy Southwest chicken, Dijon chicken, and garlicky Italian chicken. Distribute the marinades and chicken pieces among the labeled bags, seal, and freeze. [SOUTHWEST CHICKEN, DIJON CHICKEN, AND ITALIAN CHICKEN DONE]

16. Check the poached chicken. If the water is cool, remove the chicken tenders and portion them, whole or chopped, into the labeled bags and chill before freezing. [POACHED CHICKEN DONE]

17. Prepare the rubs and crumb toppings for the shrimp and fish dishes and assemble the shrimp and fish kits. [SHRIMP TACOS, CRUMB-TOPPED COD FILLET, AND TARRAGON-AND-LEMON-RUBBED FISH KITS DONE]

18. Clean up the workspace. Wipe down the counters. Once the items in the refrigerator have chilled for several hours, transfer them to the freezer.

EVERYTHING PLAN II: 1 DAY

25-plus meals serving at least 4 people

Basic Herb-Baked Chicken, page 111, 2 batches
Chicken Enchilada Bake with Green Chiles and Jalapeños, page 126, 2 batches
Chicken-Bacon Subs, page 140, 2 batches
Make-Ahead Baked Bacon, page 177, 2 batches
Queso Fundido, page 180, made with mild Italian sausage, 2 batches
Red Sauce with Sausage, page 183, 1 batch
Bean and Cheese Nacho Bake, page 192, 2 batches
Cozy Cheese and Potato Casserole, page 194, 2 batches
Homemade Cream of Celery Soup for Cooking, page 238, 4 batches
Cinnamon French Toast Dippers, page 281, 1 batch
Bacon-Cheddar Egg Bake for a Crowd, page 290, 2 batches
Chile and Sausage Oven Frittata, page 294, 2 batches
Easy Make-Ahead Garlic Bread, page 335, 2 batches

Grocery List

FRESH PRODUCE:

☐ **Onions (5 medium, for 4⅔ cups [746 g] chopped)**

☐ **Jalapeño peppers (2)**

☐ **Garlic (1 to 2 heads)**

☐ **Celery (2 to 3 ribs, for ½ cup [60 g] chopped)**

☐ **Parsley (about ⅓ cup chopped)**

☐ **Basil (about ⅓ cup chopped)**

☐ **Cilantro (2 tablespoons chopped)**

☐ **Orange (1)**

DAIRY:

- ☐ Eggs (35)
- ☐ Cheddar cheese (about 3 pounds [1362 g]; 11⅔ cups shredded)
- ☐ Milk (9 cups [2115 ml])
- ☐ Pepper Jack cheese (2 pounds [908 g]; 8 cups shredded)
- ☐ Monterey Jack cheese (6 ounces [168 g]; 1½ cups shredded)
- ☐ Mozzarella or additional Monterey Jack cheese (10 ounces [280 g] sliced)
- ☐ Sour cream (5⅓ cups)
- ☐ Ricotta cheese (16 ounces [454 g])
- ☐ Butter (1½ pounds [680 g])
- ☐ Parmesan cheese (¼ cup [25 g] shredded)

FROZEN:

- ☐ Frozen shredded potatoes (two 32-ounce [908 g] bags)

MEAT:

- ☐ Bone-in split chicken breasts (12)
- ☐ Mild Italian sausage (4½ pounds [2043 g])
- ☐ Bacon (3 pounds [1362 g])

CANNED/BOTTLED/DRY GOODS:

- ☐ Olive oil (2 tablespoons [30 ml])
- ☐ Tomato puree (four 28-ounce [784 g] cans)
- ☐ Refried beans (48 ounces [1344 g])
- ☐ Tomato sauce (two 8-ounce [224 g] cans)
- ☐ Favorite purchased salsa, or Easy Homemade Salsa, page 77 (16 ounces [454 g])
- ☐ Chopped green chiles (four 4-ounce [112 g] cans)
- ☐ Tortilla chips (13 ounces [364 g])
- ☐ Sliced black olives (about 1⅓ cups [135 g])
- ☐ Unbleached all-purpose flour (1 cup [120 g] plus 2 tablespoons [16 g])
- ☐ Light or dark brown sugar (1½ tablespoons [18 g])

SEASONINGS:

- ☐ Kosher salt, fine sea salt, and freshly ground black pepper
- ☐ Dried parsley flakes (about 2 tablespoons), if not using fresh herb
- ☐ Dried basil (about 2 tablespoons), if not using fresh herb
- ☐ Garlic powder (2 teaspoons)
- ☐ Ground cumin (2 teaspoons)
- ☐ Paprika (2½ teaspoons)
- ☐ Chili powder (4 teaspoons)
- ☐ Dried oregano (1½ teaspoons)
- ☐ Onion powder (1 teaspoon)
- ☐ Ground cinnamon (½ teaspoon)
- ☐ Crushed red pepper flakes (¼ teaspoon)
- ☐ *Herbes de Provence*, chili powder, or Italian herbs (optional; 2 teaspoons)
- ☐ Vanilla extract (1 teaspoon)

BAKERY:

☐ Italian bread (4 large loaves)

☐ Bread cubes (12 cups [600 g])

☐ French bread or sub rolls (three 8-inch [20.3 cm])

☐ Corn tortillas (24)

TO SAVE MORE TIME, PURCHASE:

☐ Shredded cheeses

☐ Chopped onions

☐ Chopped garlic

Packaging

☐ 3 quart-size (1 L) zip-top freezer bags, labeled Cooked Sausage (2), Cooked Chicken (1)

☐ 8 gallon-size (4 L) zip-top freezer bags, labeled Queso Fundido (2), Bacon (2), French Toast Dippers (2), Chile and Sausage Frittata (2)

☐ Four 8-inch (20.3 cm) pie plates, labeled Queso Fundido (2), Chile and Sausage Frittata (2)

☐ 6 or 7 pint-size (470 ml) plastic containers with lids, labeled Red Sauce

☐ Eight 9 × 13-inch (23 × 33 cm) baking pans with lids, labeled Chicken Enchilada Bake (2), Bean and Cheese Nacho Bake (2), Potato Casserole (2), Bacon-Cheddar Egg Bake (2)

☐ Heavy-duty aluminum foil

Gadgets and Small Appliances

▪ Slow cooker

▪ 2 large stockpots

▪ Food processor

Prep List

1. Assemble the storage containers and ingredients.

2. Soften the butter.

3. Shred the cheeses.

4. Slice the French bread or sub rolls for French toast.

5. Slice the 4 loaves of Italian bread horizontally.

6. Chop the herbs.

7. Make the garlic butter for the Easy Make-Ahead Garlic Bread and Chicken Bacon Subs.

Cooking Plan

1. Preheat the oven to 375°F (190°C or gas mark 5). Bake the chicken and the bacon. Be sure to set a timer and check on the pans in between the other steps. If your oven is not large enough, bake in stages.

2. Start the red sauce in the slow cooker or on the stovetop.

3. Make an 8-cup (1880 ml) batch of cream of celery soup. Allow to cool. Once cool, use in recipes or chill in refrigerator until needed.

4. Remove the casings from 2½ pounds (1135 g) of the sausage and cook the meat in a skillet on the stovetop, breaking up any chunks with the back of a spoon. Drain. Remove about one-fifth of the meat to use in the frittatas. Use the remaining cooked sausage for the queso fundido.

5. Assemble the queso fundido in the labeled pie plates. Allow the plates to cool slightly on the counter before chilling them in the refrigerator. [QUESO FUNDIDO DONE]

6. Assemble the 2 frittatas in the labeled pie plates, using the reserved cooked and cooled sausage. [FRITTATAS DONE]

7. The bacon should be cooked and cooled by now. Reserve 12 slices and package the rest for later use, dividing it between the two labeled bags. [BACON DONE]

8. Add the remaining 2 pounds (908 g) sausage links to the red sauce. Continue to simmer sauce.

9. The chicken should be baked and at least partially cooled by now. Shred or chop the chicken, according to your preference. Reserve 6 cups (840 g) for the enchilada bakes and 4 cups (560 g) for the chicken-bacon subs. Package the remaining chicken into the bag labeled Cooked Chicken for later use. [COOKED CHICKEN DONE]

10. Make the chicken-bacon subs using 4 cups (560 g) of chicken and 4 slices of bacon. At the same time, make 2 loaves of garlic bread. Wrap both bread and subs in heavy-duty foil, label, and freeze. [SUBS AND GARLIC BREAD DONE]

11. Use the remaining 6 cups (840 g) of cooked chicken to make the enchilada bakes. Cover and chill in the refrigerator before freezing. [ENCHILADA BAKES DONE]

12. Turn the oven up to 500°F (250°C or gas mark 10). Make the French toast dippers and bake them in batches. As each batch is done, cool the dippers on a rack.

13. Assemble the bacon-cheddar egg bakes. Wrap and freeze. [EGG BAKES DONE]

14. Assemble the bean and cheese nacho bakes. Cover and chill in the refrigerator before freezing. [NACHO BAKES DONE]

15. Package the cooled French toast dippers in the labeled bags and freeze. [FRENCH TOAST DONE]

16. Remove the cooked sausages from the red sauce and package them in the labeled bags. Portion the red sauce into the labeled plastic containers. Allow the sausages and sauce to cool to room temperature before chilling in the refrigerator. [RED SAUCE WITH SAUSAGE DONE]

17. Assemble the cheese and potato casseroles. Freeze immediately. [POTATO CASSEROLES DONE]

18. Clean up the workspace. Wipe down the counters. Once the items in the refrigerator have chilled for several hours, transfer them to the freezer.

EVERYTHING PLAN III: 1 DAY

25-plus meals serving at least 4 people

Mexican Beef Tortas, page 77, 1 batch
Mediterranean-Style Steak, page 81, 2 batches
Seasoned Steak with Gorgonzola-Herb Butter, page 83, 2 batches
Jamie's Spice Mix, page 98, 1 batch
Herb-Butter Chicken Tenders, page 122, 2 batches
Teriyaki Chicken Skewers, page 123, 2 batches
Spicy Shrimp and Tomatoes sauce, page 158, 1 batch
Soy-Ginger Pork Tenderloin, page 167, 2 batches
Grilled Caribbean Pork Tenderloin, page 171, 2 batches
Herb-Crusted Pork Roast, page 176, 2 batches
Ham and Swiss Potato Gratin, page 178, 1 batch
Quick and Spicy Marinara Sauce, page 216, 1 batch
Fish Chowder with Red Potatoes and Corn, page 236, 1 batch
Tortilla Soup with Shrimp, page 235, 1 batch
Homemade Cream of Celery Soup for Cooking, page 238, 4 batches

---

Grocery List

FRESH PRODUCE:

- [ ] Limes (2)
- [ ] Lemons (2)
- [ ] Onions (5 to 6 medium, for 5½ cups [880 g] chopped)
- [ ] Jalapeño pepper (1)
- [ ] Garlic (1 to 2 heads)
- [ ] Carrots (3 or 4, for 2 cups [260 g] chopped)

- [ ] Red, green, or mixed bell peppers (about 3, for 3 cups [450 g] chopped)
- [ ] Celery (about 4 ribs, for 2 cups [240 g] chopped)
- [ ] Red potatoes (2 pounds [908 g])
- [ ] Ginger (2-inch [5 cm] piece)
- [ ] Basil (3 tablespoons chopped)
- [ ] Dill (2 tablespoons chopped)
- [ ] Parsley (1 tablespoon chopped)

MEAT:

- [ ] Boneless chicken tenders (8 pounds [3632 g])
- [ ] Boneless chuck roast (4 pounds [1816 g])
- [ ] Top sirloin steaks (2 large, about 2 pounds [908 g] each)
- [ ] Tri-tip roasts (2, about 2 pounds [908 g] each)

- [ ] Pork tenderloins (4 tenderloins, 1 pound [454 g] each)
- [ ] Pork roasts (two 2-pound [908 g] roasts)
- [ ] Diced ham (8 ounces [224 g])

FROZEN FOODS:

☐ Frozen shredded potatoes (one 32-ounce [908 g] package)

☐ Frozen (or canned) corn (12 ounces [340 g])

DAIRY:

☐ Swiss cheese (8 ounces [224 g]; 2 cups shredded)

☐ Gorgonzola cheese (½ cup [60 g] crumbled)

☐ Parmesan cheese (1 ounce [28 g]; ¼ cup shredded)

☐ Heavy cream (½ cup [120 ml])

☐ Milk (1 quart [1 L])

☐ Butter (about 1½ pounds [680 g])

CANNED/BOTTLED/DRY GOODS:

☐ Crushed tomatoes (four 28-ounce [784 g] cans)

☐ Reduced-sodium chicken broth (7 cups [1645 ml])

☐ Petite diced tomatoes (two 14.5-ounce [406 g] cans)

☐ Black beans (one 15-ounce [420 g] can)

☐ Hominy (one 15.5-ounce [434 g] can)

☐ Tomato sauce (one 15-ounce [420 g] can)

☐ Olive oil (about 1 cup [235 ml])

☐ Soy sauce (about 1 cup [235 ml])

☐ Unbleached all-purpose flour (1 cup [120 g])

☐ Vegetable oil

☐ Sherry (¾ cup [180 ml])

☐ Tomato paste (one 6-ounce [168 g] can plus 1 tablespoon [15 g])

☐ Chopped green chiles (one 4-ounce [112 g] can)

☐ Rice vinegar (½ cup [120 ml])

☐ Red wine vinegar (½ cup [120 ml])

☐ Dijon mustard (3 tablespoons [33 g])

☐ Apple cider vinegar (3 tablespoons [45 ml])

☐ Sesame oil (2 tablespoons [30 ml])

☐ Light or dark brown sugar (2 teaspoons)

SEASONINGS:

☐ Garlic powder (¼ cup plus 2 teaspoons [31 g])

☐ Kosher salt, fine sea salt, and freshly ground black pepper

☐ Onion powder (2 tablespoons plus 1 teaspoon)

☐ Paprika (2 tablespoons plus 1 teaspoon)

☐ Dried thyme (2 tablespoons)

☐ Dried oregano (about 3 tablespoons)

☐ Dried basil (1 tablespoon), if not using fresh herb

☐ Dried dill (1 tablespoon), if not using fresh herb

☐ Chili powder (1 tablespoon)

☐ Dried parsley flakes (1 teaspoon), if not using fresh herb

☐ Red pepper flakes (5/8 teaspoon)

☐ Rubbed sage (2 teaspoons)

☐ Ground ginger (2 teaspoons)

☐ Dried rosemary (1½ teaspoons)

☐ Ground allspice (1 teaspoon)

☐ Celery seeds (1 teaspoon)

☐ Ground nutmeg (1 teaspoon)

☐ Smoked paprika (1 teaspoon)

☐ Cayenne pepper (1 teaspoon)

☐ Ground cinnamon (1½ teaspoons)

☐ Chipotle chile powder (½ teaspoon)

☐ Dried tarragon (½ teaspoon)

☐ Bay leaf (1)

BAKERY:

☐ Fresh bread crumbs (1 cup [50 g], or about 3 slices of bread)

TO SAVE MORE TIME, PURCHASE:

☐ Shredded cheese

☐ Chopped onions

☐ Chopped garlic

☐ Fresh bread crumbs

Packaging

☐ Plastic wrap

☐ 4 snack-size bags, labeled Steak Rub (2), Caribbean Rub (2)

☐ 2 sandwich-size bags, labeled Gorgonzola Butter

☐ 1 pint-size (470 ml) zip-top freezer bag, labeled Jamie's Spice Mix

☐ 2 to 4 quart-size (1 L) zip-top freezer bags, labeled Mexican Tortas

☐ 14 gallon-size (4 L) zip-top freezer bags, labeled Soy-Ginger Pork Tenderloin (2), Caribbean Pork Tenderloin (2), Herb-Crusted Pork Roast (2), Mediterranean-Style Steak (2), Seasoned Steak with Gorgonzola-Herb Butter (2), Teriyaki Chicken Skewers (2), Herb-Butter Chicken Tenders (2)

☐ Four 6-cup (1410 ml) plastic containers with lids, labeled Tortilla Soup (2), Fish Chowder (2)

☐ Six or seven 2-cup (470 ml) plastic containers with lids, labeled Marinara Sauce

☐ Two 3-cup (700 ml) plastic containers with lids, labeled Shrimp Sauce

☐ One 9 × 13-inch (23 × 33 cm) baking pan, labeled Ham and Swiss Gratin

Gadgets and Small Appliances

▪ Slow cooker

▪ Immersion blender

▪ 2 or 3 stockpots

Prep List

1. Assemble the storage containers and ingredients.

2. Shred the cheese.

3. Grate the lime and lemon zests.

4. Chop the herbs.

5. Chop the garlic, onions, carrots, bell peppers, celery, and jalapeños.

6. Make the bread crumbs in a blender or food processor.

7. Cook the red potatoes.

Cooking Plan

1. Start the meat for the Mexican tortas in the slow cooker.

2. Make the cream of celery soup in a stockpot on the stove. Remove 2 cups (470 ml) for the ham and Swiss gratin and chill in the refrigerator.

3. Prepare the chowder using the remaining 6 cups (1410 ml) of cream of celery soup. Instead of sautéing the vegetables in the stockpot, cook them in a small sauté pan and then add them to the cream of celery soup already in the pot. Divide the soup between the two labeled 6-cup (1410 g) plastic containers. Allow the soup to cool to room temperature and then chill it in the refrigerator before freezing. [CHOWDER DONE] Wash the pot.

4. Prepare Jaime's Spice Mix and place it in the labeled bag.

5. Start the marinara sauce on the stovetop.

6. If the reserved 2 cups (240 g) of celery soup have cooled, assemble the ham and Swiss gratin and freeze it immediately. If not, complete the next step and then come back to this one. [HAM AND SWISS POTATO GRATIN DONE]

7. Prepare the rubs for the seasoned steak, herb-crusted pork roasts, and Caribbean pork tenderloins. Make the Gorgonzola butter to go with the steaks. Assemble these meal kits by placing each piece of meat with the appropriate seasoning or condiment in the labeled bags. Freeze. [SEASONED STEAK, PORK ROASTS, AND CARIBBEAN PORK TENDERLOINS DONE]

8. Cook the sauce for the shrimp and tomatoes.

9. While the sauce is simmering, revisit previous steps, putting containers in the refrigerator to chill or cleaning up the kitchen as needed.

10. Once the shrimp sauce is done, portion the sauce into the labeled 6-cup (1410 ml) containers. Allow the sauce to cool to room temperature, then chill it in the refrigerator before freezing. [SAUCE FOR SHRIMP AND TOMATOES DONE]

11. Wash the pot.

12. Prepare the tortilla soup.

13. While the tortilla soup is simmering, prepare the marinades for the teriyaki chicken, herb-butter chicken, Mediterranean-style steak, and soy-ginger tenderloin. Assemble and freeze these meals. [TERIYAKI CHICKEN, HERB-BUTTER CHICKEN, MEDITERRANEAN STEAK, AND SOY-GINGER TENDERLOIN DONE]

14. Divide the tortilla soup between the two labeled 6-cup (1410 ml) plastic containers. Allow the soup to cool to room temperature, then chill it in the refrigerator before freezing. [TORTILLA SOUP DONE]

15. Portion the cooked meat for the tortas into the labeled quart-size (1 L) freezer bags. Allow the meat to cool to room temperature with the bag open, then chill it in the refrigerator before freezing. [TORTAS DONE]

16. Divide the marinara sauce among the labeled 2-cup (470 ml) plastic containers. Allow the sauce to cool to room temperature, then chill it in the refrigerator before freezing. [MARINARA SAUCE DONE]

17. Clean up the workspace. Wipe down the counters. Once the items in the refrigerator have chilled for several hours, transfer them to the freezer.

Creating Your Own Cooking Plan

In the Quick-Start Guide on page 7, I explained the basic steps to developing a bulk cooking plan. The previous chapter provides a number of specific cooking plans for you to follow, and those will serve you well. However, if you want to make "freezer cooking" your new regular mode of operation, you may want to bust out and create your own plans, using your own family favorite recipes. Here are the basic tenets from the Quick-Start Guide explained in greater detail, to help you create great cooking plans all your own.

1. PRINT OFF THE PLANNING PAGES.

You can copy the planning pages available on pages 69 to 71 or head to http://fishmama.com/freezer for a packet of free printable worksheets that you can download to your computer.

2. CHOOSE RECIPES YOU KNOW YOUR FAMILY LIKES.

Visit your freezer and pantry to see what ingredients you already have. Build your list from your supplies on hand first, and then consult the grocery ads to see what might be a good deal this week. Varying the types of protein (beef, pork, poultry, and so on) will help keep you from getting bored by week three. At the same time, though, you'll want to choose some dishes that have similar ingredients, so you can take advantage of bulk-buying savings. For instance, if ground beef is on sale, you might choose to make meatloaf, meatballs, and tacos, so you can buy several pounds of ground beef at a low price. It's also a time-saver: You can mix all of the meat with onions at once and then divide it up to complete the individual recipes.

Consult the list of what freezes well on pages 8 to 11. Once you've chosen your recipes, jot the recipe names down on the Freezer Cooking Master Plan sheet. As you choose your recipes, group them according to the protein or main ingredient featured. When you get cooking, you will prepare all the chicken recipes or all the beef recipes at one time, making use of common ingredients and reducing your work time. Remember the magic of the assembly line!

3. CREATE A GROCERY LIST, KEEPING MULTIPLICATION IN MIND.

The reason freezer cooking can save you time and money is that you're going to prepare multiple batches at one time, creating possibly several weeks' or a month's worth of food in one cooking session. You're also going to do a lot of grocery shopping at one time. And fewer trips to the grocery store mean fewer impulse buys and even more grocery savings.

With paper and pencil in hand, go through each recipe and create a shopping list. For duplicate items, like the aforementioned ground beef, just write tally marks next to the item until you get through the recipes and can calculate the totals for each item. Consult the contents of your pantry to make sure you don't overbuy.

Make your Grocery List reflect the multiple batches you're preparing. Use the Freezer Cooking Master Plan worksheet to keep track of your list.

4. CONSIDER HOW YOU WILL PACKAGE YOUR MEALS.

There are lots of options: freezer bags, reusable foil containers, plastic containers, and baking dishes. See my explanations on page 14. Make sure you have enough supplies for each recipe you are preparing. If you need additional dishes or packaging, add those to your Grocery List.

5. PLAN YOUR PREP CHEF LIST.

In higher-end restaurants, the chef doesn't usually do all his or her own chopping and slicing; the prep chef does this. As such, the chef has all his ingredients ready at his disposal, making recipe preparation quick and easy.

At home, you can be your own prep chef. Having the ingredients ready will make the cooking smoother, faster, and more enjoyable. Read each recipe and create a list of all the items that need to be sliced, grated, chopped, or precooked. As a shortcut, consider buying ingredients that are already prepped, like shredded cheese, chopped vegetables, and toasted nuts.

Group each family of recipes, according to core ingredient. You can use the Freezer Cooking Planning Worksheet. For example, one list might read "Freezer Cooking Planning Worksheet: Chicken" across the top. Then walk through each of your chicken recipes, jotting down in the appropriate spaces the ingredients needed as well as how those ingredients need to be prepped.

At the bottom, you can tally all the items that you need to prep ahead of time. Make sure that you double-check that needed ingredients and packaging items are on your Grocery List. As you make your tallies, move those items to the Prep Chef List and Timeline. Here you'll jot down the total ingredients that need to be prepped, giving you a working to-do list.

6. PLAN OUT THE ORDER IN WHICH YOU WILL COOK YOUR MEALS.

Use the Prep Chef List and Timeline form to map out an order of meal assembly. Consider how long something takes to cook, whether you can multitask while it's cooking, and which recipes build on one another. For instance, if you're going to make a big pot of red sauce as well as several pans of lasagna, then you need to make the sauce recipe first. The sauce will take several hours to simmer, so plan to prepare other meals while that cooks. The lasagna makes use of the red sauce, so you can assemble those when the sauce is done.

Many of the recipes in this book utilize a common cooking sauce or core protein. Those basic components will always need to be prepared first so that you can use them in later recipes. If you're making Best-Ever Chicken Pot Pie (page 127), Not Your Mother's Chicken Noodle Soup (page 223), and Green Chile Chicken Taquitos (page 139), you'll obviously need cooked chicken to prepare those meals. You work out what fits you best and then write out a plan.

7. SHOP.

Consult your Freezer Cooking Master Plan sheet. Make sure that you clean out the fridge before you go shopping. You'll be amazed at how quickly it will fill up again. And if you can stand it, just leave the nonperishables in the bags or on the counter when you return from the store. Why waste time putting them away just to get them back out again?

8. PREP.

Consult your Prep Chef List and Timeline. Before cooking, prep as many of the ingredients as you can. Do all your slicing, dicing, and chopping. Precook meats for casseroles.

9. GET COOKING AND ASSEMBLING.

Refer to both your Prep Chef List and Timeline and your Freezer Cooking Planning Worksheet to walk you through these steps. Pick some music you like, supply yourself with beverages and snacks, make sure the kids are safe and happy, and go to it. For ideas on how to include a friend, see page 291.

10. CHILL OUT.

Remember that food will freeze better and more quickly if it is really cold to begin with. You can cool the foods to room temperature, wrap them well, and then chill them in the refrigerator before freezing. Food should not sit at room temperature for more than 2 hours, so be mindful of this timeline. Once the food is very cold, it's ready for the freezer.

ADAPTING YOUR OWN RECIPES

If you cook regularly, chances are you already have an arsenal of recipes you and your family loves. Some—think soups, stews, and casseroles—will do quite well as make-ahead and freeze dishes, provided you cool and package them appropriately for the freezer. Others may need some tweaking to render them freezer friendly. Risotto, for example, doesn't freeze well, but you could precook or marinate the chicken that you'll add to it.

If you're not sure whether a family recipe is freezer friendly, then test it. The next time you prepare it, set aside a small portion. Cool it completely and wrap it well for freezing, then freeze, thaw, and reheat it. If you still like the taste and texture, you know you've got a winner.

There are bound to be a few favorite recipes that cannot be frozen either in part or in full; those will need to be relegated to days when you don't mind making everything on the spot. (A cheese soufflé would fall into this category.) And if you don't have a cache of go-to recipes, well, this book has got you covered!

▶ Covering the Bases: Sauces and Spice Mixes

Traditional recipes for freezing usually feature canned soups, prepared sauces, and foil packets of seasoning mixes. While these products are certainly quick and easy to use, they can be expensive and contain dubious ingredients. Creating your own cooking sauces and spice mixes is a great way to have flavor at your fingertips without a lot of fuss—or a lot of fake food.

The following sauces and spice blends are featured in recipes throughout this book. By preparing a bulk batch at the beginning of a cooking session, you can save yourself a great deal of time and ensure that delicious, quality ingredients are incorporated into your meals.

- Beefy Mushroom Gravy, page 87
- Basic Taco Seasoning Mix, page 97
- Chipotle Taco Seasoning Mix, page 98
- Jamie's Spice Mix, page 98
- Easy Chicken (or Turkey) Gravy, page 115
- Easy Slow Cooker Red Sauce, page 217
- Homemade Cream of Celery Soup for Cooking, page 238
- Parmesan Herb Blend, page 255

Freezer Cooking Master Plan

Main Ingredient/Protein	Recipe	Groceries

Prep Chef List and Timeline

Prep Chef List	Cooking Timeline	X
GRATE/SHRED		
CHOP/SLICE		
PREPARE		
COOK		
OTHER		

Freezer Cooking Planning Worksheet

Recipe Name/ Packaging	Ingredients Needed	Pre-Prep List		
		Cook/Prepare	Chop/Slice	Grate/Shred
{Prep-Chef List}		COOK	CHOP/SLICE	GRATE/SHRED

1

WHERE'S THE BEEF?

▸ Versatile Shredded Beef Filling ▪ 73

▸ Salsa Verde Beef ▪ 75

▸ Oven-Baked Beef Taquitos ▪ 76

▸ Easy Homemade Salsa ▪ 77

▸ Super-Simple Guacamole ▪ 77

▸ Mexican Beef Tortas ▪ 77

▸ Hearty Shredded Beef Enchiladas ▪ 79

▸ Chipotle-Rubbed Tri-Tip ▪ 80

▸ Mediterranean-Style Steak ▪ 81

▸ Easy Carne Asada ▪ 82

▸ Seasoned Steak with Gorgonzola-Herb Butter ▪ 83

▸ Quick and Easy Pepper Steak ▪ 85

▸ Cream Cheese Mashed Potatoes ▪ 86

▸ Beefy Mushroom Gravy ▪ 87

▸ Meatball Sub Kit ▪ 88

▸ Vegetable Bolognese ▪ 90

▸ Vegetable-Beef Lasagna ▪ 91

▸ Shepherd's Pie with Green Chile Mashed Potatoes ▪ 92

▸ Swedish Meatballs with Dill ▪ 94

▸ Not Your Convenience Store's Frozen Burritos ▪ 96

▸ Jamie's Spice Mix ▪ 98

▸ Sweet and Spicy Joes ▪ 99

▸ Chili-Stuffed Sweet Potatoes ▪ 99

▸ Lawnmower Taco ▪ 100

▸ Soy-Balsamic Burgers ▪ 102

▸ Outside-In Cheeseburgers ▪ 105

▸ Herbed Meatballs ▪ 106

▸ Barbecue Sauce for Meatballs ▪ 106

▸ Herbed Meatloaf ▪ 107

▸ Boules de Picolat (Catalan Meatballs) ▪ 108

Versatile Shredded Beef Filling

Seasoned, shredded beef is a wonderful filling for all sorts of sandwiches, as well as a variety of Mexican dishes like taquitos, tacos, and tostadas. It's also delicious on barbecue beef sandwiches. It's economical because beef chuck roast often goes on sale for a low price, and it's super easy to make because the slow cooker does most of the work. You can change the flavor profile of this shredded beef filling by varying the spices and aromatics used (see the variations that follow). With a few bags waiting in the freezer, you'll be able to pull a variety of meals together in just minutes. // *Serves 10 to 12*

■ **PACKAGING:** Large plastic containers or quart-size (1 L) zip-top freezer bags

1 tablespoon (15 ml) olive oil	**1 medium-size onion, chopped**
One 4-pound (1816 g) boneless chuck roast	**1 tablespoon chili powder**
or chuck steak	**1 teaspoon dried oregano**
Salt and freshly ground black pepper	**¼ cup (60 ml) water**

1. In a large skillet, heat the olive oil over medium-high heat until shimmering. Generously season the chuck roast with salt and pepper. Add the meat to the hot pan and brown it well on all sides. Transfer the roast to a 5-quart (5 L) slow cooker.

2. Add the onion to the drippings in the skillet and sauté, scraping up any browned bits. Cook until the onion is translucent. Add the chili powder and the oregano, stirring to combine well.

3. Add the water, stirring and scraping up any remaining browned bits. Scrape the onion mixture into the slow cooker.

4. Cook the roast on LOW for 6 to 8 hours or on HIGH for about 4 hours. The meat should be extremely tender and shred easily.

5. Remove the meat from the slow cooker and allow it to cool slightly. Shred the meat by chopping it into chunks and pulling it apart with two forks or small tongs.

6. Adjust the seasonings to taste. Add some of the drippings to moisten the meat, if necessary. Otherwise, strain the drippings and save them for another dish, such as soup or gravy.

FREEZING INSTRUCTIONS:

Divide the shredded beef and juices into meal-size portions in plastic containers or freezer bags. Chill the beef in the refrigerator before freezing.

TO THAW AND SERVE:

Thaw the meat in the refrigerator. Use this shredded beef for tostadas, chimichangas, burritos, tacos, enchiladas, and sandwiches. Reheat the meat in a pan on the stovetop, stirring frequently, or in a microwave-safe dish in the microwave on HIGH for 2 to 3 minutes, stirring once.

Italian Shredded Beef Filling

This variation of shredded beef is great mixed into Easy Slow Cooker Red Sauce (page 217) or used in hot Italian sandwiches. For sandwiches, spoon reheated meat and some of the juices into a crusty sub roll. Add spicy peppers and shredded Italian-blend cheese if you desire. // *Serves 10 to 12*

■ **PACKAGING:** Large plastic containers or quart-size (1 L) zip-top freezer bags

1 tablespoon (15 ml) olive oil
One 4-pound (1816 g) boneless chuck roast
   or chuck steak
Salt and freshly ground black pepper
3 cloves garlic, crushed

1 tablespoon finely shredded fresh basil
   or 1 teaspoon dried basil
1 teaspoon dried oregano
½ teaspoon freshly ground black pepper
¼ teaspoon crushed red pepper flakes
¼ cup (60 ml) water

Follow the method for Versatile Shredded Beef Filling, substituting the garlic, herbs, and spices for the onion, chili powder, and oregano in step 2.

Provençal Shredded Beef Filling

This variation on shredded beef goes well with Beefy Mushroom Gravy (page 87); you can also use it in French dip sandwiches. Save the drippings for the dipping jus. // *Serves 10 to 12*

■ **PACKAGING:** Large plastic containers or quart-size (1 L) zip-top freezer bags

1 tablespoon (15 ml) olive oil
One 4-pound (1816 g) boneless chuck roast
   or chuck steak
Salt and freshly ground black pepper

3 shallots, finely chopped
1 tablespoon *herbes de Provence*
¼ cup (60 ml) red wine

Follow the method for Versatile Shredded Beef Filling, substituting the shallots and herbs for the onion, chili powder, and oregano in step 2. Use the wine instead of water in step 3.

Salsa Verde Beef

After you serve this dish once, eyes will light up at the mere mention of it. It's hearty and filling and has a little kick—and there is rarely any left over. I love it for its versatility. Serve it simply over rice or use it as a taco or burrito filling. You can also add 5 cups of cooked pinto beans to the slow cooker near the end of the cooking time to make a delicious chili. // *Serves 6 to 8*

■ **PACKAGING:** Large plastic containers with lids

1 tablespoon (15 ml) olive oil
One 3-pound (1362 g) boneless rump
   or chuck roast, cut into 1½-inch
   (3.8 cm) cubes

½ cup (80 g) chopped onion
2 tablespoons (16 g) Basic Taco Seasoning
   Mix (page 97)
1 cup (235 ml) salsa verde

WHEN READY TO SERVE, YOU WILL NEED:
Cooked rice or flour tortillas
Shredded cheddar, Monterey Jack,
   or Mexican-blend cheese

Easy Homemade Salsa (page 77)
Super-Simple Guacamole (page 77)
Sour cream

1. Heat the oil in a large skillet. Add the beef cubes and brown on all sides, working in batches if necessary.

2. Transfer the meat to a 5-quart (5 L) slow cooker. Add the onion to the drippings in the pan and sauté until lightly browned, 3 to 4 minutes. Stir in the taco seasoning and cook for about 1 minute. Add the salsa and stir, scraping up any browned bits.

3. Add the salsa mixture to the beef. Stir to combine. Cook on LOW for 6 to 8 hours or on HIGH for about 4 hours. The meat should be very tender and shred easily when stirred.

FREEZING INSTRUCTIONS:

Divide the beef into meal-size portions in plastic containers. Chill in the refrigerator before freezing.

TO THAW AND SERVE:

Thaw the container in the refrigerator. Reheat the meat in a pan on the stovetop, stirring frequently, or in a microwave-safe dish in the microwave on HIGH for 2 to 3 minutes, stirring once. Serve with guacamole and sour cream.

Oven-Baked Beef Taquitos

I have great memories of visiting the little taco stand in my hometown. I loved going there with my dad; he'd order me two taquitos and a side of their very cold, probably-had-been-frozen guacamole. It is a precious memory of a special time with my pop. These taquitos are reminiscent of that era, only better. They're filled with a delicious beef-and-green-chile mixture. They freeze easily and bake quickly in the oven, making them the ideal quick-fix dinner. Accompany them with your own fresh, home-made guacamole. // *Serves 4 to 6*

▪ **PACKAGING:** Zip-top freezer bag or large plastic container with lid

Vegetable oil for frying the tortillas

24 corn tortillas

3 cups (675 g) Versatile Shredded Beef Filling (page 73)

One 4-ounce (112 g) can diced green chiles

2 scallions, finely chopped

Salt and freshly ground black pepper

WHEN READY TO SERVE, YOU WILL NEED:

Easy Homemade Salsa (opposite page)

Super-Simple Guacamole (opposite page)

Sour cream

1. Fill a skillet with vegetable oil to a depth of 1 inch (2.5 cm). Heat over medium heat until the oil shimmers. Fry the tortillas in the hot oil for 30 to 45 seconds each, turning once with tongs. Drain the tortillas on paper towels. Allow the tortillas to cool enough to be easily handled.

2. In a large bowl, combine the shredded beef, green chiles, and scallions. Season the mixture to taste with salt and pepper.

3. To assemble the taquitos, roll about 2 tablespoons (30 g) of filling tightly into each tortilla. Secure the taquitos with toothpicks and set them on a baking sheet.

FREEZING INSTRUCTIONS:

Place the baking sheet in the freezer for about 20 minutes, or until the taquitos are partially frozen but not so firm that you can't remove the toothpicks. If the toothpicks get frozen stuck, that's fine; you can store them with the toothpicks, though you may not be able to pack them as compactly. Once frozen, pack the taquitos into freezer bags or containers and store them in the freezer.

TO SERVE:

Preheat the oven to 475°F (240°C or gas mark 9). Place the frozen taquitos, seam side down, on a baking sheet and bake for 15 to 25 minutes, turning once. Check for crispness after 15 minutes. Serve with salsa, guacamole, and sour cream.

Easy Homemade Salsa

Makes about 4 cups (940 ml)

One 14.5-ounce (406 g) can diced tomatoes
  with juices
One 14.5-ounce (406 g) can fire-roasted
  diced tomatoes with juices
1 large handful chopped fresh cilantro

¼ cup (36 g) sliced fresh jalapeño pepper
¼ cup (25 g) chopped scallion
Juice of ½ lime
1 clove garlic
Salt

Combine all of the ingredients in the bowl of a food processor. Pulse until smooth. Season to taste with salt.

Super-Simple Guacamole

Makes about 1 cup (240 g)

2 ripe avocados, halved and pitted
Juice of ½ lemon or 1 lime
2 tablespoons (30 g) salsa

1 tablespoon finely chopped fresh jalapeño
  pepper (optional)
Salt

Scoop the flesh of the avocados into a small bowl. Sprinkle the juice over the avocados. Mash with a fork, allowing a few chunks to remain. Stir in the salsa and jalapeño, if using. Season to taste with salt.

Mexican Beef Tortas

A Mexican torta is a sandwich served on either a crisp, torpedo-shaped *bolillo* roll or a soft, round *telera* roll. It is served cold or hot, often toasted in a press like a panini or Cuban sandwich. This meat mixture is very freezer-friendly and can do double duty as a taco or burrito filling. // *Serves 10 to 12*

■ **PACKAGING:** Plastic containers with lids or zip-top freezer bags

1 tablespoon (15 ml) vegetable oil
One 4-pound (1816 g) boneless chuck roast
Salt and freshly ground black pepper
1 cup (160 g) chopped onion
One 4-ounce (112 g) can chopped
    green chiles

1 tablespoon chili powder
1 tablespoon (14 g) tomato paste
1 clove garlic, minced
1 teaspoon chipotle chile powder
1 teaspoon dried oregano

WHEN READY TO SERVE, YOU WILL NEED:

Telera or *bolillo* rolls, or other soft
    sandwich rolls
Sliced cheddar cheese

Shredded lettuce
Sliced tomatoes and avocado

1. In a large skillet, heat the oil over medium-high heat until shimmering. Season the meat to taste with salt and pepper. Brown the roast on all sides. Transfer the roast to a 5-quart (5 L) slow cooker.

2. Add the onion to the drippings in the skillet, scraping up any browned bits. Cook until the onion is translucent, about 5 minutes, stirring occasionally. Add the green chiles, chili powder, tomato paste, garlic, chipotle chile powder, and oregano. Stir to combine.

3. Add this mixture to the slow cooker. Cook the roast on LOW for 6 to 8 hours or on HIGH for about 4 hours. The meat should be very tender and shred easily.

4. Remove the roast from the slow cooker. Shred the meat. Adjust the seasoning with salt and pepper. Moisten the meat with some of the drippings.

5. Discard the drippings or strain them and save for another dish, such as a soup or stew.

FREEZING INSTRUCTIONS:

Divide the meat filling into meal-size portions in containers or freezer bags. Chill in the refrigerator before freezing.

TO THAW AND SERVE:

Thaw the meat in the refrigerator. Reheat the meat in a pan on the stovetop, stirring frequently, or in a microwave-safe dish in the microwave on HIGH for 2 to 3 minutes, stirring once. Serve on rolls with cheese, lettuce, tomatoes, and avocado slices. If you wish, heat the sandwich in a panini press before serving.

Hearty Shredded Beef Enchiladas

A friend brought us this dinner shortly after we welcomed a new baby into our family. Not only did she lighten the load, she also completely wowed us with this delicious supper. Many kids and a few tweaks later, this recipe is one of our favorite meals, especially when it's ready and waiting in the freezer. I like to cook the meat overnight in the slow cooker. That way, it's ready for shredding in the morning. // *Serves 8*

■ **PACKAGING:** Two 9 × 13-inch (23 × 33 cm) baking dishes with lids

One 4-pound (1816 g) boneless chuck roast
1 medium-size onion, chopped
Salt and freshly ground black pepper
1 cup (235 ml) warm water
1 bunch scallions, chopped
One 7-ounce (196 g) can diced green chiles
Vegetable oil, for frying the tortillas

24 corn tortillas
Two 28-ounce (784 g) cans red enchilada sauce
4 cups (480 g) shredded cheese (cheddar, Monterey Jack, or a mixture)
Sliced black olives

1. Place the chuck roast in a 5-quart (5 L) slow cooker along with the onion, salt, pepper, and water. Cook on LOW for 6 to 8 hours or on HIGH for about 4 hours. The meat should be tender and shred easily.

2. Remove the meat from the slow cooker. Remove the fat and shred the meat. Save the drippings for soup or simply discard them.

3. In a large bowl, combine the shredded beef, scallions, and green chiles. Add salt and pepper to taste. Set the mixture aside.

4. Fill a skillet with vegetable oil to a depth of 1 inch (2.5 cm). Heat over medium heat until the oil shimmers. Fry the tortillas in the hot oil for 30 to 45 seconds each, turning once with tongs. Drain the tortillas on paper towels. Allow the tortillas to cool enough to be easily handled.

5. Grease the baking dishes. Spread 1 cup (235 ml) of the enchilada sauce on the bottom of each dish.

6. To assemble, place 2 tablespoons (28 g) beef filling and 2 tablespoons cheese on a tortilla. Roll the tortilla around the filling and place the enchilada, seam side down, in a prepared baking pan. Continue until all the enchiladas are rolled and arranged in the pans.

7. Pour the remaining sauce over the enchiladas and sprinkle them with the remaining cheese and the black olives.

FREEZING INSTRUCTIONS:

Cover the pans and chill in the refrigerator before freezing.

TO THAW AND SERVE:

Thaw the enchiladas in the refrigerator. Preheat the oven to 350°F (180°C or gas mark 4). Bake the enchiladas, uncovered, for 20 minutes, or until heated through. Serve immediately.

Chipotle-Rubbed Tri-Tip

For decades on the west coast, tri-tip has been a favorite grilling cut. It's meaty and full of flavor. Thankfully, meat cutters throughout the country have caught on to what California butchers have long known: The tri-tip is a delicious cut of beef. If you don't see it in the meat case, ask your butcher. You can also use your favorite grilling cut of beef instead. Having the meat and spice rub ready to throw on the grill will help you pull off a great cookout. Serve the roast, sliced, with fresh salsa. // *Serves 4 to 8*

■ **PACKAGING:** Snack-size zip-top bag, gallon-size (4 L) zip-top freezer bag

1 teaspoon chipotle chile powder
½ teaspoon ground cumin
¼ teaspoon freshly ground black pepper
1 teaspoon fine sea salt

1 teaspoon garlic powder
One 2-pound (908 g) tri-tip roast,
    in its original wrapper

WHEN READY TO SERVE, YOU WILL NEED:

1 tablespoon (15 ml) grapeseed oil
    or olive oil

Easy Homemade Salsa (page 77)

Combine all the spices in the snack-size bag. Place the tri-tip roast and the bag of spices in the freezer bag.

FREEZING INSTRUCTIONS:

Store the roast and spice packet in the freezer until a day or two before serving.

TO THAW AND SERVE:

Thaw the roast completely on a tray in the refrigerator. Rub the tri-tip with the oil. Rub the seasoning mix into the meat, coating it thoroughly. Cook the roast on a hot grill, turning once, for 40 minutes, or until it reaches the desired doneness; the internal temperature should be 135°F (57°C) for medium-rare or 160°F (71°C) for well done. Allow the roast to rest, tented with foil, for 10 minutes. Slice the meat against the grain and serve with salsa.

Mediterranean-Style Steak

Marinated meats are quick freezer meals to put together. The meat marinates while it thaws, reducing prep time. Serve this flavorful steak as a main dish, in pita sandwiches, or atop Mediterranean Steak Salad (recipe follows). // *Serves 4 to 8*

■ **PACKAGING:** Gallon-size (4 L) zip-top freezer bag

¼ cup (60 ml) olive oil
¼ cup (60 ml) red wine vinegar
1 tablespoon (15 ml) apple cider vinegar
1 teaspoon dried oregano

2 cloves garlic, chopped
½ teaspoon freshly ground black pepper
Large top-sirloin steak, about 2 pounds
   (908 g)

1. Place the freezer bag in a medium bowl, folding the top over the edges.

2. Add the olive oil, vinegars, oregano, garlic, and pepper to the bag. Seal and massage the bag to combine the marinade ingredients.

3. Add the steak to the bag. Seal the bag carefully, squeezing out as much air as possible. Massage the bag to distribute the marinade evenly.

FREEZING INSTRUCTIONS:
Lay the bag flat to freeze.

TO THAW AND SERVE:
Place the bag on a tray or dish and thaw it in the refrigerator. Cook the thawed steak, turning once, on a hot grill until cooked through, 15 to 20 minutes.

Mediterranean Steak Salad

I love a good salad. And this one is a winner, with grilled beef, dark leafy greens, couscous, onions, tomatoes, and garbanzo beans, all drizzled with a yogurt-dill dressing. Yum! Taste-wise, this is fantastic. But work-wise, it is even better. While salads generally cannot be frozen, many of the components that make a great salad can be prepared ahead and stored in the freezer. And the other ingredients here come together in a snap. // *Serves 6*

1 recipe Mediterranean-Style Steak
  (page 81), thawed
1 cup (180 g) couscous
9 cups (270 g) spinach and mixed salad
  greens (about 1½ cups [45 g] per person)
1 small red onion, sliced

3 cups (540 g) chopped tomatoes
1 cup (245 g) canned garbanzo beans
1 cup (120 g) crumbled feta cheese
1 recipe Yogurt-Dill Dressing
  (recipe follows)

1. Cook the steak on a hot grill until it has reached the desired doneness.

2. Prepare the couscous according to the package directions.

3. While the steak rests, assemble the salads on individual plates, layering greens, sliced onion, tomatoes, garbanzo beans, and feta cheese. Spoon the couscous on the side.

4. Place the sliced steak atop the salads. Serve the dressing on the side.

Yogurt-Dill Dressing

Makes about 1¼ cups (295 ml)

½ cup (112 g) plain yogurt
½ cup (112 g) mayonnaise
1 tablespoon chopped fresh dill
  or 1 teaspoon dried dill

2 cloves garlic, minced
¼ teaspoon cayenne pepper
¼ cup (60 ml) freshly squeezed lemon juice
½ teaspoon ground cumin

In a small bowl, combine all of the ingredients. Chill the dressing until ready to serve.

Easy Carne Asada

Having grown up and lived most of my adult life in Southern California, I tend to lean toward Cal-Mex flavors. And I make no apologies! I've yet to find someone who doesn't love a great bowl of chips and salsa or an easy-to-prep carne asada dish. While many folks in the Southland might marinate their steak in Sunny Delight, I've gone the real food route with this simple but spectacular marinade. // *Serves 4 to 6*

▪ **PACKAGING:** Gallon-size (4 L) zip-top freezer bag

2 to 3 pounds (908 to 1362 g) boneless
    carne asada flap meat
½ cup (120 ml) freshly squeezed
    orange juice
¼ cup (60 ml) red wine vinegar
2 teaspoons smoked paprika

1 teaspoon garlic powder
1 teaspoon black pepper
1 teaspoon fine sea salt
1 teaspoon dried thyme
¼ cup (60 ml) olive oil

WHEN READY TO SERVE, YOU WILL NEED:

Corn tortillas
Salsa

Chopped fresh cilantro

1. Place the meat in a large zip-top plastic bag.

2. In a small bowl, whisk together the orange juice, red wine vinegar, paprika, garlic powder, black pepper, salt, and thyme. Stir in the olive oil.

3. Pour the marinade over the meat. Massage the marinade around the meat pieces.

FREEZING INSTRUCTIONS:

Lay the bag flat to freeze.

TO THAW AND SERVE:

Remove the meat from the freezer the night before serving and allow to thaw on a tray in the refrigerator. Heat a medium-hot fire in an outdoor grill. Cook the meat until no longer pink, flipping once. Remove from the heat to a cutting board. Chop the meat finely and serve in tacos with salsa and chopped fresh cilantro.

Seasoned Steak with Gorgonzola-Herb Butter

Grilled steak is simple enough to prepare. It's delicious on its own with a little salt and pepper. However, it improves in taste and elegance when you add a custom spice rub before grilling and top the cooked meat with a compound butter laden with rich Gorgonzola and fragrant herbs. If you can't find tri-tip, use your favorite grilling cut of beef instead. // *Serves 4 to 8*

- **PACKAGING:** Gallon-size (4 L) zip-top freezer bag, snack-size zip-top bag, plastic wrap, sandwich-size zip-top bag

One 2-pound (908 g) tri-tip roast,
   in its original wrapper
1 tablespoon garlic powder
1 teaspoon salt
1 teaspoon paprika
½ teaspoon plus ⅛ teaspoon freshly
   ground black pepper, divided

½ cup (112 g) (1 stick) unsalted butter,
   softened
¼ cup (30 g) crumbled Gorgonzola or other
   blue cheese
1½ teaspoons chopped fresh parsley
   or ½ teaspoon dried parsley flakes
½ teaspoon dried thyme

WHEN READY TO SERVE, YOU WILL NEED:
1 tablespoon (15 ml) grapeseed oil
   or olive oil

1. Place the packaged tri-tip in the gallon-size (4 L) freezer bag. Set aside.

2. In the snack-size bag, combine the garlic powder, salt, paprika, and ½ teaspoon of the pepper. Seal the bag and place it inside the large bag next to the tri-tip.

3. In a small bowl, combine the butter, cheese, parsley, thyme, and remaining ⅛ teaspoon black pepper. Mash together until well combined.

4. Spoon the butter mixture onto a small sheet of plastic wrap. Wrap the plastic wrap around the butter mixture, forming a small log about 1 inch (2.5 cm) in diameter. Wrap the butter log tightly and place it in the sandwich bag. Seal the bag. Place this bag in the larger bag with the roast and the seasoning packet.

FREEZING INSTRUCTIONS:
Store the large bag containing the tri-tip, seasoning packet, and Gorgonzola butter in the freezer.

TO THAW AND SERVE:
A day or two before serving, pull the bag from the freezer. Remove the tri-tip package from the bag and thaw it in the refrigerator on a tray. Thaw the butter in the refrigerator as well. About an hour before serving, brush the thawed tri-tip with the oil. Rub the spice mixture all over the meat. Cook the meat on a hot grill, turning once, for 40 minutes, or until it reaches the desired doneness; the internal temperature should be 135°F (57°C) for medium-rare or 160°F (71°C) for well done. Allow the meat to rest, tented with foil, for 10 minutes before slicing. Serve topped with slices of Gorgonzola butter.

Quick and Easy Pepper Steak

My mom found this delectable Asian-style recipe in a magazine ad more than thirty years ago. I've updated it for the freezer to make serving it quick and easy. It features seasoned beef strips in a flavorful sauce with crisp-tender bell peppers. Get a head start on it by preparing the beef and sauce ahead of time. Add the bell peppers right before serving. This is delicious served over steamed rice. You can also make this with strips of chicken breast and chicken broth instead of beef. // *Serves 4 to 6*

■ **PACKAGING:** Plastic container with lid

One 1-pound (454 g) beef round steak,
   ½ inch (1.3 cm) thick, cut into ¼-inch
   (6 mm) strips
1 tablespoon paprika
2 tablespoons (30 ml) vegetable oil
2 cloves garlic, minced

1½ cups (355 ml) beef broth
½ cup (50 g) chopped scallions
2 tablespoons (16 g) cornstarch
¼ cup (60 ml) water
¼ cup (60 ml) soy sauce

WHEN READY TO SERVE, YOU WILL NEED:
2 green bell peppers, cut into strips
1 red bell pepper, cut into strips

Hot cooked rice

1. Place the beef strips in a medium bowl and sprinkle them with the paprika. Allow the mixture to stand for 10 minutes.

2. In a large skillet, heat the oil over medium heat. Add the meat and cook until browned. Stir in the garlic and broth. Cover and simmer for 10 minutes. Stir in the scallions and cook 5 minutes more.

3. In a small bowl, combine the cornstarch, water, and soy sauce. Stir this mixture into the meat mixture and cook until smooth and thickened, 5 to 10 minutes more.

FREEZING INSTRUCTIONS:
Spoon the meat mixture into a plastic container. Chill in the refrigerator before freezing.

TO THAW AND SERVE:
Thaw the meat completely in the refrigerator. Heat through in a large saucepan over medium heat. Add the bell peppers and cook until the peppers are just crisp-tender, about 5 minutes. Serve over hot cooked rice.

Cream Cheese Mashed Potatoes

Mashed potatoes can be time-intensive to make, but they are such a comforting, ideal side dish that one doesn't want to leave them off the menu. So make a bulk batch! These freezer-friendly spuds owe their richness and flavor to the addition of cream cheese. Feel free to leave the skins on, if you prefer. // *Serves 8*

- **PACKAGING:** Two 8-inch (20.3 cm) round baking dishes with lids or one 9 × 13-inch (23 × 33 cm) baking dish with lid

5 pounds (2270 g) russet or red potatoes, peeled and quartered

8 ounces (224 g) cream cheese

1 teaspoon salt

¼ teaspoon freshly ground black pepper

1 cup (235 ml) half-and-half

2 tablespoons (28 g) butter

1. In a large pot of salted boiling water, cook the potatoes until very tender when pierced with a fork. Drain the potatoes and transfer them to the bowl of a stand mixer. Blend the potatoes until smooth.

2. Add the cream cheese and blend to combine. Stir in the salt, pepper, and half-and-half. Blend well.

3. Grease the baking dish or dishes. Spoon in the mashed potatoes. Dot the potatoes with the butter.

FREEZING INSTRUCTIONS:

Cool slightly. Cover the potatoes. Chill in the refrigerator before freezing.

TO THAW AND SERVE:

Thaw the potatoes in the refrigerator. Preheat the oven to 375°F (190°C or gas mark 5). Bake the mashed potatoes, covered, for 30 to 45 minutes or until hot. Stir the potatoes before serving.

Beefy Mushroom Gravy

Preceding generations may have relied on canned cream soups and gravies to pull together quick meals. But these soups, chock full of sodium and additives, don't do a lot for us except save some time. In reality it doesn't take very long to make up a batch of this beef and mushroom gravy. Use it as a simple sauce, in place of cream of mushroom soup, and in recipes like Shepherd's Pie with Green Chile Mashed Potatoes (page 92) and Swedish Meatballs with Dill (page 94). If you are using commercial beef broth, taste the gravy before adding salt, since such broths can vary greatly in their levels of saltiness. // ***Makes about 2 cups (470 ml)***

▪ **PACKAGING:** Plastic container with lid or pint-size (470 ml) zip-top freezer bag

4½ tablespoons (63 g) unsalted butter, divided
¼ cup (18 g) finely chopped fresh mushrooms
2 tablespoons (16 g) finely chopped onion
¼ cup (30 g) unbleached all-purpose flour

2 cups (470 ml) beef broth
2 teaspoons fresh chopped parsley or ¾ teaspoon dried parsley flakes
¾ teaspoon salt
⅛ teaspoon freshly ground black pepper
⅛ teaspoon paprika

1. In a medium skillet, melt ½ tablespoon of the butter over medium heat. Add the mushrooms and onion. Sauté the vegetables, stirring occasionally, until the mushrooms start to brown and the onion becomes translucent. Set aside.

2. In a heavy stockpot, melt the remaining 4 tablespoons (56 g) butter over medium heat. Stir in the flour and cook, stirring, until the mixture bubbles. Cook 1 minute more.

3. Whisk in the beef broth, stirring constantly, until the mixture thickens to a gravy consistency.

4. Stir in the mushroom and onion mixture, parsley, salt, pepper, and paprika. Adjust the seasonings to taste.

FREEZING INSTRUCTIONS:

Divide the gravy into desired portions in plastic containers. Chill the gravy in the refrigerator before freezing.

TO THAW AND SERVE:

Thaw the gravy in the refrigerator. Reheat in a saucepan over medium heat, whisking to recombine.

Note: To make a big batch of this gravy, simply multiply all the ingredients by four. The cooking method remains the same.

Meatball Sub Kit

Meatball subs are classic comfort food. Skip the trip to the deli by making your own—and better!—at home for less. Put together a few meatball sub kits so that you can indulge yourself whenever a craving hits. // *Makes 8 sandwiches*

- **PACKAGING:** Plastic containers with lids, gallon- (4 L), quart- (1 L) and sandwich-size zip-top freezer bags.

40 small cooked meatballs (about ½ batch Herbed Meatballs, page 106)
2 cups (470 ml) favorite marinara sauce (try Quick and Spicy Marinara Sauce, page 216)

½ cup (112 g) butter, softened
1 teaspoon chopped garlic
½ teaspoon dried parsley
8 submarine rolls or hearty hot dog buns
Mozzarella cheese, for topping (optional)

1. Place the cooled, cooked meatballs in a closed container or zip-top bag.

2. Place the sauce in a closed container or zip-top bag.

3. In a small mixing bowl, combine the butter, garlic, and parsley. Spread this mixture on both cut sides of the rolls. Wrap the rolls in foil and place in a larger zip-top bag.

4. Place the cheese in a small zip-top bag.

FREEZING INSTRUCTIONS:

Place the chilled containers or bags of meatballs, sauce, rolls, and cheese together in the freezer.

TO THAW AND SERVE:

Thaw the components in the refrigerator. Reheat the sauce and meatballs in the microwave or in a pan on the stovetop. Bake the wrapped rolls for 10 minutes in a 350°F (180°C or gas mark 4) oven. Unwrap the rolls and open them. Broil the rolls until crisp and golden. Assemble the sandwiches by piling 5 meatballs and sauce on each roll and topping with cheese. Return to the broiler if you'd like to melt the cheese a bit more. Serve immediately.

Vegetable Bolognese

One summer our CSA provided an abundance of eggplant. This Bolognese was the delicious result of my efforts to use it! Packed with vegetables, the sauce goes nicely over hot cooked noodles or rice and makes the base for a fantastic lasagna. // *Serves 6 to 8*

■ **PACKAGING:** Plastic containers with lids

¼ cup (60 ml) olive oil
1 carrot, peeled and finely chopped
1 eggplant, peeled and chopped into ½-inch
   (1.3 cm) cubes
1 medium-size onion, coarsely chopped
1 red bell pepper, coarsely chopped
1 medium-size zucchini, coarsely chopped
2 cloves garlic, minced

Salt and freshly ground black pepper
1 pound (454 g) ground beef
3½ cups (825 ml) tomato sauce
One 14.5-ounce (406 g) can diced tomatoes
   with juices
¼ cup (60 ml) red wine (optional)
3 tablespoons chopped fresh basil
   or 1 tablespoon dried basil

1. In a large stockpot, heat the olive oil over medium heat until shimmering. Add the carrot and eggplant and cook, stirring to prevent the eggplant from sticking, for 10 minutes.

2. Add the onion, bell pepper, zucchini, and garlic. Cook 5 minutes more. Add salt and pepper to taste.

3. Add the ground beef and cook, stirring often, until the meat is cooked through, about 10 minutes. Add the tomato sauce, tomatoes, red wine (if using), and basil. Add a bit of water if the mixture is too thick.

4. Adjust the seasonings to taste and bring to a bubble. Reduce the heat, cover, and simmer for 25 minutes.

FREEZING INSTRUCTIONS:

Divide the sauce into meal-size portions in plastic containers. Chill the sauce in the refrigerator before freezing.

TO THAW AND SERVE:

Thaw the sauce in the refrigerator and reheat it in a saucepan.

Vegetable-Beef Lasagna

Lasagna is a faithful friend to a freezer cook. This delicious version features cream cheese in the filling, a technique used by cookbook author Ann Hodgman. Use uncooked noodles for even quicker prep time. With an adequate amount of sauce, the uncooked noodles will soften during freezing and cook during baking. // **Serves 6 to 8**

■ **PACKAGING:** 9 × 13-inch (23 × 33 cm) baking dish with lid

3 cups (675 g) **Vegetable Bolognese (opposite page) or other favorite sauce**
3 cups (360 g) **shredded mozzarella cheese**

8 regular (not no-boil) lasagna noodles, uncooked
8 ounces (224 g) **Neufchâtel cheese**
1 cup (235 ml) **chicken broth**

1. Grease the baking dish. Spread 1½ cups (337 g) of the Bolognese sauce across the bottom of the pan. Sprinkle 1 cup (120 g) of the mozzarella cheese over the sauce. Lay 4 lasagna noodles across the cheese, overlapping slightly.

2. In a medium saucepan, heat the cream cheese and chicken broth over low heat. As the cream cheese begins to warm and soften, whisk it into the chicken broth until well blended. Pour this mixture over the noodle layer. Sprinkle 1 cup (120 g) of the mozzarella cheese over the white sauce. Lay the remaining 4 lasagna noodles across the layer of cheese.

3. Spoon the remaining Bolognese over the noodles and spread evenly. Top the sauce with the remaining 1 cup (120 g) mozzarella cheese.

FREEZING INSTRUCTIONS:

Cover the pan and chill completely in the refrigerator before freezing.

TO THAW AND SERVE:

Thaw the lasagna in the refrigerator overnight for best results. Preheat the oven to 400°F (200°C or gas mark 6). Bake for 45 minutes or until the sauce is bubbly and the cheese is melted. Allow the lasagna to rest for 10 minutes before cutting and serving.

Shepherd's Pie with Green Chile Mashed Potatoes

Shepherd's pie is a traditional English dish, made of a ground meat-and-vegetable mixture that's topped with mashed potatoes. This one is spiced up with jalapeños, cilantro, and cheddar cheese, giving it a little South of the Border flavor. // *Serves 6 to 8*

- **PACKAGING:** 9 × 13-inch (23 × 33 cm) baking dish with lid

8 medium-size red potatoes (about 2 pounds [908 g]), scrubbed and quartered (no need to peel, unless you prefer them that way)
1 pound (454 g) ground beef
1 cup (160 g) chopped onion
½ cup (75 g) chopped red bell pepper
1 tablespoon finely chopped fresh jalapeño pepper

2 cups (470 ml) Beefy Mushroom Gravy (page 87)
1 cup (150 g) fresh or frozen green peas
⅓ cup chopped fresh cilantro
1 teaspoon ground cumin
¼ cup (56 g) (½ stick) salted butter
2 tablespoons (30 ml) half-and-half
½ cup (60 g) shredded cheddar cheese
1 tablespoon canned green chiles

1. Grease the baking dish. In a large pot of boiling salted water, cook the potatoes until tender, then drain. Set aside.

2. Meanwhile, in a large skillet, cook the beef, onion, bell pepper, and jalapeño over medium-high heat until the meat is cooked and the vegetables are tender. Drain the meat and vegetables and transfer the mixture to a large bowl.

3. Add the gravy, peas, cilantro, and cumin. Stir gently to combine. Spread the meat mixture in the prepared pan.

4. Mash the potatoes with a potato masher until smooth. Blend in the butter. Stir in the half-and-half until smooth. Add the cheddar cheese and green chiles, and stir until well combined.

5. Spoon the mashed potatoes over the meat mixture, spreading to cover evenly.

FREEZING INSTRUCTIONS:
Cover the dish and chill in the refrigerator before freezing.

TO THAW AND SERVE:
Thaw the casserole in the refrigerator. Preheat the oven to 350°F (180°C or gas mark 4). Bake for 1 hour, until the filling is bubbly and the mashed potatoes are golden brown.

▶ Using Batch Cooking as a Way to Help Others

If your freezer is stocked with healthy, home-cooked meals, it's easier to be hospitable. Having folks over for dinner isn't so much of a hassle if you can pull two dozen enchiladas from the freezer and spend free time on side dishes and a pretty presentation.

Batch cooking also enables you to serve others in different ways. When we have a stockpile, it's easier to share. And sharing is always a good thing.

HELP OUT THE NEW PARENTS

Fill the freezer of a new mom and dad with a few meals. Not only will this be a gift that outlasts that first pack of diapers, it is also one that is desperately needed during those early weeks with a baby at home. New moms are ravenous—and busy with the babe in arms. So a few home-cooked meals, whether in family-size pans or individual-serving containers, are an ideal gift. You can even organize a "meal shower" by inviting other friends to bring a few frozen meals as gifts. Just coordinate a little with the others so that the new parents don't end up with a dozen pans of baked manicotti. Be sure to include cooking directions so no one is scrambling at mealtime. Also, check to make sure there's room in their freezer!

FEED THE HUNGRY

There are numerous homeless shelters that would gratefully accept meals that you've prepared and frozen. Contact your local church, synagogue, or other charitable organization to see where you can donate food to those who are less fortunate.

SERVE YOUR ELDERS

Elderly family, friends, and neighbors are also among those who could benefit from ready-made meals. If you make the meals yourself, you can ensure that the foods fit any dietary restrictions they might have and portion the food in single-serving containers. If you can stick around and keep the recipients company for a while when you drop off the meals, it will be a double kindness.

BE A GOOD NEIGHBOR

Chances are you know someone who's struggling. Military deployments, divorce, illnesses, and unemployment can make it hard for people to have regular mealtimes. There may be too much to do, too much on one's mind, or a shortage of food. Reach out to those around you with a helping hand. Some churches even stockpile meals in the church freezer to be able to share at will with those in need.

Swedish Meatballs with Dill

This meatball dish is enjoyed by diners of all ages, particularly when served with mashed potatoes or hot cooked noodles and lingonberry or cranberry sauce. The rich beef gravy will have them licking the plates clean. // *Serves 12 to 16*

■ **PACKAGING:** Quart- (1 L) or gallon-size (4 L) zip-top freezer bags, plastic containers with lids

3 pounds (1362 g) ground beef
1 pound (454 g) ground pork
3 cups (150 g) fresh bread crumbs
6 large eggs, beaten
1 cup (160 g) finely chopped onion
3 cloves garlic, minced
⅓ cup chopped fresh parsley or
   2 tablespoons dried parsley flakes

¼ cup chopped fresh dill or 1 tablespoon
   plus 2 teaspoons dried dill, divided
2 teaspoons kosher salt
¼ teaspoon ground allspice
8 cups (1880 ml) Beefy Mushroom Gravy
   (page 87)

1. Line two rimmed baking sheets with heavy-duty foil. Spray the foil lightly with nonstick cooking spray. Preheat the oven to 350°F (180°C or gas mark 4).

2. In a large bowl, mix the ground meats, bread crumbs, eggs, onion, garlic, parsley, 3 tablespoons of the fresh dill or 1 tablespoon of the dried, salt, and allspice just until everything is evenly distributed. Don't overmix, as that will make your meatballs tough.

3. Form the mixture into golf ball–size balls and place the meatballs on the prepared sheets. Bake the meatballs for 15 minutes, or until they are cooked through.

4. Pour the gravy into a large bowl. Add the remaining 1 tablespoon fresh dill or 2 teaspoons dried and stir to combine.

FREEZING INSTRUCTIONS:

Divide the meatballs into meal-size portions in freezer bags. Divide the gravy into plastic containers. Chill the meatballs and gravy in the refrigerator before freezing.

TO THAW AND SERVE:

Thaw the meatballs and gravy in the refrigerator. Reheat the gravy in a large saucepan on the stovetop, whisking to recombine. Add the meatballs and simmer until heated through. Serve immediately.

Not Your Convenience Store's Frozen Burritos

I once turned my nose up at frozen burritos, assuming they would be mushy and blah-tasting. But friends raved about making their own, so I had to try it out. And we loved them! Snacks and dinners come together so easily when the burritos are premade. Crisping them on the griddle takes them to a new level, and you'd never know they'd been frozen. // *Serves 6 to 12*

■ **PACKAGING:** Gallon-size (4 L) zip-top freezer bags

1 pound (454 g) ground beef
1 to 2 tablespoons Basic Taco Seasoning
    Mix (opposite page)
3 cups (750 g) refried beans or Seasoned
    Versatile Pinto Beans (page 189)
2 cups (240 g) shredded cheddar cheese

1 cup (235 ml) enchilada sauce
½ cup (80 g) diced onion
One 4-ounce (112 g) can chopped
    green chiles
12 burrito-size flour tortillas

1. In a large skillet, cook the meat over medium-high heat, stirring frequently, until no pink remains. Stir in the taco seasoning. Stir to blend.

2. Drain the meat and transfer it to a large bowl. Add the beans, cheese, enchilada sauce, onion, and green chiles. Stir well to combine.

3. Lay out a tortilla and spread a scant ½ cup filling in a line down one side of the tortilla. Roll the tortilla around the filling, rolling toward the middle of the tortilla. Fold in the sides and continue rolling.

4. Fill and roll the rest of the burritos in the same manner.

FREEZING INSTRUCTIONS:

Place the rolled burritos in the freezer bags. Chill in the refrigerator before freezing.

TO THAW AND SERVE:

Thaw as many burritos as desired in the refrigerator.

To reheat in the microwave: Cook thawed burritos, flipping once, 1 to 2 minutes per burrito, or until hot. You can also reheat them directly from the freezer, without thawing; just add an additional minute or two of cooking time.

To reheat on the griddle: Cook thawed burritos on a hot griddle until the filling is hot and the tortilla is crisp.

To reheat in the oven: Preheat the oven to 350°F (180°C or gas mark 4). For crispy, oven-baked burritos, bake thawed burritos for 15 to 20 minutes. For softer burritos, wrap each in foil prior to baking. If the burritos are frozen, increase the cooking time 5 to 10 minutes.

▶ Taco Seasoning Mixes and Basic Taco Meat Kit

Prepackaged spice mixes are often costly and can contain dubious ingredients. Fortunately, buying individual spices in bulk can be quite economical, and creating your own spice mixes is a great way to add flavor to any number of dishes without compromising your tastes or your budget. The flavors of spices deteriorate over long storage at room temperature. However, the flavor and intensity of spices are retained for a much longer time when the seasonings are frozen, making custom spice blends a perfect addition to your freezer cooking repertoire. They're a great way to personalize your meals.

In my house, taco seasoning is particularly popular, so I've provided two of my favorite blends, which I use with both ground beef and ground turkey. (They're also great mixed into cooked pinto beans.) Having a stash of preseasoned taco meat in your freezer opens up a world of mealtime possibilities. To prepare it, simply stir in 1 to 2 tablespoons of seasoning mix for each pound (454 g) of meat browning in a skillet. Once no pink remains, drain off the drippings, package, label, chill, and freeze.

Create a simple "taco kit" by packaging 1 pound (454 g) of precooked meat, 2 cups (240 g) of shredded cheese, and one 12-count package of soft taco-size flour tortillas. Individually wrap each component and then store them in one larger bag. On taco night, just thaw a bag and add fresh toppings like lettuce, tomatoes, salsa, and sour cream.

Basic Taco Seasoning Mix

This taco seasoning is a standard spice blend that can be mixed into ground beef, shredded chicken, soups, or chilis to give them a little punch. It is also delicious mixed into sour cream as a dip and stirred into marinades and dressings. // *Makes about ⅔ cup (65 g)*

■ **PACKAGING:** Plastic container with lid or pint-size (470 ml) zip-top freezer bag

¼ cup (30 g) chili powder	1 tablespoon (18 g) salt
2 tablespoons dried oregano	1 tablespoon garlic powder
2 tablespoons onion flakes	1 teaspoon freshly ground black pepper

Combine all of the ingredients in a small bowl. Place the mixture in an airtight plastic container or freezer bag and store in the freezer.

Chipotle Taco Seasoning Mix

Chipotle chiles, which are smoke-dried jalapeño peppers, add a little heat and a smoky flavor to foods. Once difficult to find but now widely available, they are sold canned in adobo sauce or dried in whole or ground form This seasoning mix can be used in taco meats, chilis, and soups to give a distinctive chipotle flavor. // *Makes about ½ cup (48 g)*

■ **PACKAGING:** Plastic container with lid or pint-size (470 ml) zip-top freezer bag

2 tablespoons chipotle chile powder

2 tablespoons onion flakes

1 tablespoon garlic powder

1 tablespoon (18 g) salt

1 tablespoon dried oregano

2 teaspoons ground cumin

Combine all of the ingredients in a small bowl. Place the mixture in an airtight plastic container or freezer bag and store in the freezer.

Jamie's Spice Mix

My sister Jamie has great taste in food. I love learning from her. This spice mix is based on her special blend, one that she gave as a party favor at her wedding when she married into a large Italian family. Add a few shakes to salad dressing, meat marinades, or French fries. It also goes well on pizza. // *Makes about ⅔ cup (65 g)*

■ **PACKAGING:** Pint-size (470 ml) zip-top freezer bag or plastic container with lid

2 tablespoons onion powder

2 tablespoons garlic powder

1½ tablespoons paprika

3 tablespoons chopped fresh basil
 or 1 tablespoon dried basil

1 tablespoon dried oregano

1 tablespoon (18 g) fine sea salt

2 teaspoons freshly ground black pepper

1 teaspoon celery seeds (optional)

½ teaspoon grated lemon zest

½ teaspoon cayenne pepper

Combine all of the ingredients in a small bowl. Place the mixture in an airtight plastic container or freezer bag and store in the freezer.

Sweet and Spicy Joes

Sloppy joes can be too sweet for some palates. This variation retains some of the sweet but adds a spicy kick for variety. If you do prefer a sweeter version, simply add more brown sugar. // *Serves 4 to 8*

■ **PACKAGING:** Plastic containers with lids

2 pounds (908 g) ground beef
1 to 2 cups (235 to 470 ml) tomato sauce,
    depending on how saucy you like it

2½ tablespoons (15 g) Jamie's Spice Mix
    (opposite page)
1 tablespoon brown sugar

WHEN READY TO SERVE, YOU WILL NEED:
Hamburger buns
Shredded cheddar cheese

Sliced dill pickles

1. In a large skillet, cook the meat over medium-high heat, stirring frequently, until no pink remains.

2. Stir in the tomato sauce, spice mix, and brown sugar. Bring to a bubble and then simmer for 20 minutes.

FREEZING INSTRUCTIONS:

Divide the meat mixture into meal-size portions in plastic containers. Chill in the refrigerator before freezing.

TO THAW AND SERVE:

Thaw in the refrigerator. Reheat the mixture in a saucepan. Spoon the hot mixture onto hamburger buns and top with cheese and pickles. Serve immediately.

Chili-Stuffed Sweet Potatoes

A deluxe baked potato bar comes together in a flash when you have the chili already to go in the freezer. This spicy meat blend features a hearty dose of kale to add fiber and substance. Top the baked sweet potatoes with chili and an array of colorful additions. // *Serves 4*

■ **PACKAGING:** Plastic containers with lids

1⅓ pounds (604 g) ground beef
1 medium-size onion, chopped
1 clove garlic, minced
2 tablespoons chili powder

Fine sea salt and freshly ground black pepper
4 cups (280 g) shredded kale or cruciferous
    blend
One 15-ounce (420 g) can tomato sauce

WHEN READY TO SERVE, YOU WILL NEED:
4 large baked sweet potatoes, split and
    smooshed
Sliced avocado
Sour cream

Salsa
Chopped fresh cilantro
Chopped scallions

1. In a large, heavy skillet, cook the beef, onion, garlic, and chili powder until the meat is cooked through, and the onion has become translucent. Season to taste with salt and pepper.

2. Stir in the kale and tomato sauce. Cover and simmer for 10 minutes.

FREEZING INSTRUCTIONS:
Divide the meat mixture into meal-size portions in plastic containers. Chill in the refrigerator before freezing.

TO THAW AND SERVE:
Thaw in the refrigerator. Reheat the mixture in a saucepan. Spoon the hot mixture onto the baked sweet potatoes and serve with the toppings.

Lawnmower Taco

This is a simple casserole that my kids love. It's probably in the FishFam Top 10 of Favorite Meals. We call it "lawnmower taco" because it looks, well, like a taco that got stuck in a lawnmower. How you spin the recipe name can have a positive effect on a picky eater's willingness to try something! This casserole comes together easily and is perfect for potlucks or any night when you crave a little comfort food. // *Serves 6 to 8*

■ **PACKAGING:** 9 × 13-inch (23 × 33 cm) baking dish with lid

1 pound (454 g) ground beef
1 to 2 tablespoons Basic Taco Seasoning
    Mix (page 97)
¼ cup (30 g) unbleached all-purpose flour
2 cups (470 ml) chicken broth

9 ounces (252 g) tortilla chips, crushed
    (about 4 cups)
2 cups (240 g) shredded Monterey Jack
    or cheddar cheese

WHEN READY TO SERVE, YOU WILL NEED:

Shredded lettuce

Salsa

Sour cream

Canned sliced black olives

1. In a large skillet, cook the meat over medium-high heat, stirring frequently, until no pink remains. Sprinkle the taco seasoning and the flour over the cooked meat. Stir well.

2. Stir in the broth and bring the mixture to a simmer. Simmer, stirring occasionally, until the sauce thickens, about 15 minutes.

3. Meanwhile, grease the baking dish. Spread half of the crushed chips across the bottom of the dish. Spoon half of the meat mixture over the chips.

4. Sprinkle half of the cheese over the meat layer. Repeat the layers of chips, meat, and cheese.

FREEZING INSTRUCTIONS:

Cover the dish and chill in the refrigerator before freezing.

TO THAW AND SERVE:

Thaw the casserole in the refrigerator. Preheat the oven to 325°F (170°C or gas mark 3). Bake the casserole for 20 to 30 minutes, or until bubbly. Serve with the lettuce, salsa, sour cream, and olives.

Soy-Balsamic Burgers

Burgers are a go-to supper any time of year, but particularly during the warmer months; there's something so inviting about meat that has been cooked over an open flame. Having a stash of patties in the freezer makes your prep time even quicker. These burgers are seasoned with balsamic vinegar and soy sauce, adding delicious flavor to the meat. // *Serves 8*

■ **PACKAGING:** Gallon-size (4 L) zip-top freezer bag, waxed paper, plastic wrap

2 pounds (908 g) ground beef

1 tablespoon (15 ml) balsamic vinegar

1 tablespoon (15 ml) soy sauce

1 tablespoon chopped fresh parsley
   or 1 teaspoon dried parsley flakes

½ teaspoon dried thyme

¼ teaspoon freshly ground black pepper

WHEN READY TO SERVE, YOU WILL NEED:

Hamburger buns

Lettuce leaves or shredded lettuce

Sliced tomatoes

Other toppings, as desired

1. In a large bowl, mix all of the ingredients just until everything is evenly distributed. Don't overmix, as that will make your burgers tough.

2. Divide the mixture into 8 equal portions. Form each portion into a flat hamburger patty.

FREEZING INSTRUCTIONS:

Place the patties on a baking sheet and freeze until firm. Remove the frozen patties from the sheet and place them in a freezer bag. Seal the bag carefully, removing as much air as possible. Return the burgers to the freezer. Alternatively, you can freeze the burgers in meal-size bundles, separating the patties with waxed paper. Wrap each bundle in plastic wrap and place in a freezer bag.

TO THAW AND SERVE:

If you have frozen your hamburger patties individually, simply remove the desired number of patties from the bag. There is no need to thaw them before cooking. If you used the bundle method of packaging, thaw the bundle on a dish in the refrigerator. (You may be able to cook these unthawed as well, if the frozen patties separate easily.) Place the hamburger patties on a hot grill or in a skillet. When the tops of the burgers appear wet, flip them over. Continue cooking until the burgers reach the desired doneness. Serve on buns with lettuce, tomatoes, and other toppings as desired.

▶ Prepping Hamburgers for the Freezer

You might wonder why you should bother prepping hamburgers for the freezer when you can make them up in a matter of minutes right before cooking time. The answers are manifold:

- You can take advantage of grocery sales stocking up on ground beef at a low price rather than paying a premium when the urge for burgers hits.
- Taking a few minutes now gives you the opportunity to "dude" up your burgers with different mix-ins and spices when you have more leisure to do so. This also makes it easier to offer a variety of burgers at one meal.
- Formed and frozen patties can go directly from the freezer to a hot grill, making dinner come together more quickly than a trip to the local burger stand.

There are two basic prepping methods.

1. INDIVIDUAL FREEZING

The advantage of individually freezing the burgers is that you can cook as many or as few as you like, while leaving the rest in the freezer. No need to thaw an entire package!

(continued)

Packaging: Gallon-size (4 L) zip-top freezer bag

Directions: In a large bowl, mix all of the ingredients just until the seasonings are evenly distributed. Don't overmix, as that will make your burgers tough. Divide the mixture into ¼-pound (112 g) portions, forming each portion into a flat hamburger patty.

Freezing instructions: Place the patties on a baking sheet and freeze until firm. Remove the frozen patties from the sheet and place them in a labeled zip-top freezer bag. Seal the bag carefully, removing as much air as possible. Return the patties to the freezer.

To serve: Remove the desired number of patties from the bag. There is no need to thaw them before cooking.

2. BUNDLING

The selling point of a bundle of hamburger patties is the time you save in the prep stage. You can mix, form, and freeze a number of patties in a matter of minutes. However, you have to preplan a bit. If you bundle 12 burgers, then you will probably need to thaw and cook all 12 burgers at once, as they will be more difficult to separate when they are frozen solid, even when separated by waxed paper, as I suggest here.

Packaging: Waxed paper, plastic wrap, zip-top freezer bag

Directions: In a large bowl, mix all of the ingredients just until the seasonings are evenly distributed. Don't overmix, as that will make your burgers tough. Divide the mixture into ¼-pound (112 g) portions, forming each portion into a flat hamburger patty.

Freezing instructions: Stack the burgers in meal-size bundles, separating the patties with waxed paper. Wrap each bundle in plastic wrap and place in a freezer bag. Store the patties in the freezer.

To thaw and serve: Thaw the bundle on a dish in the refrigerator and cook as desired.

Outside-In Cheeseburgers

Join two great tastes in one by mixing your cheese into this outside-in cheeseburger. The added dill is reminiscent of dill pickles, making this truly an all-in-one burger. // *Serves 8*

■ **PACKAGING:** Gallon-size (4 L) zip-top freezer bag, waxed paper, plastic wrap

2 pounds (908 g) ground beef
½ cup (80 g) finely chopped onion
½ cup (60 g) shredded cheddar cheese

1½ teaspoons fresh chopped dill
   or ½ teaspoon dried dill
½ teaspoon salt
¼ teaspoon freshly ground black pepper

WHEN READY TO SERVE, YOU WILL NEED:
Hamburger buns
Lettuce leaves or shredded lettuce

Sliced tomatoes
Other toppings, as desired

1. In a large bowl, mix all of the ingredients just until everything is evenly distributed. Don't overmix, as that will make your burgers tough.

2. Divide the mixture into 8 equal portions. Form each portion into a flat hamburger patty.

FREEZING INSTRUCTIONS:

Place the patties on a baking sheet and freeze until firm. Remove the frozen patties from the sheet and place them in a freezer bag. Seal the bag carefully, removing as much air as possible. Return the burgers to the freezer. Alternatively, you can freeze the burgers in meal-size bundles, separating the patties with waxed paper. Wrap each bundle in plastic wrap and place in a freezer bag.

TO THAW AND SERVE:

If you have frozen your hamburger patties individually, simply remove the desired number of patties from the bag. There is no need to thaw them before cooking. If you used the bundle method of packaging, thaw the bundle on a dish in the refrigerator. (You may be able to cook these unthawed as well, if the frozen patties separate easily.) Place the hamburger patties on a hot grill or in a skillet. When the tops of the burgers appear wet, flip them over. Continue cooking until the burgers reach the desired doneness. Serve on buns with lettuce, tomatoes, and other toppings as desired.

Herbed Meatballs

Meatballs are one of the handiest meal components to keep in the freezer. They can be added to soup, served atop a bowl of spaghetti, dressed in gravy over mashed potatoes, basted with barbecue sauce on the grill, or spooned into a crusty roll with red sauce for a fabulous hot sandwich. You can even serve them as meatball sliders on small dinner rolls. This recipe is easy—and just waiting to be finished with your favorite sauce. // *Serves 12 to 16*

■ **PACKAGING:** Quart- (1 L) or gallon-size (4 L) zip-top freezer bags

4 pounds (1816 g) ground beef
3 cups (150 g) fresh bread crumbs
6 large eggs, beaten
1 cup (160 g) chopped onion
⅓ cup chopped fresh parsley or
  2 tablespoons dried parsley flakes

3 tablespoons chopped fresh basil
  or 1 tablespoon dried basil
3 cloves garlic, chopped
1 teaspoon kosher salt

1. Line two rimmed baking sheets with heavy-duty foil. Spray the foil lightly with nonstick cooking spray. Preheat the oven to 350°F (180°C or gas mark 4).

2. In a large bowl, mix all of the ingredients just until everything is evenly distributed. Don't overmix, as that will make your meatballs tough.

3. Form the mixture into golf ball–size balls and place the meatballs on the prepared sheets. Bake the meatballs for 15 minutes, or until they are cooked through.

FREEZING INSTRUCTIONS:

Divide the meatballs into meal-size portions in freezer bags. Chill the bags in the refrigerator before freezing.

TO THAW AND SERVE:

Thaw the meatballs in the refrigerator. Reheat them in your choice of sauce on the stovetop.

Barbecue Sauce for Meatballs

Add a little smoky flavor to meatballs by warming them on a hot grill and basting them with this super-spicy sauce. (For less heat, reduce the cayenne pepper.) Serve over mashed potatoes or hot cooked noodles. // *Makes about 2 cups (470 ml)*

■ **PACKAGING:** 1-cup (235 ml) plastic containers with lids

2 tablespoons (30 ml) olive oil
1 cup (160 g) finely chopped onion
4 cloves garlic, minced
2 cups (470 ml) tomato sauce
½ cup (120 ml) apple cider vinegar
¼ cup (56 g) dark brown sugar
1 tablespoon chipotle chile powder

1 teaspoon cayenne pepper, or to taste
⅛ teaspoon crushed red pepper flakes
⅛ teaspoon ground ginger
⅛ teaspoon ground cloves
⅛ teaspoon dry mustard
⅛ teaspoon ground cinnamon

1. In a large saucepan, heat the oil over medium heat. Add the onion and garlic and cook for 8 minutes, or until the onion is tender and starting to caramelize.

2. Add all of the remaining ingredients and stir until well combined. Bring to a low boil, stirring constantly. Reduce the heat, cover, and simmer for 30 minutes, stirring occasionally.

3. Blend the sauce with an immersion blender or in a food processor until smooth.

FREEZING INSTRUCTIONS:

Divide the sauce into 1-cup (235 ml) plastic containers. Chill the sauce in the refrigerator before freezing.

TO THAW AND SERVE:

Thaw the sauce in the refrigerator. Reheat in the microwave or in a pan on the stovetop. Serve as a sauce for meatballs, hot or at room temperature.

Herbed Meatloaf

The basic meatball mixture can also be formed into four meatloaves. Lay out four large sheets of aluminum foil. Divide the meat mixture into four portions, placing one portion on each sheet of foil. Form each of the four portions into a loaf. Wrap each loaf well with the aluminum foil and place them into labeled zip-top freezer bags. Freeze.

TO THAW AND SERVE:

Thaw the meatloaf completely in the refrigerator. Preheat the oven to 350°F (180°C or gas mark 4). Unwrap the meatloaf, place it on a baking sheet, and bake for 45 to 60 minutes or until cooked through.

Boules de Picolat (Catalan Meatballs)

This dish is best made with porcini mushrooms, also known as *cèpes*, but I've replaced them with the more easily located and economical button mushrooms. Feel free to use your favorite variety.

// *Serves 12 to 16*

■ **PACKAGING:** Quart- (1 L) or gallon-size (4 L) zip-top freezer bags

3 pounds (1362 g) ground beef
1 pound (454 g) ground pork
2 cups (320 g) chopped onion, divided
3 tablespoons chopped fresh parsley
    or 1 tablespoon dried parsley flakes
3 cloves garlic, chopped
1 teaspoon salt
½ teaspoon freshly ground black pepper

2 tablespoons (30 ml) olive oil
½ cup (35 g) coarsely chopped fresh
    mushrooms
Two 28-ounce (784 g) cans crushed
    tomatoes in puree
One 14.5-ounce (406 g) can diced tomatoes
    with juices

WHEN READY TO SERVE, YOU WILL NEED:

1 cup (100 g) green Spanish olives with
    pimientos

Boiled potatoes or steamed rice

1. Line two rimmed baking sheets with heavy-duty foil. Spray the foil lightly with nonstick cooking spray. Preheat the oven to 350°F (180°C or gas mark 4).

2. In a large bowl, mix the meats, 1 cup (160 g) of the onion, parsley, garlic, salt, and pepper until everything is evenly distributed. Don't overmix, as that will make your meatballs tough.

3. Form the mixture into golf ball–size balls and place the meatballs on the prepared sheets. Bake the meatballs for 15 minutes, or until they are cooked through.

4. In a large stockpot, heat the oil over medium-high heat until shimmering. Add the mushrooms and the remaining 1 cup (160 g) chopped onion to the pot. Cook, stirring, until the onion becomes translucent and the mushrooms start to brown slightly, about 5 minutes. Stir in the crushed tomatoes and diced tomatoes.

5. Add the cooked meatballs to the pot and stir well. Simmer the mixture for 20 minutes.

FREEZING INSTRUCTIONS:

Divide the meatballs and sauce into meal-size portions in freezer bags. Chill the meatballs and sauce in the refrigerator before storing in the freezer.

TO THAW AND SERVE:

Thaw in the refrigerator. Reheat the meatballs and sauce in a saucepan. Stir in the olives and cook until heated through. Serve immediately, along with the potatoes.

2

WINNING CHICKEN DINNERS

▸ Basic Herb-Baked Chicken ▪ 111

▸ Versatile Chicken from the Slow Cooker ▪ 112

▸ Simply Poached Chicken ▪ 113

▸ Homemade Chicken Stock ▪ 114

▸ Easy Chicken (or Turkey) Gravy ▪ 115

▸ Spicy Southwest Chicken ▪ 118

▸ Spicy Dijon Chicken ▪ 119

▸ Tandoori Chicken ▪ 119

▸ Garlicky Italian Chicken Breasts ▪ 121

▸ Herb-Butter Chicken Tenders ▪ 122

▸ Teriyaki Chicken Skewers ▪ 123

▸ Salsa Verde Chicken ▪ 124

▸ Moo Shu–Style Chicken Wraps ▪ 125

▸ Chicken Enchilada Bake with Green Chiles and Jalapeños ▪ 126

▸ Best-Ever Chicken Pot Pie ▪ 127

▸ Garlicky Chicken Noodle Bake ▪ 128

▸ Creamy Chicken Enchiladas ▪ 129

▸ Cheesy Overnight Casserole with Chicken or Turkey ▪ 130

▸ Chicken Divan with Cheddar Crust ▪ 131

▸ Stuffed Chicken Parmesan ▪ 132

▸ Garlic Butter Chicken with Lemon Sauce ▪ 133

▸ Chicken and Wild Rice Bake ▪ 134

▸ Sesame Chicken with Snow Peas and Mushrooms ▪ 137

▸ Chipotle Chicken and Onion Wraps ▪ 138

▸ Green Chile Chicken Taquitos ▪ 139

▸ Chicken-Bacon Subs ▪ 140

▸ Make-Ahead Roast Turkey ▪ 141

▸ Spicy Taco Lasagna ▪ 142

▸ Turkey Burgers with Scallions ▪ 143

▸ Tarragon Turkey Burgers with Blue Cheese and Chipotle Mayo ▪ 144

▸ Turkey Curry ▪ 147

▸ Sweet and Sour Turkey Meatballs ▪ 148

Basic Herb-Baked Chicken

You can maximize your savings by using bone-in chicken breasts. They often go on sale, making them a very economical protein; stock up and bake a bulk batch to have on hand. I prefer bone-in chicken breasts because the meat tends to be more flavorful and doesn't dry out the way boneless, skinless chicken breasts sometimes do. // *Makes at least 6 cups (840 g) chopped cooked chicken*

■ **PACKAGING:** Quart-size (1 L) zip-top freezer bags or quart-size (1 L) plastic containers with lids

6 bone-in chicken breasts
1 teaspoon fine sea salt
1 teaspoon garlic powder

½ teaspoon freshly ground black pepper
1 teaspoon *herbes de Provence*, chili powder, or mixed Italian herbs (optional)

1. Preheat the oven to 375°F (190°C or gas mark 5).

2. Place three chicken breasts in each of two 9 × 13-inch (23 × 33 cm) baking dishes. Sprinkle the chicken with salt, garlic powder, pepper, and seasoning, if using.

3. Bake the chicken for 45 minutes to 1 hour, or until the juices run clear when the chicken is pierced with a knife.

4. Remove the chicken from the pan and set aside until cool enough to handle.

5. Remove the chicken meat from the bones. If desired, reserve the bones and skin as well as the pan drippings for making Homemade Chicken Stock (page 114).

6. Chop or shred the chicken, as desired.

FREEZING INSTRUCTIONS:

If using the chicken in a recipe, proceed with the recipe. Otherwise, place the cooked chicken in freezer bags or containers. Chill the chicken in the refrigerator before freezing.

TO THAW AND SERVE:

Thaw the chicken in the refrigerator. Use as desired in recipes.

▶ Time-Saving Tip

When you sit down to dinner, slip two pans of chicken breasts in the oven to bake while you enjoy your meal. The chicken will be finished cooking by the time you are done eating; it can cool while you clean up dinner. Prep it for the freezer quickly and you're set for several future meals.

Versatile Chicken from the Slow Cooker

On freezer-cooking day, it's best to maximize the use of every pot and appliance so that all your "servants" can be working at one time. The slow cooker is no exception. If it isn't already full of soup, chili, or pasta sauce, put the slow cooker to work on chicken. The amount of chicken you can cook at one time will depend on the size of your cooker. Slow cookers work best when filled two-thirds full. // *Makes at least 4 to 6 cups (560 to 840 g) chopped cooked chicken*

■ **PACKAGING:** Quart-size (1 L) zip-top freezer bags or quart-size (1 L) plastic containers with lids

4 to 6 bone-in chicken breasts or 1 roasting chicken, giblets removed	½ teaspoon freshly ground black pepper
1 teaspoon fine sea salt	1 teaspoon *herbes de Provence*, chili powder, or mixed Italian herbs (optional)
1 teaspoon garlic powder	

1. Sprinkle the chicken breasts or roasting chicken with salt, garlic powder, pepper, and seasoning, if using.

2. Place the chicken in the crock of a 5-quart (5 L) slow cooker. Cook on LOW for 6 to 8 hours or HIGH for 3 to 4 hours.

3. When the chicken is cooked, remove the chicken from the cooker and set aside until cool enough to handle.

4. Remove the chicken meat from the bones. If desired, reserve the bones and skin as well as the pan drippings for making Homemade Chicken Stock (page 114).

5. Chop or shred the chicken, as desired.

FREEZING INSTRUCTIONS:

If using the chicken in a recipe, proceed with the recipe. Otherwise, place the cooked chicken in freezer bags or containers. Chill the chicken in the refrigerator before freezing.

TO THAW AND SERVE:

Thaw the chicken in the refrigerator. Use as desired in recipes.

▶ Time-Saving Tip

You can start cooking the chicken in the slow cooker right before you go to bed. Set on low heat, it will be done when you awake in the morning.

Simply Poached Chicken

The two tricks to tender poached chicken are to avoid boiling it and to allow it to cool in the pan. This method lends itself well to a freezer-cooking session. Get the pan of chicken started, simmer for the allotted time, and then turn it off. While it cools, you can work on other cooking tasks. // ***Makes about 4 cups (560 g) chopped cooked chicken***

- **PACKAGING:** Quart-size (1 L) zip-top freezer bags or quart-size (1 L) plastic containers with lids

2 pounds (908 g) boneless, skinless chicken breasts or tenders
2 bay leaves

4 black peppercorns
1 clove garlic, peeled

1. In a large pot, combine the chicken, bay leaves, peppercorns, garlic, and enough water to cover the chicken by at least 1 inch (2.5 cm). Heat the water just to a boil.

2. Turn down the heat and simmer for 15 to 20 minutes, or until the chicken reaches an internal temperature of 165°F (74°C).

3. Turn off the heat and allow the chicken to cool in the liquid.

4. Chop or shred the cooked chicken, as desired.

FREEZING INSTRUCTIONS:

If using the chicken in a recipe, proceed with the recipe. Otherwise, place the cooked chicken in freezer bags or containers. Chill the chicken in the refrigerator before freezing.

TO THAW AND SERVE:

Thaw the chicken in the refrigerator. Use as desired in recipes.

▶ Ways with Cooked Chicken

Simple cooked chicken is a major building block for many meals. It finds its way into enchiladas, soups, tacos, sandwiches, and salads as a basic, adaptable protein. On busy nights, it's tempting to run for takeout or pick up a rotisserie chicken. But if I've planned ahead, I can instead go to the freezer and grab a bag of precooked shredded chicken. Meals come together in minutes and can be varied in so many ways that we never get bored.

Homemade Chicken Stock

Homemade chicken stock is amazingly easy to prepare. It is a tasty component of soups, stews, sauces, and rice dishes, and it's healthier and more economical than its canned or boxed counterparts. Use the carcass from a whole bird or the bones and skin from either the Basic Herb-Baked Chicken (page 111) or the Versatile Chicken from the Slow Cooker (page 112). // *Makes about 2 quarts (2 L)*

■ **PACKAGING:** Quart-size (1 L) plastic containers with lids

Chicken bones, skin, and drippings from
  Basic Herb-Baked Chicken (page 111) or
  Versatile Chicken from the Slow Cooker
  (page 112) or the carcass of a whole
  roasted chicken
8 cups (1880 ml) water
1 carrot, peeled and chopped
1 medium-size onion, peeled and quartered

2 ribs celery, trimmed and cut into 2-inch
  (5 cm) pieces
6 black peppercorns
2 whole cloves
1 teaspoon dried thyme
1 teaspoon kosher salt
1 bay leaf

1. Place all of the ingredients in the crock of a 5-quart (5 L) slow cooker and cook on HIGH for 4 hours or on LOW for 8 hours or overnight. Alternatively, place all of the ingredients in a large stockpot and bring to a gentle boil. Reduce the heat, cover, and simmer for about 3 hours.

2. Strain the stock and discard the solids.

3. Use the stock in your recipe as needed or pour it into containers and allow it to cool.

FREEZING INSTRUCTIONS:
Chill the chicken stock in the refrigerator. Before freezing, remove the fat that rises to the top when the broth is chilled.

TO THAW AND SERVE:
Thaw stock in the refrigerator and reheat in a pan on the stovetop, if necessary, before using in recipes.

Easy Chicken (or Turkey) Gravy

Bottled and powdered gravies may be convenient, but lots of less-than-desirable ingredients lurk in those packets and cans. Since it's quite easy to make your own gravy, there's no reason to rely on commercial versions. This gravy is a delicious accompaniment to roast chicken dinners and works well in Best-Ever Chicken Pot Pie (page 127). // *Makes about 2 cups (470 ml)*

■ **PACKAGING:** Pint-size (470 ml) plastic container or canning jar with lid

¼ cup (56 g) (½ stick) unsalted butter
   (or fat from chicken or turkey drippings)
¼ cup (30 g) unbleached all-purpose flour
2 cups (470 ml) chicken broth (or defatted
   drippings plus enough broth to make
   2 cups [470 ml])

1 teaspoon dried thyme
¼ teaspoon salt
¼ teaspoon freshly ground black pepper

1. In a large stockpot over medium heat, melt the butter. Add the flour and whisk to combine.

2. Heat until the mixture starts to bubble. Whisk in the broth and bring to a boil, stirring constantly.

3. Reduce the heat and simmer until the gravy is thickened, about 5 to 10 minutes. Add the thyme, salt, and pepper. Adjust seasoning to taste.

FREEZING INSTRUCTIONS:

If using the gravy in a recipe, cool it completely and proceed with the recipe. Otherwise, transfer the gravy to a plastic container or canning jar. Chill the gravy in the refrigerator before freezing.

TO THAW AND SERVE:

Allow the gravy to thaw completely in the refrigerator. Reheat in a saucepan over low heat, whisking to recombine.

Note: To make a big batch of this gravy, simply multiply all the ingredients by four. The cooking method remains the same, though you may have to add a few minutes to the cooking time.

▶ Naturally Gluten-Free Recipes

If you have a sensitivity or allergy to gluten, enjoying good food can involve some work. Often, suitable recipes are time-intensive or require special ingredients. While restaurants are increasing their gluten-free options, running out for takeout on a busy night is not always the best choice. Thankfully, there is a wide world of foods that are naturally gluten free. Having a stash of such meals in the freezer can be a boon to the busy, gluten-free household. Some families make a habit of stocking their gluten-sensitive college students' freezers with food they can safely eat when away at school. Please read ingredient labels carefully to make sure that you are using gluten-free products in your cooking.

- Versatile Shredded Beef Filling, page 73
- Salsa Verde Beef, page 75
- Oven-Baked Beef Taquitos, page 76
- Hearty Shredded Beef Enchiladas, page 79
- Chili-Stuffed Sweet Potatoes, page 99
- Easy Carne Asada, page 82
- Chipotle-Rubbed Tri-Tip, page 80
- Seasoned Steak with Gorgonzola-Herb Butter, page 83
- Quick and Easy Pepper Steak, page 85
- Vegetable Bolognese, page 90
- Seasoned taco meat, sidebar, page 97
- Soy-Balsamic Burgers (lettuce wrapped), page 102
- Outside-In Cheeseburgers (lettuce wrapped), page 105
- Cooked chicken: Herb-baked, from the slow cooker, or poached, pages 111 to 113
- Spicy Southwest Chicken, page 118
- Spicy Dijon Chicken, page 119

- Tandoori Chicken, page 119
- Garlicky Italian Chicken Breasts, page 121
- Herb-Butter Chicken Tenders, page 122
- Teriyaki Chicken Skewers, page 123
- Salsa Verde Chicken, page 124
- Creamy Chicken Enchiladas, page 129
- Chicken and Wild Rice Bake, page 134
- Sesame Chicken with Snow Peas and Mushrooms, page 137
- Green Chile Chicken Taquitos, page 139
- Turkey Curry, page 147
- Sweet and Sour Turkey Meatballs, page 148
- Mahi Mahi with Almond-Lime Butter, page 152
- Salmon Packets with Sun-Dried Tomato Pesto and Onions, page 151
- Shrimp and Vegetable Packets, page 156
- Grilled Tilapia or Shrimp Tacos, page 155
- Spicy Shrimp and Tomatoes, page 158

(continued)

- Versatile Slow-Cooked Carnitas, page 161
- Southwest Seasoned Pork Chops, page 162
- Pork Chile Verde with Hominy and Carrots, page 162
- Pork and Chile Tamales, page 166
- Gingery Pork and Mushroom Lettuce Wraps, page 174
- Queso Fundido, page 180
- Herbed Pork Sausage Patties, page 182
- Seasoned Versatile Pinto Beans, page 189
- Bean and Cheese Nacho Bake, page 192
- Quick and Easy Cheese Enchiladas, page 190
- Gingery Vegetable Stir-Fry Kit, page 202
- Corn and Chile Tamales, page 198
- Chile Cheese Bake, page 196
- Six-Layer Nachos, page 195
- Easy Stovetop Ratatouille, page 200
- Red Lentil Dal, page 203
- Tomato Sauce with Oregano and Kalamata Olives, page 215
- Quick and Spicy Marinara Sauce, page 216

- Easy Slow Cooker Red Sauce, page 217
- Sun-Dried Tomato Pesto, page 218
- Taco Soup with Hominy, page 222
- Tres Chiles Chili Con Quinoa, page 245
- Split Pea Soup with Bacon and Thyme, page 227
- White Bean Soup with Vegetables, page 228
- Beef and Barley Soup with Dill, page 233
- Black Bean Soup with Jalapeño, page 234
- Roasted Vegetable Soup, page 224
- Spring Vegetable Soup, page 231
- Mushroom Barley Soup, page 232
- Quick and Easy Texas Chili, page 244
- Smoky Multi-Bean Vegetarian Chili, page 247
- Parmesan Herb Blend, page 255
- Fruit, Nuts, and Oatmeal Bowls, page 273
- Savory Sausage and Quinoa Bowls, page 297
- Raspberry Baked Oatmeal, page 270
- Breakfast Smoothies, pages 287 to 289
- Slow Cooker Applesauce, page 295
- Spiced Pumpkin Custards, page 357

WINNING CHICKEN DINNERS

Spicy Southwest Chicken

This marinade is almost like a salsa. It's full of fresh flavors that miraculously withstand the cold of the freezer and come shining through later. Any leftover grilled chicken can be chopped and served in tacos or atop salads. // *Serves 4 to 6*

■ **PACKAGING:** Gallon-size (4 L) zip-top freezer bag

1 medium-size tomato, quartered
½ medium-size onion, cut into chunks
¼ cup (60 ml) vegetable oil
¼ cup (60 ml) soy sauce
¼ cup fresh cilantro leaves

¼ to ½ jalapeño pepper, chopped, to taste
2 cloves garlic
1 tablespoon (15 ml) freshly squeezed
   lime juice
4 to 6 boneless, skinless chicken breasts

1. Place the freezer bag in a medium bowl, folding the top over the edges.

2. In a blender or in a food processor fitted with a metal blade, combine the tomato, onion, oil, soy sauce, cilantro, jalapeño, garlic, and lime juice. Blend until smooth.

3. Pour the marinade into the prepared bag. Add the chicken pieces. Seal the bag and massage it gently to combine and distribute the ingredients.

4. Marinate for 2 to 8 hours in the refrigerator if cooking the same day, or freeze immediately.

FREEZING INSTRUCTIONS:

Freeze the bag flat in the freezer.

TO THAW AND SERVE:

A day or two before serving, remove the bag from the freezer and place it on a tray or dish to thaw in the refrigerator. Grill the thawed chicken breasts over a hot fire, turning once, until cooked through.

Spicy Dijon Chicken

Who would have thought that five ingredients could get together and throw a veritable party in your mouth? This Dijon chicken, loosely adapted from one in an old Williams-Sonoma grilling cookbook, pulls that off. Though I highly doubt my French *maman* would have ever added cayenne to her chicken, the Dijon and the pepper combine to give this dish a great kick. You can adjust the heat by increasing or reducing the amount of cayenne; be aware that it will taste spicier once it's cooked.
// *Serves 4 to 6*

■ **PACKAGING:** Gallon-size (4 L) zip-top freezer bag

⅓ cup (42 g) Dijon mustard
¼ cup (60 ml) olive oil
2 tablespoons (30 ml) red wine vinegar

1 teaspoon cayenne pepper
4 to 6 boneless, skinless chicken breasts

1. Place the freezer bag in a medium bowl, folding the top over the edges.

2. In a small bowl, combine the Dijon mustard, oil, vinegar, and cayenne. Whisk to blend.

3. Pour the marinade into the prepared bag. Add the chicken pieces. Seal the bag and massage gently to combine and distribute the ingredients.

4. Marinate for 2 to 8 hours in the refrigerator if cooking the same day, or freeze immediately.

FREEZING INSTRUCTIONS:
Freeze the bag flat in the freezer.

TO THAW AND SERVE:
A day or two before serving, remove the bag from the freezer and place it on a tray or dish to thaw in the refrigerator. Grill the thawed chicken breasts over a hot fire, turning once, until cooked through.

Tandoori Chicken

Teaching my children at home, I've learned about different cultures and tested out recipes of faraway lands. I wasn't sure my kids would go for tandoori chicken, but I was pleasantly surprised when they loved it. The spices gain strength in the freezer, so I've reduced the amount of seasoning that I would normally use for cooking it fresh. // *Serves 4 to 6*

■ **PACKAGING:** Gallon-size (4 L) zip-top freezer bag

¾ cup (180 g) low-fat plain yogurt
or buttermilk

2 tablespoons (30 ml) freshly squeezed
lemon juice

1 tablespoon (15 ml) olive oil

1 teaspoon paprika

1 teaspoon minced fresh ginger

1 teaspoon curry powder

1 clove garlic, finely chopped

½ teaspoon salt

½ teaspoon chili powder

4 to 6 boneless, skinless chicken breasts

1. Place the freezer bag in a medium bowl, folding the top over the edges. Combine the yogurt, lemon juice, olive oil, paprika, ginger, curry powder, garlic, salt, and chili powder in the bag. Swirl the bowl gently or use a whisk to combine.

2. Add the chicken pieces. Seal the bag and massage gently to combine and distribute the ingredients.

3. Marinate for 2 to 8 hours in the refrigerator if cooking the same day, or freeze immediately.

FREEZING INSTRUCTIONS:

Freeze the bag flat in the freezer.

TO THAW AND SERVE:

A day or two before serving, remove the bag from the freezer and place it on a tray or dish to thaw in the refrigerator. Grill the thawed chicken breasts over a hot fire, turning once, until cooked through.

Easy Caesar Salad with Garlicky Italian Grilled Chicken

In some ways, this is a "mock" Caesar salad. Gone are the raw egg and anchovies. But the dressing still packs quite a punch, and it comes together quickly, making it an ideal accent to a freezer meal. // *Serves 4 to 6*

Juice of 1 lemon (about ¼ cup [60 ml])

1 clove garlic, minced

½ cup (120 ml) olive oil

Salt and freshly ground black pepper

2 to 3 Garlicky Italian Chicken Breasts
(opposite page)

1 head romaine lettuce, torn into bite-size
pieces and refrigerated until ready
to serve

¾ cup (75 g) freshly grated Parmesan
cheese

1 cup (50 g) Homemade Croutons
(page 333)

1. In a small glass jar or bowl, combine the lemon juice and garlic. Blend well. Add the olive oil and shake or whisk well to combine. Season the dressing to taste with salt and pepper.

2. Slice the chicken breasts across the grain.

3. In a large salad bowl, toss the lettuce with the dressing. Sprinkle on the cheese and croutons and toss again. Divide the lettuce mixture among serving plates, and top each with a sliced chicken breast. Serve immediately.

Garlicky Italian Chicken Breasts

Grill up this garlicky chicken one night to serve as a main dish, reserving a couple of pieces to chop and toss on Easy Caesar Salad (opposite page) the next night. Get two meals from one, with a minimum amount of work. // *Serves 4 to 6*

■ **PACKAGING:** Gallon-size (4 L) zip-top freezer bag

¼ cup (60 ml) red wine vinegar	**½ teaspoon dried oregano**
¼ cup (60 ml) white wine or sherry	**¼ teaspoon freshly ground black pepper**
¼ cup (60 ml) olive oil	**Pinch of sugar**
2 cloves garlic, crushed	**4 to 6 boneless, skinless chicken breasts**
1 tablespoon chopped fresh basil	
or 1 teaspoon dried basil	

1. Place the freezer bag in a medium bowl, folding the top over the edges. Combine the vinegar, white wine, oil, garlic, basil, oregano, pepper, and sugar in the bag. Swirl the bowl gently to combine the ingredients.

2. Add the chicken pieces. Seal the bag and massage gently to combine and distribute the ingredients.

3. Marinate for 2 to 8 hours in the refrigerator if cooking the same day, or freeze immediately.

FREEZING INSTRUCTIONS:
Freeze the bag flat in the freezer.

TO THAW AND SERVE:
A day or two before serving, remove the bag from the freezer and place it on a tray or dish to thaw in the refrigerator. Grill the thawed chicken breasts over a hot fire, turning once, until cooked through.

▶ Marinated Chicken Pieces

One of the easiest things I pull together for freezer cooking is chicken packed in marinades. Quick to prepare, it's also a speedy meal on the other side of thawing. Cook the marinated chicken on the grill while you make a few side dishes.

Preparing marinated chicken for six dinners takes me about an hour, demonstrating the efficiency of freezer cooking. If I were prepping for one of these meals on any given night, I could easily spend a half hour just trimming the chicken, pulling out the ingredients, and mixing sauces. What could be a cumulative three hours is reduced to one by making bulk batches and preparing several items with like ingredients.

HERE'S THE BASIC METHOD FOR EASY AND QUICK MARINATED CHICKEN.

1. Prepare the marinade. Many marinades contain similar ingredients, so making several marinades at once will save time. Assemble, use, and clean up the ingredients once instead of multiple times. Mix the marinades right inside the labeled gallon-size (4 L) zip-top freezer bags that you will use to store the chicken. If you place each bag in a medium bowl, you can prevent spillage, as the bowl will support the bags while you work. Don't forget to label the bags first. You don't want to try to write on a full bag.

2. Trim the chicken as necessary for the cut you've chosen. Trimming meat is not always a pleasant job, but performing the task in bulk makes it more efficient. Some supermarket meat departments will do the trimming and slicing for you, for little or no charge. Just call and ask. This can save you valuable time in the kitchen. I prefer to marinate boneless, skinless chicken breasts that I halve horizontally into cutlets or slice into strips for stir-fries or fajitas.

3. Add the chicken pieces to the marinades. Squeeze out as much air as possible and massage the bag to distribute the marinade evenly. Lay the sealed bag flat to freeze. Placing the bags on a baking sheet in the freezer will prevent them from slipping through the slats of open freezer shelving. A day or two before serving, pull a bag from the freezer and place it on a tray or dish to thaw completely in the refrigerator.

Herb-Butter Chicken Tenders

It's amazing how tender a butter marinade can make chicken. Broil or grill the chicken and serve with a quinoa pilaf and green salad for a satisfying summer supper. For a dairy-free version, you can use olive oil in place of the butter. // **Serves 4 to 6**

■ **PACKAGING:** Gallon-size (4 L) zip-top freezer bag

¼ cup (56 g) (½ stick) unsalted butter, melted and cooled

2 tablespoons (30 ml) sherry

½ teaspoon dried thyme

½ teaspoon rubbed sage

¼ teaspoon each dried rosemary, tarragon, and oregano

10 to 12 boneless, skinless chicken breast tenders

Salt and freshly ground black pepper

1. Place the freezer bag in a medium bowl, folding the top over the edges. Combine the butter, sherry, and dried herbs in the bag. Swirl the bowl gently to combine the ingredients.

2. Add the chicken tenders. Seal the bag and massage gently to combine and distribute the ingredients.

3. Marinate for 2 to 8 hours in the refrigerator if cooking the same day, or freeze immediately.

FREEZING INSTRUCTIONS:
Freeze the bag flat in the freezer.

TO THAW AND SERVE:
A day or two before serving, remove the bag from the freezer and place on a tray or dish to thaw in the refrigerator. Grill the thawed chicken breasts over a hot fire, turning once, until cooked through. Season to taste with salt and pepper.

Teriyaki Chicken Skewers

Eating cooked meat off a stick is so much fun. There's something primeval and adventuresome about it. These chicken skewers are easy to pull together once the chicken is prepped and marinated. Grab a bag from the freezer and pack it for the next camping trip or beach cookout. // *Serves 4 to 6*

■ **PACKAGING:** Gallon-size (4 L) zip-top freezer bag

¼ cup (60 ml) soy sauce

¼ cup (60 ml) dry sherry

3 tablespoons (45 ml) vegetable oil

1 tablespoon (15 ml) sesame oil

2 cloves garlic, minced

1 teaspoon brown sugar

1 teaspoon minced ginger

2 pounds (908 g) chicken tenders, sliced in half lengthwise

1. Place the freezer bag in a medium bowl, folding the top over the edges. Combine the soy sauce, sherry, oils, garlic, brown sugar, and ginger in the bag. Swirl the bowl gently or use a whisk to combine the ingredients.

2. Add the chicken pieces. Seal the bag and massage gently to combine and distribute the ingredients.

3. Marinate for 2 to 8 hours in the refrigerator if cooking the same day, or freeze immediately.

FREEZING INSTRUCTIONS:

Freeze the bag flat in the freezer.

TO THAW AND SERVE:

Thaw the bag of chicken on a tray in the refrigerator. Thread the chicken pieces on skewers and grill them over a hot fire until cooked through.

Salsa Verde Chicken

Salsa verde, a tomatillo-and-chile-based salsa, is a staple in my cupboard. It goes so well as a condiment, but can play an even greater role as the base to a cooking sauce or marinade. This chicken is one of our favorites for summertime grilling. // *Serves 8 to 12*

■ **PACKAGING:** Gallon-size (4 L) zip-top freezer bag

½ cup (120 ml) salsa verde
Juice of 1 lime
1 teaspoon chile powder
1 teaspoon ground cumin

1 teaspoon pressed garlic
¼ cup (60 ml) olive oil
2 to 3 pounds (908 to 1362 g) chicken
    tenders

1. Place the freezer bag in a medium-size bowl, folding the top over the edges. Combine the salsa verde, lime juice, chile powder, cumin, garlic, and olive oil in the bag. Swirl the bowl gently or use a whisk to combine the ingredients.

2. Add the chicken pieces. Seal the bag and massage gently to combine and distribute the ingredients.

3. Marinate for 2 to 8 hours in the refrigerator if cooking the same day, or freeze immediately.

FREEZING INSTRUCTIONS:

Freeze the bag flat in the freezer.

TO THAW AND SERVE:

Thaw the bag of chicken on a tray in the refrigerator. Grill them over a hot fire until cooked through.

Moo Shu–Style Chicken Wraps

It's true that moo shu connotes seasoned pork served with scallions on a thin pancake. In this case, inspired by my friend Jessika, I've substituted chicken as the alternative protein and flour tortillas as the easy-to-come-by wrap. The slow cooker makes prep quick and simple. // *Serves 8*

■ **PACKAGING:** Gallon-size (4 L) zip-top freezer bag

2½ pounds (1135 g) chicken tenders
½ cup (120 ml) water
½ cup (120 ml) soy sauce
1 tablespoon (15 ml) sesame oil
1 tablespoon (15 ml) sherry

1 teaspoon fresh grated ginger
1 teaspoon chopped garlic
¼ teaspoon black pepper
½ cup (50 g) chopped scallion

ON THE DAY OF SERVING, YOU WILL NEED:
Small flour tortillas
Coleslaw mix

Hoisin sauce
Chopped fresh cilantro

1. Place the chicken tenders in the crock of a large slow cooker. In a small bowl, combine the water, soy sauce, sesame oil, sherry, ginger, garlic, and pepper. Pour this mixture over the chicken in the crock. Cover. Cook on HIGH for 4 hours or on LOW for 6 to 8 hours. The chicken will shred easily.

2. Shred the chicken and moisten with some of the juices. Add the scallions and toss gently. Place the mixture in a zip-top freezer bag.

FREEZING INSTRUCTIONS:
Freeze the bag flat in the freezer.

TO THAW AND SERVE:
Thaw the bag of chicken on a tray in the refrigerator. Reheat the chicken mixture in the microwave or in a skillet on the stove. To serve, place a small amount of chicken on each tortilla. Top with coleslaw mix. Drizzle with hoisin sauce and sprinkle with chopped cilantro.

Chicken Enchilada Bake with Green Chiles and Jalapeños

Early in our marriage, my husband made it clear that he did not care for canned cream-of-anything soup. Imagine my chagrin, as the majority of the recipes I grew up on started with canned soups. Over time, I've learned tastier and healthier ways to make our meals—without the help of canned soups. This enchilada bake would traditionally contain cream of chicken or cream of celery soup. A homemade version, however, takes only a few minutes longer to prepare on the stovetop. This casserole gets an extra kick from green chiles. // *Serves 6 to 8*

■ **PACKAGING:** Two 8-inch (20.3 cm) baking dishes with lids or one 9 × 13-inch (23 × 33 cm) baking dish with lid

3 cups (360 g) shredded cheddar or
  Monterey Jack cheese, divided
2 cups (470 ml) Homemade Cream of Celery
  Soup for Cooking (page 238)
1 cup (225 g) sour cream
One 4-ounce (112 g) can chopped
  green chiles

½ cup (80 g) chopped onion
1 fresh jalapeño pepper, seeded and finely
  chopped (optional)
2 teaspoons chili powder
12 corn tortillas, cut into bite-size pieces
3 cups (420 g) chopped cooked chicken

1. Grease the baking dish(es).

2. In a large bowl, combine 2 cups (240 g) of the cheese, the celery soup, sour cream, green chiles, onion, jalapeño (if using), and chili powder. Mix well.

3. Stir in the tortillas and the chicken. Spoon the mixture into the prepared baking dish(es).

4. Sprinkle the casserole(s) with the remaining 1 cup (120 g) cheese.

FREEZING INSTRUCTIONS:

Cover the dish(es) and chill in the refrigerator before freezing.

TO THAW AND SERVE:

Thaw completely in the refrigerator. Preheat the oven to 350°F (180°C or gas mark 4). Bake for 1 hour, or until hot and bubbly.

Best-Ever Chicken Pot Pie

THIS COZY, ONE-DISH SUPPER is frequently requested at our home. It's also a great recipe to make use of the leftovers of a big roast turkey or chicken supper. Simply put aside a few potatoes before you mash them and reserve any leftover meat, gravy, and vegetables. Fold them all together in a buttery pie crust and stash it in the freezer for dinner later in the month. Feel free to vary the vegetables according to your tastes. // *Serves 4 to 6*

■ **PACKAGING:** 9-inch (23 cm) deep-dish pie plate, heavy-duty aluminum foil

2 cups (280 g) chopped cooked
   chicken breast
½ cup (75 g) frozen peas
½ cup (60 g) diced carrots, cooked
½ cup (60 g) diced potatoes, cooked

2 cups (470 ml) Easy Chicken (or Turkey)
   Gravy (page 115)
¼ teaspoon dried sage
¼ teaspoon dried tarragon
2 recipes Versatile Buttery Pie Crust
   (page 368) or other pie crust

WHEN READY TO SERVE, YOU WILL NEED:
Milk for brushing crust

1. In a large bowl, combine the chicken, peas, carrots, potatoes, gravy, sage, and tarragon; chill the filling until cool to the touch, about 20 minutes.

2. Line the pie plate with one of the two crusts. Pour in the chilled filling. Position the second crust to cover the filling and crimp the edges to seal.

FREEZING INSTRUCTIONS:
Wrap the pie tightly with foil and freeze, making sure that the pie lies flat in the freezer.

TO SERVE:
Unwrap but do not thaw the pie before baking. Vent the top crust by slashing an *X* in the frozen crust. Brush with milk. Bake the frozen pie at 450°F (230°C or gas mark 8) for 15 minutes, then reduce the temperature to 375°F (190°C or gas mark 5) and bake until the crust is browned and the filling bubbles, 45 minutes to 1 hour.

Garlicky Chicken Noodle Bake

This noodle casserole, full of chicken and cheese with a crisp bread-crumb topping, makes for a hearty supper. Serve with a side salad or steamed vegetables for a complete meal. Be careful not to overcook the noodles. They will soften further during freezing, so cook them just al dente.

// *Serves 6 to 8*

■ **PACKAGING:** One 9 × 13-inch (23 × 33 cm) baking dish with lid or two 8-inch (20.3 cm) round baking dishes with lids

16 ounces (454 g) wide egg noodles
2½ cups (590 ml) Easy Chicken (or Turkey) Gravy (page 115)
1 cup (100 g) freshly grated Parmesan cheese
2 cloves garlic, minced

1 tablespoon chopped fresh parsley or 1 teaspoon dried parsley flakes
1 tablespoon chopped fresh basil or 1 teaspoon dried basil
4 cups (560 g) chopped cooked chicken
1 cup (50 g) fresh bread crumbs
¼ cup (56 g) (½ stick) salted butter, melted

1. Grease the baking dish(es).

2. In a large pot of salted water, cook the egg noodles until al dente, according to the package directions. Drain and cool the noodles.

3. In a large bowl, combine the gravy, Parmesan cheese, garlic, parsley, and basil.

4. Stir in the cooled noodles and chicken. Spoon this mixture into the prepared dish(es).

5. In a small bowl, combine the bread crumbs and melted butter. Sprinkle this crumb mixture over the top of the noodles.

FREEZING INSTRUCTIONS:

Cover the pans and chill in the refrigerator before freezing.

TO THAW AND SERVE:

Thaw in the refrigerator. Preheat the oven to 350°F (180°C or gas mark 4). Bake for 30 minutes, or until heated through.

Creamy Chicken Enchiladas

These creamy enchiladas are full of flavor and texture, with a little punch from the chipotle, pepper Jack cheese, and salsa verde, a tangy creaminess from the cream cheese, corn tortillas to give the dish body, and chicken to give it some heart. You'll love how easily these come together.

// *Serves 4 to 6*

■ **PACKAGING:** Snack-size zip-top freezer bag, 9 × 13-inch (23 × 33 cm) baking dish with lid

Vegetable oil, for frying tortillas
12 corn tortillas
4 cups (560 g) chopped cooked chicken
2 cups (240 g) shredded pepper Jack
    cheese, divided

8 ounces (224 g) cream cheese, softened
½ cup (80 g) chopped onion
1 teaspoon Chipotle Taco Seasoning Mix
    (page 98)
Salt and freshly ground black pepper

WHEN READY TO SERVE, YOU WILL NEED:
2 cups (470 ml) salsa verde

1. Fill a skillet with vegetable oil to a depth of 1 inch (2.5 cm). Heat over medium heat until the oil shimmers. Fry the tortillas in the hot oil for 30 to 45 seconds each, turning once with tongs. Drain the tortillas on paper towels. Allow the tortillas to cool enough to be easily handled.

2. In a bowl, combine the chicken, 1 cup (120 g) of the Jack cheese, the cream cheese, onion, and taco seasoning mix. Season the mixture to taste with salt and pepper.

3. Place the remaining 1 cup (120 g) of Jack cheese in the freezer bag and set aside.

4. Grease the baking dish.

5. Assemble the enchiladas by placing 2 tablespoons (28 g) filling on each tortilla. Roll and place the enchiladas, seam side down, in the prepared baking dish.

FREEZING INSTRUCTIONS:
Place the bag of cheese atop the enchiladas, wrap the dish for the freezer, and chill in the refrigerator before freezing.

TO THAW AND SERVE:
Thaw completely in the refrigerator. Remove the bag of Jack cheese from the dish. Preheat the oven to 350°F (180°C or gas mark 4). Pour the salsa over the enchiladas and sprinkle the reserved cheese over the enchiladas. Bake the enchiladas for 20 minutes, or until the dish is heated through and the cheese is melted.

Cheesy Overnight Casserole with Chicken or Turkey

I have fond memories of my Gramma John preparing this dish for a family reunion. I've updated her classic version with a homemade cream soup, fresh herbs, and panko bread crumbs. I love the simplicity of not having to cook the noodles first! If you are making this to serve the next day, simply store the pan in the fridge. // *Serves 6 to 8*

■ **PACKAGING:** 9 × 13-inch (23 × 33 cm) baking dish with lid

2 cups (470 ml) Homemade Cream of Celery
    Soup for Cooking (page 238)
2 cups (470 ml) milk
1 cup (225 g) sour cream
1 teaspoon freshly chopped tarragon
    or ½ teaspoon dried tarragon
1 teaspoon freshly chopped dill
    or ½ teaspoon dried dill

1 teaspoon freshly chopped sage
    or ½ teaspoon rubbed sage
Fine sea salt and freshly ground
    black pepper
16 ounces (454 g) small penne pasta,
    uncooked
2 cups (280 g) cooked and chopped chicken
1 cup (120 g) cubed cheddar cheese
½ cup (80 g) finely chopped onion

WHEN READY TO SERVE, YOU WILL NEED:

½ cup (25 g) panko bread crumbs

2 tablespoons (28 g) melted butter

1. Spray a 9 × 13-inch (23 × 33 cm) baking pan with nonstick cooking spray.

2. In a large mixing bowl, whisk together the cream of celery soup, milk, sour cream, and herbs. Season to taste with salt and pepper.

3. Stir in the uncooked pasta, chicken, cheese, and onion. Pour this mixture into the prepared pan.

FREEZING INSTRUCTIONS:

Cover the pan and chill in the refrigerator before freezing.

TO THAW AND SERVE:

Thaw in the refrigerator. Stir the mixture and pat smooth. In a small dish, combine the panko with the melted butter. Top the casserole with the buttered bread crumbs. Preheat the oven to 350°F (180°C or gas mark 4). Bake for 45 minutes, or until hot and bubbly.

Chicken Divan with Cheddar Crust

If you grew up in the 1970s and '80s, some version of broccoli-and-chicken casserole will probably be familiar to you. Many, like the one my mom used to make, contain canned soup, curry powder, and mayonnaise. Some are served over rice or noodles; some are served alone. Here, Chicken Divan gets a little makeover with a simple homemade sauce and extra broccoli and chicken. The comfort is still there, but with improved flavor and more wholesome ingredients. I like this version over steamed brown rice. // *Serves 6 to 8*

■ **PACKAGING:** One 9 × 13-inch (23 × 33 cm) baking dish with lid or two 8-inch (20.3 cm) square baking dishes with lids

1½ pounds (680 g) broccoli, cut into florets
4 cups (560 g) chopped cooked chicken
2 cups (470 ml) Homemade Cream of Celery Soup for Cooking (page 238)
½ cup (112 g) sour cream
2 tablespoons (12 g) freshly grated Parmesan cheese

1 tablespoon (15 ml) freshly squeezed lemon juice
1 tablespoon (15 ml) sherry
1 teaspoon Dijon mustard
½ cup (25 g) bread crumbs
2 tablespoons (28 g) unsalted butter, melted
1 cup (120 g) shredded sharp cheddar cheese

1. Grease the baking dish(es).

2. Steam the broccoli just until tender. Arrange the florets in the prepared dish(es).

3. Layer the cooked chicken over the broccoli.

4. In a large bowl, combine the cream of celery soup, sour cream, Parmesan cheese, lemon juice, sherry, and Dijon mustard. Whisk the mixture until smooth, then pour over the chicken layer.

5. In a small bowl, combine the bread crumbs and melted butter. Top the dish with the cheddar cheese and buttered bread crumbs.

FREEZING INSTRUCTIONS:
Cover and chill in the refrigerator before freezing.

TO THAW AND SERVE:
Thaw completely in the refrigerator. Preheat the oven to 350°F (180°C or gas mark 4). Bake for 30 to 45 minutes, until heated through.

Stuffed Chicken Parmesan

Like an outside-in chicken parmesan, this chicken is filled with mozzarella cheese, breaded, and baked. Serve it with pasta and a simple red sauce, like Easy Slow Cooker Red Sauce (page 217), and give it all a thorough dusting of Parmesan cheese. // *Serves 4 to 8*

- **PACKAGING:** 1 or 2 baking dishes with lids, depending on how many breasts you will serve at each meal

1½ cups (75 g) bread crumbs
1 tablespoon chopped fresh basil
    or 1 teaspoon dried basil
1 teaspoon garlic powder
½ teaspoon dried oregano

4 boneless, skinless chicken breasts,
    trimmed and cut in half horizontally
4 ounces (112 g) mozzarella cheese,
    cut into eight ½-ounce (14 g) sticks

WHEN READY TO SERVE, YOU WILL NEED:
2 cups (470 ml) Easy Slow Cooker Red
    Sauce (page 217)

1. Grease the baking dish(es) and set aside.

2. In a small bowl, combine the bread crumbs, basil, garlic powder, and oregano. Set the mixture aside.

3. Place the chicken pieces on a clean, flat surface and cover them with a sheet of plastic wrap. Using a kitchen mallet, pound the chicken pieces to flatten slightly.

4. Place a stick of cheese on each piece of chicken. Roll the chicken around the cheese, tucking in the sides as you roll.

5. Roll each stuffed breast in the bread crumb mixture and place it in the prepared baking dish(es).

FREEZING INSTRUCTIONS:

Once all the chicken breasts have been filled, rolled, and placed in the prepared dish(es), cover the dishes and chill in the refrigerator before freezing.

TO THAW AND SERVE:

Thaw the chicken breasts in the refrigerator. Preheat the oven to 350°F (180°C or gas mark 4). Bake for 40 minutes to 1 hour, until the chicken is cooked through and the juices run clear.

▶ Stuffed Chicken Breasts

At first glance, stuffed chicken breasts seem like a lot of work, what with the trimming, flattening, filling, rolling, and baking involved. However, stuffed chicken breasts look so elegant on a plate, it's a shame to relegate them to special occasions. Thanks to freezer cooking and assembly-line preparation, you can enjoy this dish any night. Try one of the next two recipes, then branch out with other fillings of your choice.

Garlic Butter Chicken with Lemon Sauce

My husband's favorite dinner is a lemon chicken that is quite time-intensive. It's a "once-a-year" kind of meal, but I've streamlined it here in this stuffed chicken breast recipe. Some of the garlic butter oozes out of the chicken into the pan. The garlic butter and the juices of the chicken are quickly mixed with lemon juice and a little more butter to create a delectable sauce. Enjoy this meal with rice pilaf.
// *Serves 4 to 8*

■ **PACKAGING:** 1 or 2 baking dishes with lids, depending on how many breasts you will serve at each meal

1½ cups (75 g) bread crumbs
1 tablespoon finely chopped fresh parsley
　　or 1 teaspoon plus ¼ teaspoon dried
　　parsley flakes, divided
1 teaspoon dried thyme

½ cup (112 g) (1 stick) salted butter,
　　softened
1 teaspoon minced garlic
4 boneless, skinless chicken breasts,
　　trimmed and cut in half horizontally

WHEN READY TO SERVE, YOU WILL NEED:
Juice of 1 lemon

2 tablespoons (28 g) salted butter, melted

1. Grease the baking dish(es) and set aside.

2. In a small bowl, combine the bread crumbs, 1½ teaspoons of the fresh parsley or 1 teaspoon parsley flakes, and thyme. Set the mixture aside.

3. In another small bowl, cream together the ½ cup (112 g) butter, garlic, and remaining 1½ teaspoons fresh parsley or ¼ teaspoon parsley flakes. Chill the butter mixture just until it will hold its shape when formed. Form the garlic butter into 8 logs. Chill until ready to use.

4. Place the chicken pieces on a clean, flat surface and cover with a sheet of plastic wrap. Using a kitchen mallet, pound the chicken pieces to flatten slightly.

5. Place a garlic butter log on each piece of chicken. Roll the chicken around the butter, tucking in the sides as you roll.

6. Roll each stuffed breast in the prepared bread crumb mixture and place it in the prepared baking dish(es).

FREEZING INSTRUCTIONS:

Once all the chicken breasts have been filled, rolled, and placed in the prepared dish(es), cover the pans and chill in the refrigerator before freezing.

TO THAW AND SERVE:

Thaw the chicken breasts in the refrigerator. Preheat the oven to 350°F (180°C or gas mark 4). Bake for 40 minutes to 1 hour, until the chicken is cooked through and the juices run clear. Remove the cooked chicken breasts to a platter and tent with foil. Add the lemon juice and the melted butter to the juices in the pan. Stir well to combine. Serve this sauce with the chicken.

Chicken and Wild Rice Bake

Chicken, vegetables, and herbs, as well as wild and brown rice, combine in a delicious dish that is both hearty and elegant. This dish is prepped as a kit to assemble on the day of baking. In this way, valuable time is saved by getting a lot of prep work out of the way. Quickly freezing the vegetables eliminates the need to thaw them before stirring them into the rice mixture. // *Serves 4 to 6*

■ **PACKAGING:** 2-gallon (8 L), 1-gallon (4 L), quart- (1 L), and sandwich-size zip-top freezer bags

½ cup (80 g) chopped onion
½ cup (35 g) chopped fresh mushrooms
   (optional)
1 rib celery, chopped (optional)
3 bone-in chicken breasts or mixed chicken
   pieces (about 2 pounds [908 g])

WHEN READY TO SERVE, YOU WILL NEED:
4 cups (940 ml) chicken broth or water, or a
   combination

1 recipe Herbed Vinaigrette (page 136) or
   ½ cup (120 ml) other favorite vinaigrette
2 cups (340 g) uncooked brown rice
2 tablespoons (20 g) wild rice
½ teaspoon dried thyme
¼ teaspoon freshly ground black pepper

1. Label the 2-gallon (8 L) freezer bag "Chicken and Wild Rice Bake" and include baking instructions.

2. Spread the onion, mushrooms (if using), and celery (if using) in a single layer on a parchment-lined baking sheet. Freeze for about 20 minutes.

3. Combine the chicken breasts and vinaigrette in the gallon-size (4 L) freezer bag. Seal and massage the bag to coat the chicken.

4. Combine the rice and seasonings in the quart-size (1 L) freezer bag.

5. Remove the vegetables from the freezer, place them in the sandwich bag, and seal.

6. Place all three bags in the labeled 2-gallon (8 L) bag. Freeze.

TO THAW AND SERVE:

Remove the bag containing the marinade and chicken from the larger bag. Place the bag of chicken in a dish and thaw completely in the refrigerator. The remaining ingredients can stay in the freezer.

When ready to cook, preheat the oven to 375°F (190°C or gas mark 5). Spray a 9 × 13-inch (23 × 33 cm) baking dish with nonstick cooking spray. Combine the rice mixture and the vegetables in the pan. Stir in the broth. Remove the thawed chicken pieces from the marinade and place them atop the rice. Discard the marinade. Cover the pan with foil and bake for 1 hour. Uncover the pan and bake for an additional 45 minutes to 1 hour, until the rice absorbs most of the liquid and the chicken is cooked through and the juices run clear. Remove the chicken from the pan and cut each breast in half. Serve immediately.

Herbed Vinaigrette

Makes about ½ cup (120 ml)

Juice of ½ lemon
1 tablespoon (15 ml) red wine vinegar
1 teaspoon Dijon mustard
1 clove garlic, minced

¼ teaspoon dried thyme
¼ teaspoon dried tarragon
⅛ teaspoon freshly ground black pepper
¼ cup (60 ml) extra-virgin olive oil

In a small bowl, combine the lemon juice, vinegar, mustard, garlic, herbs, and pepper. Stir well. Add the olive oil in a thin stream, whisking to combine.

Sesame Chicken with Snow Peas and Mushrooms

Sesame chicken is a takeout favorite. This chicken dish comes together easily and is fantastic to have on hand for a quick "takeout" fix without leaving the house. Serve it over rice. // **Serves 4 to 6**

■ **PACKAGING:** Freezer containers with lids or gallon-size (4 L) zip-top freezer bags

1½ pounds (680 g) boneless, skinless
    chicken breasts, sliced into 1 × ¼-inch
    (2.5 cm × 6 mm)-thick strips
2 cloves garlic, minced
1 teaspoon minced fresh ginger
⅛ teaspoon crushed red pepper flakes
1 tablespoon sesame seeds
½ cup (120 ml) chicken broth

2 tablespoons (30 ml) soy sauce
1 tablespoon (15 ml) dry sherry
1 tablespoon cornstarch
1 teaspoon sesame oil
¼ teaspoon sugar
¼ cup (60 ml) vegetable oil, divided
8 ounces (224 g) sliced fresh mushrooms
6 ounces (168 g) snow peas

1. In a medium bowl, combine the chicken strips, garlic, ginger, and crushed red pepper flakes. Set aside.

2. In a large dry skillet over medium heat, toast the sesame seeds until lightly browned. Remove them from the pan and set aside. Do not wash the pan.

3. In a small bowl, prepare the cooking sauce by combining the chicken broth, soy sauce, dry sherry, cornstarch, sesame oil, and sugar. Stir until well blended.

4. In the skillet, heat 2 tablespoons (30 ml) of the vegetable oil over high heat. Add the chicken and cook for about 3 minutes. Remove the chicken to a platter with a slotted spoon.

5. Lower the heat to medium-high and add the remaining 2 tablespoons (30 ml) of oil to the skillet. Add the mushrooms and cook, stirring, until tender and starting to brown, about 3 minutes. Add the snow peas and cook 1 minute more, stirring.

6. Add the chicken, sesame seeds, and cooking sauce to the pan. Cook over medium heat, stirring, until the sauce has thickened.

FREEZING INSTRUCTIONS:

Divide the chicken mixture into meal-size portions in plastic containers or freezer bags. Chill in the refrigerator before freezing.

TO THAW AND SERVE:

Thaw completely in the refrigerator. Heat the chicken, vegetables, and sauce in a saucepan until hot and bubbly.

Chipotle Chicken and Onion Wraps

Frozen burritos are great on-the-go food. But this particular version takes "to go" to a whole new level. Filled with a creamy chipotle chicken mixture, these burritos will disappear quickly.
// *Serves 6 to 12*

■ **PACKAGING:** Gallon-size (4 L) zip-top freezer bags

1 tablespoon (14 g) salted butter
½ cup (80 g) finely chopped onion
6 cups (840 g) diced cooked chicken
8 ounces (224 g) Neufchâtel cheese, softened

2 tablespoons (18 g) chopped chipotle chile peppers in adobo sauce
1 tablespoon chopped fresh parsley or 1 teaspoon dried parsley flakes
12 burrito-size flour tortillas

1. In a small sauté pan, melt the butter over medium heat. Add the onion and cook, stirring, until the onion is translucent. Cover the pan and reduce the heat to low. Allow the onion to cook for about 5 minutes more. Remove the lid and stir the onion, continuing to cook until it is very tender and starting to brown.

2. Combine the chicken, Neufchâtel cheese, cooked onions, chipotle chile and sauce, and parsley in a large bowl. Stir well. (You can combine these ingredients in the bowl of a stand mixer, mixing on low speed just until combined.)

3. Assemble the wraps by laying each tortilla on a flat surface. Spread a scant ½ cup (70 g) of the chicken filling down the center of each tortilla.

4. Roll the tortillas up, folding in the sides as you go. Place the wraps in the freezer bag(s).

FREEZING INSTRUCTIONS:

Seal the wraps in the bag(s), removing as much air as possible. Store in the freezer.

TO THAW AND SERVE:

The wraps can be heated directly from the freezer or thawed. Microwave a frozen wrap on a plate for 2 to 3 minutes, turning once. Or thaw the burritos in the refrigerator and then crisp them on a hot griddle until the filling is hot.

Green Chile Chicken Taquitos

Many, many moons ago, my sisters and I found a recipe that vaguely resembled chicken taquitos. We made them all through our teen years, despite the excess of not-very-spicy canned picante sauce the original recipe called for. While I still love a trip down memory lane, I've switched my allegiance to these taquitos, with their spicier and slightly more sophisticated filling. // *Serves 4 to 6*

■ **PACKAGING:** Plastic containers with lids or gallon-size (4 L) zip-top freezer bags

Vegetable oil, for frying tortillas

24 corn tortillas

2 cups (280 g) shredded cooked chicken

One 4-ounce (112 g) can diced green chiles

2 scallions, finely chopped

1 teaspoon chipotle chile powder

1 to 2 tablespoons (15 to 30 ml) chicken broth, as needed

Salt and freshly ground black pepper

WHEN READY TO SERVE, YOU WILL NEED:

Sour cream

Super-Simple Guacamole (page 77)

Easy Homemade Salsa (page 77)

1. Fill a skillet with vegetable oil to a depth of 1 inch (2.5 cm). Heat over medium heat until the oil shimmers. Fry the tortillas in the hot oil for 30 to 45 seconds each, turning once with tongs. Drain the tortillas on paper towels. Allow the tortillas to cool enough to be easily handled.

2. In a bowl, combine the shredded chicken, green chiles, scallions, and chile powder. Moisten, if necessary, with the chicken broth. Season the mixture to taste with salt and pepper.

3. To assemble the taquitos, roll 1 to 2 tablespoons (14 to 28 g) of filling tightly into each tortilla. Secure the taquitos with toothpicks and set them on a tray lined with plastic wrap or waxed paper.

FREEZING INSTRUCTIONS:

Place the tray in the freezer for about 20 minutes, or until the taquitos are partially frozen but not so firm that you can't remove the toothpicks. If the toothpicks get frozen stuck, that's fine; you can store them with the toothpicks, though you may not be able to pack them as compactly. Once frozen, pack the taquitos into freezer bags or containers and store them in the freezer.

TO SERVE:

Place the frozen taquitos, seam side down, on a baking tray and bake at 475°F (240°C or gas mark 9) for 15 to 25 minutes, turning once. Check for crispness after 15 minutes. Serve with the sour cream, guacamole, and salsa.

Chicken-Bacon Subs

Succulent chicken, crisp bacon, melted cheese, and rich garlic butter present a feast for the senses in this sandwich. Certainly, sandwiches aren't difficult to prepare. But knowing that a large gourmet sub is waiting at home, ready to be popped in the oven, is likely to deter us from stopping for fast food. Get a large, soft, Italian-style loaf for this sub, not a crusty baguette-style bread. // *Serves 4*

■ **PACKAGING:** Heavy-duty aluminum foil

1 large loaf Italian-style bread, 14 to 16 inches (25.6 to 40.6 cm) in length
½ cup (112 g) Garlic Butter (recipe follows)
2 cups (280 g) shredded cooked chicken

¼ cup (20 g) chopped bacon, cooked until crisp
5 ounces (140 g) sliced mozzarella or Monterey Jack cheese

1. Slice the bread in half horizontally and place the halves on a large sheet of heavy-duty aluminum foil. Spread the garlic butter on the bottom half of the bread.

2. Arrange the shredded chicken on top of the garlic butter. Sprinkle the chicken with the chopped bacon. Layer the cheese over the top.

3. Place the top half of the bread over the cheese.

FREEZING INSTRUCTIONS:

Wrap the sub tightly in foil and freeze.

TO THAW AND SERVE:

Thaw the sub completely in the refrigerator. Preheat the oven to 350°F (180°C or gas mark 4). Bake the sub for 25 to 30 minutes, until the cheese is melted and the filling is hot. Remove the foil and slice into four portions.

Garlic Butter

Makes ½ cup (112 g)

½ cup (112 g) unsalted butter, softened
2 cloves garlic, chopped

1½ teaspoons chopped fresh parsley or ½ teaspoon dried parsley flakes

In a small bowl, combine all of the ingredients. Blend well.

Make-Ahead Roast Turkey

Believe it or not, a roast turkey can be successfully frozen and served later—without tasting like last Christmas's leftovers. And though you may not want to make your big meal a "freezer meal," it's nice to know that you can if need be. Not only can you save yourself a great deal of work on serving day, you can also take advantage of sale prices. Cook and freeze the birds you get on special for a roast turkey dinner or turkey sandwich any night of the year. // *Serves 10 to 12 (for a 20-pound [9 kg] turkey)*

■ **PACKAGING:** Heavy-duty aluminum foil, gallon-size (4 L) zip-top freezer bags

1 tablespoon unbleached all-purpose flour	¾ cup (168 g) (1½ sticks) unsalted butter, softened, divided
1 large turkey (up to 20 pounds [9 kg]), thawed, rinsed, and giblets removed	2 teaspoons minced garlic
1 medium-size onion, quartered	Salt and freshly ground black pepper

1. Preheat the oven to 350°F (180°C or gas mark 4). Place the flour in a large turkey oven bag and shake, according to the manufacturer's directions. Place the turkey in the prepared bag and place the onions in the cavity.

2. In a small bowl, combine ½ cup (112 g) of the butter and the garlic. Spread the garlic butter all over the turkey. Season the bird generously with salt and pepper. Close the bag and bake according to the oven bag directions.

3. Carve the cooked turkey. Reserve the drippings for making soup or Easy Chicken (or Turkey) Gravy, page 115.

FREEZING INSTRUCTIONS:

Arrange the turkey slices and pieces in meal-size portions on sheets of foil. Dot the turkey portions generously with the remaining ¼ cup (56 g) butter. Wrap the turkey securely and place the bundles in freezer bags.

TO THAW AND SERVE:

Thaw the roast turkey bundles in the refrigerator. Unwrap the turkey and place it in a roasting pan; moisten with turkey drippings or broth. Cover the pan loosely with foil. Preheat the oven to 325°F (170°C or gas mark 3). Reheat the turkey until it reaches an internal temperature of 165°F (74°C), 15 to 30 minutes depending on how much turkey you are reheating.

Spicy Taco Lasagna

This turkey lasagna is an interesting twist on a classic, featuring spicy cheese and salsa as well as cream cheese in the filling. Hats off to cookbook author Ann Hodgman for the cream cheese sauce; it's the best. There's no need to cook the noodles, as they will soften during freezing and while the lasagna cooks in the oven. Serve this with sour cream, cilantro, and sliced avocado. // *Serves 6 to 8*

■ **PACKAGING:** 9 × 13-inch (23 × 33 cm) baking dish with lid

1 pound (454 g) ground turkey
2 cups (240 g) shredded pepper Jack
   cheese
2 cups (240 g) shredded cheddar cheese
3 cups (705 ml) Easy Slow Cooker Red
   Sauce (page 217) or other favorite
   red sauce

1 cup (235 ml) Easy Homemade Salsa
   (page 77) or other favorite salsa
1 cup (235 ml) chicken broth
8 ounces (224 g) cream cheese
6 to 8 regular (not no-boil) lasagna noodles

WHEN READY TO SERVE, YOU WILL NEED:
Sour cream
Sliced avocado

Chopped fresh cilantro

1. In a large skillet over medium-high heat, brown the ground turkey, breaking it up as it cooks, until it is no longer pink. Drain if necessary.

2. In a bowl, combine the shredded cheeses. In another bowl, combine the browned turkey, red sauce, and salsa.

3. In a medium saucepan, bring the chicken broth to a simmer. Add the cream cheese and whisk until smooth. Set aside.

4. Spray the baking dish with nonstick cooking spray. Spread half the turkey mixture in the bottom of the dish. Sprinkle with 1 cup (120 g) of the cheese.

5. Arrange 3 or 4 of the uncooked lasagna noodles over the cheese layer, breaking them as necessary to fit. Pour the cream cheese mixture over the noodles. Sprinkle with 1 cup (120 g) of the cheese.

6. Arrange the remaining lasagna noodles over the cream cheese layer. Spread the remaining turkey mixture over the noodles. Sprinkle on the remaining cheese.

FREEZING INSTRUCTIONS:

Cover the cooled dish and chill in the refrigerator before freezing.

TO THAW AND SERVE:

Thaw the lasagna completely in the refrigerator. Preheat the oven to 350°F (180°C or gas mark 4) and bake for 45 minutes to 1 hour, until brown and bubbly. Allow the lasagna to rest for 10 minutes before cutting. Top each serving with sour cream, sliced avocado, and chopped cilantro.

Turkey Burgers with Scallions

Turkey burgers, when well seasoned, are an excellent alternative to traditional hamburgers. These burgers are tender and juicy. Ground turkey is rather sticky, making it difficult to form. Using wet hands to shape the patties will help. // *Serves 4*

■ **PACKAGING:** Zip-top freezer bags, waxed paper, plastic wrap

1¼ pounds (568 g) ground turkey
½ cup (25 g) fresh bread crumbs
¼ cup (25 g) finely chopped scallions

1 tablespoon (15 ml) sherry
1 teaspoon salt
½ teaspoon freshly ground black pepper

WHEN READY TO SERVE, YOU WILL NEED:
Hamburger buns
Lettuce leaves or shredded lettuce

Sliced tomatoes
Other toppings, as desired

1. In a large bowl, mix all of the ingredients just until everything is evenly distributed. Don't overmix, as that will make your burgers tough.

2. Divide the mixture into 4 equal portions. Form each portion into a flat patty.

FREEZING INSTRUCTIONS:

Place the patties on a baking sheet and freeze until firm. Remove the frozen patties from the sheet and place them in a freezer bag. Seal the bag carefully, removing as much air as possible. Return the burgers to the freezer. Alternatively, you can freeze the burgers in meal-size bundles, separating the patties with waxed paper. Wrap each bundle in plastic wrap and place in a freezer bag.

TO THAW AND SERVE:

If you have frozen your hamburger patties individually, simply remove the desired number of patties from the bag. There is no need to thaw them before cooking. If you used the bundle method of packaging, thaw the bundle on a dish in the refrigerator. (You may be able to cook these unthawed as well, if the frozen patties separate easily.) Place the hamburger patties on a hot grill or in a skillet. When the tops of the burgers appear wet, flip them over. Continue cooking until the burgers reach the desired doneness. Serve on buns with lettuce, tomatoes, and other toppings as desired.

Tarragon Turkey Burgers with Blue Cheese and Chipotle Mayo

Chipotle mayonnaise and flavorful blue cheese crown these herbed burgers. No one will miss the all-beef patty. // *Serves 4*

- **PACKAGING:** Zip-top freezer bags, waxed paper, plastic wrap

1¼ pounds (568 g) ground turkey

¼ cup (25 g) chopped scallions

1½ teaspoons chopped fresh tarragon leaves or ½ teaspoon dried tarragon

½ teaspoon kosher salt

¼ teaspoon freshly ground black pepper

WHEN READY TO SERVE, YOU WILL NEED:

½ cup (60 g) crumbled blue cheese

½ cup (112 g) mayonnaise

1 chipotle chile in adobo sauce, finely chopped

Hamburger buns

Lettuce leaves or shredded lettuce

Sliced tomatoes

Sliced red onion

Other toppings, as desired

1. In a large bowl, mix all of the ingredients just until everything is evenly distributed. Don't overmix, as that will make your burgers tough.

2. Divide the mixture into 4 equal portions. Form each portion into a flat patty.

FREEZING INSTRUCTIONS:

Place the patties on a baking sheet and freeze until firm. Remove the frozen patties from the sheet and place them in a freezer bag. Seal the bag carefully, removing as much air as possible. Return the burgers to the freezer. Alternatively, you can freeze the burgers in meal-size bundles, separating the patties with waxed paper. Wrap each bundle in plastic wrap and place in a freezer bag.

TO THAW AND SERVE:

If you have frozen your hamburger patties individually, simply remove the desired number of patties from the bag. There is no need to thaw them before cooking. If you used the bundle method of packaging, thaw the bundle on a dish in the refrigerator. (You may be able to cook these unthawed as well, if the frozen patties separate easily.) Place the hamburger patties on a hot grill or in a skillet. When the tops of the burgers appear wet, flip them over. Continue cooking until the burgers reach the desired doneness.

Top the patties with the blue cheese and allow it to melt slightly before removing the burgers from the heat. In a small bowl, combine the mayonnaise with the chopped chipotle chile and its sauce. Serve the burgers on buns with the mayonnaise, lettuce, tomato, red onion, and other toppings as desired.

▶ Got Turkey?

Cooked turkey can often be used in place of cooked chicken in recipes. While turkey has a richer flavor, it is just as freezer-friendly as its barnyard counterpart. Try turkey in one of these recipes as a great way to use up holiday leftovers.

- Chicken Enchilada Bake with Green Chiles and Jalapeños, page 126
- Best-Ever Chicken Pot Pie, page 127
- Garlicky Chicken Noodle Bake, page 128
- Creamy Chicken Enchiladas, page 129
- Chicken Divan with Cheddar Crust, page 131
- Cheesy Chicken Overnight Casserole, page 130
- Chipotle Chicken and Onion Wraps, page 138
- Green Chile Chicken Taquitos, page 139
- Chicken-Bacon Subs, page 140

Turkey Curry

Enjoy a simple curry over rice with this dish that comes together quickly and freezes beautifully. Feel free to vary the vegetables based on what you have on hand. Add more serrano pepper if you like a lot of heat. // **Serves 4 to 6**

■ **PACKAGING:** Plastic containers with lids

1 tablespoon (15 ml) olive oil

1⅓ pounds (604 g) ground turkey

1 medium-size onion, chopped

1 cup (75 g) sliced mushrooms

1 serrano chile, chopped (or less to reduce heat)

1 clove garlic, chopped

Fine sea salt and freshly ground black pepper

2 teaspoons curry powder

1 teaspoon minced ginger

1 teaspoon ground turmeric

2 potatoes, diced

One 15-ounce (420 g) can tomato sauce

One 15-ounce (420 g) can petite diced tomatoes

4 cups (280 g) shredded kale or cruciferous blend

½ cup (120 ml) canned coconut milk

WHEN READY TO SERVE, YOU WILL NEED:

Hot cooked rice

Chopped fresh cilantro

Plain yogurt

1. In a large pot, heat the oil until shimmering. Add the turkey, onion, mushrooms, chile, garlic, salt and pepper to taste, curry powder, ginger, and turmeric. Cook until the turkey is browned and the onion is translucent.

2. Stir in the tomato sauce, tomatoes, and kale. Simmer for 15 to 20 minutes, covered.

3. Stir in the coconut milk and adjust the seasonings.

FREEZING INSTRUCTIONS:

Divide the curry into meal-size portions in plastic containers. Chill the curry in the refrigerator before freezing.

TO THAW AND SERVE:

Thaw the curry in the refrigerator and reheat it in a saucepan. Serve over hot cooked rice, topped with fresh cilantro and a dollop of yogurt.

Sweet and Sour Turkey Meatballs

I love sweet and sour Asian dishes. I don't love standing in line at the local restaurant or paying the high price of takeout. I've combined some of my favorite flavors into these scrumptious cilantro-scented turkey meatballs bathed in sweet and sour sauce. The colors of the peppers and pineapple are gorgeous! If you're a saucy person, double the sauce. // *Serves 4 to 6*

■ **PACKAGING:** Plastic containers with lids

1¼ pounds (568 g) ground turkey
½ cup (80 g) finely chopped onion
1 cup (50 g) bread crumbs
1 egg, beaten
¼ cup chopped fresh cilantro
¼ cup (60 ml) plus 1 tablespoon (15 ml)
    soy sauce, divided
3 tablespoons (45 ml) rice vinegar, divided
1 teaspoon minced ginger
Fine sea salt and freshly ground
    black pepper
1 tablespoon (15 ml) oil

½ cup (80 g) coarsely chopped onion
1 cup (150 g) coarsely chopped bell pepper
    (red and green mix)
1 cup (165 g) pineapple chunks,
    juice reserved
⅓ cup (80 ml) pineapple juice
⅓ cup (80 ml) chicken broth
1 tablespoon brown sugar
1 teaspoon sesame oil
¼ teaspoon red pepper flakes
4 teaspoons cornstarch

WHEN READY TO SERVE, YOU WILL NEED:
Hot cooked rice

1. Line rimmed baking sheets with heavy-duty foil. Spray the foil lightly with nonstick cooking spray. Preheat the oven to 375°F (190°C or gas mark 5).

2. In a large bowl, mix the turkey, finely chopped onion, bread crumbs, egg, cilantro, 1 tablespoon (15 ml) of the soy sauce, 1 tablespoon (15 ml) of the rice vinegar, ginger, and salt and pepper to taste. Combine just until everything is evenly distributed. Don't overmix, as that will make your meatballs tough.

3. Form the mixture into golf ball–size balls and place the meatballs on the prepared baking sheets. Bake the meatballs for 15 to 20 minutes, or until they are cooked through.

4. In a skillet, heat the oil until shimmering. Add the coarsely chopped onion and bell peppers and sauté until the onions are translucent, about 7 minutes. Add the pineapple chunks and cook a few minutes more.

5. In a small dish, whisk together the pineapple juice, chicken broth, remaining ¼ cup (60 ml) soy sauce, remaining 2 tablespoons (30 ml) rice vinegar, brown sugar, sesame oil, and pepper flakes. Whisk in the cornstarch until smooth.

6. Pour the sauce mixture into the pan and cook, stirring, until the sauce thickens, up to 5 minutes. Add the meatballs to the sauce and stir to combine.

FREEZING INSTRUCTIONS:

Divide the meatballs and sauce into meal-size portions in plastic containers with lids. Chill the containers in the refrigerator before freezing.

TO THAW AND SERVE:

Thaw the meatballs and sauce in the refrigerator. Reheat them in a pan on the stovetop. Serve with hot cooked rice.

3

THE CATCH OF THE DAY

‣ Salmon Packets with Sun-Dried Tomato Pesto and Onions ▪ 151

‣ Hoisin-Glazed Salmon Fillets ▪ 151

‣ Mahi Mahi with Almond-Lime Butter ▪ 152

‣ Crumb-Topped Cod Fillets ▪ 154

‣ Tarragon-and-Lemon-Rubbed Fish ▪ 154

‣ Grilled Tilapia or Shrimp Tacos ▪ 155

‣ Shrimp and Vegetable Packets ▪ 156

‣ Spicy Shrimp and Tomatoes ▪ 158

Salmon Packets with Sun-Dried Tomato Pesto and Onions

Salmon is a healthful fish that is readily available. It is delicious when topped with sun-dried tomato pesto and tender onions. Cooking fish in foil packets keeps it moist. Store a kit of toppings and fish in the freezer and assemble it right before cooking on the grill. // **Serves 4**

- **PACKAGING:** Gallon-size (4 L) zip-top freezer bag, 2 sandwich bags

4 salmon fillets, 5 to 8 ounces (140 to 224 g) each, wrapped securely in freezer paper

¼ cup (60 ml) Sun-Dried Tomato Pesto (page 218)
1 medium-size red onion, thickly sliced

1. Place the fish fillets in the freezer bag. Place in the freezer.

2. Place the tomato pesto in a sandwich bag and seal.

3. Place the onion slices in the other sandwich bag and seal. Place these bags in the larger bag in the freezer.

TO THAW AND SERVE:

Thaw the bag in the refrigerator. Lay out four sheets of aluminum foil. Place 1 fillet on each piece of foil. Spread 1 tablespoon (15 ml) of pesto over each fillet. Top the pesto with several slices of red onion. Fold the foil over the fish to create a sealed packet. Cook the packets on a hot grill until the fish begins to flake, 10 to 15 minutes. Serve immediately.

Hoisin-Glazed Salmon Fillets

This tangy fish is delicious served with rice and grilled vegetables. It's a grilled fish dinner that comes together in just a short time. The marinade thaws quickly at room temperature, and the salmon does not need to marinate for long. // **Serves 4**

- **PACKAGING:** Gallon-size (4 L) zip-top freezer bag, small plastic container with lid

4 salmon fillets, 5 to 8 ounces (140 to 224 g) each, wrapped securely in freezer paper
¼ cup (60 ml) rice vinegar

¼ cup (60 ml) soy sauce
1 tablespoon chopped fresh ginger
1 tablespoon (15 ml) hoisin sauce

1. Place the fish fillets in the freezer bag. Place in the freezer.

2. In the plastic container, combine the rice vinegar, soy sauce, ginger, and hoisin sauce. Mix well and seal the container. Place this container in the larger bag in the freezer.

TO THAW AND SERVE:

Thaw the bag in the refrigerator. Stir the marinade to recombine. Lay the thawed fillets in a shallow dish, then drizzle them with the thawed marinade. Allow the fish to marinate for 20 minutes. Cook the fish on a hot grill until it starts to flake, 10 to 15 minutes.

Mahi Mahi with Almond-Lime Butter

Whenever I serve this simple fish with almond-lime butter, folks just can't get enough of it. With the flavors and textures of lime zest, toasted almonds, and dill, this butter sauce blends delectably into the fish. This is my mom's favorite recipe in this entire book! // *Serves 4*

■ **PACKAGING:** Plastic wrap, gallon-size (4 L) zip-top freezer bag

4 mahi mahi fillets, 5 to 8 ounces (140 to 224 g) each, wrapped securely in freezer paper

½ cup (112 g) (1 stick) salted butter, softened

¼ cup (27 g) toasted sliced almonds

1½ teaspoons chopped fresh dill or ½ teaspoon dried dill

Grated zest of 1 lime

½ teaspoon kosher salt

Freshly ground black pepper

1. Place the fish in the freezer bag. Place the bag in the freezer.

2. In a small bowl, combine the softened butter, almonds, dill, lime zest, salt, and pepper. Blend well.

3. Lay out a small sheet of plastic wrap. Spoon the compound butter onto the center of the plastic wrap. Using the plastic wrap as a guide, form the butter into a narrow log. Wrap the butter securely in the plastic wrap and place the butter log in the freezer bag with the fish. Seal and return the bag to the freezer.

TO THAW AND SERVE:

Thaw the bag in the refrigerator. Season the thawed fillets with salt and pepper and cook them, turning once, on a hot, oiled grill until the fish starts to flake, 10 to 15 minutes. Meanwhile, allow the butter to soften. Top each fillet with a few slices of the compound butter. The butter will melt quickly atop the hot fish, forming a sauce. Serve immediately.

Crumb-Topped Cod Fillets

Fried fish is a delicious and decadent treat, but it can be a nuisance to prepare. This crumb-topped fish dish offers the crunch and flavor without much work. Having a seasoned bread crumb mixture in the freezer makes quick work of this meal. It's just as easy as frozen fish sticks, but much better. Any white fish can be used. // *Serves 4*

- **PACKAGING:** Gallon-size (4 L) zip-top freezer bag, snack-size bag

4 cod fillets or other white fish, 5 to 8 ounces (140 to 224 g) each, wrapped securely in freezer paper
½ cup (25 g) panko bread crumbs
1 tablespoon fresh chopped dill or 1 teaspoon dried dill

1 teaspoon garlic powder
Grated zest of 1 lemon
½ teaspoon sesame seeds
½ teaspoon paprika
½ teaspoon salt

WHEN READY TO SERVE, YOU WILL NEED:
1 tablespoon (15 ml) olive oil

Lemon wedges

1. Place the fish fillets in the freezer bag. Place in the freezer.

2. In a small bowl, combine the bread crumbs, dill, garlic powder, lemon zest, sesame seeds, paprika, and salt. Place the crumb mixture in the snack-size bag and place this bag in the larger bag in the freezer.

TO THAW AND SERVE:
Thaw the bag in the refrigerator. Preheat the oven to 400°F (200°C or gas mark 6) and line a rimmed baking sheet with parchment paper. Place the fish fillets on the prepared baking sheet. Brush the thawed fillets with the olive oil and sprinkle with the seasoned bread crumbs. Bake the fish in the oven until it flakes easily, 10 to 12 minutes depending on the thickness of the fillets. Serve immediately, with lemon wedges on the side.

Tarragon-and-Lemon-Rubbed Fish

Having your own custom-made spice blends on hand makes a cookout quick and easy. Store them in the freezer to preserve their freshness. This classic combination of tarragon and lemon goes well with all kinds of fish, from delicate fillets to thick, rich steaks. // *Serves 4*

- **PACKAGING:** Gallon-size (4 L) zip-top freezer bag, snack-size bag

4 fish fillets or steaks, such as salmon, 5 to 8 ounces (140 to 224 g) each, wrapped securely in freezer paper
1 tablespoon chopped fresh parsley or 1 teaspoon dried parsley flakes
1 teaspoon grated lemon zest

1 teaspoon garlic powder
1 teaspoon dried tarragon
1 teaspoon kosher salt
¼ teaspoon freshly ground black pepper
¼ teaspoon paprika

WHEN READY TO SERVE, YOU WILL NEED:
1 tablespoon (15 ml) olive oil

1. Place the fish fillets in the freezer bag. Place in the freezer.

2. In a small bowl, combine the parsley, lemon zest, garlic powder, tarragon, salt, pepper, and paprika. Place the spice mixture in the snack-size bag and place this bag in the larger bag in the freezer.

TO THAW AND SERVE:
Thaw the bag in the refrigerator. Brush the thawed fillets with the olive oil and rub the seasoning all over the fish. Cook on a hot grill or in a stovetop grill pan, turning once, until the fish starts to flake, 10 to 15 minutes.

Grilled Tilapia or Shrimp Tacos

Fish or shrimp tacos are a delicious twist on Mexican food. Popular in Baja California, they are often served with fresh cabbage and a delectable white sauce. Fried fish is popular as a taco filling, but grilling the seafood is easier and healthier. Package this meal as a kit to be assembled and cooked right before serving. // *Serves 4*

■ **PACKAGING:** Gallon-size (4 L) zip-top freezer bag, snack-size bag

1 pound (454 g) tilapia fillets or medium-size shrimp (31 to 40 count), peeled and deveined, wrapped securely in freezer paper
1 tablespoon paprika
1 teaspoon sesame seeds

½ teaspoon ground ginger
½ teaspoon freshly ground black pepper
1½ teaspoons chopped fresh dill or ½ teaspoon dried dill
½ teaspoon salt
¼ teaspoon cayenne pepper

WHEN READY TO SERVE, YOU WILL NEED:

1 tablespoon (15 ml) olive oil

Corn tortillas, warmed

Shredded green or red cabbage

Chopped fresh cilantro

Yogurt-Dill Dressing (page 82)

Easy Homemade Salsa (page 77)

Lime wedges

1. Place the fish fillets or shrimp in the freezer bag. Place in the freezer.

2. In a small bowl, combine the paprika, sesame seeds, ginger, pepper, dill, salt, and cayenne. Place the spice mixture in the snack-size bag and place this bag in the larger bag in the freezer.

TO THAW AND SERVE:

Thaw the bag in the refrigerator. Brush the thawed fillets or shrimp with the olive oil and sprinkle with the seasoning. Cook the seafood on a hot grill or in a stovetop grill pan, turning once, until the fish starts to flake or the shrimp are pink, 7 to 10 minutes. Assemble the tacos by placing a small portion of seafood on each tortilla. Top the fish with shredded cabbage and chopped cilantro. Drizzle the tacos with the yogurt-dill dressing and serve with salsa and lime wedges.

Shrimp and Vegetable Packets

An alternative to the fish packet kit is to freeze the assembled packets in advance. They take up a little more space in the freezer but the trade-off is added convenience. These shrimp packets are inspired by a great meal we enjoyed in Normandy several years ago. Succulent shrimp cooks atop a bed of carrots, accented with bell pepper, lemon, and fresh dill. // *Serves 4*

■ **PACKAGING:** Gallon-size (4 L) zip-top freezer bag, heavy-duty aluminum foil

4 cups (480 g) julienned carrots

1 pound (454 g) frozen raw shrimp
(21 to 30 count), peeled and deveined

Fine sea salt and freshly ground black
pepper or favorite spice blend

1 cup (150 g) chopped bell peppers

1 lemon, thinly sliced

4 sweet white onion slices

4 tablespoons (56 g) butter, cut into cubes

4 sprigs dill

1. Lay out four large sheets of heavy-duty aluminum foil.

2. Place 1 cup of (120 g) carrots in the center of each sheet. Divide the shrimp among the four sheets. Season to taste with salt and pepper.

3. Add ¼ cup (38 g) peppers to each pile. Layer on the lemon and onion slices. Divide the butter among the piles. Lay a sprig of dill on top of each.

4. Bring up the long sides of the foil over each pile, folding the ends together and then continuing to fold until the top is sealed tightly. Fold the sides in snugly.

FREEZING INSTRUCTIONS:

Place the bundles in large freezer bags; lay flat to freeze.

TO THAW AND SERVE:

Thaw the bags in the refrigerator. Cook the packets on a hot grill until the shrimp are cooked, 10 to 15 minutes. Serve immediately.

Spicy Shrimp and Tomatoes

Succulent shrimp and juicy tomatoes are a great combination in this dish. When you're ready to serve, the seafood cooks quickly in the tangy sauce, making for a speedy weeknight meal. Serve this spicy mixture over hot cooked rice or with cornbread. // *Serves 6 to 10*

■ **PACKAGING:** Two quart-size (1 L) plastic containers with lids

2 tablespoons (30 ml) olive oil
1 cup (150 g) chopped red or green bell
    pepper, or a combination
1 cup (160 g) chopped onion
1 cup (120 g) chopped celery
1 tablespoon chopped garlic
One 14.5-ounce (406 g) can diced tomatoes,
    with their juices
One 15-ounce (420 g) can tomato sauce
1 cup (235 ml) water

One 6-ounce (168 g) can tomato paste
1 teaspoon smoked paprika
1 teaspoon dried thyme
1 teaspoon salt
1 teaspoon dried oregano
1 bay leaf
½ teaspoon freshly ground black pepper
½ teaspoon chipotle chile powder
⅛ teaspoon crushed red pepper flakes

WHEN READY TO SERVE, YOU WILL NEED:

2 pounds (908 g) shrimp (41 to 50 count),
    peeled and deveined

1. In a large stockpot, heat the oil over medium heat until shimmering. Add the peppers, onion, celery, and garlic, and cook until the vegetables are tender and the onions are translucent, about 10 minutes.

2. Stir in the tomatoes, tomato sauce, water, tomato paste, and seasonings. Bring the mixture to a low boil. Simmer for 20 minutes.

3. Ladle the sauce into the quart-size (1 L) plastic containers. Allow the sauce to cool to room temperature.

FREEZING INSTRUCTIONS:
Cover and chill the sauce in the refrigerator before storing in the freezer.

TO THAW AND SERVE:
Thaw the sauce and the shrimp (if necessary) in the refrigerator. Heat the sauce in a large saucepan over medium heat. Add the shrimp to the sauce and cook for 3 to 5 minutes, until the shrimp are pink. Adjust the seasonings to taste.

▶ Things to Serve When You Forgot to Thaw

Water, water, everywhere, nor any drop to drink. So cried the Ancient Mariner. And you may empathize with his plight if you ever find yourself with a freezer full of food and nothing to eat for dinner! This can easily happen if you forget to pull items from the freezer in time to thaw adequately. But never fear—there is a way out of these doldrums. The following items either thaw quickly or can be cooked or reheated directly from the freezer, without thawing.

- Oven-Baked Beef Taquitos, page 76
- Mexican Beef Tortas, page 77
- Not Your Convenience Store's Frozen Burritos, page 96
- Seasoned taco meat, sidebar, page 97
- Sweet and Spicy Joes, page 99
- Herbed Meatballs, page 106, with Easy Slow Cooker Red Sauce, page 217, or Barbecue Sauce for Meatballs, page 106
- Swedish Meatballs with Dill, page 94
- Best-Ever Chicken Pot Pie, page 127
- Chipotle Chicken and Onion Wraps, page 138
- Green Chile Chicken Taquitos, page 139
- Any of the red sauces, pages 215 to 217
- Any of the soups, pages 221 to 247
- French Bread Pizza Dippers, page 260
- Deep-Dish Focaccia Pizza Your Way, page 262
- Spinach and Cheese Calzones, page 264

4

SIZZLING PORK AND SAUSAGE

▸ Versatile Slow-Cooked Carnitas ▪ 161

▸ Southwest Seasoned Pork Chops ▪ 162

▸ Pork Chile Verde with Hominy and Carrots ▪ 162

▸ Cranberry Pork Chops ▪ 163

▸ Pork and Chile Tamales ▪ 166

▸ Soy-Ginger Pork Tenderloin ▪ 167

▸ Pulled Pork Sandwiches with Asian Slaw and Tangy Barbecue Sauce ▪ 168

▸ Asian Slaw ▪ 170

▸ Tangy Asian Barbecue Sauce ▪ 171

▸ Grilled Caribbean Pork Tenderloin ▪ 171

▸ Fresh Mango Salsa ▪ 172

▸ Shells Stuffed with Pork, Mushrooms, and Onions ▪ 173

▸ Gingery Pork and Mushroom Lettuce Wraps ▪ 174

▸ Asian Dipping Sauce ▪ 176

▸ Herb-Crusted Pork Roast ▪ 176

▸ Make-Ahead Baked Bacon ▪ 177

▸ Ham and Swiss Potato Gratin ▪ 178

▸ Zesty Italian Melts ▪ 179

▸ Easy Sausage and Pepper Sandwiches ▪ 179

▸ Queso Fundido ▪ 180

▸ Herbed Pork Sausage Patties ▪ 182

▸ Red Sauce with Sausage ▪ 183

▸ Penne with Italian Sausage and Tricolor Peppers ▪ 184

▸ Wild Boar Italian Sausage with Spicy Tomato Sauce ▪ 186

Versatile Slow-Cooked Carnitas

Carnitas, while translating as "little meats" in Spanish, typically signifies a seasoned, shredded pork filling used for tacos, tostadas, and tamales. Traditionally, the pork shoulder is boiled and then roasted. Here, it is prepared in a slow cooker for a simpler, yet equally delicious result. The moist and juicy carnitas freezes and reheats quite well, making it a perfect addition to your freezer cooking arsenal. Instead of a shoulder roast, you can use country-style pork strips, which often go on sale. // *Serves 10 to 12*

■ **PACKAGING:** Quart-size (1 L) zip-top freezer bags or plastic containers with lids

One 3- to 4-pound (1362 to 1816 g) pork
    shoulder roast
Salt and freshly ground black pepper

1 medium-size onion, chopped
½ teaspoon dried oregano
¼ cup (60 ml) water

1. Place the pork roast in a 4-quart (4 L) slow cooker. Season the meat generously with salt and pepper. Add the chopped onion and sprinkle the oregano over all. Add the water to the pot.

2. Cook on LOW for 8 hours or on HIGH for about 4 hours. The meat should be very tender and shred easily.

3. Remove the meat from the pot. Strain the juices and reserve them to add to chili, stew, or soup.

4. Shred and cut the meat into bite-size pieces.

FREEZING INSTRUCTIONS:

Divide the carnitas into meal-size portions in freezer bags or containers. Chill the meat in the refrigerator before freezing.

TO THAW AND SERVE:

Thaw the meat in the refrigerator. Preheat the oven to 350°F (180°C or gas mark 4). Place the meat in a baking dish and reheat for 15 minutes, until hot. Adjust the seasonings to taste.

Southwest Seasoned Pork Chops

These pork chops gain a depth of flavor from the simple marinade and the grill. Pair these chops with fried potatoes, corn, and black beans for a hearty meal. Mix up a batch of Basic Taco Seasoning Mix (page 97) first, as that spice blend plays a starring role in the marinade. // *Serves 4*

- **PACKAGING:** Gallon-size (4 L) zip-top freezer bag

¼ cup (60 ml) red wine vinegar
¼ cup (60 ml) vegetable oil
1 tablespoon Basic Taco Seasoning Mix
   (page 97)

4 boneless pork chops, about ½ inch
   (1.3 cm) thick

1. Place the freezer bag in a medium bowl, folding the top over the edges. Pour in the vinegar and oil, and add the taco seasoning. Massage the bag to combine the marinade ingredients.

2. Add the pork chops to the bag. Seal the bag, squeezing out as much air as possible. Massage the bag to distribute the marinade evenly.

FREEZING INSTRUCTIONS:

Freeze the bag flat in the freezer.

TO THAW AND SERVE:

Thaw the chops on a tray or dish in the refrigerator. Grill or broil the thawed pork chops, turning once, until cooked through, 10 to 15 minutes. Serve hot.

Pork Chile Verde with Hominy and Carrots

This pork dish always gets rave reviews. It's simple but filling, with a touch of the Southwest. Serve it with rice, salsa, sour cream, and chopped cilantro.

A time-saving technique during a freezer cooking session is to have one or even two slow cookers going while you prepare other food items. Not only does it make good use of your time in the kitchen, it also takes advantage of the technology available to you. You can even start a stew or sauce in the slow cooker several hours before you begin your intensive cooking session. In this way, you'll have a great head start on the cooking process. // *Serves 8 to 10*

- **PACKAGING:** Plastic containers with lids

1½ pounds (680 g) boneless shoulder blade
    pork strips (also called country-style ribs)
Salt and freshly ground black pepper
1 tablespoon (15 ml) olive oil
1 cup (160 g) coarsely chopped onion
One 4-ounce (112 g) can chopped
    green chiles

½ teaspoon ground cumin
2 cups (470 ml) salsa verde
One 15.5-ounce (434 g) can hominy,
    rinsed and drained
2 cups (240 g) baby carrots

1. Season the pork generously with salt and pepper.

2. In a large skillet over medium heat, heat the oil. Brown the pork strips, turning until browned on all sides. Transfer the pork strips to a 5-quart (5 L) slow cooker or a large heavy pot.

3. Add the onion, chiles, and cumin to the drippings in the skillet. Sauté the onions until they are translucent and starting to brown, about 5 minutes. Add the onion mixture to the pork in the slow cooker or pot.

4. Stir in the salsa verde and the hominy.

5. If using the slow cooker, cover and cook on LOW for 4 to 6 hours. If using a pot, bring the mixture to a low simmer, and simmer for about 2 hours.

6. If using the slow cooker, stir in the carrots an hour before the end of cooking time. If using a pot, stir in the carrots 20 minutes before the end of cooking time.

FREEZING INSTRUCTIONS:

Divide the pork, vegetables, and sauce into meal-size portions in plastic containers. Chill in the refrigerator before storing in the freezer.

TO THAW AND SERVE:

Thaw the pork in the refrigerator. Reheat in a saucepan and serve.

Cranberry Pork Chops

This meal is ideal for a cold, blustery day. Cranberries, onions, and spices join forces to flavor the pork chops as they simmer in the slow cooker. Prep couldn't be easier, as the meat and seasonings are ready to go in one zip-top freezer bag. Just empty the bag into the cooker, turn it on, and go about your day. // *Serves 4*

    ■ **PACKAGING:** Gallon-size (4 L) zip-top freezer bag

2 tablespoons (28 g) salted butter
½ cup (80 g) chopped onion
¼ cup (30 g) chopped celery
1 clove garlic, chopped
1 cup (100 g) fresh cranberries

4 boneless pork chops, about ½ inch
   (1.3 cm) thick
¼ teaspoon freshly ground black pepper
½ teaspoon dried thyme
2 tablespoons (24 g) brown sugar

WHEN READY TO SERVE, YOU WILL NEED:
¼ cup (60 ml) chicken broth or vegetable
   broth

1. In a large skillet, melt the butter over medium heat. Add the onion, celery, and garlic, and cook, stirring, until the vegetables are tender. Set the mixture aside to cool completely.

2. Place the cooled, sautéed vegetables, cranberries, pork chops, pepper, thyme, and brown sugar in the freezer bag.

3. Seal the bag, squeezing out as much air as possible. Massage the bag to distribute the ingredients evenly.

FREEZING INSTRUCTIONS:

Freeze the bag flat in the freezer.

TO THAW AND SERVE:

Thaw the pork chops on a tray or dish in the refrigerator. On the morning of the day you plan to serve this dish, empty the contents of the bag into a 4-quart (4 L) slow cooker and add ¼ cup (60 ml) broth. Cook on LOW for 6 to 8 hours, or until the pork chops are cooked through.

▶ Tips for Cooking When You Have Kids Around

The first time I tackled a big freezer cooking day, I was seven months pregnant, with the swollen ankles to prove it. My friend Jessika and I spent two days cooking in my 50-square-foot (15.2 sq m) kitchen. We were both married without kids, and we produced about forty meals to feed ourselves and our husbands. We were freezer cooking ninjas!

The next time we tackled the job, I had a newborn. Needless to say, things were a bit different! Thankfully, I had my mother on baby duty. Jessika and I cooked while Nanna rocked the baby; I took occasional pit stops to nurse him.

(continued)

Since then my little family has almost tripled in size. With twenty years of motherhood under my belt, I can say with confidence, "This isn't my first rodeo." I think I've seen it all. While there are nights when I cook a meal from scratch to serve my brood, I love to be able to pull a full meal or just a few meal components from the freezer to make my time in the kitchen easier and quicker.

How do you cook up a storm with little people about? Over the years, I've developed a number of approaches to cooking with kids and, sometimes, in spite of them. These same strategies also come in handy when I'm preparing big holiday meals.

- Get a babysitter. Whether your Nanna comes to spend the day or weekend with the express purpose of watching the kids so that you can fill the freezer or you enlist the aid of a teenage "mother's helper," enlisting help will buy you concentrated time in the kitchen.

- Make judicious use of videos, audio resources, and computer games. Call this "free babysitting," if you will. It may not be the same as a human babysitter, but I've been okay with using electronic devices to keep my kids entertained and out of mischief while I worked toward better dinners and family nights. I've also broken up the electronic activities with Play-Doh sessions, snacks and lunches, and other independent play. If your children are school aged, cooking while they're at school may be the best way to fill your freezer.

- Have snacks ready before you start cooking. It's hard to interrupt a big cooking session to prep another meal, so have kid-friendly foods at the ready. You could even pack a little sack lunch for each child. That will give them something to look forward to.

- Cook during naptime and after the kids are in bed. There have been many nights when I've burned the midnight oil in the kitchen. I know the kids are safe, and I can work more quickly without interruptions. It's also a great time for my husband and me to catch up with each other. A freezer cooking date night? I'm all over that!

- Get your spouse or partner to plan a day out with the kiddos. Explain the benefits of a big freezer cooking day and ask that he or she take the kids out for the day. This will buy you the peace and quiet to get a lot accomplished in a short amount of time.

- Include them! I'm a firm believer in teaching kids to cook at a young age. My little ones have always loved to be in on the action. And for my bigger kids, this is about learning valuable life skills. Picky eaters might also be more excited to try new foods if they've had a hand in the preparation.

Pork and Chile Tamales

Tamales are a Christmas tradition in Mexico and southern California. Though I was born and raised in southern California, I did not grow up enjoying homemade tamales. I wish I had! Years ago, my husband suggested that we learn how to make them ourselves. Now, we often keep a few batches of tamales stashed in the freezer. They freeze beautifully and are a delicious snack, lunch, or dinner.
// *Serves 12 to 15*

■ **PACKAGING:** Quart- (1 L) or gallon-size (4 L) zip-top freezer bags

1 package dried corn husks
1⅓ cups (300 g) unsalted butter, softened
4 cups (480 g) masa harina
2 teaspoons salt
2 to 3 cups (470 to 705 ml) chicken broth

2 cups (280 g) Versatile Slow-Cooked
   Carnitas (page 161)
½ to 1 cup (120 to 235 ml) red chile sauce
   or enchilada sauce

WHEN READY TO SERVE, YOU WILL NEED:
Additional red chile sauce or enchilada
   sauce

Sour cream
Easy Homemade Salsa (page 77)

1. Soak the corn husks in warm water until pliable, up to several hours. Remove any silks or debris from the husks and rinse the husks thoroughly. Keep the husks damp until ready to use.

2. In a large bowl, whip the butter until light and fluffy. Blend in the masa harina, salt, and 2 cups (470 ml) of chicken broth. Blend well. Add more chicken broth until the dough holds together well. It should have the consistency of soft cookie dough. Cover the prepared masa with a damp cloth and keep it cool until ready to use.

3. In a medium bowl, combine the carnitas and enough of the red chile sauce to moisten it. Taste for seasoning and adjust as desired.

4. For each tamale, lay a presoaked husk flat on a work surface with the tip away from you. Spread 2 tablespoons (28 g) masa on the husk, in a 5 × 4-inch (12.7 × 10 cm) rectangle. Spoon 2 tablespoons (28 g) carnitas filling in a line down the center of the masa rectangle.

5. Fold the right side of the corn husk over the center of the filling, then fold the left side over the filling, wrapping any uncovered husk around the tamale. Fold the ends over.

6. Lay each tamale in a steamer basket, folded side down to hold it shut. Once all the tamales are folded and arranged in the steamer, place the steamer basket in a large pot over a few inches of boiling water. Make sure that the steam can move freely around the tamales; don't pack them in too tightly.

7. Cover the pot and turn the heat to medium so that the water will boil gently. Steam the tamales for 45 minutes to 1 hour.

8. To test for doneness, remove one tamale from the top of the stack and one from the middle. Open them; they are done if the masa dough is firm, does not stick to the husk, and does not have a raw, doughy taste.

FREEZING INSTRUCTIONS:

Cool the tamales completely and package them in freezer bags. Chill in the refrigerator before freezing.

TO SERVE:

Steam the frozen tamales for 20 to 30 minutes or until heated through. Or microwave frozen tamales on a plate, covered with a damp paper towel, for 1 to 2 minutes per tamale. Serve the tamales with red chile sauce, sour cream, and salsa.

Soy-Ginger Pork Tenderloin

This Asian-flavored pork tenderloin marinates as it thaws in the refrigerator, making for simple last-minute preparation. Once thawed, this easy but elegant meal can go from refrigerator to table in about 30 minutes. Serve with rice and vegetables on the side. // *Serves 4*

■ **PACKAGING:** Gallon-size (4 L) zip-top freezer bag

¼ cup (60 ml) rice vinegar
¼ cup (60 ml) vegetable oil
3 tablespoons (45 ml) soy sauce
1 teaspoon minced fresh ginger

½ teaspoon crushed garlic
¼ teaspoon freshly ground black pepper
¼ teaspoon crushed red pepper flakes
One 1-pound (454 g) pork tenderloin

1. Place the freezer bag in a medium bowl, folding the top over the edges. Pour in the vinegar, oil, and soy sauce, and add the ginger, garlic, black pepper, and red pepper flakes. Massage the bag to combine the marinade ingredients.

2. Add the tenderloin to the bag. Seal the bag, squeezing out as much air as possible. Massage the bag to distribute the marinade evenly.

FREEZING INSTRUCTIONS:

Freeze the bag flat in the freezer.

TO THAW AND SERVE:

Thaw the tenderloin on a tray in the refrigerator. Preheat the oven to 375°F (190°C or gas mark 5). Remove the tenderloin from the bag and place it in a baking dish. Cook the tenderloin until an instant-read thermometer registers 145°F (63°C) for medium or 160°F (71°C) for well done, 30 to 40 minutes. Alternatively, the tenderloin can be cooked on a grill for about 30 minutes, turning once. Allow the tenderloin to rest for about 10 minutes after cooking. Slice and serve.

Pulled Pork Sandwiches with Asian Slaw and Tangy Barbecue Sauce

A dinner that might take hours to prepare requires only minutes to assemble when you have succulent pulled pork ready in the freezer. Pair the tender meat with a tangy barbecue sauce and an Asian-inspired coleslaw for a great dinner. // *Serves 8 to 12*

■ **PACKAGING:** Quart- (1 L) or gallon-size (4 L) zip-top freezer bags

1½ teaspoons garlic powder
1 teaspoon onion powder
1 teaspoon chili powder
1 teaspoon salt
½ teaspoon freshly ground black pepper

½ teaspoon ground cumin
½ teaspoon ground ginger
One 2½-pound (1135 g) boneless
    pork shoulder

WHEN READY TO SERVE, YOU WILL NEED:
Kaiser rolls or hamburger buns
Asian Slaw (recipe follows)

Tangy Asian Barbecue Sauce
    (recipe follows)

1. In a small bowl, combine the garlic powder, onion powder, chili powder, salt, pepper, cumin, and ginger.

2. Rub the spice mixture all over the pork shoulder.

3. Place the seasoned pork shoulder in a 5-quart (5 L) slow cooker. Turn the slow cooker to HIGH for 30 minutes. Then reduce it to LOW and continue to cook for 6 to 8 hours, or until the meat is pull-apart tender.

4. Remove the meat from the pot. Strain the juices and save them to add to chili, stew, or soup.

5. Cut and shred the meat into bite-size pieces.

FREEZING INSTRUCTIONS:

Cool the meat completely and divide into meal-size portions in freezer bags. Squeeze out the excess air and chill in the refrigerator before freezing.

TO THAW AND SERVE:

Thaw the meat in the refrigerator, then place it in a baking dish. Adjust the seasonings to taste. Preheat the oven to 350°F (180°C or gas mark 4). Reheat the meat for 15 minutes, or until heated through. Serve immediately on buns, topped with slaw and sauce.

Asian Slaw

Makes about 4 cups (454 g)

■ **PACKAGING:** Quart-size (1 L) zip-top freezer bag

½ cup (120 ml) rice vinegar
2 tablespoons (30 ml) soy sauce
1 tablespoon (15 ml) sesame oil
1 tablespoon minced fresh ginger

1 tablespoon (15 ml) olive oil
1 pound (454 g) coleslaw mix
½ cup (50 g) chopped scallions

WHEN READY TO SERVE, YOU WILL NEED:

¼ cup chopped fresh cilantro
2 tablespoons (16 g) sesame seeds, toasted

One 8-ounce (224 g) can water chestnuts, drained and chopped

1. In a large bowl, combine the rice vinegar, soy sauce, sesame oil, ginger, and olive oil. Whisk to blend.

2. Stir in the coleslaw mix and scallions. Toss to coat.

FREEZING INSTRUCTIONS:

Spoon the slaw into the freezer bag and seal. Freeze.

TO THAW AND SERVE:

Thaw the slaw in the refrigerator on a tray to catch any drips. Just before serving, stir in the chopped cilantro, sesame seeds, and water chestnuts.

Tangy Asian Barbecue Sauce

This sauce comes together quickly on the stovetop. It's a delicious accompaniment to pulled pork, grilled meats, and meatballs. // **Makes about 2½ cups (590 ml)**

■ **PACKAGING:** Plastic containers with lids

2 tablespoons (30 ml) olive oil	¼ cup (60 ml) soy sauce
½ cup (80 g) chopped onion	1 tablespoon chopped fresh ginger
One 15-ounce (420 g) can tomato sauce	1 tablespoon (15 ml) sesame oil
½ cup (120 ml) hoisin sauce	¼ teaspoon red pepper flakes

1. In a large saucepan, heat the oil over medium heat. Add the onion and cook for 8 minutes, or until the onions are tender and starting to caramelize.

2. Add the remaining ingredients and stir until well combined. Bring to a low boil, stirring constantly. Reduce the heat and simmer, covered, for 30 minutes, stirring occasionally.

FREEZING INSTRUCTIONS:

Divide the sauce into meal-size portions in plastic containers. Chill in the refrigerator before freezing.

TO THAW AND SERVE:

Thaw the sauce in the refrigerator. Reheat in a saucepan. Serve immediately.

Grilled Caribbean Pork Tenderloin

Exotic spice rubs can pack a pricey punch if you buy them premixed. But you can make your own, saving you money and time. This pork rub was a pleasant surprise to my family. They were initially skeptical of the Caribbean spices, but the proof was on the empty plate! Serve this taste of the Caribbean with a side of rice and Fresh Mango Salsa (recipe follows). // **Serves 4**

■ **PACKAGING:** Gallon-size (4 L) zip-top freezer bag, snack-size zip-top freezer bag

One 1- to 1½-pound (454 to 680 g) boneless pork tenderloin, in its original wrapper	½ teaspoon ground nutmeg
	½ teaspoon kosher salt
1 teaspoon garlic powder	¼ teaspoon cayenne pepper
1 teaspoon dried thyme	¼ teaspoon ground cinnamon
1 teaspoon grated lime zest	¼ teaspoon freshly ground black pepper
½ teaspoon ground allspice	

WHEN READY TO SERVE, YOU WILL NEED:

2 tablespoons (30 ml) olive oil

Fresh Mango Salsa (recipe follows)

1. Place the tenderloin in the large freezer bag.

2. In the snack-size bag, combine all of the remaining ingredients. Seal the bag, removing as much air as possible.

3. Place the spice rub bag into the larger bag. Seal the larger bag, squeezing out as much air as possible.

FREEZING INSTRUCTIONS:

Store the bag in the freezer.

TO THAW AND SERVE:

Thaw the bag in the refrigerator on a tray to catch any drips. Remove the tenderloin from its wrappings and brush all over with some of the olive oil. Shake the spice mix to recombine the spices. Rub the spice mixture all over the tenderloin. Allow the meat to sit for 15 minutes. Brush a grill grate with the remaining oil. Cook the tenderloin on a hot grill until it reaches an internal temperature of 145°F (63°C) for medium and 160°F (71°C) for well done, 20 to 30 minutes. Allow the meat to rest for 10 minutes before slicing. Serve with Fresh Mango Salsa.

Fresh Mango Salsa

Makes about 2 cups (470 ml)

1 mango, peeled, pitted, and chopped
¼ cup chopped fresh cilantro
Juice of 1 lime

1 jalapeño pepper, finely chopped
2 tablespoons (16 g) chopped red onion

In a small bowl, combine all of the ingredients. Stir gently. Serve immediately.

Shells Stuffed with Pork, Mushrooms, and Onions

These shells have a magical quality. Even the pickiest of eaters will devour them in seconds. I know, because I've watched it happen numerous times. The delicately seasoned pork is mild without being bland. Use a great sauce like Easy Slow Cooker Red Sauce (page 217) for an exceptional meal. And do not overcook the noodles; they will soften further during freezing and baking. For smaller portions, simply divide the shells into smaller baking dishes. // **Serves 4 to 6**

■ **PACKAGING:** 9 × 13-inch (23 × 33 cm) baking dish with lid

12 ounces (340 g) jumbo pasta shells
1¼ pounds (568 g) ground pork
½ cup (80 g) diced onion
1 cup (75 g) finely chopped fresh
    mushrooms
¼ teaspoon dried oregano
¼ teaspoon dried thyme
Salt and freshly ground black pepper

3 cups (360 g) shredded mozzarella cheese,
    divided
¼ cup (25 g) freshly grated Parmesan
    cheese
3 cups (705 ml) Easy Slow Cooker Red
    Sauce (page 217) or other favorite
    red sauce

1. In a large pot of boiling, salted water, cook the shells according to the package directions just until al dente. Drain and set aside to cool.

2. In a large skillet over medium heat, cook the pork, onion, and mushrooms for about 10 minutes or until the meat is no longer pink. Stir in the oregano and thyme. Season the mixture to taste with salt and pepper. Transfer to a large bowl to cool.

3. Add 2 cups (240 g) of the mozzarella cheese and the Parmesan cheese to the cooled pork mixture and stir to combine.

4. Grease the baking dish. Fill the cooled shells with the pork mixture and arrange them in the prepared baking dish. Top the filled shells with the pasta sauce. Sprinkle the shells with the remaining 1 cup (120 g) mozzarella cheese.

FREEZING INSTRUCTIONS:

Cover and chill the casserole in the refrigerator before freezing.

TO THAW AND SERVE:

Thaw the shells in the refrigerator. Preheat the oven to 375°F (190°C or gas mark 5). Bake for 15 to 20 minutes, until hot and bubbly. Serve immediately.

Gingery Pork and Mushroom Lettuce Wraps

You might not expect a meal involving a lettuce wrap to be freezer-friendly. But it can be if you prepare the cooked component first and store it in the freezer. Add the lettuce leaves and other fresh elements right before serving. The ginger-seasoned pork and mushrooms come together quickly and easily for a light summertime supper or elegant appetizer. // *Serves 4*

■ **PACKAGING:** Quart-size (1 L) zip-top freezer bag or plastic container with lid

1 pound (454 g) ground pork
8 ounces (224 g) fresh mushrooms,
   finely chopped
2 teaspoons minced fresh ginger
2 cloves garlic, minced

⅛ teaspoon red pepper flakes
1 tablespoon (15 ml) sherry
1 tablespoon (15 ml) soy sauce
1 tablespoon (15 ml) water
1 tablespoon cornstarch

WHEN READY TO SERVE, YOU WILL NEED:

Lettuce leaves
Chopped fresh cilantro
Chopped scallions

Shredded carrots
Asian Dipping Sauce (recipe follows),
   soy sauce, sriracha sauce, or chili sauce

1. In a large skillet, cook the pork and mushrooms over medium-high heat until the pork is cooked through and the mushrooms start to brown slightly, about 10 minutes.

2. Stir in the ginger, garlic, and red pepper.

3. In a small bowl, combine the sherry, soy sauce, water, and cornstarch. Add the sauce to the skillet and cook, stirring, until the sauce thickens.

FREEZING INSTRUCTIONS:

Cool the pork mixture to room temperature. Spoon the mixture into a freezer bag or plastic container. Chill the mixture in the refrigerator before freezing.

TO THAW AND SERVE:

Thaw the pork mixture in the refrigerator. Reheat the mixture in a large skillet or in the microwave. Spoon several spoonfuls of the pork mixture into each lettuce leaf. Top with cilantro, scallion, and carrot. Serve with the sauce of your choice.

Asian Dipping Sauce

This recipe from my friend Jessika also makes a great dipping sauce for pot stickers or spring rolls. // *Makes about 1 cup (235 ml)*

⅓ cup (80 ml) soy sauce
¼ cup (60 ml) rice vinegar
3 cloves garlic, minced
2 tablespoons (30 ml) sesame oil

2 tablespoons (25 g) sugar
1 tablespoon minced fresh ginger
¼ teaspoon freshly ground black pepper
¼ teaspoon crushed red pepper flakes

Combine all of the ingredients in a glass bowl and microwave until warmed through. Alternatively, heat the sauce over low heat in a small saucepan.

Herb-Crusted Pork Roast

Dijon mustard and apple cider vinegar flavor this hearty main dish. The roast is preseasoned and then frozen uncooked. On the morning of serving day, place the thawed roast in the slow cooker and await the enticing aromas that will fill your home. // *Serves 4*

■ **PACKAGING:** Gallon-size (4 L) zip-top freezer bag

1 tablespoon Dijon mustard
½ teaspoon dried thyme
1½ teaspoons cider vinegar
½ teaspoon rubbed sage

½ teaspoon dried rosemary
⅛ teaspoon freshly ground black pepper
One 2-pound (908 g) pork loin roast

1. In a small bowl, combine the mustard, thyme, cider vinegar, sage, rosemary, and black pepper. Stir until a smooth paste forms.

2. Rub the paste all over the pork roast. Place the roast inside the freezer bag. Seal the bag, squeezing out as much air as possible.

FREEZING INSTRUCTIONS:
Store the roast in the freezer.

Thaw the bag on a tray in the refrigerator. Place the roast in a 4-quart (4 L) slow cooker. Cook the roast on LOW for 6 to 8 hours or until cooked through. Alternatively, the pork can be roasted the oven. Preheat the oven to 375°F (190°C or gas mark 5), cover the roast with foil, and cook for 45 minutes to 1 hour. Remove the foil for the last 15 minutes to brown the roast. The pork should reach an internal temperature of 145°F (63°C) for medium and 160°F (71°C) for well done. Remove the roast from the slow cooker (or oven) and allow it to rest for 10 minutes before slicing and serving.

Make-Ahead Baked Bacon

Bacon for the freezer? Really? Yes, really. Having precooked bacon on hand enables you to make a quick BLT or breakfast sandwich. It also helps you prepare in advance for weekend brunches or a houseful of guests. And everything is better with bacon! Grab a few slices whenever you want to add a little smoky crunch to a dish.

The easiest way to cook bacon is in the oven, not in a pan on the stove. The mess and time are both greatly reduced. Just watch it carefully to prevent burning. // *Serves 4*

▪ **PACKAGING:** Gallon-size (4 L) zip-top freezer bag

1 pound (454 g) sliced bacon

1. Preheat the oven to 375°F (190°C or gas mark 5). Line a rimmed baking sheet with aluminum foil.

2. Separate the slices of bacon and lay them on the sheet. Avoid overlapping the slices if possible.

3. Bake for 15 to 20 minutes, turning the slices over about midway through the cooking time. As oven temperatures and thickness of bacon can vary, check often to prevent burning. Once the bacon is cooked to your desired doneness, remove the pan from the oven.

4. Drain the bacon on paper towels.

FREEZING INSTRUCTIONS:

Place the strips of bacon on a foil-lined tray in the freezer and freeze. Once the bacon is frozen, place the slices in the freezer bag. Seal the bag, squeezing out as much air as possible.

TO THAW AND SERVE:

Remove the desired number of bacon slices from the freezer bag and reheat in a pan on the stovetop or between paper towels in the microwave until hot. Serve immediately.

Ham and Swiss Potato Gratin

This cheesy, meaty gratin is perfect for a cold winter's night. It's filling and rich and just begging for a nice glass of wine, a crisp salad, and a roaring fire to eat it by. This casserole uses a homemade cream of celery soup that brings flavor and richness without the dubious ingredients of the canned version. // *Serves 4*

■ **PACKAGING:** 9 × 13-inch (23 × 33 cm) baking dish with lid

2 cups (470 ml) Homemade Cream of Celery
    Soup for Cooking (page 238)
1 tablespoon Dijon mustard
½ cup (120 ml) heavy cream
One 32-ounce (908 g) bag frozen shredded
    potatoes (do not thaw)

2 cups (240 g) shredded Swiss cheese
8 ounces (224 g) diced ham
1 cup (50 g) bread crumbs
2½ tablespoons (35 g) unsalted butter,
    melted

1. Grease the baking dish.

2. In a large bowl, combine the celery soup, Dijon mustard, and cream. Stir in the potatoes, cheese, and ham. Spoon the mixture into the prepared baking dish.

3. In a small bowl, combine the bread crumbs and butter. Sprinkle the buttered bread crumbs over the potato mixture.

FREEZING INSTRUCTIONS:

Cover and freeze.

TO THAW AND SERVE:

Thaw the dish in the refrigerator. Preheat the oven to 350°F (180°C or gas mark 4). Bake for about 1 hour, or until bubbly. Serve immediately.

Zesty Italian Melts

My husband's favorite sandwich features Italian meats and herbed mayonnaise on a roll, which we often eat cold and freshly made. I've transformed it here into a freezer-friendly sub that's baked or grilled before serving, resulting in hot, melty, meaty goodness. Serve this one with a salad or a cup of vegetable soup. // *Serves 8*

- **PACKAGING:** Heavy-duty aluminum foil, 3 to 4 gallon-size (3 to 4 L) zip-top freezer bags

½ cup (112 g) (1 stick) unsalted butter, softened

2 teaspoons chopped fresh basil or ½ teaspoon dried basil

1 teaspoon minced garlic

¼ teaspoon dried oregano

8 Italian rolls, sliced lengthwise, with one long edge attached

8 slices ham

24 slices salami

8 slices mozzarella cheese

1. In a small bowl, combine the softened butter, basil, garlic, and oregano. Blend well. Spread a thin layer of the garlic butter on each roll.

2. Layer one slice of ham, three slices of salami, and one slice of cheese on each roll. Close the rolls and wrap each tightly with aluminum foil.

FREEZING INSTRUCTIONS:

Place all the wrapped rolls in the freezer bags. Store the sandwiches in the freezer.

TO THAW AND SERVE:

Thaw the desired number of sandwiches in the refrigerator. Preheat the oven to 325°F (170°C or gas mark 3). Bake the wrapped sandwiches for 15 to 25 minutes, or until the bread is crusty and the cheese is melted. Alternatively, you can cook the thawed sandwiches in a panini press until hot.

Easy Sausage and Pepper Sandwiches

Freezer sandwiches are some of my favorite recipes to make ahead. Like the Chicken Bacon Subs, page 140, and the Zesty Italian Melts, above, these Easy Sausage and Pepper Sandwiches provide a hot, filling meal that really hits the spot. Depending on your schedule, you can even reheat them in the slow cooker, returning home to find dinner all ready to go. // *Serves 6*

- **PACKAGING:** Heavy-duty aluminum foil, gallon-size (4 L) zip-top bags

6 hot or mild Italian sausages	Salt and pepper
1 tablespoon (15 ml) olive oil	6 ciabatta rolls, split horizontally,
1 bell pepper, any color, sliced	with a hinge
1 onion, sliced	6 slices pepper Jack cheese
1 teaspoon Italian herb blend	

1. Place the sausages in a large, nonstick skillet and cook until done, about 10 minutes. Add water to the pan occasionally to prevent burning. Remove the cooked sausages from the pan and allow to cool. Slice the sausages thinly across.

2. Heat the oil in the pan and add the bell pepper and onion slices. Season with the Italian herbs and salt and pepper to taste. Cook until crisp tender. Allow the vegetables to cool.

3. Lay out the rolls and place one slice of cheese on each bottom half. Divide the cooled sausage and vegetables among the rolls.

4. Place the tops on the rolls and wrap each sandwich tightly with aluminum foil.

FREEZING INSTRUCTIONS:

Place all the wrapped rolls in the freezer bags. Store the sandwiches in the freezer.

TO THAW AND SERVE:

Thaw the desired number of sandwiches in the refrigerator. Preheat the oven to 350°F (180°C or gas mark 4). Bake the wrapped sandwiches for 30 minutes, or until the bread is crusty and the cheese is melted. Alternatively, you can cook the thawed sandwiches in a panini press until hot or cook them on LOW in a slow cooker for 2 to 3 hours.

Queso Fundido

This meal has been a mainstay in our family for almost 20 years. Delicious and easy to prepare, it's got a little kick, thanks to the spicy cheese and the hot sausage. It's ideal for taking to a potluck or to share with a friend. Serve a green salad, beans, and rice as side dishes. For milder flavor, use mild Italian sausage and Monterey Jack cheese. // *Serves 4*

■ **PACKAGING:** 8-inch (20.3 cm) pie plate or other 1-quart (1 L) baking dish with lid or foil, gallon-size (4 L) zip-top freezer bag

1 pound (454 g) hot Italian sausage,	2 cups (240 g) shredded pepper Jack
casings removed	cheese
1 cup (160 g) chopped onion	

WHEN READY TO SERVE, YOU WILL NEED:

12 corn tortillas or soft taco-size flour
    tortillas

Sour cream
Easy Homemade Salsa (page 77)

1. In a large skillet, brown the sausage and onion over medium-high heat, breaking up any big chunks of meat with the back of a spoon, for about 10 minutes, or until the meat is just cooked and no longer pink. Drain off any grease.

2. Grease the pie plate. Spoon the mixture into the pie plate and set aside to cool.

3. Cover the cooled sausage with the shredded cheese.

FREEZING INSTRUCTIONS:

Wrap the pie plate in foil and place it inside a zip-top freezer bag. Chill the dish in the refrigerator before freezing.

TO THAW AND SERVE:

Thaw the pie plate in the refrigerator. Preheat the oven to 350°F (180°C or gas mark 4). Bake, uncovered, for 15 to 20 minutes, or until the cheese is melted and bubbling. Serve with the tortillas, sour cream, and salsa.

Herbed Pork Sausage Patties

Want a change of pace from your regular burger? Looking for a spicy accompaniment to your eggs in the morning? How about a simple homemade sausage? You can't go wrong with this version, which mixes up quickly and freezes beautifully. Store the patties, cooked or uncooked, in the freezer for quick breakfast or lunch fare. // *Serves 6*

■ **PACKAGING:** Waxed paper, plastic wrap, gallon-size (4 L) zip-top freezer bag

1 pound (454 g) lean ground pork
2 tablespoons (28 g) salted butter, softened
2 cloves garlic, chopped
1 teaspoon salt
½ teaspoon onion powder
¼ teaspoon freshly ground black pepper

¼ teaspoon rubbed sage
⅛ teaspoon dried thyme
⅛ teaspoon paprika
⅛ teaspoon cayenne pepper
⅛ teaspoon dry mustard

1. In the bowl of a stand mixer, mix all of the ingredients until the mixture is well blended and starts to bind together.

2. With wet hands, divide the pork mixture into six equal portions. Pat each portion into a flat patty.

FREEZING INSTRUCTIONS:

If freezing uncooked, stack the patties with a square of waxed paper between each one. Wrap the stack in plastic wrap and place in a freezer bag.

If freezing precooked, preheat the oven to 400°F (200°C or gas mark 6) and cook the patties on a foil-lined rimmed baking sheet, flipping once, for 10 to 15 minutes, or until cooked through. Drain the cooked patties on paper towels. Cool completely. Freeze the patties on a tray, and then transfer to a freezer bag. Seal the bag, squeezing out as much air as possible. Return the patties to the freezer.

TO THAW AND SERVE:

For uncooked patties, thaw in the refrigerator. Preheat the oven to 400°F (200°C or gas mark 6). Bake the unwrapped patties on a foil-lined rimmed baking sheet, flipping once, for 10 to 15 minutes, or until cooked through.

For cooked patties, thaw in the refrigerator. Preheat the oven to 400°F (200°C or gas mark 6). Reheat the patties 5 to 10 minutes, or until heated through. You can also reheat them without thawing; add about 5 minutes to the oven time.

Red Sauce with Sausage

This meaty red sauce is simple and delicious. It freezes well and complements pasta dishes beautifully. One of the secrets to its rich flavor is cooking the sausages *in* the sauce, a trick I owe to a fellow homeschool mom, Carla Luffman. This recipe is an adaptation of one her family has long enjoyed. Feel free to use sweet sausage, spicy sausage, or a mixture. If you are pressed for time, omit the sausages, stir in some beef broth, and reduce the cooking time to 2 hours total. // *Serves 10 to 12*

■ **PACKAGING:** Glass jars or plastic containers with lids, quart-size (1 L) zip-top freezer bags for the sausages

2 tablespoons (30 ml) olive oil
1 cup (160 g) chopped onion
2 cloves garlic, chopped
Four 28-ounce (784 g) cans tomato puree
3 cups (705 ml) water
1 tablespoon (18 g) salt
3 tablespoons chopped fresh Italian parsley
   or 1 tablespoon dried parsley flakes

3 tablespoons chopped fresh basil
   or 1 tablespoon dried basil
1½ teaspoons dried oregano
¼ teaspoon red pepper flakes
2 pounds (908 g) Italian sausage links

WHEN READY TO SERVE, YOU WILL NEED:
Cooked pasta

1. In a large pot, heat the olive oil over medium heat and cook the onion and garlic until softened. Add the tomato puree and water. Stir to mix thoroughly, then add the salt, parsley, basil, oregano, and red pepper flakes.

2. Cover and simmer for 2 hours, stirring occasionally. Add the sausages and cook, covered, for another 2 hours.

FREEZING INSTRUCTIONS:
Divide the sausages into meal-size portions in freezer bags. Squeeze out as much air as possible and seal the bags. Pour the sauce into containers. Chill the sausages and the sauce in the refrigerator before storing in the freezer.

TO THAW AND SERVE:
Thaw a container of sauce and a bag of sausages in the refrigerator. Reheat them together in a saucepan and serve over pasta.

Penne with Italian Sausage and Tricolor Peppers

When we were broke college students living in France, my friend Sarah and I often prepared a simple pasta dish with tomatoes and vegetables. We didn't have the extra coin to add meat. This dish is reminiscent of what we ate in those days, only with mild Italian sausage added to give it a little more oomph. This sauce freezes beautifully. It's delicious over pasta, served with sliced baguette for soaking up the juices. // *Serves 6 to 8*

   ■ **PACKAGING:** Plastic containers with lids

1 tablespoon (15 ml) olive oil
12 ounces (340 g) bulk mild Italian sausage
2 cloves garlic, minced
½ cup (75 g) each diced green, red,
   and yellow bell pepper
½ cup (30 g) julienned sun-dried tomatoes
One 15-ounce (420 g) can tomato sauce
One 6-ounce (168 g) can tomato paste

1 tablespoon chopped fresh basil
   or 1 teaspoon dried basil
1 tablespoon chopped fresh parsley
   or 1 teaspoon dried parsley flakes
¼ teaspoon freshly ground black pepper
¼ teaspoon red pepper flakes
2 cups (470 ml) water

WHEN READY TO SERVE, YOU WILL NEED:
Cooked penne

1. In a large saucepan, heat the oil over medium heat. Add the sausage and garlic. Cook, stirring, until the sausage just starts to brown, about 10 minutes.

2. Add the bell peppers. Cook, stirring, until the peppers have softened, about 5 minutes more.

3. Stir in the sun-dried tomatoes, tomato sauce, tomato paste, basil, parsley, black pepper, red pepper flakes, and water.

4. Bring the sauce to a low boil. Reduce the heat and simmer for 20 minutes.

FREEZING INSTRUCTIONS:
Divide the sauce into meal-size portions in plastic containers. Chill in the refrigerator before freezing.

TO THAW AND SERVE:
Thaw the sauce in the refrigerator. Reheat in a saucepan and serve over pasta.

Wild Boar Italian Sausage with Spicy Tomato Sauce

Freezer meals don't need to be boring. In this case, reheating the sausage on the grill gives it a smoky flavor you wouldn't get from the stovetop. If you can't find wild boar sausage, Italian pork sausages will work just as well. The red pepper gives the sauce a nice kick, but you can reduce it to tone down the spiciness, if you prefer. Serve the sausages and sauce with pasta or polenta and lots of grated Parmesan for sprinkling. // *Serves 4 to 6*

■ **PACKAGING:** Plastic containers with lids, quart-size (1 L) zip-top freezer bags

1 tablespoon (15 ml) olive oil	2 tablespoons chopped fresh basil
½ cup (60 g) finely chopped carrot	or 2 teaspoons dried basil
½ cup (80 g) chopped onion	¼ teaspoon red pepper flakes
One 15-ounce (420 g) can tomato sauce	1 teaspoon kosher salt
One 14.5-ounce (406 g) can diced tomatoes	⅛ teaspoon freshly ground black pepper
with juices	4 wild boar Italian sausage links

WHEN READY TO SERVE, YOU WILL NEED:

Cooked pasta or polenta   Freshly grated Parmesan cheese

1. In a large pot, heat the olive oil over medium heat until shimmering. Add the carrot and onion. Sauté the vegetables until very tender, about 10 minutes.

2. Add the tomato sauce, diced tomatoes, basil, red pepper flakes, salt, and black pepper. Stir to combine. Bring to a low boil.

3. Submerge the sausage links in the sauce. Cover the pot slightly. Simmer for 1 hour.

FREEZING INSTRUCTIONS:

Divide the sausages into meal-size portions in freezer bags. Squeeze out as much air as possible and seal the bags. Pour the sauce into containers. Chill the sauce and the sausages in the refrigerator before storing in the freezer.

TO THAW AND SERVE:

Thaw a container of sauce and a bag of sausages in the refrigerator. Reheat the sauce in a saucepan. Brown the sausages on a hot grill. Slice the sausages on the diagonal. Serve the hot sausages and sauce over cooked pasta or polenta. Top with Parmesan.

► How Freezer Cooking Helps Me

Here's how readers of my blog Life as Mom answered these questions: How does freezer cooking help you? How does it help your family eat better? How do you make it work for your life?

"Freezer cooking has benefited our family greatly. With four kids, three of whom are very active in sports, and tending to a sick mother, freezer cooking has saved our budget countless times. When I have a day that isn't quite as full as others, I sneak some extra time in the kitchen and prepare the main parts of a meal, or an extra meal at dinnertime, and pop it in the freezer. Considering we are still on a mission to pay down our debt, I've been able to consistently keep my eat-out budget close to nothing! Knowing a meal is waiting in the freezer is enough to curb the 'I wanna eat outs,' and it means fewer dishes on an already busy night."

—Phoebe H., mom of 4

"Freezer cooking has been a big part of my life for over ten years and has helped me serve my family healthy home-cooked meals when I did not have the time or energy to cook. I have relied on freezer cooking during times of sickness, through the years of having three kids under five, and now through the struggles of gluten-free eating and other food allergies. My style of freezer cooking may have changed over the years, but the overall concept of having meals ready and waiting in the freezer is the same."

—Lynn W., mom of 3

5

MEATLESS MARVELS

- Seasoned Versatile Pinto Beans ▪ 189
- Quick and Easy Cheese Enchiladas ▪ 190
- Bean and Cheese Nacho Bake ▪ 192
- Whole Wheat Black Bean and Pepper Wraps ▪ 192
- Cozy Cheese and Potato Casserole ▪ 194
- Six-Layer Nachos ▪ 195
- Chile Cheese Bake ▪ 196
- Green Chile Rice Casserole ▪ 197
- Pepper Jack and Chile Burritos ▪ 197
- Corn and Chile Tamales ▪ 198
- Easy Stovetop Ratatouille ▪ 200
- Italian-Spiced Cheesewiches ▪ 201
- Gingery Vegetable Stir-Fry Kit ▪ 202
- Red Lentil Dal ▪ 203
- Tahini Vegetable Patties ▪ 204

- Potatoes Stuffed with Caramelized Onions and Dubliner Cheese ▪ 206
- Broccoli Gratin with Tarragon and Buttered Bread Crumbs ▪ 207
- Roasted Vegetable Quiche ▪ 208
- Individual Greek Egg Casseroles ▪ 209
- Alfredo Mac and Cheese ▪ 210
- Pesto Penne and Cheese ▪ 211
- Baked Manicotti with Sun-Dried Tomatoes and Thyme ▪ 212
- Spinach and Feta Manicotti with Lemon and Oregano ▪ 214
- Tomato Sauce with Oregano and Kalamata Olives ▪ 215
- Quick and Spicy Marinara Sauce ▪ 216
- Easy Slow Cooker Red Sauce ▪ 217
- Sun-Dried Tomato Pesto ▪ 218

Seasoned Versatile Pinto Beans

Our family battled its way out of debt years ago. Today we live debt-free, in part because we enjoyed a "rice and beans" diet for a time. This recipe, so easy and satisfying, is still a mainstay in our menu rotation. It's an ideal freezer staple to have on hand. Although canned beans are certainly convenient, they can be high in sodium, and more expensive than cooking your own. It is quite simple to cook dried beans and freeze them in 2-cup (520 g) portions. Reheating them is just as easy as opening a can.

// *Makes 6 cups (1550 g) cooked beans*

■ **PACKAGING:** Pint-size (470 ml) containers with lids or pint-size (470 ml) zip-top freezer bags

1 pound (454 g) dried pinto beans, rinsed and picked over	**2 teaspoons chopped garlic**
1 cup (160 g) chopped onion	**1 tablespoon (18 g) salt**
	¼ teaspoon freshly ground black pepper

Place the beans in a pot and add enough water to cover by at least 2 inches (5 cm). Allow the beans to soak for at least 6 hours, or as long as overnight. Drain and rinse the beans.

TO COOK IN A SLOW COOKER:

Place the beans in a 5-quart (5 L) slow cooker. Add the chopped onion, garlic, and enough water to cover the beans by about 1 inch (2.5 cm). Cook on LOW for 6 to 8 hours. Drain the beans partially, leaving a small amount of water in the pot. Season with salt and pepper. Mash the beans slightly.

TO COOK ON THE STOVETOP:

Place the soaked and rinsed beans, the chopped onion, garlic, and water to cover in a large stockpot. Bring to a boil. Reduce the heat to a simmer and partially cover. Cook for about 2 hours, stirring frequently, adding more water if necessary. Once the beans are tender, drain them, mash them slightly, and season with salt and pepper.

FREEZING INSTRUCTIONS:

If using in a recipe, proceed with the recipe. Otherwise, divide the beans into 2-cup (520 g) portions (about the amount of beans in a typical can) in containers or freezer bags. Chill in the refrigerator before freezing.

TO THAW AND SERVE:

Thaw the beans in the refrigerator or reheat them directly from the freezer. Reheat them in a pan on the stovetop or in a microwave-safe dish in the microwave.

Quick and Easy Cheese Enchiladas

Imagine delicious Mexican fare for supper—without having to wait hours for a table. This meal is it! Partnered with rice and beans and a green salad, cheese enchiladas make an ideal meatless meal. This recipe yields two large pans of a dozen enchiladas each. But you can package them in whatever size baking dishes best suit the number of people you're serving. // *Serves 8 to 12*

■ **PACKAGING:** Two 9 × 13-inch (23 × 33 cm) baking dishes with lids

Vegetable oil, for frying
24 corn tortillas
4 cups (480 g) shredded cheddar and/or
    Monterey Jack cheese, divided

One 28-ounce (784 g) can red enchilada
    sauce
One 2.25-ounce (63 g) can sliced
    black olives
¼ cup (25 g) sliced scallions

1. Fill a skillet with vegetable oil to a depth of 1 inch (2.5 cm). Heat over medium heat until the oil shimmers. Fry the tortillas in the hot oil until the texture is a bit leathery but not crisp, 20 to 30 seconds, turning once. Drain the tortillas on paper towels and set aside until cool enough to handle.

2. Grease the baking dishes.

3. Set aside 1 cup (120 g) of cheese. For each enchilada, place a small handful of cheese down the center of each tortilla, roll up, and place, seam side down, in a greased baking dish. Continue until all the tortillas are rolled and the baking dishes are filled. You should be able to fit 12 enchiladas in each dish.

4. Pour the enchilada sauce over the tops of the rolled tortillas. Sprinkle the reserved 1 cup (120 g) cheese as well as the olives and scallions over the top.

FREEZING INSTRUCTIONS:

Cover the enchiladas and chill in the refrigerator before freezing.

TO THAW AND SERVE:

Thaw the enchiladas in the refrigerator. Preheat the oven to 350°F (180°C or gas mark 4). Bake the enchiladas until they are heated through and the cheese is melted, about 15 minutes. You can also bake this directly from the freezer; allow an extra 15 to 30 minutes of baking time.

Bean and Cheese Nacho Bake

This versatile bean and cheese casserole can be served as a main dish, accompanied by salad and rice, or as an appetizer with chips. Using homemade salsa will give it a fresher taste. // *Serves 6 to 8*

■ **PACKAGING:** 9 × 13-inch (23 × 33 cm) baking dish with lid

3 cups (750 g) canned refried beans
⅓ cup (53 g) finely chopped onion
1 teaspoon chopped garlic
1 cup (235 ml) Easy Homemade Salsa
    (page 77) or other favorite salsa
⅔ cup (65 g) canned sliced black olives,
    drained
1 cup (235 ml) tomato sauce

2 cups (240 g) shredded pepper Jack
    cheese, divided
1 cup (225 g) ricotta cheese
⅔ cup (155 g) sour cream
½ teaspoon ground cumin
6½ ounces (182 g) crushed tortilla chips
    (about 3 cups)

1. Grease the baking dish.

2. In a large bowl, combine the beans, onion, garlic, salsa, black olives, and tomato sauce.

3. In another bowl, combine 1 cup (120 g) of the Jack cheese, the ricotta, sour cream, and cumin.

4. Place half of the chips in the bottom of the baking dish, spreading to cover. Spread half of the bean mixture over the chips. Spread all of the cheese mixture over the bean layer. Repeat the layers, using the remaining chips, bean mixture, and remaining 1 cup (120 g) Jack cheese.

FREEZING INSTRUCTIONS:

Cover and chill in the refrigerator before freezing.

TO THAW AND SERVE:

Thaw the casserole in the refrigerator. Preheat the oven to 350°F (180°C or gas mark 4). Bake for 40 minutes, or until the casserole is hot and the cheese is bubbly.

Whole Wheat Black Bean and Pepper Wraps

Munching on these wraps while I type, I encourage you to make a batch of these right now! The peppers, black beans, cumin, and cheese just play so well together in a whole wheat tortilla. Mmmm. Good! // *Serves 8*

■ **PACKAGING:** Gallon-size (4 L) zip-top freezer bags, aluminum foil or plastic wrap (optional)

1 tablespoon (15 ml) oil	**½ teaspoon ground cumin**
1 large onion, chopped	**Fine sea salt and freshly ground**
1 green bell pepper, chopped	**black pepper**
1 red bell pepper, chopped	**Dash red pepper flakes**
2 cloves garlic, chopped	**8 burrito size whole wheat tortillas**
Two 15-ounce (420 g) cans black beans,	**2 cups (240 g) shredded pepper Jack**
rinsed and drained	**cheese**
½ cup (16 g) chopped cilantro	

1. In a large skillet over medium-high heat, heat the oil until shimmering. Cook the onion until translucent, about 5 minutes. Add the peppers and garlic and cook, stirring, for another 5 minutes. Add the black beans, cilantro, and seasonings to taste. Remove from the heat and cool.

2. Fill the wraps by spooning ½ cup (125 g) of the bean filling down the center of each tortilla and top with ¼ cup (30 g) of the cheese. Roll it up, tucking in the sides as you go. As each wrap is rolled, place it in a freezer bag. If you like, you can wrap each wrap in aluminum foil or plastic wrap before placing it in the freezer bag.

FREEZING INSTRUCTIONS:

Seal the wraps in the bags, squeezing out as much air as possible. Store the bags of wraps in the freezer.

TO THAW AND SERVE:

Thaw as many wraps as desired in the refrigerator.

To reheat in the microwave: Cook thawed wraps, flipping once, for 1 to 2 minutes per wrap, or until hot. You can also reheat them directly from the freezer, without thawing; just add an additional minute or two of cooking time.

To reheat on the griddle: Cook thawed wraps on a hot griddle until the filling is hot and the tortilla is crisp.

To reheat in the oven: Preheat the oven to 350°F (180°C or gas mark 4). For crispy wraps, bake thawed wraps for 15 to 20 minutes. For softer wraps, wrap each in foil prior to baking. If the wraps are frozen, increase the cooking time by 5 to 10 minutes.

▶ If Your Freezer Has Experienced a Power Failure

Once you pack your freezer with the fruits of your labor, the last thing you want is to lose it all to a power failure. It happened to me once when the ground fault interrupter, or GFI, in the garage tripped the breaker and broke power to the freezer. I called my husband, crying. All he could get out of my mumbling was the word "died." Needless to say, he had a minor panic attack until I was able to clarify that it was an appliance that was the victim and not a child or parent.

Since then, we've installed a small, inexpensive freezer alarm. It lets out a loud wail any time the freezer gets too warm. It's fairly sensitive, able to detect the slightest changes in temperature when I load it with food, so I rest easy, trusting that it will let me know—loud and clear—when it starts to get hot under the collar.

To help provide a buffer in case of a power failure, fill any empty spots in the freezer with water bottles or milk jugs filled with water. They will act as insulation, helping the freezer run more efficiently. (A full freezer runs better than an empty one.) In case of a power failure, the frozen water bottles should keep the contents of the freezer cold until the power comes back on. Add water bottles to your freezer gradually, as the appliance has to work harder if a lot of unfrozen items are added at one time.

If the power does go out or the door is left open, all is not lost. The food may be safe to use if there are still ice crystals present. If the power is out, keep the freezer closed and do not open it. According to the USDA, a full freezer that is kept shut can keep food safe for up to two days. You can refreeze food that is partly frozen, still has ice crystals, and/or is no warmer than 40°F (4.4°C). Discard any food that has been warmer than 40°F (4.4°C) for longer than 2 hours, as well as anything that has been touched by raw meat juices.

Cozy Cheese and Potato Casserole

At first glance, you might confuse this delectable concoction of potatoes and cheese with the "church potatoes" or hash brown casseroles of yore. However, unlike its predecessors, this potato bake features a homemade cream of celery soup that puts the canned version to shame. It's important to use frozen potatoes in this dish; uncooked fresh potatoes will blacken in the freezer. Commercially frozen hash brown potatoes work exceptionally well here. Don't let them thaw as you mix up this casserole. Stir it up quickly, spoon it into the pan, and pop it into the freezer. // *Serves 6 to 8*

■ **PACKAGING:** 9 × 13-inch (23 × 33 cm) baking dish with lid

2 cups (470 ml) Homemade Cream of Celery
    Soup for Cooking (page 238), chilled
1½ cups (180 g) shredded cheddar cheese
1 cup (225 g) sour cream
1 teaspoon kosher salt

¼ teaspoon freshly ground black pepper
One 32-ounce (908 g) bag frozen shredded
    potatoes
1 teaspoon paprika

1. Grease the baking dish.

2. In a large bowl, combine the celery soup, cheese, sour cream, salt, and pepper. Stir in the frozen shredded potatoes, combining well.

3. Spoon the potato mixture into the prepared dish. Sprinkle the paprika over the top.

FREEZING INSTRUCTIONS:

Cover and freeze.

TO THAW AND SERVE:

Thaw the casserole in the refrigerator. Preheat the oven to 375°F (190°C or gas mark 5). Bake the casserole for about 1 hour, or until it is heated through and the cheese is melted.

Six-Layer Nachos

This nacho plate is always a hit. Whether served as an appetizer or a "snacky" dinner, it's a crowd-pleaser. For the meat-eaters, you can add a layer of seasoned taco meat (sidebar, page 97), but it's not necessary; it's packed full of flavor as it is. Make several pans at once so that you always have a quick appetizer, snack, or dinner on hand. // *Serves 4 as a main dish, 6 to 8 as an appetizer*

■ **PACKAGING:** 8-inch (20.3 cm) pie plate, foil, gallon-size (4 L) zip-top freezer bag

1 cup (250 g) canned refried beans
½ cup (120 ml) enchilada sauce
1 cup (120 g) shredded cheddar cheese

2 tablespoons (18 g) chopped green chiles
2 tablespoons sliced black olives
2 tablespoons (20 g) chopped onion

WHEN READY TO SERVE, YOU WILL NEED:

Tortilla chips
Sour cream
Easy Homemade Salsa (page 77)
Sliced avocado or Super-Simple Guacamole
    (page 77)

Other toppings as desired, such as chopped
    tomatoes or shredded lettuce

1. Grease the pie plate.

2. Spread the refried beans across the bottom of the plate. Drizzle the enchilada sauce over the beans. Sprinkle the cheese over the sauce. Sprinkle the green chiles, black olives, and chopped onion over the cheese layer.

FREEZING INSTRUCTIONS:

Cover the pan with foil and slip the pan inside the freezer bag, taking care not to tip the pan. Freeze.

TO THAW AND SERVE:

Thaw the nachos in the refrigerator. Preheat the oven to 350°F (180°C or gas mark 4). Bake the nachos for 15 to 20 minutes, until hot and bubbly. Serve with the tortilla chips and toppings.

Chile Cheese Bake

I never turn my nose up at a casserole; they are hearty comfort food that freezes and bakes up beautifully. This Chile Cheese Bake is a particular favorite; it gets its kicky flavor from home-roasted poblano chiles. Yum!

■ **PACKAGING:** One 9 × 13-inch (23 × 33 cm) baking dish with lid

1½ cups (338 g) sour cream
12 ounces (340 g) bottled salsa verde
12 corn tortillas, cut into bite-size pieces
8 ounces (224 g) shredded cheddar cheese
    (about 2 cups)

3 roasted poblano chiles, peeled, seeded,
    and diced
½ teaspoon dried parsley
⅛ teaspoon paprika

1. Grease a large baking dish.

2. In a large mixing bowl, combine the sour cream and salsa verde. Add the tortillas, cheese, and chiles.

3. Spoon the mixture into the prepared dish. Sprinkle the parsley and paprika over the top.

FREEZING INSTRUCTIONS:

Cover and freeze.

TO THAW AND SERVE:

Thaw the casserole in the refrigerator. Preheat the oven to 350°F (180°C or gas mark 4). Bake the casserole for 30 to 45 minutes, or until it is hot and bubbly.

Green Chile Rice Casserole

Rice, cheese, and chiles combine in a comfort-food dish that will disappear quickly. Brown rice boasts a denser texture and a nuttier flavor than white rice. It also holds up better in the freezer, making it the perfect base for this rich and creamy casserole. You will want to cook the rice ahead of time so that it can cool before you assemble the casserole. Sour cream adds great flavor, but Greek yogurt has it beat with less fat and extra protein. // *Serves 4 to 6*

■ **PACKAGING:** 8-inch (20.3 cm) square baking dish or 3-quart (3 L) baking dish with lid

3 cups (510 g) cooked brown rice, at room temperature
16 ounces (454 g) plain Greek-style yogurt or sour cream
2 cups (240 g) shredded cheddar cheese
One 4-ounce (112 g) can chopped green chiles

1 tablespoon finely chopped jalapeño peppers
¼ teaspoon ground cumin
⅛ teaspoon freshly ground black pepper

Grease the baking dish. Combine all of the ingredients in a large bowl. Spoon the mixture into the prepared pan.

FREEZING INSTRUCTIONS:

Cover and chill in the refrigerator before freezing.

TO THAW AND SERVE:

Thaw the dish in the refrigerator. Preheat the oven to 350°F (180°C or gas mark 4). Bake the casserole for 25 to 40 minutes, or until heated through.

Pepper Jack and Chile Burritos

Frozen burritos make quick snacks or main dishes. After an overnight thaw in the refrigerator, these will crisp perfectly on a hot griddle, for a healthier alternative to chimichangas. Top with enchilada sauce, shredded lettuce, tomatoes, and sour cream. For even quicker eats, simply microwave the frozen burritos for a minute or two. To prevent the burritos from cracking when you roll them, use fresh tortillas that are at room temperature. // *Serves 6 to 12*

■ **PACKAGING:** Gallon-size (4 L) zip-top freezer bags, aluminum foil or plastic wrap (optional)

4 cups (1000 g) canned refried beans
    or Seasoned Versatile Pinto Beans
    (page 189)
2 cups (240 g) shredded pepper Jack
    cheese

One 4-ounce (112 g) can chopped
    green chiles
12 burrito-size flour tortillas

1. In a large bowl, combine the beans, cheese, and green chiles.

2. Fill the burritos by spooning a scant ½ cup (125 g) of the filling down the center of each tortilla. Roll it up, tucking in the sides as you go. As each burrito is rolled, place it in a freezer bag. If you like, you can wrap each burrito in aluminum foil or plastic wrap before placing it in the freezer bag.

FREEZING INSTRUCTIONS:
Seal the burritos in the bags, squeezing out as much air as possible. Store the bags of burritos in the freezer.

TO THAW AND SERVE:
Thaw as many burritos as desired in the refrigerator.

To reheat in the microwave: Cook thawed burritos, flipping once, 1 to 2 minutes per burrito, or until hot. You can also reheat them directly from the freezer, without thawing; just add an additional minute or two of cooking time.

To reheat on the griddle: Cook thawed burritos on a hot griddle until the filling is hot and the tortilla is crisp.

To reheat in the oven: Preheat the oven to 350°F (180°C or gas mark 4). For crispy burritos, bake thawed burritos for 15 to 20 minutes. For softer burritos, wrap each in foil prior to baking. If the burritos are frozen, increase the cooking time 5 to 10 minutes.

Corn and Chile Tamales

The Pork and Chile Tamales featured on page 166 are delicious, but, truth be told, sometimes it feels like "work" to make them. That's when this "cheater" tamale recipe comes in handy. Instead of filling the corn husk with a layer of masa and a layer of filling, the filling is incorporated into the masa, making for a quick and easy preparation—a marvelous meatless one, too, I might add. // **Makes about 20 tamales**

■ **PACKAGING:** Quart- (1 L) or gallon-size (4 L) zip-top freezer bags

Dried corn husks
3½ cups (420 g) masa harina (I use Maseca)
1 cup (225 g) butter, softened
1½ teaspoons salt
3 cups (705 ml) vegetable broth

2 cups (240 g) shredded pepper Jack
   cheese
7-ounce (196 g) can chopped green chiles
1 cup (150 g) corn kernels

WHEN READY TO SERVE, YOU WILL NEED:

Additional red chile sauce or enchilada
   sauce

Sour cream
Easy Homemade Salsa (page 77)

1. Soak the corn husks in hot water for a couple of hours to soften. They float, so you may need to weight them down with a frying pan to keep them submerged. Rinse the corn husks, removing any silt or other debris. Keep wet until ready to use.

2. Prepare a large stockpot by placing a steamer in the bottom. Add enough hot water to reach the bottom of the steamer. In a large mixing bowl, combine the masa harina, butter, and salt. With a mixer (a stand mixer is okay), blend the ingredients together until coarse crumbs are formed.

3. Add enough broth (I used all 3 cups [705 ml] last time) to make a light and fluffy batter, similar to cookie dough.

4. Mix in the cheese, chiles, and corn.

5. On a work surface, lay out several corn husks. Place several scoops of the masa mixture in the center of the husk. Wrap the sides of the husk around the mixture, and fold the ends over. Place the tamales seam-side down in the steamer basket.

6. Continue wrapping the tamales and placing them in the basket. Leave some space between tamales in the basket so the hot air can circulate.

7. Cover the pot and turn the heat to medium-high. You want the pot hot enough to steam continually without burning off all the liquid. Add more water if necessary.

8. Steam the tamales for 45 minutes to 1 hour. They are done when the husk doesn't stick to the dough or vice versa and it doesn't taste "doughy."

FREEZING INSTRUCTIONS:

Cool the tamales completely and package them in freezer bags. If you like, you can wrap each tamale in aluminum foil or plastic wrap before placing in the freezer bag. Chill in the refrigerator before freezing.

TO SERVE:

Steam the frozen tamales for 20 to 30 minutes, or until heated through. Or microwave frozen tamales on a plate, covered with a damp paper towel, for 1 to 2 minutes per tamale. Serve the tamales with red chile sauce, sour cream, and salsa.

Easy Stovetop Ratatouille

A traditional french vegetable stew, ratatouille is summer captured in a bowl. There is great debate over the proper preparation of ratatouille—vegetables cooked together or separately? This simple version is mixed in one pot and simmered on the stovetop. A vegan dish that is good served hot or even at room temperature, it's a delicious way to preserve the bounty of the summer garden. Provide lots of sliced baguette for soaking up the juices. Avoid overcooking the vegetables, so that they are not soggy when reheated. // *Serves 6 to 8*

■ **PACKAGING:** Plastic containers with lids

¼ cup (60 ml) olive oil
1 cup (160 g) chopped onion
1 tablespoon chopped garlic
1 red bell pepper, chopped
1 green bell pepper, chopped
1 medium zucchini, sliced into ¼-inch
   (6 mm)-thick half-moons

1 small yellow squash, sliced
1 eggplant, peeled and cubed
4 ounces (112 g) fresh mushrooms, sliced
Two 14.5-ounce (406 g) cans petite diced
   tomatoes with juices
1½ teaspoons *herbes de Provence*
1 teaspoon kosher salt

1. In a large heavy pot, heat the oil over medium heat until shimmering. Add the onion and garlic, and cook until the onions are translucent.

2. Add the peppers, zucchini, yellow squash, eggplant, and mushrooms, and sauté for about 5 minutes, stirring occasionally.

3. Add the tomatoes, *herbes de Provence*, and salt. Stir to combine. Cook for about 30 minutes, or until the vegetables are just tender.

FREEZING INSTRUCTIONS:

Divide the ratatouille into meal-size portions in plastic containers and chill in the refrigerator before freezing.

TO THAW AND SERVE:

Thaw the ratatouille in the refrigerator. Reheat in a saucepan. Serve hot, warm, or at room temperature.

Italian-Spiced Cheesewiches

My mom made something similar to these cheesewiches when I was a kid. We loved them; they were like cheese pizza undercover. The updated version is even better! I've freshened up the seasonings and replaced canned soup with tomato sauce and fresh garlic. These toasty, flavorful cheese sandwiches are the perfect complement to a cup of soup or a bowl of salad for a hearty lunch or supper. // *Serves 6 to 12*

■ **PACKAGING:** Heavy-duty aluminum foil, gallon-size (4 L) zip-top freezer bags

4 cups (480 g) shredded sharp cheddar cheese
2 cups (470 ml) tomato sauce
½ cup (50 g) canned chopped black olives, drained
¼ cup (60 ml) olive oil
2 teaspoons chopped garlic

1½ teaspoons chopped fresh basil or ½ teaspoon dried basil
½ teaspoon dried oregano
½ teaspoon dried thyme
¼ teaspoon freshly ground black pepper
12 kaiser rolls

1. In a large bowl, combine the cheese, tomato sauce, olives, olive oil, garlic, basil, oregano, thyme, and black pepper.

2. Slice each roll in half, leaving the top and bottom attached on one side. Scoop out the insides of the rolls, leaving a 1-inch (2.5 cm) shell. Crumble the inner bread portions and add to the cheese mixture. Stir the mixture to combine all the ingredients well.

3. Fill the rolls with the cheese mixture. Close each roll and wrap in foil.

FREEZING INSTRUCTIONS:

Place all the foil-wrapped rolls in one or two freezer bags and freeze.

TO THAW AND SERVE:

Thaw the desired number of rolls in the refrigerator. Preheat the oven to 350°F (180°C or gas mark 4). Bake thawed, foil-wrapped rolls for 15 to 25 minutes, until the bread is crusty and the cheese is melted.

Gingery Vegetable Stir-Fry Kit

Asian takeout is one of my kids' favorite treats. However, one child's nut allergy can put a damper on its frequent enjoyment. Making my own stir-fries at home not only saves us money, but also allows me to make an allergen-friendly meal that's safe for everyone at our table. How handy to have a few stir-fry kits at the ready! Using commercially frozen vegetables allows for quick assembly of these stir-fry kits without the blanching involved in preparing fresh vegetables for freezing. // *Serves 4*

■ **PACKAGING:** Gallon-size (4 L) zip-top freezer bag, pint-size (470 ml) zip-top freezer bag

3 cups (460 g) frozen broccoli florets
2 cups (250 g) frozen green beans
1 cup (150 g) frozen bell pepper strips
½ cup (120 ml) vegetable or chicken broth
2 tablespoons (30 ml) soy sauce
2 tablespoons (30 ml) cooking sherry

1 teaspoon sesame oil
1 teaspoon minced ginger
1 teaspoon minced garlic
1 teaspoon honey
1 tablespoon cornstarch

WHEN READY TO SERVE, YOU WILL NEED:
2 tablespoons (30 ml) vegetable oil
One 8-ounce (224 g) can sliced water
    chestnuts, drained

Hot cooked rice

1. Combine the broccoli, green beans, and pepper strips in a gallon-size (4 L) zip-top bag. Place in the freezer immediately.

2. In a small mixing bowl, whisk together the vegetable broth, soy sauce, sherry, sesame oil, ginger, garlic, and honey. Whisk in the cornstarch. Place the mixture in the pint-size (470 ml) bag and close, removing as much air as possible.

FREEZING INSTRUCTIONS:

Store the two bags in the freezer.

TO THAW AND SERVE:

Thaw the bag of sauce in the refrigerator on a plate to catch drips or on the counter for 15 minutes. Heat the oil in a large skillet until shimmering. Add the frozen vegetables and cook, stirring, until hot throughout, 10 to 15 minutes. Massage the bag of sauce to recombine and add the sauce to the pan. Cook, stirring, until the sauce is thickened. Stir in the water chestnuts. Serve the vegetables and sauce over the rice.

Red Lentil Dal

Seasoned lentils, or dal, are staples in much of India. While this preparation is not as spicy as some, it has a warmth that will please the palate. Cooked lentils freeze and reheat well, making this an ideal dish for bulk cooking. Thanks to my Indian pen pal and fellow blogger Prerna Malik, for her tips on Indian cuisine. Serve the dal with rice and roti (Indian flat bread). // *Serves 4 to 6*

■ **PACKAGING:** Plastic containers with lids

2 cups (380 g) red lentils, rinsed
   and picked over
2 tablespoons (30 ml) olive oil
1 cup (160 g) chopped onion
1 teaspoon chopped fresh ginger
1 teaspoon ground cumin
1 teaspoon chopped garlic

1 teaspoon red curry powder
1 teaspoon salt
½ teaspoon ground turmeric
One 14.5-ounce (406 g) can petite diced
   tomatoes with juices
4 cups (940 ml) water

1. Soak the lentils for 20 minutes.

2. Meanwhile, in a large stockpot, heat the oil over medium heat until shimmering. Add the onion and cook until translucent. Stir in the ginger, cumin, garlic, curry powder, salt, and turmeric. Cook for about 1 minute, stirring.

3. Add the tomatoes, stirring and scraping up any browned bits.

4. Drain the lentils and add them to the pot, along with the 4 cups (940 ml) water. Simmer for about 20 minutes, or until the lentils are tender.

FREEZING INSTRUCTIONS:

Divide the dal into meal-size portions in plastic containers. Chill in the refrigerator before freezing.

TO THAW AND SERVE:

Thaw the dal in the refrigerator. Reheat in a saucepan until heated through.

Tahini Vegetable Patties

These veggie patties combine the flavors of falafel and fresh vegetables, making for a delicious and filling dish. Serve them with Greek yogurt, chopped fresh cilantro, and crumbled feta cheese, or stuff them into pita breads, if you like. Make smaller patties to serve as appetizers. // *Serves 4*

■ **PACKAGING:** Waxed paper, quart-size (1 L) zip-top freezer bag

1 tablespoon (15 ml) olive oil
½ cup (60 g) shredded zucchini
½ cup (75 g) chopped red bell pepper
½ cup (80 g) chopped onion
1 tablespoon finely chopped jalapeño pepper
1 teaspoon chopped garlic

One 15-ounce (420 g) can garbanzo beans, drained
1¾ cups (85 g) fresh bread crumbs
2 large eggs, beaten
2 tablespoons (28 g) tahini
1 teaspoon kosher salt

WHEN READY TO SERVE, YOU WILL NEED:

Olive oil, for frying
Plain Greek-style yogurt

Chopped fresh cilantro
Crumbled feta cheese

1. In a large skillet over medium-high heat, heat the olive oil. Sauté the zucchini, bell pepper, onion, jalapeño, and garlic. Cook the mixture until the vegetables are tender, about 7 minutes. Remove from the heat and set aside to cool.

2. In the bowl of a food processor, pulse the garbanzo beans until coarsely chopped. Alternatively, you can mash them with a potato masher.

3. In a large bowl, combine the sautéed vegetables, garbanzo beans, bread crumbs, eggs, tahini, and salt. Stir gently to combine. Form the mixture into 4 patties.

FREEZING INSTRUCTIONS:

Stack the patties with a square of waxed paper between each one. Place in a freezer bag and freeze.

TO THAW AND SERVE:

Thaw the patties in the refrigerator. Heat 1 to 2 tablespoons (15 to 30 ml) olive oil in a skillet and fry the patties in the hot oil until hot and browned. Serve with the yogurt, cilantro, and feta for toppings.

Potatoes Stuffed with Caramelized Onions and Dubliner Cheese

Twice-baked potatoes reach new heights of deliciousness with the addition of caramelized onions and sharp Dubliner cheese. Since these potatoes freeze and reheat so well, it's worth making a big batch so you can enjoy an elegant potato dish any night of the week. Serve these stuffed potatoes with a side salad. You can substitute sharp cheddar cheese for the Dubliner if you'd rather.

// *Serves 8*

■ **PACKAGING:** Plastic wrap, gallon-size (4 L) zip-top freezer bags

8 large baking potatoes
2 tablespoons (30 ml) olive oil
1 cup (160 g) chopped onion
1 teaspoon chopped garlic
1 cup (225 g) sour cream
1 cup (120 g) shredded Dubliner
　or sharp cheddar cheese, divided

¼ cup (56 g) (½ stick) unsalted butter,
　softened
1 tablespoon chopped fresh parsley
　or 1 teaspoon dried parsley flakes
½ teaspoon kosher salt
½ teaspoon freshly ground black pepper

1. Pierce each potato several times with a fork. Bake the potatoes in the oven at 350°F (180°C or gas mark 4) for 1 hour or until tender, or microwave them until cooked through. Set the potatoes aside until cool enough to handle.

2. In a medium skillet, heat the olive oil over medium heat until shimmering. Add the onions and garlic, and cook until the onions are translucent. Turn the heat to low, cover, and cook 5 minutes more. Remove the lid and stir. Continue to cook until the onions start to brown lightly around the edges. Remove the pan from the heat and set the mixture aside to cool.

3. Cut ¼ inch (6 mm) off the top of each baked potato and discard or reserve for another use. Scoop out the insides of each potato, leaving a ¼-inch (6 mm)-thick shell. Place the scooped-out potato in a large bowl and mash with a potato masher.

4. Stir the onion mixture, sour cream, ¾ cup (90 g) of the Dubliner cheese, the butter, parsley, salt, and pepper into the mashed potatoes. Stir well to combine.

5. Fill the potato shells with the mixture. Sprinkle the remaining ¼ cup (30 g) of Dubliner cheese over the tops of the potatoes.

FREEZING INSTRUCTIONS:

Allow the potatoes to cool to room temperature. Wrap each potato in plastic wrap and place the potatoes in freezer bags. Chill in the refrigerator before freezing.

TO THAW AND SERVE:

Thaw the potatoes in the refrigerator. Preheat the oven to 375°F (190°C or gas mark 5). Unwrap the potatoes and place them on a baking sheet. Reheat the potatoes for 15 to 20 minutes, until heated through. Serve immediately.

Broccoli Gratin with Tarragon and Buttered Bread Crumbs

This creamy broccoli-and-cheese casserole makes a delicious meatless main dish when accompanied by a salad and bread. Homemade cream of celery soup replaces the canned variety often seen in traditional casseroles. // *Serves 4 to 6*

- **PACKAGING:** 9 × 13-inch (23 × 33 cm) baking dish with lid

1½ pounds (680 g) broccoli florets
    (about 9 cups)
2 cups (470 ml) Homemade Cream of Celery
    Soup for Cooking (page 238)
½ teaspoon dried tarragon

1 cup (120 g) shredded cheddar cheese,
    divided
1 cup (50 g) fresh bread crumbs
2 tablespoons (28 g) salted butter, melted

1. Grease the baking dish. Steam the broccoli florets until crisp-tender, 8 to 10 minutes.

2. In a large bowl, combine the broccoli, cream of celery soup, tarragon, and ½ cup (60 g) of the cheddar cheese. Stir gently to combine. Spread the mixture in the bottom of the prepared baking dish. Sprinkle the remaining ½ cup (60 g) cheddar cheese over the top.

3. In a small bowl, combine the bread crumbs and melted butter. Sprinkle this over the cheese layer.

FREEZING INSTRUCTIONS:

Cover and chill in the refrigerator before freezing.

TO THAW AND SERVE:

Thaw the dish in the refrigerator. Preheat the oven to 350°F (180°C or gas mark 4). Bake the gratin for 30 to 45 minutes, or until hot and bubbly.

Roasted Vegetable Quiche

Full of protein and flavor, a quiche goes wonderfully with a fresh salad on the side. This savory pie is bursting with roasted vegetables and creamy eggs and cheese. Although you can use a store-bought crust, consider making the Versatile Buttery Pie Crust (page 368) to take this dish over the top. // *Makes one 9-inch (23 cm) quiche*

■ **PACKAGING:** 9-inch (23 cm) pie plate, heavy-duty aluminum foil

2 cups (240 g) chopped vegetables, such as zucchini, onion, bell pepper, or broccoli, or a combination
2 tablespoons (30 ml) olive oil
Salt and freshly ground black pepper
1 unbaked 9-inch (23 cm) single pie shell

1 cup (120 g) shredded cheddar cheese tossed with 2 tablespoons (16 g) unbleached all-purpose flour
3 large eggs
1½ cups (355 ml) cream or half-and-half

1. Preheat the oven to 400°F (200°C or gas mark 6). In a large bowl, combine the vegetables and olive oil. Season the vegetables generously with salt and pepper. Transfer the vegetables to a shallow baking dish and roast them in the preheated oven for 15 to 30 minutes, or until tender, stirring occasionally to prevent sticking. Transfer the cooked vegetables to a plate to cool.

2. Once the vegetables have cooled, spread them in the bottom of the unbaked pie shell. Sprinkle the cheddar cheese over the top.

3. In a bowl, beat the eggs. Stir in the cream and ⅛ teaspoon black pepper. Pour the egg mixture over the vegetables and cheese in the pie shell.

FREEZING INSTRUCTIONS:
Place the pie plate flat in the freezer. Freeze until firm. Wrap the frozen quiche well with foil. Return to the freezer.

TO SERVE:
Preheat the oven to 400°F (200°C or gas mark 6). Bake the frozen quiche, uncovered (no need to thaw), for 30 to 45 minutes, or until a knife inserted in the center comes out clean.

Individual Greek Egg Casseroles

In my husband's hometown, there used to be a delightful family owned Greek restaurant where we often ate as newlyweds. One of my favorite meals at Pavlako's was the Greek eggs, which featured the delicious combination of spinach and feta. I've re-created Pavlako's Greek eggs in this individual egg casserole, which makes a delicious lunch or dinner when served with a side salad and a roll. Make several individual casseroles at one time by multiplying the recipe, lining up all the dishes and ingredients, and preparing them assembly-line style. // *Serves 1*

■ **PACKAGING:** 2-cup (470 ml) baking dish with lid

1 cup (50 g) soft bread cubes from an
    Italian loaf
⅓ cup (40 g) crumbled feta cheese
¼ cup chopped frozen spinach, thawed and
    squeezed dry

2 large eggs, beaten
½ cup (120 ml) milk
Pinch of freshly ground black pepper

1. Grease the baking dish. Spread the bread cubes across the bottom of the dish. Sprinkle the feta cheese and spinach over the bread cubes.

2. In a small bowl, whisk together the eggs, milk, and black pepper. Pour the egg mixture over the bread and cheese.

FREEZING INSTRUCTIONS:

Cover and freeze.

TO THAW AND SERVE:

Thaw the casserole in the refrigerator. Preheat the oven to 350°F (180°C or gas mark 4). Bake the casserole for 25 minutes or until the top is puffy and a tester inserted in the center comes out clean. Alternatively, bake directly from the freezer for 40 to 45 minutes.

Alfredo Mac and Cheese

Mac and cheese is a classic comfort dish. I've scaled it up with an Alfredo sauce, redolent with garlic. This is no boxed mac and cheese! Make it just a little fancier by serving the noodles and sauce in individual ramekins. // **Serves 6 to 8**

■ **PACKAGING:** One 9 × 13-inch (23 × 33 cm) baking dish with lid OR six 2-cup (470 ml) baking dishes with lids

1 pound (454 g) elbow macaroni
¼ cup (56 g) butter
⅓ cup (40 g) unbleached, all-purpose flour
4 cloves garlic, crushed, or 1 heaping
    teaspoon crushed garlic from a jar
2½ cups (590 ml) milk

2 cups (240 g) shredded mozzarella
    or Jack cheese, divided
1 cup (100 g) shredded Asiago, Romano,
    or Parmesan cheese
Fine sea salt and freshly ground
    black pepper, to taste
Chopped scallions, for garnish (optional)

1. Grease the pan(s) you are using.

2. In a large pot of boiling, salted water, cook the macaroni according to package directions, then drain.

3. Meanwhile, in a medium saucepan, melt the butter. Add the flour and garlic, whisking until smooth. Cook over medium-high heat until bubbly.

4. Slowly whisk in the milk, whisking until smooth. Cook over medium-high heat until thickened into a sauce. Whisk in 1 cup (120 g) of the mozzarella cheese as well as the Asiago. Season to taste with salt and pepper.

5. Combine the cheese sauce with the cooked noodles, stirring to distribute the sauce throughout. (It will be pretty stringy thanks to the mozzarella.)

6. Transfer to the prepared baking dish(es). Sprinkle on the remaining 1 cup (120 g) mozzarella cheese and scatter the scallions, if using, over the top.

FREEZING INSTRUCTIONS:

Cover and chill the dish(es) in the refrigerator before freezing.

TO THAW AND SERVE:

Thaw the casserole(s) in the refrigerator. Preheat the oven to 400°F (200°C or gas mark 6). Bake the pasta until heated through, about 30 minutes. Adjust the baking time down to 15 to 20 minutes for individual serving dishes.

Pesto Penne and Cheese

Rich pesto and intense sun-dried tomatoes take the humble mac-and-cheese casserole up a few notches. Serve this with a green salad and a glass of great wine. // **Serves 6 to 8**

■ **PACKAGING:** 9 × 13-inch (23 × 33 cm) baking dish with lid

One 16-ounce (454 g) package penne
1½ cups (180 g) shredded mozzarella
   cheese, divided
8 ounces (224 g) cubed Monterey Jack
   cheese

1 cup (225 g) sour cream
¾ cup (41 g) julienned sun-dried tomatoes
½ cup (120 ml) pesto
Salt and freshly ground black pepper

WHEN READY TO SERVE, YOU WILL NEED:
1 tablespoon chopped fresh parsley
   or 1 teaspoon dried parsley flakes

1. Grease the baking dish. Cook the pasta just until al dente, according to the package directions. Drain.

2. Meanwhile, in a large bowl, combine 1 cup (120 g) of the mozzarella cheese, the Monterey Jack, sour cream, sun-dried tomatoes, and pesto. Season the mixture to taste with salt and pepper. Stir in the drained noodles.

3. Spoon the mixture into the baking dish. Sprinkle the remaining ½ cup (60 g) mozzarella cheese over the top.

FREEZING INSTRUCTIONS:

Cover and chill the pan in the refrigerator before freezing.

TO THAW AND SERVE:

Thaw the macaroni and cheese in the refrigerator. Preheat the oven to 350°F (180°C or gas mark 4). Bake the casserole until heated through, about 30 minutes. Stir to recombine the cheese sauce and noodles before serving. Sprinkle the parsley over the top.

Baked Manicotti with Sun-Dried Tomatoes and Thyme

Noodles and cheese are a beautiful combination. They can be prepared casually, as in a pasta salad or mac and cheese, or they can be dressed up, as in this manicotti. Manicotti can seem intimidating to prepare, since the large pasta tubes tear easily. To help them hold their shape, cook the noodles just until al dente or a tad firmer. The noodles will soften upon freezing and with further baking in the oven. I've called for one large pan here, but feel free to package the manicotti in smaller baking dishes or store them in freezer bags without the sauce (freeze the sauce separately). That way, you can bake whatever quantity you want at serving time. // **Serves 5 to 7**

■ **PACKAGING:** 9 × 13-inch (23 × 33 cm) baking dish with lid

1 package manicotti (about 14 manicotti)
2 cups (240 g) shredded mozzarella cheese, divided
15 ounces (420 g) ricotta cheese
½ cup (27 g) finely chopped sun-dried tomatoes

½ teaspoon dried thyme
¼ teaspoon freshly ground black pepper
3 cups (705 ml) Easy Slow Cooker Red Sauce (page 217) or other favorite sauce

1. Grease the baking dish.

2. Cook the manicotti just until al dente, according to the package directions. Drain the noodles.

3. In a large bowl, combine 1 cup (120 g) of the mozzarella cheese, the ricotta, sun-dried tomatoes, thyme, and black pepper. Stir well to combine.

4. Fill the cooked manicotti by spooning a heaping tablespoon of the mixture into each one. You can also fill the manicotti using a piping bag made out of a quart-size (1 L) freezer bag. Spoon the cheese filling into the bag and seal. Snip off one corner of the bag and pipe the filling into the cooked manicotti.

5. Arrange the manicotti in the prepared baking dish. Pour the sauce over the manicotti. Sprinkle the remaining 1 cup (120 g) mozzarella cheese over the sauce.

FREEZING INSTRUCTIONS:
Cover and chill the pan in the refrigerator before freezing.

TO THAW AND SERVE:
Thaw the manicotti in the refrigerator. Preheat the oven to 350°F (180°C or gas mark 4). Bake the pasta until heated through, about 30 minutes.

Spinach and Feta Manicotti with Lemon and Oregano

Spinach and feta cheese are happy companions in a number of Greek dishes. But they steal the show in this easy baked pasta dish. As with the Baked Manicotti with Sun-Dried Tomatoes and Thyme (page 212), remember to cook the noodles just until al dente or a tad firmer. The noodles will soften upon freezing and with further baking in the oven. And, if you like, package them in smaller baking dishes or store them in freezer bags without the sauce (freeze the sauce separately). That way, you can bake whatever quantity you want at serving time. // *Serves 5 to 7*

■ **PACKAGING:** 9 × 13-inch (23 × 33 cm) baking dish with lid

1 package manicotti (about 14 manicotti)
One 16-ounce (454 g) package frozen
    chopped spinach, thawed and
    squeezed dry
2 cups (240 g) shredded mozzarella cheese,
    divided
2 cups (450 g) ricotta cheese
1 cup (120 g) crumbled feta cheese

1 large egg, beaten
Grated zest of 1 lemon
¼ teaspoon dried oregano
3 to 4 cups (705 to 940 ml) Tomato Sauce
    with Oregano and Kalamata Olives
    (opposite page) or other favorite
    red sauce

1. Grease the baking dish.

2. Cook the manicotti just until al dente, according to the package directions. Drain the noodles.

3. In a large bowl, combine the spinach, 1 cup (120 g) of the mozzarella cheese, the ricotta, feta cheese, egg, lemon zest, and oregano. Stir well to combine.

4. Fill the cooked manicotti by spooning a heaping tablespoon of the mixture into each one. You can also fill the manicotti using a piping bag made out of a quart-size (1 L) freezer bag. Spoon the cheese filling into the bag and seal. Snip off one corner of the bag and pipe the filling into the cooked manicotti.

5. Arrange the manicotti in the prepared baking dish. Pour the sauce over the manicotti. Sprinkle the remaining 1 cup (120 g) mozzarella cheese over the sauce.

FREEZING INSTRUCTIONS:

Cover and chill the pan in the refrigerator before freezing.

TO THAW AND SERVE:

Thaw the manicotti in the refrigerator. Preheat the oven to 350°F (180°C or gas mark 4). Bake the pasta until heated through, about 30 minutes.

Tomato Sauce with Oregano and Kalamata Olives

This mediterranean-style sauce is delicious served over pasta, as a dipping sauce for bread, or even on pizza. It also makes a delicious topping for the Spinach and Feta Manicotti with Lemon and Oregano (opposite page). // *Makes about 6 cups (1410 ml)*

■ **PACKAGING:** Plastic containers with lids

2 tablespoons (30 ml) olive oil
½ cup (80 g) chopped onion
1 teaspoon chopped garlic
¼ cup (60 ml) white wine
Two 14.5-ounce (406 g) cans petite diced
    tomatoes with juices

One 15-ounce (420 g) can tomato sauce
⅓ cup (35 g) chopped kalamata olives
2 teaspoons dried oregano
⅛ teaspoon freshly ground black pepper

1. In a large stockpot, heat the olive oil over medium heat until shimmering. Add the onion and garlic, and cook, stirring, until the onion becomes translucent, about 5 minutes.

2. Add the white wine and stir, scraping up any brown bits. Add the diced tomatoes, tomato sauce, olives, oregano, and black pepper. Simmer the mixture for 30 minutes. Taste and adjust the seasonings.

FREEZING INSTRUCTIONS:

Divide the sauce into meal-size portions in plastic containers. Chill in the refrigerator before freezing.

TO THAW AND SERVE:

Thaw the sauce in the refrigerator. Reheat in a saucepan on the stovetop or in a microwave-safe dish in the microwave.

Quick and Spicy Marinara Sauce

Making homemade pasta sauces is one of the easiest and most satisfying of cooking pursuits. Not only can you tailor them to your preference, you also control all the ingredients. No high-fructose corn syrup here! While many jarred sauces are full of sweeteners, sodium, and additives, this one tastes of vegetables and spices. It also comes together in a flash. You can certainly let it simmer for several hours, but you don't have to, since the flavors blend during freezing. This sauce can also be prepared in a 5-quart (5 L) slow cooker; cook it on HIGH for 4 hours or LOW for 6 to 8 hours. // **_Makes 14 to 16 cups sauce (3290 to 3760 ml)_**

■ **PACKAGING:** Plastic containers with lids

¼ cup (60 ml) olive oil
2 cups (320 g) chopped onion
1 tablespoon chopped garlic
1 cup (120 g) finely chopped carrot
½ cup (75 g) chopped bell pepper (red, green, or a combination)

½ cup (60 g) chopped celery
Four 28-ounce (784 g) cans crushed tomatoes
⅓ cup (32 g) Jamie's Spice Mix (page 98)
2 to 3 cups (470 to 705 ml) water

1. In a large stockpot, heat the olive oil over medium heat until shimmering. Add the onion and garlic, and cook, stirring, for about 5 minutes, or until the onions are translucent.

2. Add the carrot, pepper, and celery, and cook, stirring occasionally, 5 minutes more.

3. Stir in the crushed tomatoes, spice mix, and enough water to achieve the desired consistency. Stir well to blend.

4. Simmer the sauce on the stovetop for 1 hour, or until the carrots are tender.

5. For a smoother sauce, blend it in batches in a blender or food processor, or puree it using an immersion blender.

FREEZING INSTRUCTIONS:

Divide the sauce into meal-size portions in plastic containers. Chill in the refrigerator before freezing.

TO THAW AND SERVE:

Thaw the sauce in the refrigerator. Reheat it in a saucepan over low heat, whisking to recombine. Add a small amount of water if necessary to achieve the desired consistency.

Easy Slow Cooker Red Sauce

When my family needed to economize years ago, I started making my own pasta sauce, and I haven't looked back. About once a month I cook up a big batch, divide it into 2-cup (470 ml) portions, and freeze it. I never buy jarred sauce; we enjoy the homemade version so much more. Serve this sauce over your favorite noodles, or use it in lasagna and other casseroles. // ***Makes 14 to 16 cups (3290 to 3760 ml)***

■ **PACKAGING:** Plastic containers with lids

¼ cup (60 ml) olive oil
2 large onions, diced
1 tablespoon chopped garlic
Four 28-ounce (784 g) cans crushed
   tomatoes
1 to 2 cups (235 to 470 ml) water

1 tablespoon (18 g) salt
⅓ cup (16 g) chopped fresh basil
   or 2 tablespoons dried basil
3 tablespoons chopped fresh parsley
   or 1 tablespoon dried parsley flakes
½ teaspoon red pepper flakes

In a large skillet, heat the olive oil over medium heat. Add the onions and garlic and cook until softened. Spoon the onion mixture into a 5-quart (5 L) or larger slow cooker. Add the crushed tomatoes, water, salt, basil, parsley, and red pepper flakes. Cover and cook on LOW for at least 4 hours. Adjust the seasonings to taste.

FREEZING INSTRUCTIONS:

Divide the sauce into meal-size portions in plastic containers. Chill in the refrigerator before freezing.

TO THAW AND SERVE:

Thaw the sauce in the refrigerator. Reheat in a saucepan over low heat, whisking to recombine.

Sun-Dried Tomato Pesto

Sun-dried tomatoes create a vibrant pesto that works beautifully on pizza, hot pasta, and pasta salads; you can mix it into hamburgers or use it as a topping for chicken breasts. A little goes a long way in adding sunny summer flavor. // *Makes 2½ cups (590 g)*

■ **PACKAGING:** Plastic containers with lids or pint-size (470 ml) zip-top freezer bags

2 cups (110 g) sun-dried tomatoes
1 cup (100 g) freshly grated Parmesan
   cheese
¾ cup (90 g) walnuts or pine nuts
3 tablespoons chopped fresh basil
   or 1 tablespoon dried basil

1 tablespoon chopped garlic
1 teaspoon freshly ground black pepper
¼ teaspoon red pepper flakes
¾ cup (180 ml) olive oil

1. In a food processor fitted with a metal blade, combine the sun-dried tomatoes, cheese, nuts, basil, garlic, black pepper, and red pepper flakes. Process until smooth.

2. With the machine running, pour in the olive oil in a slow stream. Process until combined.

FREEZING INSTRUCTIONS:

Divide into ½-cup (120 ml) portions in plastic containers or pint-size (470 ml) zip-top freezer bags and chill in the refrigerator before freezing.

TO THAW AND SERVE:

Thaw in the refrigerator. Stir to recombine the ingredients before using.

► Potluck-Friendly Main Dishes

One of the goals of bulk cooking is to free up your time so you can spend it on other things. If you have a freezer full of homemade convenience foods, you can easily attend potlucks and other group meals, feast in hand. You're more likely to arrive with a smile on your face if you haven't spent the previous few hours fussing over food.

The following items travel well in a slow cooker or covered dish. Use insulated carriers to keep both slow cookers and baking dishes warm between home and your destination.

- Hearty Shredded Beef Enchiladas, page 79
- Vegetable-Beef Lasagna, page 91
- Shepherd's Pie with Green Chile Mashed Potatoes, page 92
- Sweet and Spicy Joes, page 99
- Lawnmower Taco, page 100
- Chicken Enchilada Bake with Green Chiles and Jalapeños, page 126
- Best-Ever Chicken Pot Pie, page 127
- Garlicky Chicken Noodle Bake, page 128
- Creamy Chicken Enchiladas, page 129
- Chicken Divan with Cheddar Crust, page 131
- Sweet and Sour Turkey Meatballs, page 148
- Ham and Swiss Potato Gratin, page 178
- Easy Sausage and Pepper Sandwiches, page 179
- Bean and Cheese Nacho Bake, page 192
- Quick and Easy Cheese Enchiladas, page 190
- Cozy Cheese and Potato Casserole, page 194
- Roasted Vegetable Quiche, page 208
- Pesto Penne and Cheese, page 211
- Spinach and Feta Manicotti with Lemon and Oregano, page 214
- Tres Chiles Chili Con Quinoa, page 245
- Bacon-Cheddar Egg Bake, page 289
- Eggs Florentine Casserole, page 292
- Savory Ham and Swiss Clafouti, page 293
- Chile and Sausage Oven Frittata, page 294

6

SOUP'S ON

‣ Cheddar Soup with Zucchini, Broccoli, and Carrots ▪ 221

‣ Taco Soup with Hominy ▪ 222

‣ Not Your Mother's Chicken Noodle Soup ▪ 223

‣ Roasted Vegetable Soup ▪ 224

‣ Cheesy Butternut Squash Soup with Herbs ▪ 226

‣ Split Pea Soup with Bacon and Thyme ▪ 227

‣ White Bean Soup with Vegetables ▪ 228

‣ Creamy Cauliflower Soup ▪ 229

‣ Spring Vegetable Soup ▪ 231

‣ Mushroom-Barley Soup ▪ 232

‣ Beef and Barley Soup with Dill ▪ 233

‣ Black Bean Soup with Jalapeño ▪ 234

‣ Tortilla Soup with Shrimp ▪ 235

‣ Fish Chowder with Red Potatoes and Corn ▪ 236

‣ Homemade Cream of Celery Soup for Cooking ▪ 238

‣ Chicken Cacciatore Stew ▪ 239

‣ Our Favorite Irish Stew ▪ 240

‣ Hearty Beef Stew with Olives ▪ 241

‣ Beef Stew with Eggplant and Carrots ▪ 242

‣ Quick and Easy Texas Chili ▪ 244

‣ Chihuahua Chili ▪ 244

‣ Tres Chiles Chili Con Quinoa ▪ 245

‣ Smoky Multi-Bean Vegetarian Chili ▪ 247

Cheddar Soup with Zucchini, Broccoli, and Carrots

Fancy cafés charge a pretty penny for their cheese and broccoli soup. Save money and eat at home in style. Keep single-serving containers of this soup on hand for quick lunches and suppers. Or have the girlfriends over and enjoy the whole pot! // *Serves 4 to 6*

■ **PACKAGING:** Plastic containers with lids

¼ cup (56 g) (½ stick) unsalted butter, divided
2 cloves garlic, minced
½ medium-size zucchini, shredded
1 carrot, peeled and shredded
½ medium-size onion, shredded
1 head broccoli, chopped into small florets (about 3 cups [215 g])

3 cups (705 ml) reduced-sodium chicken broth
¼ cup (30 g) unbleached all-purpose flour
2 cups (470 ml) milk
2 cups (240 g) shredded cheddar cheese
Salt and freshly ground black pepper

1. In a large saucepan, melt 2 tablespoons (28 g) of the butter. Add the garlic, zucchini, carrot, and onion. Sauté until the vegetables are tender, about 10 minutes.

2. Stir in the broccoli and broth. Simmer until the broccoli is tender, about 10 minutes.

3. Meanwhile, melt the remaining 2 tablespoons (28 g) butter in a large pot over medium heat. Whisk in the flour and cook for a minute or two. Whisk in the milk until smooth. Simmer until thickened. Whisk in the cheddar cheese gradually, stirring to incorporate.

4. Pour the vegetable mixture into the cheese mixture, stirring to combine. Season to taste with salt and pepper.

FREEZING INSTRUCTIONS:

Portion the soup into meal-size plastic containers. Cool to room temperature. Cover and chill in the refrigerator before freezing.

TO THAW AND SERVE:

Thaw the soup in the refrigerator. Reheat in a saucepan until heated through, stirring to recombine. Serve immediately.

Taco Soup with Hominy

Taco soup is generally a winner with children. However, many recipes call for packaged seasoning mixes, which are laden with sodium. I've tweaked those recipes to suit my family's tastes and budget. This cooks in the slow cooker, and it's so easy my son put it together all by himself when he was five! Well, I cooked the meat and opened the cans, but he did all the rest. How simple is that?

// *Serves 6 to 8*

■ **PACKAGING:** Plastic containers with lids

1 pound (454 g) ground beef or turkey
One 28-ounce (784 g) can crushed tomatoes
Two 15-ounce (420 g) cans black beans, rinsed and drained
One 15.5-ounce (434 g) can hominy, drained
One 15-ounce (420 g) can kidney beans, rinsed and drained
One 15-ounce (420 g) can pinto beans, rinsed and drained

1 to 2 cups (235 to 470 ml) water
1 cup (235 ml) red enchilada sauce
3 tablespoons chopped fresh parsley or 1 tablespoon dried parsley flakes
1 tablespoon dried oregano
1 tablespoon onion powder
1 teaspoon garlic powder
Freshly ground black pepper

WHEN READY TO SERVE, YOU WILL NEED:
Salsa
Shredded cheddar cheese

Sour cream

1. In a large skillet over medium heat, brown the meat until it is no longer pink, breaking it up with the back of a spoon as it cooks. Drain.

2. Combine all of the ingredients in a 5-quart (5 L) slow cooker. Cook on HIGH for 4 to 6 hours.

FREEZING INSTRUCTIONS:

Divide the soup into meal-size portions in plastic containers. Chill in the refrigerator before freezing.

TO THAW AND SERVE:

Thaw the soup in the refrigerator. Reheat in a saucepan until heated through, stirring to recombine. Serve immediately with the salsa, cheese, and sour cream.

Not Your Mother's Chicken Noodle Soup

Canned soup was a standard for many of us growing up. But keeping a freezer full of soup is just as easy as stocking the pantry with cans—and much healthier and more delicious. This version is loaded with tender bits of vegetables and chicken and boasts a slightly Asian twist with sesame oil, cilantro, and spicy red pepper. The noodles will absorb more water and soften in the freezer, so it is fine to cook them al dente. // *Serves 6 to 8*

■ **PACKAGING:** Plastic containers with lids

2 tablespoons (30 ml) sesame oil
1 medium-size onion, grated
1 teaspoon chopped garlic
1 teaspoon chopped fresh ginger
2 carrots, shredded
1 small zucchini, shredded

8 cups (1880 ml) reduced-sodium or
   homemade chicken broth
2 cups (280 g) chopped cooked chicken
⅛ to ¼ teaspoon red pepper flakes
Salt and freshly ground black pepper
8 ounces (224 g) wide egg noodles

WHEN READY TO SERVE, YOU WILL NEED:
2 tablespoons chopped fresh cilantro

Lime wedges

1. In a large stockpot, heat the sesame oil over medium heat. Add the onion, garlic, and ginger, and sauté until translucent, about 5 minutes. Stir in the carrots and zucchini and cook a few minutes more.

2. Stir in the chicken broth. Bring the soup to a boil and stir in the chicken, red pepper flakes, and salt and pepper to taste. Simmer for 15 minutes. Stir in the egg noodles and continue to simmer the soup until noodles are al dente.

FREEZING INSTRUCTIONS:

Divide the soup into meal-size portions in plastic containers. Chill in the refrigerator before freezing.

TO THAW AND SERVE:

Thaw the soup in the refrigerator. Reheat in a saucepan until heated through. Sprinkle the fresh cilantro over the top before serving. Serve with the lime wedges.

Roasted Vegetable Soup

I'm pretty sure that you could make a different kind of soup every day of the year and not repeat yourself. There are just so many options—smooth, chunky, noodle, vegetable, chicken—the choices are endless. I love the rich flavors that roasted vegetables bring to this blended soup. While you may not be in the mood for eating soup in the summer when these veggies are at their peak, your Fall Weather Self will thank you that you filled the freezer when you could. // *Serves 4*

■ **PACKAGING:** Plastic containers with lids

1 eggplant, trimmed and split lengthwise
1 large patty pan squash or 2 yellow
   squash, trimmed and split in half
2 ribs celery, trimmed
2 bell peppers, seeded and halved
1 cup (120 g) baby carrots or 2 large
   carrots, peeled and cut into 2-inch
   (5 cm) chunks
1 cup (150 g) cherry tomatoes or 2 medium
   tomatoes, halved

4 large cloves garlic, unpeeled
2 tablespoons (30 ml) olive oil
1 tablespoon chopped fresh oregano
   or 1 teaspoon dried oregano
1 bay leaf
3 to 5 cups (705 to 1175 ml) vegetable
   or chicken broth
Fine sea salt and freshly ground
   black pepper

1. Preheat the oven to 400°F (200°C or gas mark 6). Place the vegetables on a rimmed baking sheet. Brush the vegetables with the oil.

2. Roast the vegetables for 45 minutes, until tender and spotted with brown.

3. Scoop the eggplant pulp from the skin and place it in a large stockpot. Remove the garlic from its skins and add to the pot as well as the other vegetables, oregano, and bay leaf.

4. Add 3 cups (705 ml) of the broth and bring to a simmer. Simmer the mixture for about 45 minutes, or until the vegetables are very tender.

5. Remove the bay leaf and discard. Use an immersion blender to blend the vegetables until smooth. (You can also blend the soup in a blender or in a food processor.) Thin with more stock, if desired. Season to taste with salt and pepper.

FREEZING INSTRUCTIONS:

Divide the soup into meal-size portions in plastic containers. Chill in the refrigerator before freezing.

TO THAW AND SERVE:

Thaw the soup in the refrigerator. Reheat in a saucepan until heated through, stirring to recombine.

Cheesy Butternut Squash Soup with Herbs

Believe it or not, I had never eaten butternut squash until our CSA provided an abundance of them one fall. We are fast friends now. The squash plays so nicely with cheddar in this soup. Happiness in a spoon! I like to package it in single servings for quick lunches on the go. // *Serves 6 to 8*

- **PACKAGING:** Plastic containers with lids

5 tablespoons (70 g) salted butter, divided
One 2-pound (908 g) butternut squash, peeled, seeded, and cubed, or two 12-ounce (340 g) packages cubed squash
1½ cups (270 g) chopped onion
1 cup (120 g) chopped celery
1 cup (120 g) chopped carrot
1 cup (120 g) diced potato

5 cups (1175 ml) reduced-sodium chicken broth or water
¼ teaspoon rubbed sage
¼ teaspoon dried thyme
⅛ teaspoon dried marjoram
¼ cup (30 g) unbleached all-purpose flour
2 cups (470 ml) milk
2 cups (240 g) shredded cheddar cheese
Salt and freshly ground black pepper

1. In a large stockpot, melt 3 tablespoons (42 g) of the butter over medium heat. Add the butternut squash and onion. Cook for about 5 minutes, stirring occasionally.

2. Add the celery, carrot, and potato. Cook 5 minutes more, stirring occasionally.

3. Add the chicken broth, sage, thyme, and marjoram, and bring to a boil. Reduce the heat and simmer until the vegetables are tender, about 30 minutes.

4. Meanwhile, melt the remaining 2 tablespoons (28 g) butter in a large pot over medium heat. Whisk in the flour and cook for a minute or two. Whisk in the milk until smooth. Simmer until thickened. Whisk in the cheddar cheese gradually, stirring to incorporate. Remove from the heat.

5. Puree the vegetable mixture with an immersion blender or in a food processor, in batches if necessary. Stir in the cheese mixture. Season with salt and pepper to taste.

FREEZING INSTRUCTIONS:
Divide the soup into meal-size portions in plastic containers. Chill in the refrigerator before freezing.

TO THAW AND SERVE:
Thaw the soup in the refrigerator. Reheat in a saucepan until heated through.

Split Pea Soup with Bacon and Thyme

In this hearty, flavorful split pea soup, the bacon and thyme go particularly well with the creamy goodness of the peas, making for a delightful supper. // *Serves 8*

■ **PACKAGING:** Plastic containers with lids

4 slices lower-salt bacon, finely chopped
1½ cups (270 g) chopped onion
1 cup (120 g) chopped carrot
3 quarts (2.7 L) water
1 pound (454 g) split peas, picked over
   and rinsed

1 bay leaf
1 tablespoon (18 g) fine sea salt
½ teaspoon dried marjoram
½ teaspoon dried thyme
¼ teaspoon freshly ground black pepper

1. In a large stockpot, cook the bacon and onion over medium heat until the bacon is crisp and the onion has begun to turn translucent, about 5 to 10 minutes.

2. Add the carrot, reduce the heat to low, and cook for about 2 minutes.

3. Add the water, peas, bay leaf, salt, marjoram, thyme, and pepper. Bring to a boil. Reduce the heat to low, cover, and simmer for 2 hours.

4. Remove the bay leaf. Puree the soup with an immersion blender or in a food processor or blender, in batches if necessary. Adjust the seasonings to taste.

FREEZING INSTRUCTIONS:

Divide the soup into meal-size portions in plastic containers. Chill in the refrigerator before freezing.

TO THAW AND SERVE:

Thaw the soup in the refrigerator. Reheat in a saucepan until heated through.

White Bean Soup with Vegetables

Though i grew up in a meat-and-potatoes family, I've been pleasantly surprised to discover how satisfying meatless meals can be. Not only are they less expensive, there's a freshness that always shines through. This filling, flavorful white bean soup contains no meat or dairy, making it a great dish to serve to vegetarian or vegan friends. Omit the jalapeño for a less spicy soup. // *Serves 6 to 8*

■ **PACKAGING:** Plastic containers with lids

¼ cup (60 ml) olive oil
½ cup (80 g) chopped onion
1½ teaspoons crushed garlic
1 cup (120 g) chopped red potato
½ cup (60 g) chopped carrot
½ cup (60 g) chopped celery
¼ cup (38 g) chopped red bell pepper
1 tablespoon chopped jalapeño pepper
    (optional)

1 pound (454 g) Great Northern white
    beans, rinsed, picked over, and soaked
    according to package directions,
    then drained
6 cups (1410 ml) water
3 tablespoons chopped fresh parsley
    or 1 tablespoon dried parsley flakes
1 tablespoon Jamie's Spice Mix (page 98)
1 teaspoon salt
Freshly ground black pepper

1. In a large stockpot, heat the oil over medium heat until shimmering. Sauté the onion and garlic until the onion start to turn translucent, about 5 minutes.

2. Add the potato, carrot, celery, bell pepper, and jalapeño, if using, to the pot, and cook, stirring occasionally, 5 minutes more.

3. Add the beans, water, parsley, spice mix, salt, and pepper to the pot. Bring to a low boil and simmer, covered, for 2 to 3 hours, until the beans are tender. Alternatively, the soup can be cooked in a 4- or 5-quart (4 or 5 L) slow cooker on LOW for 6 to 8 hours or on HIGH for 4 hours. Adjust the seasonings to taste.

FREEZING INSTRUCTIONS:

Divide the soup into meal-size portions in plastic containers. Chill in the refrigerator before freezing.

TO THAW AND SERVE:

Thaw the soup in the refrigerator. Reheat in a saucepan until heated through.

Creamy Cauliflower Soup

This creamy soup makes a perfectly simple supper for cold winter nights. Just add bread and a green salad. Full of vegetables and cheese, it can also be served as a starter for a more elegant meal.
// *Serves 8*

■ **PACKAGING:** Plastic containers with lids

2 tablespoons (28 g) plus ⅓ cup (75 g)
   salted butter, divided
1 cup (120 g) chopped celery
½ cup (60 g) chopped carrot
⅓ cup (55 g) chopped onion
4 cups (940 ml) water
1 head cauliflower, cut into florets
   (about 5 cups [500 g])

1½ teaspoons chopped fresh dill
   or ½ teaspoon dried dill
1 teaspoon salt
1½ teaspoons Jamie's Spice Mix (page 98)
½ cup (60 g) unbleached all-purpose flour
4 cups (940 ml) milk
4 ounces (112 g) cream cheese, cubed
Salt and freshly ground pepper

1. In a large stockpot, melt the 2 tablespoons (28 g) butter over medium heat. Add the celery, carrot, and onion, and cook, stirring occasionally, until the onion turns translucent, about 5 minutes.

2. Add the water, cauliflower, dill, salt, and spice mix. Bring to a low boil. Reduce the heat and simmer for 30 to 40 minutes, or until the vegetables are tender.

3. Meanwhile, melt the remaining ⅓ cup (75 g) butter in a large pot over medium heat. Whisk in the flour and cook for a minute or two. Whisk in the milk until smooth. Simmer until thickened. Whisk in the cream cheese, stirring to incorporate.

4. Once the cauliflower and other vegetables are tender, blend the mixture with an immersion blender, leaving some chunks of vegetables.

5. Add the milk mixture to the vegetable mixture, stirring to incorporate. Adjust the seasonings to taste.

FREEZING INSTRUCTIONS:

Divide the soup into meal-size portions in plastic containers. Chill in the refrigerator before freezing.

TO THAW AND SERVE:

Thaw the soup in the refrigerator. Reheat in a saucepan until heated through, stirring to recombine.

▶ How Freezer Cooking Helps Me

Here's how readers of my blog LifeasMOM.com answered these questions: How does freezer cooking help you? How does it help your family eat better? How do you make it work for your life?

"The key is to be flexible. When I have time and my husband has time, I will cook for an entire day while he watches the kids. Other times, I simply double a recipe in the slow cooker or on the stove and freeze half. I make whatever I can in a very limited time, such as cooking up beans when I am doing other things around the house. Then I freeze them and I save money by not having to buy canned beans."
     —Melissa B., mom of 3

"Freezer cooking is rarely something I set out to do but just what happens when cooking nearly every dinner from scratch. Huge batches of soup, for example, are just as easy as small batches, so to avoid wasting the leftovers, freezing becomes a necessity. On the other end of the process, it's a joy to have a quick and easy meal for those nights when I've just not planned well, have no inspiration, or am simply tired. I'm not as tempted to eat out or use convenience foods, which helps our budget and our overall nutrition, and I also freeze a lot of 'parts' of meals, like chicken stock and chopped vegetables, so I can cook fresh more quickly and healthfully."
     —Katie K., mom of 4

"Freezer cooking is like an emergency fund for my freezer. Having a stash of meal components at the ready turns my foodie crisis moments into mere inconveniences. It keeps us eating well and for a lot less!"
     —Amy M., mom of 6

Spring Vegetable Soup

Blended soups are one of the frugal cook's best friends. You can easily clean out the veggie drawer and waste not a carrot. Feel free to vary the veggies in this dish based on what you have on hand. This Spring Vegetable Soup is a perfect starter to a larger meal or a hearty accompaniment to a simple sandwich supper. // **Serves 4**

■ **PACKAGING:** Plastic containers with lids

¼ cup (60 ml) olive oil or butter
2 cups (200 g) thinly sliced leeks
2 teaspoons crushed garlic
2 large potatoes, chopped
   (about 2 cups [240 g])
2 large carrots, chopped
   (about 2 cups [240 g])

1 pound (454 g) asparagus spears,
   cut into ½-inch (1.3 cm) pieces
6 cups (1410 ml) vegetable broth
   or chicken stock, more as needed
Fine sea salt and freshly ground
   black pepper

1. In a large heavy pot over medium-high heat, heat the oil or melt the butter. Decrease the heat to low and cook the leeks and garlic until the leeks are tender, about 5 minutes.

2. Add the potatoes, carrot, asparagus, and broth. Bring to a boil. Reduce the heat and simmer, uncovered, for 20 minutes, or until the vegetables are tender.

3. Using an immersion blender, blend the soup until smooth. Alternatively, you can blend the soup in batches in a food processor.

4. Add more broth, if desired, to achieve your preferred consistency. Season to taste with salt and pepper.

FREEZING INSTRUCTIONS:

Divide the soup into meal-size portions in plastic containers. Chill in the refrigerator before freezing.

TO THAW AND SERVE:

Thaw the soup in the refrigerator. Reheat in a saucepan until heated through, stirring to recombine.

Mushroom-Barley Soup

Mushroom soup is earthy and hearty, the perfect option for a cold day. This version features an array of veggies and a dose of barley for good measure. Serve crackers or toast alongside for a simple soup supper. // *Serves 4*

6 tablespoons (84 g) butter
8 ounces (224 g) mushrooms, sliced
2 leeks, chopped
½ cup (80 g) chopped onion
1 cup (120 g) chopped carrots
1 cup (120 g) chopped celery
¼ cup (30 g) unbleached, all-purpose flour
6 cups (1410 ml) chicken or vegetable broth

1 cup (235 ml) milk
½ teaspoon fine sea salt
½ teaspoon paprika
½ teaspoon dried summer savory
½ teaspoon dried tarragon
¼ teaspoon black pepper
1 cup (200 g) quick-cooking barley
1 cup (150 g) frozen peas (no need to thaw)

1. In a large stockpot over medium heat, melt the butter. Add the mushrooms, leeks, and onion, cooking until the onions start to turn translucent, about 5 minutes. Add the carrots and celery and continue cooking another 5 minutes. The mushrooms should be tender and have given up their liquid.

2. Sprinkle the flour over the vegetables and stir. The flour will absorb the butter and other vegetable liquid. Add the chicken broth and milk as well as the salt, paprika, summer savory, tarragon, and pepper, stirring to combine. Bring the soup to a simmer, stirring occasionally.

3. Stir in the barley and cook over low heat for 15 minutes, or until the barley is soft. Stir in the peas in the last few minutes of cooking. Adjust the seasonings.

FREEZING INSTRUCTIONS:

Divide the soup into meal-size portions in plastic containers. Chill in the refrigerator before freezing.

TO THAW AND SERVE:

Thaw the soup in the refrigerator. Reheat in a saucepan until heated through, stirring to recombine.

Beef and Barley Soup with Dill

Beef and barley are a classic combination. They bring iron, protein, and that stick-to-your-ribs comfort that we often look for in soups. The addition of vegetables and dill to this soup makes it shine a little more brightly. Package it in 2-cup (470 ml) portions for easy lunches to take to the office or enjoy at home. // *Serves 8*

■ **PACKAGING:** Plastic containers with lids

2 tablespoons (30 ml) olive oil
2 pounds (908 g) boneless chuck roast,
    finely cubed
1 cup (160 g) chopped onion
1 teaspoon chopped garlic
½ cup (60 g) chopped celery
½ cup (38 g) chopped mushrooms

½ cup (60 g) chopped carrot
¾ cup (150 g) pearl barley, rinsed
½ cup (120 ml) white wine
8 cups (1880 ml) reduced-sodium beef broth
1 tablespoon chopped fresh dill
    or 1 teaspoon dried dill
Salt and freshly ground black pepper

1. In a large stockpot, heat the oil over medium heat until shimmering. Add the beef cubes and cook, stirring, for 5 minutes. Add the onion and garlic, and cook 5 minutes more. Add the celery, mushrooms, and carrot, and cook 5 minutes more.

2. Add the barley and cook, stirring, until the barley is lightly browned, 5 to 10 minutes.

3. Add the white wine and cook a minute or two, scraping up any browned bits. Stir in the beef broth and dill. Season to taste with salt and pepper.

4. Simmer the soup, partially covered, for 1 hour, or until the barley and beef are tender. Adjust the seasonings to taste.

FREEZING INSTRUCTIONS:

Divide the soup into meal-size portions in plastic containers. Chill in the refrigerator before freezing.

TO THAW AND SERVE:

Thaw the soup in the refrigerator. Reheat in a saucepan until heated through, stirring to recombine.

Black Bean Soup with Jalapeño

Some black bean soups are laden with bacon. While bacon is certainly not a bad thing, this soup is different in that the flavor of vegetables and beans shines through. Serve it with crusty bread and cheddar cheese or a dollop of sour cream. The soup can be prepared with dried beans, but for quicker cooking, use canned black beans. // *Serves 6 to 8*

■ **PACKAGING:** Plastic containers with lids

1 pound (454 g) dried black beans, rinsed, picked over, and soaked according to package directions, then drained, or four 15-ounce (420 g) cans black beans, rinsed and drained

6 cups (1410 ml) reduced-sodium chicken broth or vegetable broth

1 tablespoon (15 ml) olive oil

1 cup (120 g) shredded carrot

1 cup (160 g) chopped onion

1 cup (120 g) chopped celery

1 tablespoon finely chopped jalapeño pepper

1 teaspoon chopped garlic

1 cup (120 g) shredded potato

1 bay leaf

1 to 2 teaspoons kosher salt

1 teaspoon dried oregano

½ teaspoon ground cumin

¼ teaspoon freshly ground black pepper

1 tablespoon (15 ml) freshly squeezed lemon juice or lime juice

1. In a large stockpot, combine the soaked dried beans and broth. Bring to a boil and simmer for 2 hours, or until the beans are tender. If you're using canned beans, simply combine the beans and broth and move on to step 2.

2. In a large heavy skillet, heat the oil over medium heat until shimmering. Sauté the carrot, onion, celery, jalapeño, and garlic until crisp-tender, about 5 minutes.

3. Transfer the sautéed vegetables to the pot along with the shredded potato, bay leaf, salt, oregano, cumin, and pepper. Stir well and simmer for 1 hour.

4. Remove the bay leaf and discard it. Stir in the lemon juice. This is a chunky soup. If you prefer it smoother, puree the soup with an immersion blender or in a food processor or blender, in batches if necessary. Adjust the seasonings to taste.

FREEZING INSTRUCTIONS:

Divide the soup into meal-size portions in plastic containers. Chill in the refrigerator before freezing.

TO THAW AND SERVE:

Thaw the soup in the refrigerator. Reheat in a saucepan until heated through, stirring to recombine.

Tortilla Soup with Shrimp

Vegetables, seasonings, and broth combine to make a flavorful soup base that is frozen; shrimp are stirred in during the last few minutes of cooking to make it an extra-special bowl of goodness. For a less spicy soup, reduce or omit the jalapeños. // *Serves 8*

■ **PACKAGING:** Plastic containers with lids

2 tablespoons (30 ml) olive oil
1 cup (160 g) chopped onion
1 cup (120 g) sliced carrot
½ cup (75 g) chopped bell pepper
    (red, green, or a combination)
1 jalapeño pepper, finely chopped (optional)
One 14.5-ounce (406 g) can petite diced
    tomatoes with juices

One 15-ounce (420 g) can black beans,
    rinsed and drained
One 15.5-ounce (434 g) can hominy,
    rinsed and drained
7 cups (1645 ml) reduced-sodium
    chicken broth
1 teaspoon dried oregano
Salt and freshly ground black pepper

WHEN READY TO SERVE, YOU WILL NEED:

8 ounces (224 g) medium shrimp, shelled
    and deveined

Crushed tortilla chips
Chopped fresh cilantro

1. In a large stockpot, heat the oil over medium heat until shimmering. Add the onion and sauté until it starts to turn translucent, about 5 minutes.

2. Add the carrot, bell pepper, and jalapeño, and cook about 5 minutes more.

3. Stir in the tomatoes, black beans, hominy, broth, and oregano. Simmer for 20 minutes. Season with salt and pepper to taste.

FREEZING INSTRUCTIONS:

Divide the soup into meal-size portions in plastic containers. Chill in the refrigerator before freezing.

TO THAW AND SERVE:

Thaw the soup in the refrigerator. Reheat in a saucepan until heated through. Stir the shrimp into the soup. Continue cooking until the shrimp has turned pink, about 10 minutes. Place a small handful of crushed tortilla chips into each bowl. Ladle the hot soup over the chips. Top with chopped cilantro and serve immediately.

Fish Chowder with Red Potatoes and Corn

This chowder is full of flavor, with bell pepper, onion, potatoes, dill, and corn. Chunks of cod or salmon take it up a few notches. Prepare the base soup or sauce and freeze it, then add the fish right before serving. The fish cooks perfectly without getting overcooked. This method is a perfect blend of flavor and convenience. This chowder can easily make dinner for two nights. Consider dividing the chowder into two plastic containers with lids. // *Serves 8*

■ **PACKAGING:** Plastic containers with lids

1 tablespoon (15 ml) olive oil
½ cup (80 g) chopped onion
1 cup (150 g) chopped bell pepper
   (red, green, or a combination)
6 cups (1410 ml) Homemade Cream of
   Celery Soup for Cooking (page 238)
1½ cups (225 g) frozen or canned corn
   kernels, drained if canned

Grated zest of 1 lemon
2 tablespoons chopped fresh dill
   or 1 tablespoon dried dill
4 cups (about 2 pounds [908 g]) cooked
   and cubed red potatoes (microwave
   or steam them)
Water
Salt and freshly ground black pepper

WHEN READY TO SERVE, YOU WILL NEED:
10 ounces (280 g) salmon or cod fillets, cut
   into 1-inch (2.5 cm) cubes

1. In a large stockpot, heat the oil over medium heat until shimmering. Add the onion and sauté until the onion starts to become translucent, 3 to 4 minutes. Add the bell pepper and cook until tender, about 5 minutes.

2. Stir in the cream of celery soup, corn, lemon zest, dill, and potatoes. Add water to thin the soup to the desired consistency. Simmer the soup for 20 minutes. Season to taste with salt and pepper.

FREEZING INSTRUCTIONS:

Divide the chowder into meal-size portions in plastic containers. Chill in the refrigerator before freezing.

TO THAW AND SERVE:

Thaw the chowder in the refrigerator. Reheat in a saucepan until heated through, stirring to recombine. Stir the fish chunks into the hot chowder. Continue cooking until the fish is cooked through, 10 to 15 minutes. Adjust the seasonings to taste. Serve immediately.

Homemade Cream of Celery Soup for Cooking

Canned cream soup has been a resource for busy home cooks for more than 50 years. However, a quick glance at the label tells us that there might be better foods to feed our bodies. Cook up a bulk batch of this vegetarian cream of celery soup to use in cooking instead. For a richer flavor, use chicken broth or vegetable broth instead of water. // *Makes about 2 cups (470 ml)*

■ **PACKAGING:** Plastic container with lid

¼ cup (56 g) (½ stick) salted butter
¼ cup (30 g) unbleached all-purpose flour
1 cup (235 ml) milk
1 cup (235 ml) water
2 tablespoons (16 g) chopped celery

1 tablespoon freshly grated Parmesan cheese
1 teaspoon salt
¼ teaspoon freshly ground black pepper
¼ teaspoon onion powder
⅛ teaspoon paprika

1. In a large stockpot, melt the butter over medium heat. Stir in the flour and cook until the mixture bubbles. Cook 1 minute more, stirring.

2. Whisk in the milk and water, stirring constantly, until the mixture thickens to a sauce-like consistency.

3. Stir in the celery, Parmesan cheese, salt, black pepper, onion powder, and paprika. Simmer for 5 minutes.

FREEZING INSTRUCTIONS:

If using the soup in a recipe, cool it completely and proceed with the recipe. Otherwise, transfer the soup to a plastic container. Chill the soup in the refrigerator before freezing.

TO THAW AND SERVE:

Thaw the soup in the refrigerator. Use as directed in recipes.

Note: To make a big batch of this soup, simply multiply all the ingredients by four. The cooking method remains the same.

Chicken Cacciatore Stew

This chicken stew, made with tender white meat, sweet tomatoes, and woodsy mushrooms, is sure to please everyone at your table. And since you don't have to break a sweat to make it, you'll have a smile on your face as well. Serve it with crusty bread for a hearty meal. // *Serves 6 to 8*

■ **PACKAGING:** Plastic containers with lids

¼ cup (60 ml) olive oil
1 cup (160 g) chopped onion
1 red bell pepper, chopped
1 green bell pepper, chopped
8 ounces (224 g) fresh mushrooms,
    cleaned and quartered
One 14.5-ounce (406 g) can petite diced
    tomatoes with juices

One 15-ounce (420 g) can tomato sauce
4 pounds (1816 g) chicken tenders or
    boneless, skinless chicken breasts,
    cut into 1-inch (2.5 cm) chunks
1 teaspoon dried rosemary
Salt and freshly ground black pepper

1. In a large stockpot, heat the oil over medium heat until shimmering. Add the onion, bell peppers, and mushrooms, and cook until the vegetables are very tender, about 7 minutes.

2. Stir in the tomatoes, tomato sauce, chicken, and rosemary. Season generously with salt and pepper.

3. Bring to a simmer. Cover and cook on low heat for about 20 minutes, stirring occasionally, until the chicken is cooked through.

FREEZING INSTRUCTIONS:

Divide the stew into meal-size portions in plastic containers. Chill in the refrigerator before freezing.

TO THAW AND SERVE:

Thaw the stew in the refrigerator. Reheat it in a saucepan until heated through, stirring to recombine.

Our Favorite Irish Stew

This is our family's traditional St. Patrick's Day fare. The saint of the Emerald Isle had, of course, been a shepherd, and so this simple, authentic meal is one we share in his honor. It is delicious served with slices of Irish soda bread and chunks of Dubliner cheese. // *Serves 6 to 8*

■ **PACKAGING:** Plastic containers with lids

¼ cup (30 g) unbleached all-purpose flour
1 teaspoon salt
½ teaspoon freshly ground black pepper
2 pounds (908 g) chuck roast, cut into
   1-inch (2.5 cm) cubes
2 tablespoons (30 ml) vegetable oil

1 cup (160 g) finely chopped onion
½ cup (120 ml) beef broth
1 bay leaf
2 cups (240 g) baby carrots
4 medium potatoes, peeled and cut into
   1-inch (2.5 cm) chunks

1. Combine the flour, salt, and pepper in a large zip-top bag. Add the beef cubes, seal, and shake to coat all the cubes with the flour.

2. In a large skillet, heat the oil over medium heat until shimmering. Brown the beef cubes on all sides, in batches if necessary. As the meat browns, transfer it to a 5-quart (5 L) slow cooker.

3. Add the onion to the drippings in the skillet and sauté until tender, 5 to 7 minutes. Add the onions to the slow cooker.

4. Stir in the beef broth and the bay leaf. Cook the stew on LOW for 4 hours.

5. Add the carrots and potatoes and stir gently to combine. Cook on LOW 4 hours more, or until the meat and vegetables are tender. Adjust the seasonings to taste.

FREEZING INSTRUCTIONS:
Divide the stew into meal-size portions in plastic containers. Chill in the refrigerator before freezing.

TO THAW AND SERVE:
Thaw the stew in the refrigerator. Reheat in a saucepan until heated through.

Hearty Beef Stew with Olives

My four boys are self-proclaimed "meat-atarians." Though they do enjoy meatless meals, they absolutely devour this hearty beef stew boasting the bright flavor of lime and spicy chiles from the enchilada sauce. Serve it over rice or boiled potatoes. // *Serves 6 to 8*

■ **PACKAGING:** Plastic containers with lids

½ cup (60 g) unbleached all-purpose flour
1 teaspoon salt
½ teaspoon freshly ground black pepper
2 pounds (908 g) boneless chuck roast,
  cubed
2 tablespoons (30 ml) olive oil
½ cup (80 g) chopped onion

¼ cup (60 ml) freshly squeezed lime juice
¼ cup (60 ml) canned red chile sauce
  or enchilada sauce
1½ teaspoons dried oregano
One 5-ounce (140 g) jar green Spanish
  olives (with or without pimientos),
  drained

1. Combine the flour, salt, and pepper in a large zip-top bag. Add the beef cubes, seal, and shake to coat all the cubes with the flour.

2. In a large skillet, heat the oil over medium heat until shimmering. Brown the beef cubes, in batches if necessary. Transfer the browned beef to a 4-quart (4 L) slow cooker.

3. Add the onion to the skillet and cook, stirring, until it starts to become translucent, about 5 minutes. Add the lime juice, stirring to scrape up any browned bits. Add the enchilada sauce and oregano and stir to combine.

4. Transfer this mixture to the slow cooker. Cook the stew on LOW for 6 to 8 hours. In the last 20 minutes of cooking, stir in the green olives. Adjust the seasonings to taste.

FREEZING INSTRUCTIONS:

Divide the stew into meal-size portions in plastic containers. Chill in the refrigerator before freezing.

TO THAW AND SERVE:

Thaw the stew in the refrigerator. Reheat in a saucepan until heated through.

Beef Stew with Eggplant and Carrots

For a cozy supper of comfort food, this stew hits the mark; it is absolutely delicious, especially when served over mashed potatoes. The eggplant adds richness and great flavor. // *Serves 8*

SOUP'S ON

■ **PACKAGING:** Plastic containers with lids

¼ cup (60 ml) olive oil, divided
3 pounds (1362 g) boneless chuck roast,
    cut into 1-inch (2.5 cm) cubes
Salt and freshly ground black pepper
1 medium-size onion, diced
3 cloves garlic, minced
2 bay leaves

3 tablespoons (24 g) unbleached
    all-purpose flour
2 teaspoons dried thyme
2 cups (470 ml) reduced-sodium beef broth
2 cups (165 g) peeled and diced eggplant
2 cups (240 g) peeled and sliced carrots

WHEN READY TO SERVE, YOU WILL NEED:
Cream Cheese Mashed Potatoes (page 86)
    or other favorite mashed potatoes

1. In a large skillet, heat 2 tablespoons (30 ml) of the oil over medium heat until shimmering. Brown the beef cubes on all sides, in batches if necessary. Transfer the beef to a 5-quart (5 L) slow cooker and season with salt and pepper.

2. Add the onion and garlic to the drippings in the skillet. Sauté until translucent, about 5 minutes. Add the bay leaves, flour, and thyme. Stir to combine. Stir in the beef broth, scraping up any browned bits. Transfer the broth and onion mixture to the slow cooker. Cook on LOW for 4 hours.

3. In a large skillet, heat the remaining 2 tablespoons (30 ml) olive oil over medium-high heat until shimmering. Sauté the eggplant, stirring, for about 7 minutes. Stir the eggplant and the carrots into the stew in the slow cooker. Continue to cook 2 hours more. Season to taste with salt and pepper.

FREEZING INSTRUCTIONS:

Divide the stew into meal-size portions in plastic containers. Chill in the refrigerator before freezing.

TO THAW AND SERVE:

Thaw the stew in the refrigerator. Reheat in a saucepan until heated through. Serve over mashed potatoes.

Quick and Easy Texas Chili

A traditional bowl of red is simply meat and chiles—no beans. While beans certainly fill the dish with fiber, they aren't acceptable as a chili ingredient in some parts of the country. And the no-beans variety is extremely tasty and freezer-friendly. Serve this Texas-style chili over chips or with cornbread. It can even fill up burritos or be served over hot cooked noodles. Feel free to make this with ground turkey; simply reduce the cayenne pepper to ¼ teaspoon, to complement the milder flavor of turkey. // *Serves 4 to 6*

■ **PACKAGING:** Plastic containers with lids

2½ pounds (1135 g) ground beef or ground turkey	**2 tablespoons chili powder**
1 medium-size onion, chopped	**1 teaspoon salt**
2 cloves garlic, minced	**1 teaspoon dried oregano**
One 15-ounce (420 g) can tomato sauce	**1 teaspoon ground cumin**
	½ teaspoon cayenne pepper

1. In a large pot, cook the ground beef, onion, and garlic over medium heat, stirring, until the meat is browned and the onion starts to turn translucent, about 10 minutes.

2. Stir in the tomato sauce, chili powder, salt, oregano, cumin, and cayenne pepper. Simmer for 15 minutes, stirring occasionally. Adjust the seasonings to taste.

FREEZING INSTRUCTIONS:

Divide the chili into meal-size portions in plastic containers. Chill in the refrigerator before freezing.

TO THAW AND SERVE:

Thaw the chili in the refrigerator. Reheat in a saucepan until heated through. Serve immediately.

Chihuahua Chili

I've been making this chili for more than two decades. It's flavorful and filling, with just enough kick. When I'm going to feed a crowd, this is my go-to, easy-to-serve recipe. Just dish up bowls of red, offer a selection of toppings and a basket of bread and butter, and you're good to go. If you'd like, you can make this in the slow cooker. After you sauté the onions and garlic, simply combine all of the ingredients in a 5-quart (5 L) slow cooker and cook on LOW for 6 to 8 hours // *Serves 8 to 12*

■ **PACKAGING:** Plastic containers with lids

1 pound (454 g) ground beef

2 cups (320 g) chopped onion

3 tablespoons (24 g) chopped garlic

Two 29-ounce (812 g) cans or four 15-ounce (420 g) cans pinto beans, rinsed and drained

Two 15-ounce (420 g) cans black beans, rinsed and drained

2 cups (470 ml) tomato sauce

1 cup (235 ml) enchilada sauce

One 12-ounce (340 ml) bottle beer

1 tablespoon ground cumin

1 tablespoon chili powder

WHEN READY TO SERVE, YOU WILL NEED:

Sour cream

Shredded cheddar cheese

Chopped fresh cilantro

1. In a large pot, cook the ground beef, onion, and garlic over medium heat, stirring, until the meat is browned and the onion starts to turn translucent, about 10 minutes.

2. Add the beans, tomato sauce, enchilada sauce, beer, cumin, and chili powder. Stir the mixture well to combine.

3. Bring the chili to a low boil. Reduce the heat to low. Simmer, partially covered, until the chili is slightly thickened and the flavors have mingled, about 1 hour.

FREEZING INSTRUCTIONS:

Divide the chili into meal-size portions in plastic containers. Chill in the refrigerator before freezing.

TO THAW AND SERVE:

Thaw the chili in the refrigerator. Reheat in a saucepan until heated through. Serve immediately with the sour cream, cheese, and cilantro.

Tres Chiles Chili Con Quinoa

Quinoa, that pseudo-cereal that's hard to pronounce, is packed with protein, which makes it a great addition to a meatless chili. While it can have a strong flavor by itself on a plate, blended into a robust chile sauce? Trust me, your kids won't even notice it. I love the spicy flavors of this three-chile chili. If you can't find pasilla chile powder, feel free to use ancho chile powder instead.

■ **PACKAGING:** Plastic containers with lids

2 tablespoons (30 ml) olive oil
½ cup (80 g) chopped onion
1 jalapeño chile, seeded and chopped
1 clove garlic, minced
2 tablespoons pasilla chile powder
1 teaspoon ground cumin
1 teaspoon dried oregano
One 15-ounce (420 g) can tomato sauce
2 cups (470 ml) chicken stock
¾ cup (135 g) uncooked quinoa, rinsed
Two 15.5-ounce (434 g) cans black beans,
    rinsed and drained

Two 15.5-ounce (434 g) cans kidney beans,
    rinsed and drained
Two 15.5-ounce (434 g) cans pinto beans,
    rinsed and drained
One 14.5-ounce (406 g) can diced tomatoes
    with their juices
One 4-ounce (112 g) can chopped
    green chiles with juices
Fine sea salt and freshly ground
    black pepper

WHEN READY TO SERVE, YOU WILL NEED:

Shredded cheese
Salsa
Sour cream

Chopped avocado
Chopped fresh cilantro

1. In a large stockpot over medium heat, heat the oil until shimmering. Cook the onion, jalapeño, and garlic until the onions start to become translucent, about 5 minutes.

2. Add the pasilla chile powder, cumin, and oregano. Stir to combine. Stir in the tomato sauce and then the chicken stock. Bring to a low simmer.

3. Add the quinoa, beans, tomatoes, and green chiles. Bring to a simmer. Reduce the heat to low and cover. Simmer for about 20 minutes, or until the quinoa is tender. Adjust the seasonings with salt and pepper to taste.

FREEZING INSTRUCTIONS:

Divide the chili into meal-size portions in plastic containers. Chill in the refrigerator before freezing.

TO THAW AND SERVE:

Thaw the chili in the refrigerator. Reheat in a saucepan until heated through. Serve with the accompaniments.

Smoky Multi-Bean Vegetarian Chili

Going meatless can be a great way to cut costs and improve health. This chili, adapted from one Jessika shared with me years ago, is full of fiber from beans and lentils. It also boasts a warm, smoky flavor from the ground chipotle chile powder. You can certainly use regular chili powder, but you'll miss out on the smoked flavor of the chipotles. // *Serves 8 to 10*

■ **PACKAGING:** Plastic containers with lids

2 tablespoons (30 ml) olive oil
1 cup (160 g) chopped onion
3 cloves garlic, chopped
½ cup (75 g) chopped red or green
   bell pepper
One 4-ounce (112 g) can chopped
   green chiles
2 teaspoons ground cumin
1 teaspoon chipotle chile powder
1 teaspoon fine sea salt
½ teaspoon dried oregano

2 cups (470 ml) water
Two 15-ounce (420 g) cans black beans,
   rinsed and drained
One 15-ounce (420 g) can red beans, rinsed
   and drained
1½ cups (225 g) frozen or canned corn,
   drained if canned
1 cup (200 g) lentils, rinsed and picked over
1 cup (235 ml) tomato sauce
Salt and freshly ground black pepper

1. In a large stockpot over medium heat, heat the oil until shimmering. Cook the onions and garlic until the onion starts to become translucent, about 5 minutes.

2. Add the bell pepper, chiles, cumin, chipotle chile powder, salt, and oregano. Stir to combine, reduce the heat to low, and cook for about a minute.

3. Add the water, beans, corn, lentils, and tomato sauce. Bring to a boil. Reduce the heat to low and cover. Simmer for about 1 hour, or until the lentils are tender. Alternatively, you can cook the chili in a 5-quart (5 L) slow cooker on LOW for 4 to 6 hours. Adjust the seasonings with salt and pepper to taste.

FREEZING INSTRUCTIONS:

Divide the chili into meal-size portions in plastic containers. Chill in the refrigerator before freezing.

TO THAW AND SERVE:

Thaw the chili in the refrigerator. Reheat in a saucepan until heated through.

7

PERFECT PIZZAS

▸ Basic Pizza Dough ▪ 249

▸ Tomato and Herb Pizza Sauce ▪ 251

▸ Easy-Peasy Cheesy Pizza ▪ 253

▸ Burrito Pizza ▪ 254

▸ Jalapeño Burn Pizza ▪ 256

▸ Pesto Pizza with Shrimp, Feta, and Tomatoes ▪ 258

▸ Barbecue Cheeseburger Pizza ▪ 259

▸ French Bread Pizza Dippers ▪ 260

▸ Deep-Dish Focaccia Pizza Your Way ▪ 262

▸ Chicken and Sun-Dried Tomato Pizza with Goat Cheese ▪ 262

▸ Pepperoni Calzones ▪ 263

▸ Spinach and Cheese Calzones ▪ 264

Basic Pizza Dough

Many grocery stores now sell pizza dough in the refrigerated section. But it's not difficult to make your own. By doing so, you can customize the ingredients and save money. To speed things up, I use a bread machine or stand mixer to prepare the dough. This gives me a more consistent texture and keeps the kitchen cleaner. But you can very easily mix and knead this dough by hand, if you prefer.

Preparing the dough takes about 2 hours from start to finish. However, I can break up that prep time by mixing and freezing the dough one day and letting it thaw and rise another day. This helps me use my time in the kitchen more efficiently.

For bulk dough making, I usually start one batch in the bread machine and then get my KitchenAid stand mixer going on another. I freeze the dough after it has risen for only 30 minutes, placing each greased dough ball in a plastic sandwich bag and then storing them in a larger freezer bag or paired with other ingredients in a pizza kit. // ***Makes enough dough for four 12-inch (30.5 cm) pizzas or 8 individual-size pizzas***

> ■ **PACKAGING:** Zip-top sandwich bags, gallon-size (4 L) zip-top freezer bag

1½ cups (355 ml) water
¼ cup (60 ml) olive oil
2 tablespoons (40 g) honey or (25 g) sugar
4½ cups (540 g) unbleached all-purpose
    flour (you can substitute up to 1 cup
    [120 g] whole-wheat flour for an
    equivalent amount of all-purpose flour)

1 tablespoon (18 g) salt
1 tablespoon active dry yeast

IF MAKING DOUGH IN A BREAD MACHINE:

Combine all of the ingredients in the bread machine pan in the order recommended by the manufacturer. Set the machine to the dough cycle and start it, checking after 10 minutes to make sure all of the ingredients have been incorporated and are not stuck to the side of the pan. Once the mixing cycle is complete, allow the dough to rise for 30 minutes.

IF MAKING DOUGH IN A STAND MIXER:

Combine the water and honey in the bowl of the stand mixer. Sprinkle the yeast over the top and allow it to proof for 5 minutes. Add the oil, 2 cups (240 g) of the flour, and the salt. Fit the mixer with the dough hook and beat on low speed. Once the dough starts to come together, 1 to 2 minutes, increase the speed a notch. Knead the dough, gradually adding more flour until a dough ball forms. Knead the dough 2 minutes more. Transfer the dough to a greased bowl and turn it to coat it with oil. Allow the dough to rise for 30 minutes.

IF MAKING DOUGH BY HAND:

In a large bowl, combine the water, oil, honey, and yeast, and allow to proof for 5 minutes. Add the flour and salt, stirring with a wooden spoon until a stiff dough forms. Turn the dough out onto a lightly floured surface and knead for 5 minutes, or until the dough has a smooth, elastic feel. Add more flour if necessary. Transfer the dough to a greased bowl and turn it to coat it with oil. Allow the dough to rise for 30 minutes.

TO FINISH THE DOUGH:

When the dough is ready, use greased hands to divide it into 4 or 8 portions, as desired. Shape each portion into a ball. Place each dough ball into a sandwich bag and freeze immediately. The dough will continue to rise and you want to arrest that process, so the sooner it is frozen, the better.

FREEZING INSTRUCTIONS:

Package the dough balls with other pizza ingredients to make kits or in one large zip-top freezer bag.

TO THAW AND SERVE:

Remove the frozen dough from the freezer. Remove the dough from the bag and place in a greased bowl; if thawing more than one dough ball, place on a greased baking pan. Allow the dough to rise for 6 to 8 hours in the refrigerator or for 3 hours at room temperature. If the dough has risen in the refrigerator, let it sit at room temperature for 30 minutes before forming, topping, and baking.

▶ Make Your Own Sauce Ahead of Time

I almost always have several pints or quarts of Easy Slow Cooker Red Sauce (page 217) in the freezer. It's a multipurpose sauce that works well for pizza, lasagna, and pasta.

But when I want to make things a little extra-special, I mix up a bulk batch of the following pizza sauce. You can portion it into ½-cup containers—just the right amount for a 12-inch (30.5 cm) pizza—and store them in the freezer. It's also good on pasta.

Tomato and Herb Pizza Sauce

This flavorful sauce comes together in minutes. Inspired by the sauce at California Pizza Kitchen, it is a delicious topping for pizzas and dip for Calzones (pages 263 to 265) and French Bread Pizza Dippers (page 260). // *Makes about 4½ cups (1060 ml)*

▪ **PACKAGING:** Plastic containers with lids

¼ cup (60 ml) olive oil
2 teaspoons minced garlic
One 28-ounce (784 g) can petite diced
    tomatoes with juices
3 tablespoons chopped fresh basil
    or 1 tablespoon dried basil

1 teaspoon salt
½ teaspoon dried oregano
¼ teaspoon red pepper flakes
One 6-ounce (168 g) can tomato paste

1. In a large saucepan, heat the olive oil over medium heat until shimmering. Stir in the garlic and cook until just barely browned.

2. Add the tomatoes, basil, salt, oregano, and red pepper flakes. Simmer until the juices have started to evaporate slightly, about 10 minutes.

3. Stir in the tomato paste and cook 3 minutes more. This is a chunky sauce. Use it as is or puree it with an immersion blender or in a food processor. Let cool.

FREEZING INSTRUCTIONS:

Divide the sauce into desired portions in plastic containers. Cool completely. Cover and chill in the refrigerator before freezing.

TO THAW AND SERVE:

Thaw the sauce in the refrigerator. Use as a topping or dip.

▶ Pizza Night Is a Highlight of Our Week—with Pizza Kits on Hand

For many folks, pizza night is a great way to kick off the weekend, celebrate a team's victory, or otherwise enjoy a casual meal with friends and family. And many of us rely on the pizza parlor or the frozen-food section of the grocery store to provide this culinary delight.

But homemade pizza can be as good as or better than commercial versions. And if you've got a few pizza kits in your freezer, you'll be set for a delicious dinner with a minimal amount of work.

I often spend Friday afternoons assembling the makings of homemade pizza, which I bake in the oven or cook on the grill. We enjoy it with vegetable dippers and homemade ranch dressing or a mixed salad. Then after kitchen cleanup (or not), we watch a movie and officially enter the weekend.

Most members of my younger crew prefer simple cheese or pepperoni pizzas, while the more mature ones in our family opt for the Jalapeño Burn Pizza (page 256), Burrito Pizza (page 254), or Pesto Pizza with Shrimp, Feta, and Tomatoes (page 258).

The trick to making these pizza nights relaxing is to have pizza kits at the ready. Homemade sauce, pizza dough, shredded cheese, and other toppings can be prepared ahead and stored in the freezer, ready to grab and thaw in the refrigerator.

All kinds of frozen meal components can come together in a beautiful way for pizza night. A barbecue sauce pairs well with shredded chicken on one pizza, while a homemade sauce and shredded cheese come together on another. It's easy to make several kinds of pizza on one night if you have the fixings portioned and ready to go.

Creating pizza kits also helps you make good use of your bulk shopping items, like those large bags of cheese you might buy at a warehouse club. Don't fear the 5-pound (2270 g) bag of cheese. That's the most economical way to buy shredded mozzarella. Simply divide the cheese into quart-size (1 L) freezer bags when you bring it home. Put ½ pound (224 g, about 2 cups) of cheese in each bag, enough for a pizza, depending on how cheesy you like it. Stash the bags in the freezer or, for even greater efficiency, combine them with other components in a pizza kit.

The easiest way to put together pizza kits is to bundle all the components together in a gallon-size (4 L) zip-top freezer bag. Label the bag (be sure to note what kind of pizza fixings it contains), and include a bag of pizza dough, a bag of cheese, a container of sauce, and any other freezable toppings you would like.

Easy-Peasy Cheesy Pizza

This cheese pizza is delicious—and easy. It's utterly simple, but it still packs a punch of flavor. The combination of cheeses makes it especially delicious. My baby girl, now nine, deems it her favorite pizza EVER, though she does like to bake an egg on top from time to time. // *Makes one 12-inch (30.5 cm) pizza*

- **PACKAGING:** Quart- (1 L) or pint-size (470 ml) bag, snack-size bag, plastic container with lid or additional snack-size bag, gallon-size (4 L) zip-top freezer bag

¾ cup (90 g) shredded mozzarella cheese

¾ cup (90 g) shredded Monterey Jack cheese

¼ cup (25 g) Parmesan Herb Blend (page 255)

½ cup (120 ml) Tomato and Herb Pizza Sauce (page 251)

¼ batch frozen, bagged Basic Pizza Dough (page 249)

1. Place the mozzarella and Jack cheeses in the quart- (1 L) or pint-size (470 ml) bag. Place the Parmesan Herb Blend in the snack-size bag. Place the pizza sauce in a plastic container or a snack-size bag.

2. Place the two bags of cheese and the container of sauce, along with the frozen pizza dough, in the gallon-size (4 L) zip-top freezer bag. Store in the freezer.

TO THAW AND SERVE:

Remove the pizza kit from the freezer. Grease a medium bowl. Unwrap the pizza dough and place it in the greased bowl. Thaw it in the refrigerator for 6 to 8 hours, covered. Thaw the other items in the kit in the refrigerator. Preheat the oven to 475°F (240°C or gas mark 9). Allow the dough to sit at room temperature for about 30 minutes. Stretch the dough to fit a 12-inch (30.5 cm) pizza pan. Spread the sauce over the prepared dough. Sprinkle the mozzarella mixture over the sauce. Sprinkle the Parmesan Herb Blend over the top. Bake the pizza for 10 to 12 minutes, or until the crust is crisp and the cheese is melted and starting to brown. Cool slightly before slicing and serving.

Burrito Pizza

It is such a fun surprise to serve this pizza to friends and family. My brother and sister-in-law were stunned at the idea, but they were fast fans. For this simple and delicious pizza, black beans are layered on the crust and topped with cheese and vegetables. Serve it with shredded lettuce, sour cream, salsa, and guacamole. SO good! // *Makes one 12-inch (30.5 cm) pizza, serves 4*

■ **PACKAGING:** Quart- (1 L) or pint-size (470 ml) bag, two snack-size bags, gallon-size (4 L) zip-top freezer bag

1 cup (120 g) shredded mozzarella cheese
½ cup (60 g) shredded cheddar cheese
½ cup (80 g) chopped onion

1 jalapeño pepper, thinly sliced
¼ batch frozen, bagged Basic Pizza Dough (page 249)

WHEN READY TO SERVE, YOU WILL NEED:
One 15-ounce (420 g) can black beans, rinsed and drained
½ cup (90 g) diced tomato
¼ cup (25 g) sliced black olives

Shredded lettuce
Easy Homemade Salsa (page 77)
Super-Simple Guacamole (page 77)
Sour cream

1. Place the mozzarella and cheddar cheeses in the quart- (1 L) or pint-size (470 ml) bag. Place the chopped onion in a snack-size bag and seal. Place the sliced jalapeño in another snack-size bag and seal.

2. Place the bagged cheese, jalapeño, and onion, along with the bag of frozen pizza dough, in the gallon-size (4 L) zip-top freezer bag. Store in the freezer.

TO THAW AND SERVE:

Remove the pizza kit from the freezer. Grease a medium bowl. Unwrap the pizza dough and place it in the greased bowl. Thaw it in the refrigerator for 6 to 8 hours, covered. Thaw the other items in the kit in the refrigerator. Preheat the oven to 475°F (240°C or gas mark 9). Allow the dough to sit at room temperature for about 30 minutes. Stretch the dough to fit a 12-inch (30.5 cm) pizza pan. Spread the black beans over the prepared dough. Sprinkle with 1 cup (120 g) of the mozzarella mixture. Layer the tomato, onion, jalapeño, and black olives over the cheese. Sprinkle the remaining ½ cup (60 g) cheese over the top. Bake for 10 to 12 minutes, or until the crust is crisp and the cheese is melted and golden in spots. Cool slightly before slicing. Serve with the shredded lettuce, salsa, guacamole, and sour cream.

Parmesan Herb Blend

This mixture is delicious stirred into sauces, sprinkled on salads or steamed vegetables, or used to season herb butters. Toss hot cooked pasta with olive oil and a few tablespoons of this mixture for an easy side dish. Mix up a batch at the beginning of a freezer cooking session and use it to add instant flavor to a number of dishes, including Easy-Peasy Cheesy Pizza (page 253). // *Makes about 1 cup (100 g)*

■ **PACKAGING:** Pint-size (470 ml) zip-top freezer bag or plastic container with lid

1 cup (100 g) grated Parmesan cheese
1 tablespoon chopped fresh parsley
   or 1 teaspoon dried parsley flakes
1 teaspoon garlic powder
¾ teaspoon chopped fresh basil
   or ¼ teaspoon dried basil

¼ teaspoon dried oregano
¼ teaspoon dried thyme
⅛ teaspoon freshly ground black pepper

In a small bowl, gently mix all of the ingredients.

FREEZING INSTRUCTIONS:
Freeze the cheese blend in a freezer bag or airtight container.

▶ Pizza Baking and Grilling Tips

Make sure the oven is hot! Preheat the oven for at least 30 minutes to ensure a great crust.

You can use a pizza stone if you like, but it isn't necessary. I don't use a special stone, and I've been able to cook beautiful pizzas on regular baking sheets, greased and sometimes sprinkled with cornmeal. I also have a couple of perforated round pizza pans and pizza screens, which I love, and they serve as my go-to pizza tools.

Consider cooking pizza on the grill. If you have the dough and sauce prepared in advance, grilled pizzas come together in a very short time. This method works best for individual pizzas. Brush the grill grate with oil to prevent sticking. Heat the grill. Place the formed pizza dough on the hot grill and close the lid. Cook until the bottom of the dough appears cooked, 5 to 10 minutes, depending on how hot your grill is. Flip the crust and add your sauce and toppings on the cooked side. Continue to cook until the crust is crisp and browned and the toppings are hot, another 5 to 15 minutes, depending on the heat inside your grill.

Jalapeño Burn Pizza

Those who love spicy food will get a real kick out of this pizza. Red pepper flakes and sliced jalapeños offer heat, while the tomatoes refresh your palate and the cheese helps cool the burn. It's particularly good served with chopped fresh avocado added after the pizza comes out of the oven.
// *Makes one 12-inch (30.5 cm) pizza, serves 4*

- **PACKAGING:** Quart- (1 L) or pint-size (470 ml) bag, two snack-size bags, sandwich bag, gallon-size (4 L) zip-top freezer bag

1 cup (120 g) shredded mozzarella cheese
½ cup (60 g) shredded cheddar cheese
½ cup (80 g) chopped onion
2 jalapeño peppers, thinly sliced

1 cup (140 g) chopped cooked chicken
¼ batch frozen, bagged Basic Pizza Dough
  (page 249)

WHEN READY TO SERVE, YOU WILL NEED:
1 tablespoon (15 ml) olive oil
Red pepper flakes
1 medium tomato, diced

¼ cup (25 g) sliced black olives
1 medium avocado, peeled, pitted,
  and chopped

1. Place the mozzarella and cheddar cheeses in the quart- (1 L) or pint-size (470 ml) bag. Place the chopped onion in a snack-size bag. Place the sliced jalapeño in another snack-size bag. Place the chopped chicken in the sandwich bag and seal.

2. Place the bagged cheese, onion, jalapeño, and chicken, along with the bag of frozen pizza dough, in the gallon-size (4 L) zip-top freezer bag. Store in the freezer.

TO THAW AND SERVE:

Remove the pizza kit from the freezer. Grease a medium bowl. Unwrap the pizza dough and place it in the greased bowl. Thaw it in the refrigerator for 6 to 8 hours, covered. Thaw the other items in the kit in the refrigerator. Preheat the oven to 475°F (240°C or gas mark 9). Allow the dough to sit at room temperature for about 30 minutes. Stretch the dough to fit a 12-inch (30.5 cm) pizza pan. Spread the oil over the prepared pizza dough. Sprinkle with red pepper flakes to taste and 1 cup (120 g) of the mozzarella mixture. Layer the chicken, tomato, onion, jalapeños, and black olives over the cheese. Sprinkle the remaining ½ cup (60 g) cheese over the top. Bake for 10 to 12 minutes, or until the crust is crisp and the cheese is melted and golden in spots. Cool slightly, sprinkle chopped avocado over the pizza, slice, and serve.

Pesto Pizza with Shrimp, Feta, and Tomatoes

A restaurant I once worked in served a pasta dish with pesto, shrimp, and some salty garnishes. I've re-created it on a pizza, adding feta for tang and tomatoes for sweetness and juicy texture.
// *Makes one 12-inch (30.5 cm) pizza, serves 4*

■ **PACKAGING:** Quart-size (1 L) zip-top freezer bag, sandwich-size bag, plastic container with lid or snack-size bag, gallon-size (4 L) zip-top freezer bag

16 medium-size shrimp, peeled and deveined
½ cup (60 g) crumbled feta cheese

½ cup (120 ml) pesto
¼ batch frozen, bagged Basic Pizza Dough (page 249)

WHEN READY TO SERVE, YOU WILL NEED:
1 cup chopped tomatoes

1. Place the shrimp in the quart-size (1 L) zip-top freezer bag. Place the feta cheese crumbles in the sandwich-size bag. Place the pesto in a plastic container or snack-size bag.

2. Place the bags of shrimp and cheese and the container of pesto, along with the bag of frozen pizza dough, in the gallon-size (4 L) zip-top freezer bag. Store in the freezer.

TO THAW AND SERVE:
Remove the pizza kit from the freezer. Grease a medium bowl. Unwrap the pizza dough and place it in the greased bowl. Thaw it in the refrigerator for 6 to 8 hours, covered. Thaw the other items in the kit in the refrigerator. Preheat the oven to 475°F (240°C or gas mark 9). Allow the dough to sit at room temperature for about 30 minutes. Stretch the dough to fit a 12-inch (30.5 cm) pizza pan. Spread the pesto over the prepared dough. Scatter the shrimp over the sauce. Sprinkle the feta cheese over the shrimp. Sprinkle the tomatoes over the top of the pizza. Bake the pizza for 10 minutes, or until the crust is crisp, the shrimp are pink, and the cheese is slightly melted and starting to brown. Cool slightly before slicing and serving.

Barbecue Cheeseburger Pizza

It's amazing what flavors you can put on a pizza! You really can re-create some of your favorite meals on a flatbread. Fresh toppings make this pie extra-special. This pizza tastes like a barbecue cheeseburger, complete with a smoky sauce, seasoned ground beef, cheddar cheese, and a topping of red onion, tomatoes, and shredded lettuce. // *Makes one 12-inch (30.5 cm) pizza, serves 4*

■ **PACKAGING:** Quart-size (1 L) zip-top freezer bag, quart- (1 L) or pint-size (470 ml) bag, plastic container with lid or snack-size bag, gallon-size (4 L) zip-top freezer bag

1 cup (200 g) seasoned taco meat
   (sidebar, page 97)
1 cup (120 g) shredded mozzarella cheese
½ cup (60 g) shredded cheddar cheese

½ cup (120 ml) Barbecue Sauce for
   Meatballs (page 106)
¼ batch frozen, bagged Basic Pizza Dough
   (page 249)

WHEN READY TO SERVE, YOU WILL NEED:
1 cup (180 g) chopped tomato
1 cup (70 g) shredded lettuce

¼ cup (40 g) chopped red onion

1. Place the taco meat in the quart-size (1 L) zip-top freezer bag. Place the mozzarella and cheddar cheese in the quart- (1 L) or pint-size (470 ml) bag. Place the barbecue sauce in a plastic container or snack-size bag.

2. Place the bags of meat and cheese and the container of sauce, along with the bag of frozen pizza dough, in the gallon-size (4 L) zip-top freezer bag. Store in the freezer.

TO THAW AND SERVE:

Remove the pizza kit from the freezer. Grease a medium bowl. Unwrap the pizza dough and place it in the greased bowl. Thaw it in the refrigerator for 6 to 8 hours, covered. Thaw the other items in the kit in the refrigerator. Preheat the oven to 475°F (240°C or gas mark 9). Allow the dough to sit at room temperature for about 30 minutes. Stretch the dough to fit a 12-inch (30.5 cm) pizza pan. Spread the barbecue sauce over the prepared dough. Sprinkle the taco meat over the sauce. Sprinkle the mozzarella mixture over the meat. Bake the pizza for 10 minutes, or until the crust is crisp and the cheese is slightly melted and starting to brown. Cool slightly before slicing. Serve topped with the tomato, lettuce, and red onion.

French Bread Pizza Dippers

I love to experiment with pizza, and one way to do that is with different pizza bases. Large flour tortillas work in a pinch for quick lunchtime thin-crust pizzas. And bagel and English muffin pizzas have long been a kids' standby. When I set out to find a way to make French bread pizza work for freezer meals, the answer was a baguette pizza "dipper." Similar in spirit to the *tartine*, or baguette spread with butter and jam that I dipped into my breakfast coffee when I lived in France, this is a pizza baguette spread with garlic butter and mozzarella cheese that's dipped in a homemade pizza sauce. The result is a deliciously crisp, cheesy pizza bread that waits happily in the freezer until a pizza craving hits.

// *Serves 2 generously*

■ **PACKAGING:** Gallon-size (4 L) zip-top freezer bag

¼ cup (56 g) (½ stick) salted butter, softened
1 teaspoon chopped garlic

1 traditional French baguette, about 24 inches (61 cm) long, cut into thirds and split horizontally
8 ounces (224 g) sliced mozzarella cheese

WHEN READY TO SERVE, YOU WILL NEED:
1 cup (235 ml) Tomato and Herb Pizza Sauce (page 251) or other favorite red sauce, warmed

1. In a small mixing bowl, combine the butter and garlic. Spread the garlic butter on each of the six baguette pieces.

2. Layer the mozzarella cheese over the garlic butter.

FREEZING INSTRUCTIONS:

Place the cheese-topped bread pieces in the freezer bag. Remove as much air as possible and seal. Freeze.

TO THAW AND SERVE:

Thaw the bread in the refrigerator. Preheat the oven to 475°F (240°C or gas mark 9). Place the bread on a baking sheet. Bake for 5 to 10 minutes, until the cheese is melted and starting to brown slightly and the crust is crisp. Serve with the warmed sauce on the side for dipping.

Deep-Dish Focaccia Pizza Your Way

Focaccia makes a wonderful base for pizza that's reminiscent of pizza parlor deep-dish pizza. Keep rounds of freshly baked focaccia in your freezer for pizza that comes together almost as quickly as opening a box of frozen pizza. // *Makes three 8-inch (20.3 cm) deep-dish-style pizzas*

- **PACKAGING:** Plastic wrap, plastic container with lid, quart- (1 L) or pint-size (470 ml) zip-top freezer bag, 2-gallon-size (8 L) zip-top freezer bag

1 recipe Garlic Focaccia (page 331)
¾ cup (180 ml) Tomato and Herb Pizza
  Sauce (page 251)

1½ cups (180 g) shredded mozzarella
  cheese

WHEN READY TO SERVE, YOU WILL NEED:
Your favorite toppings, such as sliced
  pepperoni, sliced mushrooms, sliced

tomatoes, chopped onions, chopped
  tomatoes—you name it

1. Wrap the baked and cooled focaccia rounds in plastic wrap. Place the sauce in a small plastic container with a lid. Place the cheese in a quart- (1 L) or pint-size (470 ml) zip-top freezer bag.

2. Place the focaccia, the container of sauce, and the bag of cheese in the 2-gallon (8 L) bag. Freeze.

TO THAW AND SERVE:
Thaw the pizza kit in the refrigerator. Preheat the oven to 475°F (240°C or gas mark 9). Place the focaccia rounds on baking sheets. Spread the sauce over the bread. Sprinkle the cheese over the sauce. Add any other toppings you desire. Bake the pizza for 5 to 10 minutes, or until the crust is crisp and the cheese is slightly melted and starting to brown. Cool slightly before slicing and serving.

Chicken and Sun-Dried Tomato Pizza with Goat Cheese

I love baked goat cheese; something about it just makes the food taste special. This upscale pizza combines rich sun-dried tomato pesto and chicken with goat cheese. // *Makes one 12-inch (30.5 cm) pizza, serves 4*

- **PACKAGING:** Two sandwich-size bags, plastic container with lid or snack-size bag, quart- (1 L) or pint-size (470 ml) bag, gallon-size (4 L) zip-top freezer bag

1 cup (140 g) chopped cooked chicken

½ cup (60 g) crumbled goat cheese

½ cup (120 ml) Sun-Dried Tomato Pesto (page 218)

¼ batch frozen, bagged Basic Pizza Dough (page 249)

1. Place the cooked chicken in a sandwich-size bag. Place the goat cheese crumbles in another sandwich-size bag. Place the pesto in a plastic container or snack-size bag.

2. Place the bags of chicken and cheese and the container of pesto, along with the bag of frozen pizza dough, in the gallon-size (4 L) zip-top freezer bag. Store in the freezer.

TO THAW AND SERVE:

Remove the pizza kit from the freezer. Grease a medium bowl. Unwrap the pizza dough and place it in the greased bowl. Thaw it in the refrigerator for 6 to 8 hours, covered. Thaw the other items in the kit in the refrigerator. Preheat the oven to 475°F (240°C or gas mark 9). Allow the dough to sit at room temperature for about 30 minutes. Stretch the dough to fit a 12-inch (30.5 cm) pizza pan. Spread the pesto over the prepared dough. Sprinkle the chicken over the sauce. Sprinkle the goat cheese crumbles over the chicken. Bake the pizza for 10 to 12 minutes, or until the crust is crisp and the cheese is slightly melted and starting to brown. Cool slightly before slicing and serving.

Pepperoni Calzones

A calzone is simply a pizza folded in half. Make them with any number of fillings, provided that the fillings do not have a lot of water in them, which would make the crust soggy. Since these are baked prior to freezing, they make great snacks or lunches: Simply reheat them in a toaster oven or microwave.

// *Serves 8*

■ **PACKAGING:** Plastic wrap, two gallon-size (4 L) zip-top freezer bags

1 batch Basic Pizza Dough (page 249), prepared through step 1

Cornmeal for sprinkling

4 cups (480 g) shredded mozzarella cheese

Two 6-ounce (168 g) packages sliced pepperoni (about 64 slices)

WHEN READY TO SERVE, YOU WILL NEED:

Easy Slow Cooker Red Sauce (page 217) or other favorite red sauce, warmed

1. Once the pizza dough is mixed, allow it to rise for 1 hour or until doubled in bulk.

2. Preheat the oven to 475°F (240°C or gas mark 9). Grease 2 or 3 baking sheets and sprinkle them with cornmeal.

3. Transfer the dough to a lightly floured surface and divide it into 8 equal portions. Form each portion into a tight ball. Once all the portions are formed, flatten each one into a 6- to 8-inch (15 to 20.3 cm) round.

4. Sprinkle ½ cup (60 g) mozzarella cheese over half of each dough round, leaving a ½-inch (1.3 cm) border around the edge. Arrange 8 slices of pepperoni over the cheese.

5. Fold the other half of the dough over the pepperoni and press to seal the edges. You should have a half-moon shape. Gently turn the bottom crust over the top in sections to further seal the rounded edge. As you work your way around the edge of the dough, each turned-up section should build on the previous one, creating a type of braided effect.

6. Place all the formed calzones on the prepared baking sheets. Cut 2 or 3 slits in the top of each one. Bake for 10 to 12 minutes or until crisp. Remove from the baking sheets and cool on a rack.

FREEZING INSTRUCTIONS:

Wrap each cooled calzone in plastic wrap. Package 4 calzones in each freezer bag and store in the freezer.

TO THAW AND SERVE:

Thaw calzones in the refrigerator overnight. Preheat the oven to 350°F (180°C or gas mark 4). Unwrap the calzones and reheat for 5 to 10 minutes, or until heated through. Serve with the warmed sauce for dipping.

Spinach and Cheese Calzones

Spinach and ricotta are natural partners and combine into a delicious filling in these calzones, which make an elegant appetizer or light main course. Pair them with Tomato Sauce with Oregano and Kalamata Olives (page 215) for a fresh twist. These are great to pack in lunches and reheat at work or school. // *Serves 8*

> ▪ **PACKAGING:** Plastic wrap, two gallon-size (4 L) zip-top freezer bags

1 batch Basic Pizza Dough (page 249),
   prepared through step 1
Cornmeal for sprinkling
2 cups (450 g) ricotta cheese

One 16-ounce (454 g) package frozen
   chopped spinach, thawed and
   squeezed dry
1 tablespoon Jamie's Spice Mix (page 98)

WHEN READY TO SERVE, YOU WILL NEED:
Tomato Sauce with Oregano and Kalamata
   Olives (page 215) or other favorite
   tomato sauce, warmed

1. Once the pizza dough is mixed, allow it to rise for 1 hour or until doubled in bulk.

2. Preheat the oven to 475°F (240°C or gas mark 9). Grease 2 or 3 baking sheets and sprinkle them with cornmeal.

3. Transfer the dough to a lightly floured surface and divide it into 8 equal portions. Form each portion into a tight ball. Once all the portions are formed, flatten each one into a 6- to 8-inch (15 to 20.3 cm) round.

4. In a large bowl, combine the ricotta cheese, spinach, and spice mix. Divide the cheese mixture among the 8 dough rounds, spreading it over half of each dough round and leaving a ½-inch (1.3 cm) border around the edge.

5. Fold the other half of dough over the cheese filling and press to seal the edges. You should have a half-moon shape. Gently turn the bottom crust over the top in portions to further seal the rounded edge. As you work your way around the edge of the dough, each turned-up section should build on the previous one, creating a type of braided effect.

6. Place all the formed calzones on the prepared baking sheets. Cut 2 or 3 slits in the top of each one. Bake for 10 to 12 minutes or until crisp. Remove from the baking sheets and cool on a rack.

FREEZING INSTRUCTIONS:
Wrap each calzone in plastic wrap. Package 4 calzones in each freezer bag and store in the freezer.

TO THAW AND SERVE:
Thaw calzones in the refrigerator overnight. Preheat the oven to 350°F (180°C or gas mark 4). Unwrap the calzones and reheat for 5 to 10 minutes, or until heated through. Serve with the warmed sauce for dipping.

8

BREAKFASTS FOR CHAMPIONS

‣ Milk and Honey Granola ▪ 267

‣ Maple Granola with Oats, Nuts, and Seeds ▪ 267

‣ Cranberry-Orange Granola ▪ 269

‣ Raspberry Baked Oatmeal ▪ 270

‣ Fruit, Nut, and Oatmeal Bowls ▪ 273

‣ Better Instant Oatmeal Packets ▪ 274

‣ Bulk-Batch Pancakes ▪ 275

‣ Oatmeal–Chocolate Chip Pancakes ▪ 276

‣ Maple-Oat Waffles ▪ 277

‣ Lemon-and-Honey Flax Waffles ▪ 278

‣ Spiced Whole-Grain Waffles ▪ 280

‣ Cinnamon French Toast Dippers ▪ 281

‣ Sweet Almond Toasts (Poorman's Bostock) ▪ 282

‣ Buttered French Toast Casserole with Almonds and Ginger ▪ 284

‣ Breakfast Cookies ▪ 286

‣ Breakfast Smoothies ▪ 287

‣ Bacon-Cheddar Egg Bake ▪ 289

‣ Bacon-Cheddar Egg Bake for a Crowd ▪ 290

‣ Eggs Florentine Casserole ▪ 292

‣ Bacon and Spinach Quiche ▪ 293

‣ Savory Ham and Swiss Clafouti ▪ 293

‣ Chile and Sausage Oven Frittata ▪ 294

‣ Slow Cooker Applesauce ▪ 295

‣ Breakfast Sliders ▪ 296

‣ Savory Sausage and Quinoa Bowls ▪ 297

Milk and Honey Granola

Granola can be a pretty pricey grocery store item. However, it is very easy to make this breakfast cereal yourself at home. If you can buy the ingredients in bulk and/or on sale, you will enjoy further savings. An added benefit is that you can add whatever nuts and seeds you like. This basic recipe is flavored with honey and cooks slowly in the oven. Enjoy it as a breakfast cereal, in parfaits layered with yogurt and fruit, or just for snacking. // *Serves 6 to 8*

■ **PACKAGING:** Plastic containers with lids or gallon-size (4 L) zip-top freezer bag

5 cups (400 g) old-fashioned rolled oats (do
   not use quick-cooking oats)
½ cup (60 g) wheat bran
1 cup (80 g) wheat germ
½ cup (72 g) sesame seeds

½ teaspoon salt
1 cup (320 g) honey
½ cup (120 ml) vegetable oil
½ cup (60 g) powdered nonfat milk
2 teaspoons lemon zest

1. Preheat the oven to 300°F (150°C or gas mark 2). Grease a large, rimmed baking sheet or line it with parchment paper.

2. In a very large bowl, combine the oats, wheat bran, wheat germ, sesame seeds, and salt. In a separate bowl, combine the honey, oil, powdered milk, and lemon zest. Pour the wet mixture over the dry and toss to coat evenly.

3. Spread the mixture on the prepared baking sheet. Bake for 40 to 45 minutes, stirring every 15 minutes. Do not let the mixture brown too much.

4. Remove the pan from the oven and allow the granola to cool completely.

FREEZING INSTRUCTIONS:

Store in a plastic container or freezer bag in the freezer.

TO THAW AND SERVE:

Thaw the granola in its container on the counter.

Maple Granola with Oats, Nuts, and Seeds

I love granola. And I love it even more with yogurt and fresh fruit. Yum! Almost like dessert—and a great way to get lots of whole grains. If I have a stash of granola, breakfast—or dessert—comes together in a matter of seconds. This granola, inspired by a recipe from cookbook author Ellie Krieger, is the simplest one I've ever made. Just toss oats, nuts, and seeds with a little salt and maple syrup. Bake until crisp. Delicious! // *Serves 6 to 8*

■ **PACKAGING:** Plastic containers with lids or gallon-size (4 L) zip-top freezer bag

4 cups (320 g) old-fashioned rolled oats (do not use quick-cooking oats)
½ cup (70 g) pecans
½ cup (70 g) walnuts
½ cup (120 g) whole raw almonds

½ cup raw (70 g) sunflower seeds
½ cup (70 g) raw pumpkin seeds
⅜ teaspoon salt
1 cup (235 ml) maple syrup

1. Preheat the oven to 300°F (150°C or gas mark 2). Grease a large rimmed baking sheet or line it with parchment paper.

2. Combine all of the ingredients in a large bowl, tossing to coat everything with the maple syrup.

3. Spread the mixture on the prepared baking sheet. Bake for 30 to 45 minutes, stirring often, until toasted and crisp. Cool completely.

FREEZING INSTRUCTIONS:

Store in a plastic container or freezer bag in the freezer.

TO THAW AND SERVE:

Thaw the granola in its container on the counter.

▶ Quick Tips for Bulk Cooking

"Messy stations slow things down, food doesn't go, orders pile up, disaster! I will make this easier to remember: Keep your station clean—or I will kill you!" —Colette, *Ratatouille*

- Start with a clean kitchen and a stack of clean kitchen towels and sponges.

- Buy in bulk and large containers whenever possible. This saves money because the unit price is usually lower for bulk goods. You'll save time because you can open one gigantic can instead of five smaller ones. And you send less waste to the landfill.

- Call the butcher in advance and ask if he will cube/preslice any meats that you're buying in bulk. This also helps ensure they have the quantities you want when you arrive.

- Wear an apron to protect your clothes; you can also dry your hands on it.

- Gather all your containers and wrappings ahead of time.

- If space allows, assemble all your nonperishable ingredients on the counters.

(continued)

- Prep all the ingredients before assembling your meals.

- Remember that the assembly line is your friend. Use it whenever you can. Don't repeat actions unnecessarily.

- Clean as you go, or at least load the dishwasher or drop dirty dishes into a sink of soapy water.

- Play music to keep you inspired.

Cranberry-Orange Granola

This granola makes a beautiful gift at the holidays, as well as a fantastic breakfast any time of year. Store the cranberries separately from the granola until you're ready to serve it, so they retain their tenderness and moisture. // *Serves 6 to 8*

- **PACKAGING:** Plastic containers with lids or gallon-size (4 L) zip-top freezer bag

5 cups (400 g) old-fashioned rolled oats (do not use quick-cooking oats)
1 cup (140 g) chopped nuts, such as walnuts or pecans
1 cup (225 g) light brown sugar
½ cup (120 ml) vegetable oil

½ cup (60 g) powdered nonfat milk, optional
¼ cup (60 ml) water
1 tablespoon ground cinnamon
Grated zest of 1 orange
1 teaspoon vanilla extract
½ teaspoon salt

WHEN READY TO SERVE, YOU WILL NEED:
1 cup (150 g) dried cranberries

1. Preheat the oven to 300°F (150°C or gas mark 2). Grease a large rimmed baking sheet or line it with parchment paper.

2. In a large bowl, combine the oats and nuts.

3. In a medium saucepan over low heat, combine the brown sugar, oil, powdered milk (if using), water, cinnamon, orange zest, vanilla, and salt. Heat, stirring, until just simmering. Pour this mixture over the oats and nuts, stirring to combine.

4. Spread the mixture on the prepared baking sheet. Bake for 40 to 45 minutes, stirring every 10 to 15 minutes. Cool completely.

FREEZING INSTRUCTIONS:

Store in a plastic container or freezer bag in the freezer.

TO THAW AND SERVE:

Thaw the granola in its container on the counter. Add the cranberries right before serving.

Raspberry Baked Oatmeal

I was a skeptic about baked oatmeal, but Lynn's Kitchen Adventures made me a believer. My friend Lynn has created over TWENTY different versions of baked oatmeal! This raspberry-studded version is one I adapted from her standard, based on what I had on hand and what my kids liked. I was so pleased to see how freezer-friendly these oatmeal casseroles are! // *Serves 8 to 10*

■ **PACKAGING:** One 9 × 13-inch (23 × 33 cm) baking pan with lid

3 cups (240 g) old-fashioned oats
¼ cup (60 g) brown sugar
2 teaspoons baking powder
¾ teaspoon salt
½ cup (112 g) applesauce
½ cup (112 g) plain yogurt

½ cup (120 ml) nonfat milk
¼ cup (60 ml) oil or (56 g) butter
1 teaspoon vanilla extract
2 eggs
2 cups (300 g) raspberries
(can use frozen, no need to thaw)

WHEN READY TO SERVE, YOU WILL NEED:
Heavy cream, whipped or plain

1. Grease a 9 × 13-inch (23 × 33 cm) baking pan.

2. In a large mixing bowl, combine the oats, brown sugar, baking powder, and salt.

3. In a second mixing bowl, whisk together the applesauce, yogurt, milk, oil, vanilla, eggs.

4. Pour the wet ingredients onto the dry, and add the raspberries. Fold gently to combine. Spoon the mixture into the prepared pan.

FREEZING INSTRUCTIONS:

Cover and freeze.

TO THAW AND SERVE:

Thaw the casserole overnight in the refrigerator. Preheat the oven to 350°F (180°C or gas mark 4) and bake for 30 to 40 minutes, or until golden. To bake from frozen, add 10 to 15 minutes to the baking time.

▶ Breakfast of Champions

Breakfast can be a tough meal. You know it's beneficial for you to eat a good breakfast each morning, but getting it together can be a difficult job to tackle. Freezer cooking comes to the rescue! You'll be pleasantly surprised to see what great breakfasts you can pull off if you do some advance prep work.

Here are a few ways you can make breakfast ahead of time:

PREPARE YOUR OWN INSTANT BREAKFAST CEREALS

My kids love this, especially the younger ones. I make a million little packets of homemade instant oatmeal, and breakfast for the early birds is ready before my coffee is brewed. Homemade granola is another easy cereal solution.

ENJOY THE BEAUTY OF THE BOWL

Breakfast bowls, whether they contain a smoothie or an oatmeal base, topped with fruit and nuts, or a quinoa base, topped with sautéed vegetables and sausage, make for fabulous, quick, on-the-go morning meals. Just thaw your smoothie bowl overnight in the fridge or zap the oatmeal or quinoa in the microwave for a few minutes. Breakfast is ready before you are!

ASSEMBLE BREAKFAST SANDWICHES

Make a detour from the fast-food lane in the morning by assembling your own English muffin or biscuit sandwiches. Wrap them in foil and freeze them to reheat on a busy morning.

ENJOY HOMEMADE BAKED GOODS

Homemade cinnamon rolls are a staple at our house since my friend Amy McGuire (who blogs at AmysFinerThings.com) taught me the best way to freeze them. Simply freeze individual unbaked rolls on a tray and store them in a bag in the freezer. The night before you want fresh-baked rolls, thaw the rolls overnight in a pan, and bake them in the morning. Brilliant! I keep a bag of cinnamon rolls in the freezer at all times (see page 324 for my whole-grain recipe). And I use this same freezing method for a multitude of scone recipes as well.

FREEZE EGG DISHES TO BAKE LATER

Easy-to-prepare recipes like quiche and egg casseroles also go from freezer to oven in a flash, making brunch or a hearty breakfast simple to pull off.

MAKE A MIX

Waffle, pancake, and muffin mixes can be made efficiently via the assembly-line method. Keep a stash of homemade baking mixes on hand for fast and healthy breakfasts any day.

Fruit, Nut, and Oatmeal Bowls

These bowls are such a time-saver! I love grabbing one from the freezer and just zapping it for a few minutes in the microwave. I don't even have to think to make breakfast! The butter-sugar-spice mixture melts into the steel-cut oats and fruit, making this hearty breakfast taste almost like dessert!

// *Serves 10*

- **PACKAGING:** Ten 1-cup (235 ml) containers with lids

4 cups (940 ml) water
½ teaspoon fine sea salt
2 cups (80 g) quick-cooking steel-cut oats
½ cup (112 g) brown sugar
¼ cup (56 g) (½ stick) butter, softened
½ teaspoon ground ginger
½ teaspoon ground cinnamon

2½ cups (375 g) frozen fruit, such as blueberries, raspberries, and/or pineapple tidbits
5 tablespoons (45 g) chopped nuts, such as pecans
5 tablespoons (15 g) coconut chips

1. Heat the water and salt in a saucepan until bubbly. Whisk in the oats. Cook, covered, for 5 minutes, or until most of the water is absorbed, stirring occasionally. Remove from the heat and let stand for 5 minutes, covered.

2. Meanwhile, in a small mixing bowl, cut the brown sugar into the butter, using a pastry blender. You want coarse crumbs. Sprinkle and mix in the ginger and cinnamon.

3. Divide the oats among the 10 dishes. Chill completely in the refrigerator.

4. Divide the fruit, sugar mixture, nuts, and coconut among the 10 dishes. Cover and freeze immediately.

FREEZING INSTRUCTIONS:
Store the dishes in the freezer.

TO SERVE:
Heat the oatmeal bowls in the microwave until hot throughout, 2 to 4 minutes, depending on the size of the container and the power of your microwave.

Better Instant Oatmeal Packets

I love breakfast in a box! It makes our mornings go so much more smoothly when I serve food that is easy to prepare and clean up. Even the little kids can do it all by themselves! Cold cereal and instant oatmeal are favorites, but since my children can eat through one box of instant oatmeal packets in a single morning, I've learned to make my own, inspired by a recipe on the blog The Simple Dollar. It takes just minutes to assemble a few dozen packets. I store the packets in a bin the pantry, but you can freeze them for longer storage. To reduce waste, save the empty snack-size bags to refill next month or next week. // *Serves 1*

■ **PACKAGING:** Snack-size zip-top bag

¼ cup (20 g) quick-cooking rolled oats
1½ teaspoons brown sugar
1 tablespoon raisins, dried cranberries, or
  dried blueberries (optional)

1 teaspoon powdered nonfat milk (optional)
⅛ teaspoon salt

Place the oats, brown sugar, fruit (if using), milk (if using), and salt in the bag. Shake gently to combine. Repeat to make as many additional servings as desired.

FREEZING INSTRUCTIONS:

Store the bags in the freezer.

TO SERVE:

Empty the contents of one bag into a heatproof bowl. Add ¼ to ½ cup (60 to 120 ml) boiling water. If you omitted the milk powder, you can use hot milk instead of boiling water. Let sit for 1 to 2 minutes, then stir before serving.

Bulk-Batch Pancakes

One thing I love about pancakes is that I can vary the batter recipe as well as the toppings to suit my mood or whatever's in the pantry. I've even been known to prepare them for a quick dinner when my other plans don't pan out.

You can combine the dry ingredients in this bulk pancake recipe ahead of time, for a mix that can be stored in the pantry or freezer. Or cook and cool the pancakes, wrap them in stacks of three, and store them in the freezer. Simply reheat cooked pancakes in the microwave or oven before serving.

If you decide to package the recipe as a mix, be sure to mark the bag with a list of the wet ingredients to add right before cooking, as well as the cooking instructions. // **Serves 4 to 6**

■ **PACKAGING:** Quart-size (1 L) zip-top freezer bag or plastic wrap and gallon-size (4 L) zip-top freezer bags

DRY INGREDIENTS:
1½ cups (180 g) unbleached all-purpose flour
1½ cups (180 g) whole-wheat pastry flour
¼ cup (50 g) sugar

1 tablespoon baking powder
1 teaspoon baking soda
1 teaspoon salt

WET INGREDIENTS:
3 to 3½ cups (705 to 825 ml) buttermilk
2 large eggs

⅓ cup (75 g) unsalted butter, melted
Melted butter, for the griddle

TO PACKAGE AS A MIX:
Place all of the dry ingredients in the quart-size (1 L) freezer bag. Seal the bag and shake it gently to combine. Store in the freezer.

COOKING INSTRUCTIONS:
1. In a large bowl, combine the buttermilk, eggs, and melted butter, blending well. Stir in the dry ingredients. There may be a few small lumps, but that's fine. Add some more buttermilk if the batter is too thick.

2. Heat a large skillet or griddle over medium heat until a few droplets of water sizzle when sprinkled onto the cooking surface. Brush the griddle with melted butter. Pour the batter onto the griddle in ¼-cup (60 ml) portions.

3. Cook the pancakes until bubbles form in the batter and start to pop. Flip the pancakes with a pancake turner. Brush the cooked tops of the cakes with more melted butter. Cook a minute or two more. Stack on a plate and continue until all are cooked.

FREEZING INSTRUCTIONS:

Cool completely. Wrap pancakes in plastic wrap in stacks of three and place in the large freezer bag. Freeze.

TO THAW AND SERVE:

Thaw the pancakes in the refrigerator or on the counter. Reheat in the microwave or oven until hot.

Oatmeal–Chocolate Chip Pancakes

These delicious, whole-grain pancakes are reminiscent of oatmeal–chocolate chip cookies, with a tad less guilt. You can combine the dry ingredients ahead of time, for a mix that can be stored in the pantry or freezer. Or cook and cool the pancakes, wrap them in stacks of three, and store them in the freezer. Simply reheat cooked pancakes in the microwave or oven before serving. If you decide to package the recipe as a mix, be sure to mark the bag with a list of the wet ingredients to add right before cooking, as well as the cooking instructions. // *Serves 4 to 6*

- **PACKAGING:** Quart-size (1 L) zip-top freezer bag or plastic wrap and gallon-size (4 L) zip-top freezer bags

DRY INGREDIENTS:

1 cup (120 g) unbleached all-purpose flour
1 cup (120 g) whole-wheat pastry flour
1 cup (120 g) oat flour
½ cup (40 g) quick-cooking oats
¼ cup (56 g) brown sugar

1 tablespoon baking powder
1 teaspoon baking soda
1 teaspoon salt
½ cup (88 g) mini chocolate chips

WET INGREDIENTS:

3½ cups (825 ml) buttermilk
2 large eggs
⅓ cup (80 ml) vegetable oil

1 teaspoon vanilla extract
1 teaspoon grated orange zest
Butter, for the griddle

TO PACKAGE AS A MIX:

Place all of the dry ingredients in the quart-size (1 L) freezer bag. Seal the bag and shake it gently to combine the ingredients. Store in the freezer.

COOKING INSTRUCTIONS:

1. In a large bowl, combine the buttermilk, eggs, oil, vanilla, and orange zest, blending well. Add the dry ingredients, whisking until smooth. There may be a few lumps, but that's fine. Add some more buttermilk if the batter is too thick or 1 to 2 tablespoons (8 or 16 g) of flour if it is too thin.

2. Heat a large skillet or griddle over medium heat until a few droplets of water sizzle when sprinkled onto the cooking surface. Brush the griddle with melted butter. Pour the batter onto the griddle in ¼-cup (60 ml) portions.

3. Cook the pancakes until bubbles form in the batter and start to pop. Flip the pancakes with a pancake turner. Brush the cooked tops of the cakes with more melted butter. Cook a minute or two more. Stack on a plate and continue until all are cooked.

FREEZING INSTRUCTIONS:

Cool completely. Wrap pancakes in plastic wrap in stacks of three and place in the large freezer bag. Freeze.

TO THAW AND SERVE:

Thaw the pancakes in the refrigerator or on the counter. Reheat in the microwave or oven until hot.

Maple-Oat Waffles

These tasty waffles get even better under cold storage. The tang of the buttermilk mellows and the maple flavor shines through. Full of whole grains, they are a hearty way to start your morning. Serve them with butter and a little more maple syrup to make the day sing. Prepare the dry ingredients as a mix, or cook and freeze the waffles to reheat later for breakfasts on the go. If you decide to package the recipe as a mix, be sure to mark the bag with a list of the wet ingredients to add right before cooking, as well as the cooking instructions. // *Serves 4 to 6*

■ **PACKAGING:** Gallon-size (4 L) zip-top freezer bag

DRY INGREDIENTS:

2½ cups (300 g) unbleached all-purpose flour
2 cups (240 g) whole-wheat pastry flour
1 cup (120 g) oat flour

½ cup (40 g) quick-cooking oats
¼ cup (60 g) baking powder
1½ teaspoons salt

WET INGREDIENTS:

5 cups (1175 ml) buttermilk

1 cup (225 g) (2 sticks) unsalted butter, melted

¼ cup (60 ml) maple syrup

4 large eggs

TO PACKAGE AS A MIX:

Place all of the dry ingredients in the freezer bag. Seal the bag and shake it gently to combine the ingredients. Store in the freezer.

COOKING INSTRUCTIONS:

In a large bowl, combine the dry ingredients with the wet ingredients. Allow the batter to rest for 5 minutes before cooking in your waffle iron according to the manufacturer's instructions. Cool the cooked waffles on a rack.

FREEZING INSTRUCTIONS:

Place the cooked waffles in the labeled freezer bag and store in the freezer.

TO SERVE:

Reheat frozen waffles (no need to thaw) in the toaster or toaster oven.

Lemon-and-Honey Flax Waffles

Talk about your day-brighteners! These waffles positively buzz with honey and lemon zest. The touch of flax brings fiber, antioxidants, and omega-3s to the table. These waffles are out of this world when served with berries and freshly whipped cream. Prepare the dry ingredients as a mix, or cook and freeze the waffles to reheat later for breakfasts on the go. If you decide to package the recipe as a mix, be sure to mark the bag with a list of the wet ingredients to add right before cooking, as well as the cooking instructions. // *Serves 4 to 6*

■ **PACKAGING:** Gallon-size (4 L) zip-top freezer bag

DRY INGREDIENTS:

3 cups (360 g) whole-wheat pastry flour

3 cups (360 g) unbleached all-purpose flour

¼ cup (30 g) baking powder

½ tablespoon salt

WET INGREDIENTS:

3½ cups (825 ml) milk

1 cup (235 ml) olive oil

3 large eggs

¼ cup (80 g) honey

1 tablespoon ground flax seed meal,
    combined with 3 tablespoons
    (45 ml) water

Grated zest of 1 lemon

TO PACKAGE AS A MIX:

Place all of the dry ingredients in the freezer bag. Seal the bag and shake it gently to combine the ingredients. Store in the freezer.

COOKING INSTRUCTIONS:

In a large bowl, combine the dry ingredients with the wet ingredients. Allow the batter to rest for 5 minutes before cooking in your waffle iron according to the manufacturer's instructions. Cool the cooked waffles on a rack.

FREEZING INSTRUCTIONS:

Place the cooked waffles in the freezer bag and store in the freezer.

TO SERVE:

Reheat frozen waffles (no need to thaw) in the toaster or toaster oven.

Spiced Whole-Grain Waffles

Waffles are a wonderful make-ahead meal. You can prepare this recipe as a mix or cook all the waffles at one time, cool, and freeze. Either way, you've cut out a significant amount of prep time. These spiced waffles are packed with whole grains and have so much flavor that you can eat them out of hand, without any toppings. My mother, however, says they beg for a scoop of vanilla ice cream. (Obviously, not all your mother's ideas need be discarded.) If you decide to package the recipe as a mix, be sure to mark the bag with a list of the wet ingredients to add right before cooking, as well as the cooking instructions. // *Serves 4 to 6*

■ **PACKAGING:** Gallon-size (4 L) zip-top freezer bag

DRY INGREDIENTS:

3½ cups (420 g) unbleached all-purpose
    flour

2 cups (240 g) whole-wheat pastry flour

¼ cup (20 g) quick-cooking oats

¼ cup (30 g) cornmeal

¼ cup (56 g) dark brown sugar

¼ cup (30 g) baking powder

1½ teaspoons salt

1½ teaspoons ground cinnamon

1 teaspoon ground nutmeg

1 teaspoon grated orange zest

1 teaspoon ground ginger

WET INGREDIENTS:

4 cups (940 ml) milk

1 cup (225 g) (2 sticks) unsalted butter,
    melted

4 large eggs

1 teaspoon vanilla extract

TO PACKAGE AS A MIX:

Place all of the dry ingredients in the freezer bag. Seal the bag and shake it gently to combine the ingredients. Store in the freezer.

COOKING INSTRUCTIONS:

In a large bowl, combine the milk, melted butter, eggs, and vanilla until well blended. Stir in the dry ingredients. Allow the batter to rest for 5 minutes before cooking in your waffle iron according to the manufacturer's instructions. Cool the cooked waffles on a rack.

FREEZING INSTRUCTIONS:

Place the cooked waffles in the freezer bag and store in the freezer.

TO SERVE:

Reheat frozen waffles (no need to thaw) in the toaster or toaster oven.

Cinnamon French Toast Dippers

French toast is a tasty way to make use of day-old bread. With this recipe you can prepare a large batch of this crispy, crunchy, battered bread at one time, making it a perfect recipe for a crowd. I've updated a vintage recipe by stirring in some spices and using large French rolls sliced on the diagonal, which creates ideal "dippers." // *Serves 6 to 8*

■ **PACKAGING:** Gallon-size (4 L) zip-top freezer bag

5 large eggs
1 cup (235 ml) milk
1½ tablespoons (18 g) brown sugar
½ teaspoon salt
1 teaspoon vanilla extract

¼ teaspoon grated orange zest
½ teaspoon ground cinnamon
Three 8-inch (20.3 cm) French or sub rolls, sliced on the diagonal into 8 slices each

1. Preheat the oven to 500°F (250°C or gas mark 10). Line 2 to 3 baking sheets with parchment paper or silicone baking mats.

2. In a wide, shallow dish, mix the eggs, milk, brown sugar, salt, vanilla, orange zest, and cinnamon until well blended.

3. Dip both sides of the bread pieces into the egg mixture and arrange them on the prepared baking sheets.

4. Bake the bread slices until the undersides are golden, about 5 minutes. Turn the slices over. Bake until the bread is golden brown, 2 to 5 minutes more. Watch carefully to prevent burning.

FREEZING INSTRUCTIONS:
Cool the French toast dippers completely on a wire rack. Place the dippers in the zip-top freezer bag and freeze.

TO SERVE:
Preheat the oven to 375°F (190°C or gas mark 5). Place the frozen dippers (no need to thaw) on an ungreased baking sheet. Bake until heated through, 8 to 10 minutes. You can warm smaller quantities in the toaster or toaster oven.

Sweet Almond Toasts (Poorman's Bostock)

Bostock is a French pastry of frangipane baked atop thick slices of brioche that have been brushed with almond syrup and coated with jam. I've simplified the process as well as frugal-ified it, skipping the almond syrup and using a homemade almond cream instead of the more expensive almond paste. These are a delightful addition to your brunch or *petit dejeuner* table. // *Serves 12*

■ **PACKAGING:** Large plastic container with lid

12 thick slices day-old bread or toast
Jam or Nutella (optional)
½ cup (60 g) super-fine almond flour
½ cup (112 g) (1 stick) softened butter
⅓ cup (65 g) granulated sugar
Pinch of salt

1 egg, beaten
½ teaspoon vanilla extract
Zest of 1 lemon
¼ cup (30 g) cake flour
¾ cup (75 g) sliced almonds

WHEN READY TO SERVE, YOU WILL NEED:
Confectioners' sugar

1. Preheat the oven to 350°F (180°C or gas mark 4). Line baking sheets with parchment paper.

2. Lay the bread or toast on the baking sheet. Spread a small amount of jam or Nutella on each slice, if desired.

3. In a small mixing bowl, cream together the almond flour, butter, granulated sugar, and salt. Add the egg, vanilla, and lemon zest and mix well. Stir in the cake flour until smooth and spreadable. Spread this mixture over the toast, covering well from edge to edge. Sprinkle the almonds generously over the top.

4. Bake for 15 to 20 minutes, until the almond cream is set and golden. Remove from the oven and cool on a rack.

5. Layer the baked toasts between sheets of waxed paper in the plastic container. Cover and chill.

FREEZING INSTRUCTIONS:
Store the container in the freezer.

TO THAW AND SERVE:
Thaw the toasts in the refrigerator. You can recrisp them in a toaster oven if you desire. Cool on a rack. Sift confectioners' sugar over the cooled toasts and serve.

Buttered French Toast Casserole with Almonds and Ginger

A breakfast casserole is one of the easiest ways to start the morning. This elegant dish is bursting with color and sweetness from the cranberries and raisins, crunch from the almonds, and a little kick from the ginger. Leftovers are delicious served cold. For a crisper texture, omit the dried fruit and leave the dish uncovered for the entire baking time. Use a softer, Italian-style bread rather than a crusty French loaf for this dish, and serve with maple syrup, if you like. // *Serves 4 to 6*

■ **PACKAGING:** One 9 × 13-inch (23 × 33 cm) baking dish with lid

1 loaf Italian or brioche bread, 14 to 16 inches long (35.6 to 40.6 cm), sliced into 1½-inch (3.8 cm) slices

¼ cup (56 g) (½ stick) unsalted butter, softened

¼ cup (38 g) golden raisins or dark raisins, or a combination

2 tablespoons (16 g) dried cranberries

2 tablespoons (18 g) sliced almonds

2 tablespoons chopped crystallized ginger

3 large eggs, beaten

1 cup (235 ml) half-and-half

¼ cup (50 g) sugar

2 tablespoons (16 g) unbleached all-purpose flour

1. Spray the baking dish with nonstick cooking spray.

2. Butter the bread slices on one side and fit the slices, buttered side up, in the bottom of the prepared baking dish.

3. Sprinkle the raisins, cranberries, almonds, and ginger over the top of the bread.

4. In a bowl, combine the eggs, half-and-half, sugar, and flour, whisking well to combine. Pour the egg mixture over the bread slices.

FREEZING INSTRUCTIONS:

Cover and freeze.

TO THAW AND SERVE:

Thaw the casserole in the refrigerator. Preheat the oven to 350°F (180°C or gas mark 4). Bake, covered, for 25 minutes, then remove the cover and bake 20 minutes more.

Breakfast Cookies

My husband leaves for work before most of the household is awake. He often grabs a cup of coffee and a protein bar, then hits the road. I am always on the hunt for a more economical yet still nourishing option. I took one of my favorite cookie recipes and tweaked it by substituting healthier ingredients like honey, whole-wheat flour, and lots of nuts and grains. The result is a hearty, portable breakfast cookie. Whole-wheat pastry flour can usually be found in the bulk section of your health food store and in larger supermarkets. If you can't find it, you can substitute regular whole-wheat flour, though the cookie will be denser. If you don't have coconut oil, use butter or your preferred vegetable oil instead. // *Makes 3 dozen cookies*

- **PACKAGING:** Gallon-size (4 L) zip-top freezer bag

½ cup (160 g) honey
¾ cup (150 g) light or dark brown sugar
¾ cup (150 g) coconut oil
2 large eggs
2 teaspoons (10 ml) vanilla extract
½ cup (60 g) ground flaxseed meal
1½ cups (180 g) whole-wheat pastry flour
1 teaspoon salt

1 teaspoon baking soda
2 cups (160 g) quick-cooking oats
¼ cup (38 g) dried cranberries
¼ cup (45 g) semisweet chocolate chips
¼ cup (35 g) raw pumpkin seeds
¼ cup (35 g) sunflower seeds
¼ cup (35 g) chopped nuts of your choice

1. Preheat the oven to 350°F (180°C or gas mark 4). Line 2 or 3 baking sheets with silicone baking mats or parchment paper.

2. In a large bowl, combine the honey, brown sugar, and coconut oil. Blend well. Beat in the eggs and vanilla. Stir in all of the remaining ingredients.

3. Drop the batter by tablespoonfuls onto the prepared baking sheets. Bake for 10 to 15 minutes or until the tops are set and golden. Cool on racks.

FREEZING INSTRUCTIONS:

Place the cooled cookies into the freezer bag. Store in the freezer. Cookies can also be packed into sandwich-size bags and then placed in a larger freezer bag, to make them that much easier to grab and go.

TO THAW AND SERVE:

The cookies thaw in a few minutes at room temperature.

Breakfast Smoothies

While blending a smoothie doesn't take that long, it's nice to be able to grab a quick, cold snack or breakfast. Freezer smoothies are just the ticket! Dishwasher- and microwave-safe 8-ounce (224 g) plastic freezer jars with screw-on lids are perfect for storing freezer smoothies.

Making smoothies can be really simple. Just blend different combinations of fruits, juices, and ice. To make dairy-based smoothies, add yogurt and/or milk. Or use soy milk or almond milk, for creaminess without dairy. I even use homemade fruit jam to flavor milk-based smoothies. Test out some of your favorite fruits and see what combinations you like best. And then keep your freezer stocked for all sorts of cool snacking.

A smoothie is great to pack in the lunch box or to grab and go. Thaw in the refrigerator for 4 hours before serving or on the counter for about an hour, or microwave it for 20 seconds on 50 percent power for a perfect slushy consistency.

> **Smoothie Bowl Variation:** Smoothie bowls have seen quite a bit of popularity in recent years. Consider packing your smoothie as a bowl, not a drink. Blend the smoothie on the thicker side and pour into plastic containers. Top with your favorite frozen fruit, nuts, and seeds. Cover and freeze.

The Red Banana

There's a smoothie bar in Santa Barbara that serves up some of the best smoothies on the planet, including the Red Banana, a milk-based smoothie with strawberries and bananas. It is delicious simplicity.
// *Serves 6*

■ **PACKAGING:** Six plastic freezer jars with lids

2½ cups (590 ml) nonfat milk   2 bananas, broken into pieces
1 cup (170 g) sliced strawberries

Mix the milk, strawberries, and bananas in the blender until smooth. Pour the mixture into the freezer jars, leaving ½ inch (1.3 cm) headspace.

FREEZING INSTRUCTIONS:
Cover the jars and freeze.

TO THAW AND SERVE:
Thaw smoothies in the refrigerator for 4 hours or on the counter for about an hour, or microwave them for 20 seconds on 50 percent power. Serve immediately.

The Red Orange

This nondairy fruit-based smoothie is a great way to get one of your five daily servings of produce. The riper the strawberries, the sweeter the treat. Add a teaspoon or two of honey to adjust the sweetness, if desired. // *Serves 6*

- **PACKAGING:** Six plastic freezer jars with lids

2 cups (470 ml) orange juice

2 cups (340 g) sliced strawberries

½ cup (120 ml) raspberry-grape juice blend

1 to 2 teaspoons honey (optional)

Mix the orange juice, strawberries, and raspberry-grape juice in the blender until smooth. Taste and adjust the sweetness if necessary by adding honey. Pour the mixture into the freezer jars, leaving ½ inch (1.3 cm) headspace.

FREEZING INSTRUCTIONS:

Cover the jars and freeze.

TO THAW AND SERVE:

Thaw smoothies in the refrigerator for 4 hours or on the counter for about an hour, or microwave them for 20 seconds on 50 percent power. Serve immediately.

The Blue Maple

This milky treat features blueberries and gets a little zip from the maple syrup. // *Serves 6*

- **PACKAGING:** Six plastic freezer jars with lids

2 cups (470 ml) milk

1½ cups (225 g) blueberries

¾ cup (180 g) plain yogurt

2 tablespoons (30 ml) maple syrup

Mix the milk, blueberries, yogurt, and maple syrup in the blender until smooth. Pour the mixture into the freezer jars, leaving ½ inch (1.3 cm) headspace.

FREEZING INSTRUCTIONS:

Cover the jars and freeze.

TO THAW AND SERVE:

Thaw smoothies in the refrigerator for 4 hours or on the counter for about and hour, or microwave them for 20 seconds on 50 percent power. Serve immediately.

The Blue Pineapple

Canned pineapple and fresh blueberries blend beautifully with plain yogurt for a nutritious smoothie. // *Serves 6*

■ **PACKAGING:** Six plastic freezer jars with lids

One 20-ounce (560 g) can sliced or chunk
    pineapple in juice

1 cup (150 g) blueberries
8 ounces (224 g) plain yogurt

Mix the pineapple, blueberries, and yogurt in the blender until smooth. Pour the mixture into the freezer jars, leaving ½ inch (1.3 cm) headspace.

FREEZING INSTRUCTIONS:
Cover the jars and freeze.

TO THAW AND SERVE:
Thaw smoothies in the refrigerator for 4 hours or on the counter for about an hour, or microwave them for 20 seconds on 50 percent power. Serve immediately.

Bacon-Cheddar Egg Bake

The egg bake is a fantastic make-ahead breakfast dish. It's basically bread, cheese, and cooked meat and/or vegetables soaked in a custard mixture, refrigerated overnight, and then baked in the morning. An egg bake is ideal to serve for brunch or, paired with a salad, as an elegant lunch. Egg dishes also freeze well, further freeing up your time.

Usually egg bakes are prepared in 9 × 13-inch (23 × 33 cm) baking dishes. However, I enjoy making them in individual servings as well. Following are instructions for both a single serving and a bigger batch. You can customize the individual egg bakes by adding different cheeses, meats, or precooked vegetables and prepare as many as you would like. Just lay out several small baking dishes and assemble a variety of egg bakes at one time. // *Serves 1*

■ **PACKAGING:** One 2-cup (470 ml) baking dish with lid

1 cup (50 g) soft bread cubes
⅓ cup (40 g) shredded cheddar cheese
2 slices bacon, cooked and chopped
2 large eggs, beaten

½ cup (120 ml) milk
Pinch of freshly ground black pepper

1. Grease the baking dish. Spread the bread cubes across the bottom of the dish. Sprinkle the cheese and bacon over the bread cubes.

2. In a small bowl, combine the eggs, milk, and black pepper. Pour the egg mixture over the bread and cheese.

FREEZING INSTRUCTIONS:
Cover and freeze.

TO THAW AND SERVE:
Thaw the egg bake in the refrigerator. Preheat the oven to 350°F (180°C or gas mark 4). Bake for 25 minutes, or until the top is puffy and a tester inserted in the center comes out clean.

Bacon-Cheddar Egg Bake for a Crowd

Serves 6 to 8

■ **PACKAGING:** One 9 × 13-inch (23 × 33 cm) baking dish with lid

6 cups (300 g) soft bread cubes
1⅓ cups (160 g) shredded cheddar cheese
4 slices bacon, cooked and chopped

9 large eggs, beaten
2 cups (470 ml) milk
¼ teaspoon freshly ground black pepper

1. Grease the baking dish. Spread the bread cubes across the bottom of the dish. Sprinkle the cheese and bacon over the bread cubes.

2. In a large bowl, combine the eggs, milk, and black pepper. Pour the egg mixture over the bread and cheese.

FREEZING INSTRUCTIONS:
Cover and freeze.

TO THAW AND SERVE:
Thaw the casserole in the refrigerator. Preheat the oven to 350°F (180°C or gas mark 4). Bake for 45 minutes to 1 hour, or until the top is puffy and a tester inserted in the center comes out clean.

► Cooking with Friends

Cooking is a very relaxing pursuit for me. If I have a nice drink and a snack, soft music and someone to talk with while I work, I am happy as can be. And while filling my freezer for a week or a month might be considered "work," the load is lightened when I have a cooking partner.

Years ago, my friend Jessika and I cooked together, split the costs, and shared the benefits. Since our husbands had similar tastes in food, we were able to make quite a few dishes to please everyone. We enjoyed talking girl talk while we chopped and mixed and cooked—and when we were done, we had a month's worth of dinners at our fingertips. We've both since moved to different cities, but we still get together a couple times a year to eat and talk.

I introduced my friend Tami to this method of batch cooking at about the same time Jessika and I started. Tami found a cooking buddy, too, and they've been dishing together for almost 20 years! They've perfected their routine after all this time. Four times a year, the husbands watch the kids while the ladies cook enough meals to last for three months. Tami and Margie only make about 25 meals at each session, but they stretch those meals with leftovers, takeout, and dinners with friends mixed in. They've even been able to accommodate one family's switch to a paleo diet. They are a great example of tweaking bulk cooking to fit individual lifestyles.

Cooking with friends can be a great habit. Not only do you experience the companionship and camaraderie of spending time with a friend, you also have someone to share the workload and another kitchen full of equipment to draw upon. I've heard from some people, though, whose experiences haven't been so positive or long-lasting. Consider the following tips to make your cooking partnership a success:

1. Discuss recipes carefully. Spend a fair amount of time talking about the foods that your respective households prefer. Flip through this book, making lists of the recipes you want to make. Choose the recipes that you *both* want to try.

2. Keep a careful record of receipts. When you are buying so much food in bulk, it can be easy to lose track of purchases, but it's important to make sure no one feels stiffed. Collect the receipts after shopping, or better yet, set a budget before you go shopping, so that you can each pay your fair share.

3. Split the meals evenly. As you assemble the meals, use the same packaging for both families whenever possible. Even though you may have different needs or appetites, you are sharing the workload and costs equally, so it's important to remember to split the benefits evenly. Sour grapes don't make for tasty dinners.

4. Prepare adequately for transporting the food. You probably aren't going to cook at both homes, so there will be some transportation of utensils, ingredients, and prepared meals involved. Plan for this. Large coolers are ideal for carrying home chilled

(continued)

food. Laundry baskets or plastic totes are good for carrying spices, utensils, and other shared items.

5. Plan to eat out or get takeout afterward. Depending on how long your cooking session lasts, you may be too tired to do anything but eat food someone else has prepared! Celebrate your accomplishment by ordering a couple of pizzas and putting your feet up.

6. Be flexible about the cooking relationship. Bulk cooking doesn't work for everybody all the time. Seasons change, and so do the needs, food tastes, and preferences of every family. It's okay if this doesn't become a shared activity that stretches over decades. But be sure to enjoy it if it does.

Eggs Florentine Casserole

Breakfast has always been an enjoyable meal for our family. One of my favorite morning meals is this easy make-ahead casserole. It was served to my husband and me at a little bed and breakfast where we stayed on our honeymoon. It's a delicious way to get your children to eat spinach. Thanks to hearty portions of rich cheeses, it is both filling and flavorful. // *Serves 6 to 10*

- **PACKAGING:** One 9 × 13-inch (23 × 33 cm) baking dish with lid or two 8-inch (20.3 cm) round baking dishes with lids

9 large eggs
16 ounces (454 g) cottage cheese
2 cups (240 g) shredded Swiss cheese
2 cups (240 g) crumbled feta cheese

One 10-ounce (280 g) package frozen chopped spinach, thawed and squeezed dry

1. Spray the baking dish(es) with nonstick cooking spray.

2. In a large bowl, beat the eggs. Add the cheeses and stir to combine well. Stir in the spinach. Pour the mixture into the prepared dish(es).

FREEZING INSTRUCTIONS:
Cover and freeze.

TO THAW AND SERVE:
Thaw the casserole in the refrigerator. Preheat the oven to 350°F (180°C or gas mark 4). Bake the casserole for 45 minutes to 1 hour, or until the eggs are cooked through. Cool slightly before cutting into squares. Serve hot or warm.

Bacon and Spinach Quiche

Quiche, a french classic, is a basic custard pie that can be varied in any number of ways. It's also unbelievably easy to make ahead and freeze. Just make sure you can store the unbaked pie level in your freezer until it freezes solid. Then wrap it tightly in foil and slip the frozen quiche into a freezer bag before returning it to the freezer. To make it even easier, feel free to use a frozen pie shell—but it won't be as good as my Buttery Pie Crust. An 8-inch (20.3 cm) pie pan works best for this recipe. // *Serves 4 to 6*

■ **PACKAGING:** One 9-inch (23 cm) pie plate, heavy-duty aluminum foil, gallon-size (4 L) zip-top freezer bag

1 cup (120 g) shredded Swiss cheese mixed with 2 tablespoons (16 g) unbleached all-purpose flour

½ cup (30 g) frozen chopped spinach, thawed and squeezed dry

2 tablespoons crumbled cooked bacon

1 recipe Versatile Buttery Pie Crust (page 368) or other favorite pie crust, pressed into an 8-inch (20.3 cm) pie plate

3 large eggs

1½ cups (355 ml) cream or half-and-half

⅛ teaspoon freshly ground black pepper

1. Sprinkle the cheese, spinach, and bacon over the bottom of the unbaked pie shell.

2. In a bowl, beat the eggs with the cream and pepper. Pour the egg mixture into the pie shell.

FREEZING INSTRUCTIONS:

Place the pie plate flat in the freezer. Freeze until firm. Cover the frozen quiche with foil and then place in the freezer bag. Return to the freezer.

TO SERVE:

Preheat the oven to 400°F (200°C or gas mark 6). Unwrap the frozen quiche and bake it (no need to thaw) for 30 to 45 minutes, or until a knife inserted in the center comes out clean.

Savory Ham and Swiss Clafouti

A clafouti is traditionally a fruit-and-custard dessert. However, savory clafouti has recently arrived on the scene. Similar to a crustless quiche, this rich ham-and-cheese custard makes an elegant breakfast or brunch entrée. // *Serves 4 to 6*

■ **PACKAGING:** One 9-inch (23 cm) baking dish with lid, heavy-duty aluminum foil

3 large eggs
1½ cups (355 ml) cream or half-and-half
1 teaspoon Dijon mustard
1 tablespoon chopped fresh parsley
   or 1 teaspoon dried parsley flakes

⅛ teaspoon freshly ground black pepper
1 cup (120 g) shredded Swiss cheese mixed
   with 2 tablespoons (16 g) unbleached
   all-purpose flour
1¾ cups diced ham (about 8 ounces [224 g])

1. Grease the baking dish.

2. In a large bowl, beat the eggs. Stir in the cream, Dijon mustard, parsley, and pepper. Stir in the shredded cheese and diced ham. Pour the egg mixture into the prepared baking dish.

FREEZING INSTRUCTIONS:

Place the baking dish flat in the freezer. Freeze until firm. Cover the frozen clafouti or wrap well with foil. Return to the freezer.

TO THAW AND SERVE:

Thaw the clafouti in the refrigerator. Preheat the oven to 350°F (180°C or gas mark 4). Bake the thawed clafouti, uncovered, for 30 to 45 minutes. Alternatively, bake the frozen clafouti for 45 minutes to 1 hour, or until a knife inserted in the center comes out clean.

Chile and Sausage Oven Frittata

This oven-baked egg dish is full of flavor from the sausage and green chiles. It is also a breeze to prepare. Mix up and freeze several at a time, and enjoy this easy, protein-packed main dish later. The frittata also makes a delicious and simple lunch or dinner when served with a side salad or a bowl of soup.
// *Serves 4 to 6*

■ **PACKAGING:** One 9-inch (23 cm) deep-dish pie plate, heavy-duty aluminum foil

4 ounces (112 g) sweet Italian sausage,
   casings removed
¾ cup (90 g) shredded Monterey Jack
   cheese mixed with 1 tablespoon
   unbleached all-purpose flour

One 4-ounce (112 g) can diced green chiles
6 large eggs, beaten
½ teaspoon ground cumin
⅛ teaspoon freshly ground black pepper
1 tablespoon chopped fresh cilantro

1. In a large skillet over medium-high heat, cook the sausage until no longer pink, breaking up the chunks with the back of a spoon. Drain the sausage and let cool.

2. Grease the deep-dish pie plate. Sprinkle the sausage, cheese, and chiles over the bottom of the pie plate.

3. In a large bowl, beat the eggs. Stir in the cumin and pepper. Pour the egg mixture into the pie plate. Sprinkle the cilantro over the top.

FREEZING INSTRUCTIONS:

Place the pie plate flat in the freezer. Freeze until firm. Cover the frozen frittata with foil. Return to the freezer.

TO THAW AND SERVE:

Thaw frittata in the refrigerator. Preheat the oven to 400°F (200°C or gas mark 6). Remove the foil from the frittata and bake it for 20 to 30 minutes, or until the eggs are set.

Slow Cooker Applesauce

When apples are in season, stock up. Make several batches of this easier-than-pie applesauce and stash them in 2-cup (470 ml) portions in the freezer. You can eat the applesauce straight up or use it in recipes; try it in Applesauce-Walnut Bread (page 300).

If you don't have a slow cooker, you can make this on the stovetop. Cook it over low heat in a heavy saucepan for about an hour, checking often to make sure the water doesn't completely evaporate.

// *Serves 12*

■ **PACKAGING:** Plastic containers with lids

16 large apples, such as Granny Smith, Gravenstein, or Braeburn, peeled, cored, and cut into quarters

¼ cup (60 ml) water
¼ cup (56 g) brown sugar (optional)

1. Place the apples and water in a 5-quart (5 L) slow cooker. Cook on HIGH for about 4 hours or until the apples have softened.

2. Mash the apples with a potato masher to achieve a chunky consistency. Use an immersion blender if you prefer a smooth texture. Stir in the brown sugar, if desired.

FREEZING INSTRUCTIONS:

Divide the applesauce into 2-cup (470 ml) portions in plastic containers. Cool completely before covering and freezing.

TO THAW AND SERVE:

Thaw the applesauce in the refrigerator. Serve warm, at room temperature, or chilled.

Breakfast Sliders

Breakfast sandwiches are a favorite with everyone. However, a quick morning trip to the drive-through can leave your wallet empty and your blood pressure elevated. Instead, prepare and freeze your own breakfast sandwiches to reheat while you get ready for the day. These sandwiches contain homemade pork sausage, but feel free to use commercially made sausage or substitute a different breakfast meat, such as bacon or Canadian bacon. // *Serves 6*

- **PACKAGING:** Plastic wrap or heavy-duty aluminum foil, gallon-size (4 L) zip-top freezer bag

6 Herbed Pork Sausage Patties (page 182), cooked and cooled	**6 slices cheddar cheese**
	6 English muffins, split

Assemble the breakfast sandwiches by placing one sausage patty and one slice of cheese between two English muffin halves.

FREEZING INSTRUCTIONS:

Wrap each sandwich individually, using plastic wrap if you plan to reheat in the microwave or foil if you plan to reheat in the oven. Place all the sandwiches in the freezer bag, squeezing out as much air as possible from the bag, and freeze.

TO THAW AND SERVE:

Sandwiches can be reheated thawed or frozen. For microwave heating, heat thawed plastic-wrapped sandwiches for 1 to 2 minutes or until heated through. Increase cooking time by 30 seconds to 1 minute for frozen sandwiches. For oven heating, preheat the oven to 375°F (190°C or gas mark 5). Reheat thawed foil-wrapped sandwiches for 15 minutes or until heated through. Increase cooking time by 10 minutes for frozen sandwiches.

Savory Sausage and Quinoa Bowls

I love a hearty, savory breakfast, complete with sautéed vegetables. I don't love an enormous amount of work or fuss first thing in the morning. That's just one of the reasons I love these Savory Sausage and Quinoa Bowls. The fact that they taste amazing would be another. // *Serves 5*

■ **PACKAGING:** 5 individual plastic containers with lids

1 cup (180 g) uncooked quinoa
5 Italian sausage links
2 tablespoons (30 ml) vegetable oil
2 cups (320 g) coarsely chopped onion
1 cup (70 g) sliced mushrooms

1 cup (150 g) coarsely chopped red
   bell pepper
1 cup (150 g) coarsely chopped green
   bell pepper
Fine sea salt and freshly ground
   black pepper

WHEN READY TO SERVE, YOU WILL NEED:
Optional toppings: baby spinach or kale,
   fried eggs, sliced avocado, hot sauce

1. Cook the quinoa according to package directions.

2. In a large, lightly greased skillet, prick the sausages with a fork and fry them until cooked through and golden, about 15 minutes. Add a bit of water to the pan, if needed, to prevent scorching. Remove to a cutting board and slice thinly.

3. Wipe out the skillet and heat the vegetable oil over medium-high heat. Add the onions and mushrooms. Cook until the onions start to turn translucent, about 5 minutes. Add the peppers and cook for another 2 to 3 minutes. Season to taste with salt and pepper.

4. Lay out the five containers. Divide the quinoa among the five containers, then add the sausage, then the vegetables. Chill the containers completely.

FREEZING INSTRUCTIONS:
Cover and freeze.

TO SERVE:
Heat the bowls in the microwave until hot throughout, about 5 minutes. Serve hot. If desired, add a handful of spinach and cover. The spinach will steam in the residual heat. Serve with fried eggs, avocado slices, and hot sauce, if desired.

9

BREADS, MUFFINS, SCONES, ROLLS, AND THEN SOME

- Buttermilk Cornbread ▪ 299
- Honey Butter ▪ 299
- Applesauce-Walnut Bread ▪ 300
- Chocolate Chip Banana Bread with Oats ▪ 301
- Spiced Pumpkin Flax Bread ▪ 303
- Nutty Zucchini Bread ▪ 305
- Cinnamon Banana Bread ▪ 306
- Vanilla Cranberry Bread ▪ 307
- Mix-and-Match Muffins ▪ 309
- Coconut-Lime Muffins with Chocolate Chips ▪ 310
- Crumb-Topped Zucchini Muffins ▪ 311
- Lemon-Blueberry Scones ▪ 313
- Raspberry Jam Cream Scones ▪ 314
- Ginger-Coconut Scones ▪ 316
- Lime Chocolate Chip Scones ▪ 317
- Garlic-Parmesan Swirl Biscuits ▪ 320
- Make-Ahead Drop Biscuits ▪ 322
- Cheddar Coins ▪ 323
- Whole-Grain Cinnamon Rolls ▪ 324
- Crystal's Butterhorn Rolls ▪ 326
- Cinnamon Twist Loaves ▪ 327
- Chocolate Butterhorn Rolls ▪ 329
- Honey Multigrain Rolls ▪ 330
- Garlic Focaccia ▪ 331
- Wholesome Energy Bars ▪ 333
- Easy Make-Ahead Garlic Bread ▪ 335

Buttermilk Cornbread

This buttermilk-and-brown-sugar cornbread is a favorite with friends and family. I serve it as a side dish with dinner, but we also love it for breakfast with a little honey butter. Since this recipe mixes and bakes so quickly, it's most efficient to package several batches of the "dry team" and store them in the freezer for later use, rather than freezing a finished bread. The honey butter can be prepared ahead of time and stored in the refrigerator. // ***Makes one 8-inch (20.3 cm) square pan***

■ **PACKAGING:** Quart-size (1 L) freezer bag

DRY INGREDIENTS:

¾ cup (90 g) whole-wheat pastry flour

¾ cup (90 g) unbleached all-purpose flour

½ cup (60 g) cornmeal

½ cup (112 g) dark brown sugar

1 tablespoon baking powder

½ teaspoon salt

WET INGREDIENTS:

½ cup (120 ml) vegetable oil or melted
    unsalted butter

2 large eggs

1¼ cups (295 ml) buttermilk

Honey Butter (recipe follows)

TO PACKAGE AS A MIX:

Place all of the dry ingredients in the freezer bag. Seal the bag and shake it gently to combine the ingredients. Store it in the pantry or freezer.

BAKING INSTRUCTIONS:

Preheat the oven to 350°F (180°C or gas mark 4). Grease an 8-inch (20.3 cm) square baking pan. In a large bowl, combine the oil, eggs, and buttermilk. Whisk to blend. Add the bag of cornbread mix. Mix well. Pour the batter into the prepared pan and bake for about 30 minutes, or until the cornbread is golden and a tester inserted in the center comes out with only a few crumbs attached. Serve with the honey butter.

Honey Butter

½ cup (112 g) (1 stick) salted butter,
    softened

2 tablespoons (40 g) honey

In a small bowl, blend the butter and honey. Spoon the butter into a small plastic container with a lid. Store in the refrigerator.

Applesauce-Walnut Bread

Quick breads are wonderful to keep on hand in the freezer. They make delicious breakfasts, snacks, and hostess gifts. This bread, adapted from a *Silver Palate* cake recipe, is a comfort, full of apple-sauce, spices, and crunchy nuts. It's delicious with or without the icing. For best flavor, use home-made Slow Cooker Applesauce (page 295). Commercial applesauce just doesn't cut it. Oh my! Yummy and good for you. // ***Makes two short 4½ × 8½ (11.4 × 21.6 cm) loaves***

■ **PACKAGING:** Plastic wrap, two gallon-size (4 L) zip-top freezer bags

¾ cup (180 ml) vegetable oil

1 cup (225 g) dark brown sugar

2 large eggs

2 cups (450 g) Slow Cooker Applesauce (page 295; don't include the optional brown sugar) or other favorite unsweetened applesauce

1 teaspoon vanilla extract

1 cup (120 g) whole-wheat pastry flour

2 cups (240 g) unbleached all-purpose flour

2 teaspoons ground cinnamon

2 teaspoons baking soda

1 cup (140 g) chopped walnuts

WHEN READY TO SERVE, YOU WILL NEED:

1 cup (120 g) confectioners' sugar

½ teaspoon ground cinnamon

3 tablespoons (45 ml) freshly squeezed orange juice

1. Preheat the oven to 325°F (170°C or gas mark 3). Spray two 4½ × 8½-inch (11.4 × 21.6 cm) loaf pans with nonstick cooking spray.

2. In a large bowl, combine the oil and brown sugar. Add the eggs and beat until combined. Stir in the applesauce and vanilla extract.

3. In another large bowl, whisk together the flours, cinnamon, and baking soda. Add this dry mixture to the wet mixture. Before stirring, sprinkle the walnuts over the dry ingredients. Gently fold everything together until well combined.

4. Pour the batter into the prepared pans. Bake for 60 to 65 minutes, or until a tester inserted in the center comes out with only a few crumbs attached. Transfer the pans to a rack and let cool for 10 minutes, then remove the loaves from the pans and place on a rack to cool completely.

FREEZING INSTRUCTIONS:

Wrap the cooled loaves in plastic wrap and place them in the zip-top freezer bags. Store in the freezer.

TO THAW AND SERVE:

Thaw the breads, wrapped, at room temperature for about 1 hour. Unwrap and place on a rack. In a small bowl, stir together the confectioners' sugar, cinnamon, and orange juice, and drizzle this icing over the tops of the breads. Once the icing is set, transfer the loaves to a serving tray. Slice and serve.

Chocolate Chip Banana Bread with Oats

In college there was always a mad dash at the cafeteria when this bread was on the menu. Precollege, I had never heard of such a thing. Now it's an item regularly stashed in my freezer. Banana bread is wonderfully adaptable for bulk baking and freezing. // ***Makes one 9 × 5-inch (23 × 12.7 cm) loaf***

▪ **PACKAGING:** Plastic wrap, gallon-size (4 L) zip-top freezer bag

1 cup (200 g) sugar
⅔ cup (160 ml) vegetable oil
2 large eggs
¼ cup (60 ml) buttermilk
1 teaspoon baking soda
1 cup (225 g) mashed banana

⅔ cup (80 g) unbleached all-purpose flour
⅔ cup (80 g) whole-wheat flour
⅓ cup (27 g) quick-cooking rolled oats
1 teaspoon vanilla extract
½ cup (88 g) chocolate chips

1. Preheat the oven to 350°F (180°C or gas mark 4). Spray a 9 × 5-inch (23 × 12.7 cm) loaf pan with nonstick cooking spray.

2. In a large bowl, combine all of the ingredients until well blended.

3. Pour the batter into the prepared pan. Bake for about 1 hour, or until a tester inserted in the center comes out clean.

4. Transfer to a rack and let cool for 10 minutes, then remove from the pan and place on a rack to cool completely.

FREEZING INSTRUCTIONS:

Wrap the cooled loaf in plastic wrap and place it in the zip-top freezer bag. Store in the freezer.

TO THAW AND SERVE:

Thaw the loaf, wrapped, at room temperature for about 1 hour. Slice and serve.

Note: To make a big batch (four loaves) of this banana bread, simply multiply all the ingredients by four. The cooking method remains the same. You should be able to fit two wrapped loaves into a gallon-size (4 L) freezer bag.

▶ Should You Buy a Deep Freezer?

Not all refrigerators are created equal. In fact, some are equipped with freezer compartments that won't even hold a 9 × 13-inch (23 × 33 cm) pan. If this describes your situation, you have to get creative if you want to cook and freeze in bulk. But never fear! There are a number of ways to make bulk cooking work, even with a small freezer.

1. Do shorter, more frequent cooking sessions. Chances are you can fit 10 meals into your freezer, even if it is a smaller model. Two or three times a month, you can spend an hour or two prepping those 10 meals, then stash them away to use over the coming weeks. When your supply dwindles, hold another mini cooking session.

2. Use zip-top freezer bags as your main form of packaging, as these are the most compact option. Seal the bag carefully and freeze the food flat. Once the package is frozen, you can flip the bags on their sides and line them up like books on a shelf.

If you'd like to expand your frozen storage resources, having a dedicated freezer might be the best route. Owning a deep freezer can be very useful, especially if you want to cook a month's worth of meals, are feeding large numbers of people, or would like to invest in significant bulk purchases, such as a side of beef.

There are two basic styles of deep freezer to choose from: the chest freezer and the upright. There are pros and cons to both.

We have owned a chest freezer for almost 20 years. It has served us well through everyday life with a large family, two cross-country moves, one power failure, and a few sides of beef. We bought our freezer used from a friend, so there wasn't a ton of research involved in our purchase. I had investigated upright freezers, but this was simply too good of a deal to pass up.

A chest freezer has a number of potential drawbacks:

1. It can be a safety hazard if small children try to remove items unsupervised. Yes, there have been cases of children falling in and becoming trapped. Our freezer can be locked, which is an excellent safety feature.

2. It can accumulate ice crystals on the walls. I defrost it once or twice a year. Since this requires emptying it completely, we do "a freezer challenge" and eat everything up, thereby rotating our stock and making sure nothing gets lost in the depths.

(continued)

3. Things can get "lost," since you have to pile the frozen entrees on top of one another and can't see beneath them.

In its defense, however, a chest freezer can't be left open accidentally, causing the contents to thaw.

Consider these pros and cons to the different styles of freezers:

CHEST FREEZERS

Pros

- Energy Star chest freezers are more efficient in energy usage than uprights.
- They are less expensive than uprights.

Cons

- They are too deep for short people to reach the bottom.
- They are difficult to organize efficiently.
- They need to be defrosted regularly.

UPRIGHT FREEZERS

Pros

- All the contents are visible.
- They are easy to organize.
- They are more flexible for storage.
- They have a smaller footprint than a chest freezer.

Cons

- Upright freezers can be left ajar accidentally.
- They are less energy efficient because ambient air pours in when the door is opened.

Spiced Pumpkin Flax Bread

This recipe is an egg-free, nut-free spiced pumpkin bread that is not overly sweet. (And if you use vegetable oil, it's also vegan.) It mixes up quickly, fills your home with a tantalizing aroma, and freezes beautifully. Flax seed meal is a great source of omega-3 fatty acids. If you prefer to use eggs, just substitute 3 beaten eggs for the flax seed meal and water. If you use canned pumpkin, make sure it is solid-pack pumpkin and NOT pumpkin pie filling. // *Makes two 9 × 5-inch (23 × 12.7 cm) loaves*

■ **PACKAGING:** Plastic wrap, gallon-size (4 L) zip-top freezer bag

3 tablespoons (20 g) flaxseed meal

½ cup (120 ml) plus 1 tablespoon (15 ml) water

2 cups (400 g) sugar

¾ cup (150 g) (1½ sticks) plus 2 tablespoons (28 g) melted unsalted butter or vegetable oil

2 cups (450 g) pumpkin puree or solid-pack pumpkin (one 15-ounce [420 g] can is fine)

3 cups (360 g) unbleached all-purpose flour

½ teaspoon ground ginger

½ teaspoon ground cinnamon

½ teaspoon ground nutmeg

1 teaspoon baking soda

½ teaspoon salt

½ teaspoon baking powder

1. Preheat the oven to 350°F (180°C or gas mark 4). Grease two 9 × 5-inch (23 × 12.7 cm) loaf pans.

2. In a small bowl, combine the flax seed meal and the water. Let it rest for 2 minutes.

3. In a large bowl, beat together the sugar and the butter. Mix in the flax seed mixture and the pumpkin.

4. In another large bowl, sift together the flour, ginger, cinnamon, nutmeg, baking soda, salt, and baking powder. Stir the flour mixture into the pumpkin mixture in two additions.

5. Pour the batter into the prepared pans. Bake for 50 minutes to 1 hour, or until a tester inserted in the center comes out clean.

6. Transfer to racks and let cool for 10 minutes. Loosen the loaves from the edges of the pans. Remove from the pans and place on racks to cool completely.

FREEZING INSTRUCTIONS:

Wrap the cooled loaves in plastic wrap. Place both loaves in the freezer bag and freeze.

SERVING INSTRUCTIONS:

Thaw the bread, wrapped, at room temperature for about 1 hour. Slice and serve.

Nutty Zucchini Bread

Ah, zucchini. The vegetable you love to hate, or hate to love. They are such prolific little buggers. When I have a wealth of zucchini from his garden, I bake up a big batch of this bread. A food processor is very handy for this sort of thing, making quick work of grating zucchini. Feel free to stir in chopped nuts or chocolate chips, or both. Still got extra zucchini? Be sure to make the Chocolate-Zucchini Cake (page 351). // *Makes four 9 × 5-inch (23 × 12.7 cm) loaves*

■ **PACKAGING:** Plastic wrap, two gallon-size (4 L) zip-top freezer bags

3 cups (705 ml) vegetable oil

9 large eggs, beaten

5 cups (1000 g) sugar

2 tablespoons (30 ml) vanilla extract

9 cups (1080 g) unbleached all-purpose flour

6 cups (720 g) shredded zucchini

1 tablespoon baking soda

¾ teaspoon baking powder

1 tablespoon (18 g) salt

1 tablespoon ground cinnamon

1½ cups (210 g) chopped nuts of your choice, chocolate chips, or a combination

1. Preheat the oven to 325°F (170°C or gas mark 3). Spray four 9 × 5-inch (23 × 12.7 cm) loaf pans with nonstick cooking spray.

2. In a very large bowl, combine the oil, eggs, sugar, and vanilla. Mix well.

3. Stir in the flour, shredded zucchini, baking soda, baking powder, salt, cinnamon, and nuts. Stir until just mixed.

4. Pour the batter into the prepared pans and bake for 1 hour or until a tester inserted in the center comes out clean. Transfer to a rack and let cool for 10 minutes, then remove from the pan and place on a rack to cool completely.

FREEZING INSTRUCTIONS:

Wrap the cooled loaves in plastic wrap. Place two wrapped loaves in each freezer bag and freeze.

TO THAW AND SERVE:

Thaw the bread, wrapped, at room temperature for about 1 hour. Slice and serve.

Cinnamon Banana Bread

I love baking banana bread in big batches. When you're rich in golden loaves fragrant with cinnamon and banana, it's easy to share—and to stash a few away for a rainy day. Baking in muffin tins can save you time and provide you with individual breads, ready to pack for work, school, or play. // *Makes four 9 × 5-inch (23 × 12.7 cm) loaves or 36 to 40 mini breads*

■ **PACKAGING:** Plastic wrap, gallon-size (4 L) zip-top freezer bags

6 bananas, mashed	3 cups (360 g) unbleached all-purpose flour
1½ cups (355 ml) half-and-half	3 cups (360 g) whole-wheat pastry flour
3 large eggs	1 tablespoon baking powder
¾ cup (180 ml) vegetable oil or melted unsalted butter	1½ teaspoons baking soda
	1½ teaspoons salt
2 cups (450 g) light or dark brown sugar	1½ teaspoons ground cinnamon

1. Preheat the oven to 350°F (180°C or gas mark 4). Spray four loaf pans with nonstick cooking spray or line muffin tins with paper liners. You can bake some of both sizes, if you prefer.

2. In a very large bowl, blend the bananas, half-and-half, eggs, and oil until smooth. Add the brown sugar and stir, smoothing out any lumps.

3. Add the flours, baking powder, baking soda, salt, and cinnamon. Fold the wet and dry ingredients together just until mixed.

4. Pour the batter into the prepared pans. Bake the loaves for about 1 hour, or until a tester inserted in the center comes out clean. Bake the mini breads for 20 to 22 minutes, or until a tester inserted in the center comes out clean.

5. Transfer the pans to a rack and let cool for 10 minutes, then remove the breads from the pans and place on a rack to cool completely.

FREEZING INSTRUCTIONS:

Wrap each cooled loaf in plastic wrap. Place two wrapped loaves in each freezer bag and freeze. Mini breads can be placed in freezer bags; remove as much air as possible before sealing the bags.

TO THAW AND SERVE:

Thaw banana bread, wrapped, at room temperature for about 1 hour.

Vanilla Cranberry Bread

This cranberry bread is delightful at tea or breakfast, and makes a perfect addition to a holiday breadbasket. The sweet bread, tangy cranberries, and warm vanilla blend together harmoniously. Keep several loaves stashed in the freezer for a tasty snack anytime. // ***Makes three 9 × 5-inch (23 × 12.7 cm) loaves***

■ **PACKAGING:** Plastic wrap, gallon-size (4 L) zip-top freezer bags

1 cup (225 g) (2 sticks) unsalted butter, softened

2¼ cups (250 g) sugar

6 large eggs

1 cup (225 g) plain yogurt

1 cup (235 ml) milk

1 tablespoon (15 ml) vanilla extract

4 cups (480 g) unbleached all-purpose flour

2 cups (240 g) whole-wheat pastry flour

1½ teaspoons salt

1½ teaspoons baking soda

1½ teaspoons baking powder

3 cups (300 g) fresh cranberries

1. Preheat the oven to 350°F (180°C or gas mark 4). Spray three loaf pans with nonstick cooking spray.

2. In a very large bowl, cream the butter and sugar until smooth. Add the eggs and beat until well incorporated. Stir in the yogurt, milk, and vanilla.

3. Add the flours, salt, baking soda, and baking powder. Fold the wet and dry ingredients together just until mixed. Fold in the cranberries.

4. Spoon the batter into the prepared pans. Bake the breads for 50 minutes to 1 hour, or until a tester inserted in the center comes out clean.

5. Transfer the pans to a rack and let cool for 10 minutes, then remove the loaves from the pans and place on a rack to cool completely.

FREEZING INSTRUCTIONS:
Wrap each cooled loaf in plastic wrap and store them in freezer bags. Freeze.

TO THAW AND SERVE:
Thaw the bread, wrapped, at room temperature for about 1 hour. Slice and serve.

► Make Your Own Mixes

I love to bake, and I know that baking from scratch is usually the most frugal option. But I confess, I'm often lazy and just don't want to haul out the flour and leavening and measuring cups. A boxed mix could come to my rescue, but there is a better, healthier, less expensive way: homemade baking mixes. Any of the recipes in this chapter can be prepared as mixes, except for the yeast breads.

About once a month, I spend an hour or so making and packaging my own mixes. In assembly-line fashion, I measure out the dry ingredients for some of my favorite recipes. I make two to four batches of each, storing them in quart- (1 L) or gallon-size (4 L) freezer bags. I mark the bags clearly, noting which wet ingredients and mix-ins to add later, as well as the baking instructions; I don't want to have to hunt down a recipe at baking time. I often store my mixes in the freezer since many of them contain whole-wheat flour, which doesn't have as long a shelf life as all-purpose white flour. Then, when Coconut-Lime Muffins with Chocolate Chips (page 310) sound good one morning, or the family is begging for Buttermilk Cornbread (page 299) with dinner, I just mix up the wet ingredients, dump in a bag of mix, and we're good to go. You can even take some baking mixes camping with you!

Homemade mixes also play a major role in my gift giving. When I need a hostess gift or a quick thank-you, I can grab a mix from the freezer, pair it with a jar of jam or a bag of coffee, tie it all with a ribbon, and have a gift ready in just minutes. Instant friendship in a gift bag!

GREAT RECIPES FOR MIX-MAKING:

- Bulk-Batch Pancakes, page 275
- Oatmeal–Chocolate Chip Pancakes, page 276
- Spiced Whole-Grain Waffles, page 280
- Maple-Oat Waffles, page 277
- Lemon-and-Honey Flax Waffles, page 278
- Buttermilk Cornbread, page 299
- Mix-and-Match Muffins, page 309
- Coconut-Lime Muffins with Chocolate Chips, page 310
- Crumb-Topped Zucchini Muffins, page 311

- Raspberry Jam Cream Scones, page 314
- Lemon-Blueberry Scones, page 313
- Ginger-Coconut Scones, page 316
- Lime Chocolate Chip Scones, page 317
- Make-Ahead Drop Biscuits, page 322
- Garlic-Parmesan Swirl Biscuits, page 320
- Cocoa Brownies, page 346

Mix-and-Match Muffins

Home-baked muffins are hard to beat—unless you add more sugar and call them cupcakes. This recipe, inspired by one from bakery owner and cookbook author Joanne Chang, has endless possibilities. I've adapted it by adding plain yogurt and a little whole-wheat flour. Prepare the baking mix ahead of time for fresh muffins in a matter of minutes on busy mornings. If you decide to package the recipe as a mix, be sure to mark the bag with a list of the wet ingredients to add right before baking, as well as the baking instructions. // *Makes 24 muffins*

■ **PACKAGING:** Zip-top freezer bags (gallon size [4 L] for baked muffins, quart size [1 L] for mix)

DRY INGREDIENTS:

3 cups (360 g) unbleached all-purpose flour
½ cup (60 g) whole-wheat flour
4 teaspoons (15 g) baking powder
½ teaspoon baking soda
½ teaspoon salt
1 cup (200 g) granulated or (225 g) light
  brown sugar

WET INGREDIENTS:

½ cup (120 ml) vegetable oil
1 cup (235 ml) milk
½ cup (112 g) plain yogurt
2 large eggs

Mix-ins: Your choice of 1 teaspoon extract (such as vanilla, almond, butterscotch, or coconut), 1½ cups (225 g) any combination of fruit (such as mashed bananas, finely chopped apples, blueberries, raspberries, or fresh or dried cranberries), chopped nuts, and/or chocolate chips

TO PACKAGE AS A MIX:

Place all of the dry ingredients in the quart-size (1 L) freezer bag. Seal the bag and shake it gently to combine the ingredients. Store in the freezer.

BAKING INSTRUCTIONS:

1. Preheat the oven to 350°F (180°C or gas mark 4). Line two muffin tins with paper liners or spray them with nonstick cooking spray.

2. In a large bowl, combine the oil, milk, yogurt, and eggs. Whisk to blend. Add the dry ingredients to the wet ingredients and fold gently with a rubber spatula just until combined. Fold in the desired mix-ins.

3. Scoop the batter into the prepared muffin tins. Bake for 25 to 30 minutes, until the muffins are golden brown and a tester comes out clean. Cool the muffins on a rack.

FREEZING INSTRUCTIONS:

Place the cooled muffins in the gallon-size (4 L) freezer bags, removing as much air as possible before sealing the bag. Freeze.

TO THAW AND SERVE:

Thaw the muffins in bags at room temperature.

Coconut-Lime Muffins with Chocolate Chips

When we were newlyweds, my husband and I enjoyed a local restaurant that served flourless choco-late cake with a lime sauce. It was heavenly. While we can't have chocolate cake for breakfast, I can re-create some of those flavors in these delectable muffins bursting with tart lime, buttery coconut, and sweet chocolate. Use the dry ingredients from Mix-and-Match Muffins (page 309), then add the wet ingredients and mix-ins right before baking. Alternatively, bake up these muffins and stash them in the freezer for on-the-go snacking. Just before serving, you can drizzle the icing over the tops, though the muffins are delicious without it as well. // *Makes 24 muffins*

■ **PACKAGING:** Two gallon-size (4 L) zip-top freezer bags

½ cup (120 ml) vegetable oil
1 cup (235 ml) coconut milk
½ cup (112 g) plain yogurt
2 large eggs
1 tablespoon (15 ml) freshly squeezed
    lime juice

Grated zest of 1 lime
1 batch Mix-and-Match Muffins,
    dry ingredients only (page 309)
1 cup (175 g) chocolate chips

WHEN READY TO SERVE, YOU WILL NEED:

1 cup (120 g) confectioners' sugar
Juice of 1 lime

Grated zest of 1 lime

1. Preheat the oven to 350°F (180°C or gas mark 4). Line two muffin tins with paper liners or spray them with nonstick cooking spray.

2. In a large bowl, combine the oil, coconut milk, yogurt, eggs, the 1 tablespoon (15 ml) lime juice, and zest of 1 lime. Whisk to blend.

3. Add the dry ingredients. Fold gently until mostly moistened but still lumpy. Fold in the chocolate chips.

4. Scoop the batter into the prepared muffin tins. Bake for 25 to 30 minutes, until the muffins are golden brown and a tester comes out clean. Cool the muffins on a rack.

FREEZING INSTRUCTIONS:

Place the cooled muffins in the freezer bags, removing as much air as possible before sealing the bags. Freeze.

TO THAW AND SERVE:

Thaw the muffins in bags at room temperature. Stir together the confectioners' sugar, remaining lime juice, and remaining lime zest. Drizzle this icing over the muffins.

Crumb-Topped Zucchini Muffins

I love the versatility of baking mixes because I can stir in all kinds of goodies, like zucchini. Your kids might not think of zucchini as a "goodie," but when it's baked into these muffins they will! Summertime tip: If you don't feel like baking up your whole zucchini harvest at once, simply freeze the shredded vegetable in quart-size (1 L) zip-top freezer bags. Thaw and drain the zucchini before adding it to recipes. // *Makes 24 muffins*

■ **PACKAGING:** Two gallon-size (4 L) zip-top freezer bags

½ cup (120 ml) vegetable oil
1 cup (235 ml) milk
½ cup (112 g) plain yogurt
2 large eggs
1 teaspoon vanilla extract

½ teaspoon ground nutmeg
1 batch Mix-and-Match Muffins,
 dry ingredients only (page 309)
1½ cups (180 g) shredded zucchini

STREUSEL TOPPING:

½ cup (60 g) unbleached all-purpose flour
2 tablespoons (28 g) unsalted butter, cubed
¼ cup (56 g) brown sugar

½ cup (70 g) chopped walnuts, pecans,
 or almonds
1 teaspoon ground cinnamon
½ teaspoon almond extract

1. Preheat the oven to 350°F (180°C or gas mark 4). Line two muffin tins with paper liners or spray them with nonstick cooking spray.

2. In a large bowl, combine the oil, milk, yogurt, eggs, vanilla, and nutmeg. Whisk to blend.

3. Add the bag dry ingredients. Fold gently until mostly moistened but still lumpy. Fold in the zucchini.

4. To prepare the streusel topping, place all the topping ingredients in the bowl of a food processor. Pulse until coarse crumbs are formed. Alternatively, combine the flour and butter in a small bowl. Cut the butter into the flour with a pastry blender or two knives. Stir in the sugar, nuts, cinnamon, and almond extract.

5. Scoop the batter into the prepared muffin tins. Sprinkle the streusel topping over the batter. Bake for 25 to 30 minutes, until the muffins are golden brown and a tester comes out clean. Cool the muffins on a rack.

FREEZING INSTRUCTIONS:

Place the cooled muffins in the freezer bags, removing as much air as possible before sealing the bag. Freeze.

TO THAW AND SERVE:

Thaw the muffins in bags at room temperature.

▶ Scones and Biscuits

Scones and biscuits are easy shortbreads to pull together, but making them still involves mess and time. I've found three successful methods for preparing scones and biscuits ahead of time. Each allows me flexibility in baking—and makes good use of my freezer.

MAKE A MIX

Combine the dry ingredients in a quart-size (1 L) freezer bag. Label it with a list of the wet ingredients to be added later and the baking instructions. Half the work is already done next time you want a fresh scone or biscuit.

QUICK FREEZE

This method involves mixing and forming the dough and then freezing it. Frozen unbaked scones can be pulled from the freezer and slid into the oven. They are hot on the table within 20 minutes.

BAKE AND FREEZE

For this method, completely prepare the scone or biscuit recipe. Once the baked goods have cooled, wrap them well and freeze. This method allows for quick breakfasts, lunches, and snacks on the go.

Lemon-Blueberry Scones

Lemons and blueberries are a classic flavor combination, and for good reason. They just burst with sunshiny flavor. What better way to start a morning than with fresh-baked lemony scones, popping with blueberries? Mix up a batch to freeze. On a busy morning, you can pull them from the freezer and pop them in the oven. They'll be ready in no time. // *Makes 12 scones*

- **PACKAGING:** Zip-top freezer bags (gallon size [4 L] for preformed or baked scones, quart size [1 L] for mix)

DRY INGREDIENTS:

3 cups (360 g) whole-wheat pastry flour

2 cups (240 g) unbleached all-purpose flour

1 cup (200 g) sugar

1 tablespoon baking powder

1 teaspoon baking soda

½ teaspoon salt

WET INGREDIENTS:

Grated zest of 1 lemon

1 cup (225 g) (2 sticks) unsalted butter, cut into cubes

2 cups (470 ml) buttermilk

1½ cups (225 g) frozen blueberries (no need to thaw)

TO PACKAGE AS A MIX:

Place all of the dry ingredients in the quart-size (1 L) freezer bag. Seal the bag and shake it gently to combine the ingredients. Store in the pantry or freezer.

TO PREPARE SCONES:

1. Line baking sheets with parchment paper.

2. In a large bowl, combine the dry ingredients and lemon zest. Cut in the butter with a pastry blender or two knives until coarse crumbs form. (To speed up the process, you can do this in batches in a food processor, then remove the mixture to a large bowl.)

3. Add the buttermilk and blueberries. Fold gently until combined. The dough will be sticky.

4. Turn the dough out onto a floured surface and fold 2 or 3 turns, or until the dough comes together.

5. Gently pat or roll the dough into a 1-inch (2.5 cm)-thick rectangle, taking care not to squash the berries. Cut the dough into 12 rectangles. Scones can be baked at this point.

FREEZING INSTRUCTIONS:

Place the unbaked scones on parchment-lined baking sheets and freeze until firm. Once the scones are firm, transfer them to the gallon-size (4 L) freezer bags, removing as much air as possible. Freeze. Baked scones can also be frozen in an airtight container or freezer bag.

TO SERVE:

Preheat the oven to 375°F (190°C or gas mark 5). Bake scones for 20 minutes, or 25 minutes for frozen scones (no need to thaw). Cool and serve. Thaw prebaked scones in bags at room temperature.

Raspberry Jam Cream Scones

My husband loves the raspberry scones at a certain coffee shop. I found a way to make them at home, and now I can freeze them and pop them in the oven at any time. Feel free to make scone "bites" by cutting the dough into smaller squares. // ***Makes 12 scones***

- **PACKAGING:** Zip-top freezer bags (gallon size [4 L] for preformed or baked scones, quart size [1 L] for mix)

DRY INGREDIENTS:

2 cups (240 g) whole-wheat pastry flour

3 cups (360 g) unbleached all-purpose flour

1 cup (200 g) sugar

1 tablespoon baking powder

1 teaspoon baking soda

½ teaspoon salt

WET INGREDIENTS:

1 teaspoon grated orange zest

¾ cup (170 g) (1½ sticks) unsalted butter, cut into cubes

1¾ cups (415 ml) cream

⅓ cup (75 g) seedless raspberry jam

TO PACKAGE AS A MIX:

Place all of the dry ingredients in the quart-size (1 L) freezer bag. Seal the bag and shake it gently to combine the ingredients. Store in the pantry or freezer.

TO PREPARE SCONES:

1. Line baking sheets with parchment paper.

2. In a large bowl, combine dry ingredients and orange zest. Cut in the butter with a pastry blender or two knives until coarse crumbs form. (To speed up the process, do this in batches in a food processor, then transfer to a large bowl.)

3. Add the cream. Fold gently until combined. The dough will be sticky.

4. Turn the dough out onto a floured surface and fold 2 or 3 turns, or until the dough comes together.

5. Pat or roll the dough into a 1-inch (2.5 cm)-thick rectangle. Spread the jam over one half of the dough. Fold the side without jam over the jam side and press to flatten again to a 1-inch (2.5 cm) thickness. The jam and dough should swirl together a bit. Cut the dough into 12 rectangles. Scones can be baked at this point.

FREEZING INSTRUCTIONS:

Place the unbaked scones on parchment-lined baking sheets and freeze until firm. Once the scones are firm, transfer them to the gallon-size (4 L) freezer bags, removing as much air as possible. Freeze. Baked scones can also be frozen in an airtight container or freezer bag.

TO SERVE:

Preheat the oven to 375°F (190°C or gas mark 5). Bake scones for 20 minutes, or 25 minutes for frozen scones (no need to thaw). Cool and serve. Thaw prebaked scones in bags at room temperature.

Ginger-Coconut Scones

I love the way ginger and coconut work together. There's a warm, buttery zip to these scones, making them perfect with a cup of tea. Feel free to cut them into smaller squares for snack-size scones. // **Makes 12 large or 24 small scones**

■ **PACKAGING:** Zip-top freezer bags (gallon size [4 L] for preformed or baked scones, quart size [1 L] for mix)

DRY INGREDIENTS:

2 cups (240 g) whole-wheat pastry flour

3 cups (360 g) unbleached all-purpose flour

1 cup (200 g) sugar

1 tablespoon baking powder

½ teaspoon ground ginger

½ teaspoon salt

WET INGREDIENTS:

1 cup (225 g) (2 sticks) unsalted butter,
  cut into cubes

1½ cups (355 ml) light coconut milk

½ cup (40 g) unsweetened shredded
  coconut

¼ cup (25 g) chopped crystallized ginger

TO PACKAGE AS A MIX:

Place all of the dry ingredients in the quart-size (1 L) freezer bag. Seal the bag and shake it gently to combine the ingredients. Store in the pantry or freezer.

TO PREPARE SCONES:

1. Line baking sheets with parchment paper.

2. Place the dry ingredients in a large bowl. Cut in the butter with a pastry blender or two knives until coarse crumbs form. (To speed up the process, you can do this in batches in a food processor, then remove the mixture to a large bowl.)

3. Add the coconut milk, shredded coconut, and crystallized ginger. Fold gently until combined. The dough will be sticky.

4. Turn the dough out onto a floured surface and fold 2 or 3 turns, or until the dough comes together.

5. Pat or roll the dough into a 1-inch (2.5 cm)-thick rectangle. Cut into 12 or 24 squares. Scones can be baked at this point.

FREEZING INSTRUCTIONS:

Place the unbaked scones on parchment-lined baking sheets and freeze until firm. Once the scones are firm, transfer them to the gallon-size (4 L) freezer bags, removing as much air as possible. Freeze. Baked scones can also be frozen in an airtight container or freezer bag.

TO SERVE:

Preheat the oven to 375°F (190°C or gas mark 5). Bake scones for 20 minutes, or 25 minutes for frozen scones (no need to thaw). Cool and serve. Thaw prebaked scones in bags at room temperature.

Lime Chocolate Chip Scones

No scone repertoire is complete without a chocolate recipe. These make use of the ease of self-rising flour and combine lime zest and chocolate, two friends that go very well together. If you make the smaller scones, consider using mini chocolate chips. // *Makes 12 large or 24 small scones*

■ **PACKAGING:** Zip-top freezer bags (gallon size [4 L] for preformed or baked scones, quart size [1 L] for mix)

DRY INGREDIENTS:

4 cups (480 g) self-rising flour

**½ cup (100 g) granulated sugar
or light brown sugar**

WET INGREDIENTS:

**½ cup (112 g) (1 stick) unsalted butter,
    cubed**
½ cup (120 ml) milk
¼ cup (60 ml) cream

2 large eggs
Zest of 2 limes
1 cup (175 g) chocolate chips

TO PACKAGE AS A MIX:

Place all of the dry ingredients in the quart-size (1 L) freezer bag. Seal the bag and shake it gently to combine the ingredients. Store in the pantry or freezer.

TO PREPARE SCONES:

1. Line baking sheets with parchment paper.

2. Place the dry ingredients in a large bowl. Cut in the butter with a pastry blender or two knives until coarse crumbs form. (To speed up the process, you can do this in batches in a food processor, then remove the mixture to a large bowl.)

3. In another mixing bowl, combine the milk, cream, eggs, and lime zest. Add this to the dry mixture. Sprinkle the chocolate chips over the dough and fold gently until combined. The dough will be sticky.

4. Turn the dough out onto a floured surface and fold 2 or 3 turns, or until the dough comes together.

5. Pat or roll the dough into a 1-inch (2.5 cm)-thick rectangle. Cut into 12 or 24 rectangles. Scones can be baked at this point.

FREEZING INSTRUCTIONS:

Place the unbaked scones on parchment-lined baking sheets and freeze until firm. Once the scones are firm, transfer them to the gallon-size (4 L) freezer bags, removing as much air as possible. Freeze. Baked scones can also be frozen in an airtight container or freezer bag.

TO SERVE:

Preheat the oven to 375°F (190°C or gas mark 5). Bake scones for 20 minutes, or 25 minutes for frozen scones (no need to thaw). Cool and serve. Thaw prebaked scones in bags at room temperature.

► Forming a Bulk Cooking Co-Op

"If more of us valued food and cheer and song above hoarded gold, it would be a merrier world." —J.R.R. Tolkien

Food is a great equalizer. We all need it. We all love it. And we know it's fun to share it. A bulk cooking co-op can be a great way to do just that.

A co-op can take different forms, but the general idea is that each person in the group makes one or two recipes in quantities large enough to share with everyone in the group. Like a traditional Christmas cookie exchange, the group members gather with their pre-made, prefrozen meals and then swap, so that everyone goes home with one container of each meal. This method of bulk cooking allows you to capitalize on the assembly-line method of cooking and bulk buying while adding more variety to your freezer choices.

Certainly you can make your co-op as big and complicated, or as small and simple, as you like. The point is to help one another serve great food at home and create a little community spirit at the same time.

Here are some basic tips to help you start a bulk freezer cooking cooperative:

1. Decide on the size of the group. Four to six people is ideal. You'll need to make that number of batches of one recipe at a time, and you don't want the adventure to become too unwieldy by including too many people.

2. Choose the recipes. Coordinating the tastes and food preferences of several households is a little more complicated than cooking on your own or with just one friend. Be diplomatic, as well as respectful of food allergies and aversions. You aren't doing your partners any favors if you make food their families can't or won't eat.

3. Assign the recipes. This is a great way to build on one another's strengths. Does someone in the group just rock the tamale making? Assign that dish to her. Is someone else a whiz with pastry? Let him make the Best-Ever Chicken Pot Pie (page 127). Arrange who will cook what, and then choose a day to convene to swap meals. At the same time, find out what kind of freezer storage each person has at home. Some freezers can't hold larger pans easily, so make sure that the other group members will be able to stash your meals.

4. Cook up a storm on your own. Remember to label carefully and make each share more or less the same size, even if you need to use smaller pans to accommodate smaller freezers. Two 8-inch (20.3 cm) square pans are about equal to one 9 × 13-inch (23 × 33 cm) baking dish.

5. Get together to swap. Bring coolers full of frozen meals to one location; go home with those coolers full of different frozen meals.

(continued)

6. Compare notes. As you prepare for the next round of cooking, discuss what meals worked—or didn't—in the previous go-round. Try to have a thick skin about this. Different folks like different flavors. If you thoroughly discussed the recipes at the outset, this shouldn't be a big problem. But things will invariably come up ("Oh, I forgot that Joe doesn't like olives."). Go with it.

Garlic-Parmesan Swirl Biscuits

These biscuits take a little extra work, but they look elegant and really dress up the plate. I have found that preparing and freezing them in advance of baking is the best approach. // *Makes 12 biscuits*

▪ **PACKAGING:** Gallon-size (4 L) zip-top freezer bag

GARLIC BUTTER:

¼ cup (56 g) (½ stick) unsalted butter, softened

3 cloves garlic, crushed

2 tablespoons freshly grated Parmesan cheese

¼ teaspoon dried parsley flakes

BISCUIT DOUGH:

2 cups (240 g) unbleached all-purpose flour

1 teaspoon salt

1 tablespoon baking powder

⅓ cup (75 g) unsalted butter

¾ cup (180 ml) milk

1. Grease a 12-cup muffin tin.

2. In a small bowl, combine the garlic butter ingredients. Set aside.

3. In a large bowl, combine the flour, salt, and baking powder. Cut in the ⅓ cup (75 g) butter with a pastry blender or two knives until coarse crumbs are formed. Stir in the milk until combined.

4. Turn the dough out onto a floured surface. Knead the dough a few times and flatten into a 9 × 12-inch (23 × 30.5 cm) rectangle.

5. Spread the garlic butter over the surface of the dough. Roll the dough up from the long side and pinch the edges to seal.

6. Cut the rolled dough into twelve 1-inch (2.5 cm)-wide pieces. Place each spiral in a prepared muffin cup.

FREEZING INSTRUCTIONS:

Place the muffin pan in the freezer. Freeze until the biscuits are firm to the touch. Pop the biscuits out of the pan and store them in the freezer bag in the freezer.

TO SERVE:

Preheat the oven to 425°F (220°C or gas mark 7). Place the desired number of frozen biscuits (no need to thaw) on a baking sheet and bake for 15 minutes, or until golden brown. Serve warm.

Make-Ahead Drop Biscuits

My kids love biscuits. One night they ate a full dozen before I could get dinner on the table. Time to make these babies in bulk! Homemade biscuits are so much tastier and healthier than the kind you buy in a can. Although it's nice to make the fluffy cutout variety, drop biscuits are much easier and more forgiving. // *Makes 12 biscuits*

▪ **PACKAGING:** Quart-size (1 L) zip-top freezer bag, gallon-size (4 L) zip-top freezer bag

DRY INGREDIENTS:
1 cup (120 g) unbleached all-purpose flour
1 cup (120 g) whole-wheat pastry flour

1 tablespoon baking powder
½ teaspoon salt

WET INGREDIENTS:
3 tablespoons (45 ml) olive oil
1 large egg

¾ cup (180 ml) milk

TO PACKAGE AS A MIX:

Place all of the dry ingredients in the quart-size (1 L) freezer bag. Seal the bag and shake it gently to combine the ingredients. Store in the pantry or freezer.

TO PREPARE THE BISCUITS:

1. Preheat the oven to 450°F (230°C or gas mark 8) and line a baking sheet with parchment paper or a silicone baking mat.

2. Place the dry ingredients in a large bowl. In another bowl, combine the oil, egg, and milk.

3. Fold the wet mixture into the dry gently until combined.

4. Drop the batter by scant ¼-cupfuls (60 ml) onto the prepared baking sheet. See directions below for freezing unbaked biscuits.

5. Bake for 10 to 15 minutes, or until golden brown. Cool the biscuits completely on a rack.

FREEZING INSTRUCTIONS:
Place the cooled biscuits in the gallon-size (4 L) freezer bag, removing as much air as possible. Freeze.

TO THAW AND SERVE:
Thaw the biscuits at room temperature and warm in a low oven until heated through.

TO FREEZE UNBAKED BISCUITS:
Place the unbaked biscuits on baking sheets or trays in the freezer. Once they are firm, transfer them to the gallon-size (4 L) freezer bag, removing as much air as possible. Freeze.

TO SERVE:
Preheat the oven to 450°F (230°C or gas mark 8). Bake frozen biscuits (no need to thaw) on a baking sheet lined with parchment paper or a silicone baking mat for 15 to 20 minutes.

VARIATION: HERB BISCUITS
Stir the following into the dry ingredients:

¼ teaspoon garlic powder
¼ teaspoon dried basil

⅛ teaspoon dried oregano
⅛ teaspoon dried thyme

Proceed as directed.

Cheddar Coins

Most of us can go through a box of cheesy snack crackers in one sitting. To combat the expense and the number of ingredients whose names I can't pronounce in store-bought snack crackers, I experimented with making a healthier cheese cracker. This is adapted from a version I found in *Fine Cooking* magazine; I make it with whole-wheat flour and simplify the process. The end result was a crisp, salty, cheddary cracker that smacks of the "I-could-eat-the-whole-box" packaged cheese crackers. // *Makes about 4 dozen crackers*

■ **PACKAGING:** Quart-size (1 L) zip-top freezer bag

1 cup (120 g) unbleached all-purpose flour
⅓ cup (40 g) whole-wheat flour
1⅓ cups (160 g) finely shredded sharp
    cheddar cheese
1 teaspoon salt

½ teaspoon garlic powder
½ cup (112 g) (1 stick) unsalted butter,
    cubed
1 large egg

1. In the bowl of a food processor, combine the flours, cheese, salt, and garlic powder. Add the butter cubes and pulse until crumbs are formed. Blend in the egg until the dough comes together around the blade.

2. Turn the dough out onto a sheet of plastic wrap. Form the dough into a 1-inch (2.5 cm)-diameter log. Wrap tightly in plastic wrap and chill in the refrigerator for at least 2 hours.

3. Preheat the oven to 375°F (190°C or gas mark 5). Line baking sheets with parchment paper or silicone baking mats.

4. Slice the log into thin coins, rolling the log on the cutting board so as to maintain its rounded shape.

5. Place the coins on the prepared baking sheets and bake for 15 minutes. Cool on a rack.

FREEZING INSTRUCTIONS:

Store the cooled crackers in the freezer bag, removing as much air as possible from the bag. Freeze.

TO THAW AND SERVE:

These crackers thaw quickly. They will be ready to devour after just a few minutes on the counter.

Whole-Grain Cinnamon Rolls

I used to mix up cinnamon rolls every Saturday night so we could enjoy them on Sunday mornings. While we loved the morning ritual, I wasn't crazy about the messy Saturday night kitchen. My friend Amy McGuire, from AmysFinerThings.com, taught me how to adapt my cinnamon rolls for the freezer. Now we can enjoy cinnamon rolls any day of the week—without the huge mess! I use a bread machine to make the process even easier. // *Makes 18 rolls*

■ **PACKAGING:** Gallon-size (4 L) zip-top freezer bags

DOUGH:

2 cups (470 ml) milk
4½ tablespoons (63 g) unsalted butter
1½ teaspoons vanilla extract
¼ cup (50 g) granulated sugar
3¾ teaspoons active dry yeast

½ cup (40 g) quick-cooking rolled oats
1 cup (120 g) whole-wheat flour
3 to 3½ cups (360 to 420 g) unbleached
    all-purpose flour
1¾ teaspoons salt

FILLING:

3½ tablespoons (50 g) unsalted butter,
    softened

¾ cup (150 g) light or dark brown sugar
1 tablespoon ground cinnamon

WHEN READY TO SERVE, YOU WILL NEED:

¾ cup (90 g) confectioners' sugar
1 to 2 tablespoons (15 to 30 ml) milk

½ teaspoon vanilla extract

1. Line baking sheets with parchment paper.

2. If making the dough in the bread machine, combine the dough ingredients in the bread machine according to the manufacturer's instructions. Program the machine for the dough setting and start it.

If making the dough by hand, place the milk and butter in a medium saucepan and warm slightly. Transfer the mixture to a large bowl or the bowl of a stand mixer and add the vanilla, sugar, and yeast. Stir and allow the yeast to proof for 5 minutes. Add the oats, whole-wheat flour, 3 cups (360 g) of the all-purpose flour, and the salt. Stir to combine well. Knead in the stand mixer with the dough hook or turn the mixture out onto a lightly floured surface and knead by hand. Continue kneading for 5 minutes to create a smooth, elastic dough, adding more of the all-purpose flour as necessary. Transfer to a greased bowl and turn the dough ball to coat. Let rise until doubled in bulk, about 1 hour.

3. When the dough is ready, roll it out on a lightly floured surface to form a 12 × 15-inch (30.5 × 38 cm) rectangle.

4. Spread the softened butter over the surface.

5. In a small bowl, combine the brown sugar and cinnamon. Sprinkle this mixture over the butter.

6. Roll up the dough, jelly-roll fashion, starting from a long edge and pinching the seam to seal.

7. Cut the rolled dough into 18 slices, each about ⅔ inch (1.7 cm) wide, and arrange them on the prepared baking sheets 1 to 2 inches (2.5 to 5 cm) apart.

FREEZING INSTRUCTIONS:

Place the trays in the freezer and freeze the rolls until they are firm. Remove the trays from the freezer and place the rolls on their sides in the freezer bags, in stacks of six. Place the bags in the freezer immediately.

TO THAW AND SERVE:

The night before baking, remove as many rolls as desired from the freezer and place them in a greased 9 × 13-inch (23 × 33 cm) baking dish. You may need two pans if you bake all 18 rolls at once. Cover the dish with plastic wrap and refrigerate overnight. The rolls will thaw and rise in the refrigerator. In the morning, remove the dish from the refrigerator and let the rolls rest for 20 minutes at room temperature. Preheat the oven to 350°F (180°C or gas mark 4). Bake the rolls until browned, 20 to 30 minutes. Remove the pans from the oven and cool on a wire rack. To make the icing, stir together the confectioners' sugar, milk, and vanilla until smooth. Glaze with the icing before serving.

Crystal's Butterhorn Rolls

Crystal, the blogger from Money Saving Mom, shared her butterhorn recipe years ago, and my family was instantly smitten with them. These rolls freeze, thaw, rise, and bake beautifully; they can be frozen baked or unbaked. I adapted her recipe to work in my bread machine, thereby enabling me to multitask a little bit better in the kitchen. The bread machine can do most of the work while I do something else. // *Makes 32 rolls*

- **PACKAGING:** Gallon-size (4 L) zip-top freezer bags

1 cup (235 ml) warm milk
½ cup (112 g) (1 stick) unsalted butter, melted, plus additional for brushing
2 large eggs
½ cup (100 g) sugar

4 to 4½ cups (480 to 540 g) unbleached all-purpose flour
1 teaspoon salt
1 heaping tablespoon active dry yeast

1. Grease baking sheets or line them with parchment paper or silicone baking mats.

2. Combine the milk, ½ cup (112 g) butter, eggs, sugar, 4 cups (480 g) of the flour, the salt, and yeast in your bread machine, according to the manufacturer's instructions. Program the machine for the dough setting and start it. If the dough is very sticky during the mixing phase, add up to ½ cup (60 g) additional flour, until a soft dough is formed.

If making the dough in a stand mixer, place the milk, sugar, and yeast in the bowl of the mixer and stir. Allow to proof for 5 minutes. Add the butter, eggs, flour, and salt and mix with the dough hook. Knead for about 5 minutes until a smooth dough ball forms. Transfer the dough to a greased bowl and let rise until doubled in bulk, about 1 hour.

3. When the dough is ready, transfer it to a lightly floured surface. Divide it into four equal parts.

4. Roll each piece of dough into a 12-inch (30.5 cm) circle and cut each circle into 8 wedges. Brush the melted butter over the surface of each wedge. Roll each wedge like a crescent roll, starting with the wide bottom of the triangular wedge and ending with the point.

5. Place the rolls, point down, on the prepared baking sheets, about 2 inches (5 cm) apart.

FREEZING INSTRUCTIONS:

To bake and freeze: Allow the rolls to rise for 30 minutes. Preheat the oven to 375°F (190°C or gas mark 5). Bake for 12 to 15 minutes, or until lightly browned. Let cool, then place in freezer bags and seal, removing as much air as possible. Freeze.

To freeze unbaked rolls: Place the rolls on their sheets or trays in the freezer and freeze until firm. Place the frozen rolls in freezer bags and store in the freezer.

TO THAW AND SERVE:

To serve baked rolls: Thaw the rolls at room temperature in their bags before warming in a low oven.

To serve unbaked rolls: Grease baking sheets or line them with parchment paper or silicone baking mats. Place the frozen rolls on the prepared sheets. Let thaw and rise, covered, in the refrigerator for at least 5 hours or as long as overnight, until doubled in size. Preheat the oven to 375°F (190°C or gas mark 5) and bake the rolls for 12 to 15 minutes, or until lightly browned. Cool on wire racks.

Cinnamon Twist Loaves

Our family loves Crystal's Butterhorn Rolls (opposite page) so much that I experimented with the dough and came up with several variations. This one is a delicious braided cinnamon loaf. For variety in your freezer stash, prepare one batch of dough and make Butterhorn Rolls, Chocolate Butterhorns (page 329), and these Cinnamon Twist Loaves. // ***Makes 4 large braids***

- **PACKAGING:** Gallon-size (4 L) zip-top freezer bags

1 cup (235 ml) warm milk
½ cup (112 g) (1 stick) unsalted butter, melted
2 large eggs
½ cup (100 g) sugar

4 to 4½ cups (480 to 540 g) unbleached all-purpose flour
1 teaspoon salt
1 heaping tablespoon active dry yeast
½ cup (100 g) sugar mixed with 2 tablespoons ground cinnamon

1. Line 2 baking sheets with parchment paper.

2. Combine the milk, cubed butter, eggs, sugar, 4 cups (480 g) of the flour, the salt, and yeast in your bread machine, according to the manufacturer's instructions. Program the machine for the dough setting and start it. If the dough is very sticky during the mixing phase, add up to ½ cup (60 g) additional flour, until a soft dough is formed.

If making the dough in a stand mixer, place the milk, sugar, and yeast in the bowl of the mixer and stir. Allow to proof for 5 minutes. Add the butter, eggs, flour, and salt and mix with the dough hook. Knead for about 5 minutes until a smooth dough ball forms. Transfer the dough to a greased bowl and let rise until doubled in bulk, about 1 hour.

3. When the dough is ready, transfer it to a lightly floured surface. Divide it into four equal parts.

4. Roll each piece of dough into a 12-inch (30.5 cm)-long oval and sprinkle 2 tablespoons cinnamon sugar over the surface of each oval.

5. Slice each oval into three strips, leaving them attached at the top edge. Braid the dough, press the ends to seal, and tuck under slightly.

FREEZING INSTRUCTIONS:

Place the braided loaves on prepared baking sheets and freeze. Once the braids are frozen, place them in freezer bags and store in the freezer until needed.

TO THAW AND SERVE:

Grease a baking sheet or line it with parchment paper or a silicone baking mat. Place 1 or 2 cinnamon braids on the prepared sheet, leaving several inches of space between the loaves on the pan. Let thaw and rise for at least 5 hours and as long as overnight in the refrigerator, until doubled in size. Preheat the oven to 375°F (190°C or gas mark 5) and bake the braid(s) for 12 to 15 minutes, or until lightly browned. Cool on wire racks.

You can also freeze the baked braids. Simply place cooled, baked bread braids in gallon-size (4 L) zip-top freezer bags and seal, removing as much air as possible before closing the bag. Thaw in bags at room temperature.

Chocolate Butterhorn Rolls

Since i have a little bit of a sweet tooth, I played around with that butterhorn dough a little more, adding chocolate to the finished product. Oh, my word! In my initial recipe testing, the first batch of 32 small rolls never even made it to the freezer. Easy, make-ahead, and delicious—what more could you ask for in a recipe? Reminiscent of chocolate croissants, these rolls will make you a star at your next brunch get-together. // *Makes 32 rolls*

■ **PACKAGING:** Gallon-size (4 L) zip-top freezer bags

1 cup (235 ml) warm milk
½ cup (112 g) (1 stick) unsalted butter,
    melted
2 large eggs
½ cup (100 g) sugar
4 to 4½ cups (480 to 540 g) unbleached
    all-purpose flour

1 teaspoon salt
1 heaping tablespoon active dry yeast
1 to 2 cups (175 to 350 g) chocolate chips,
    depending on how chocolaty you want
    the rolls

1. Grease baking sheets or line them with parchment paper or silicone baking mats.

2. Combine the milk, cubed butter, eggs, sugar, 4 cups (480 g) of the flour, the salt, and yeast in your bread machine, according to the manufacturer's instructions. Program the machine for the dough setting and start it. If the dough is very sticky during the mixing phase, add up to ½ cup (60 g) additional flour until a soft dough is formed.

If making the dough in a stand mixer, place the milk, sugar, and yeast in the bowl of the mixer and stir. Allow to proof for 5 minutes. Add the butter, eggs, flour, and salt and mix with the dough hook. Knead for about 5 minutes until a smooth dough ball forms. Transfer the dough to a greased bowl and let rise until doubled in bulk, about 1 hour.

3. When the dough is ready, transfer it to a lightly floured surface. Divide it into four equal parts.

4. Roll each piece of dough into a 12-inch (30.5 cm) circle and cut each circle into 8 wedges. Sprinkle chocolate chips over the surface of each wedge. Roll each wedge like a crescent roll, starting with the wide bottom of the triangular wedge and ending with the point.

5. If baking before freezing, place the rolls, point down, on the prepared baking sheets, about 2 inches (5 cm) apart. If freezing unbaked rolls, place the rolls on trays or baking sheets (no need to line with parchment paper or use a mat).

FREEZING INSTRUCTIONS:

To bake and freeze: Allow the rolls to rise for 30 minutes. Preheat the oven to 375°F (190°C or gas mark 5). Bake for 12 to 15 minutes, or until lightly browned. Let cool, then place in freezer bags and seal, removing as much air as possible. Freeze.

To freeze unbaked rolls: Place the rolls on their sheets or trays in the freezer and freeze until firm. Place the frozen rolls in freezer bags and store in the freezer.

TO THAW AND SERVE:

To serve baked rolls: Thaw the rolls at room temperature in their bags before warming in a low oven.

To serve unbaked rolls: Grease baking sheets or line them with parchment paper or silicone baking mats. Place the frozen rolls on the prepared sheets. Let thaw and rise, covered, in the refrigerator for at least 5 hours or as long as overnight, until doubled in size. Preheat the oven to 375°F (190°C or gas mark 5) and bake the rolls for 12 to 15 minutes, or until lightly browned. Cool on wire racks.

Honey Multigrain Rolls

These rolls don't taste overly "healthy," but they are packed with whole-grain goodness. Oat flour, whole-wheat flour, and ground corn combine in a hearty roll that is perfect alongside a bowl of soup on a rainy day. // *Makes 8 large rolls*

■ **PACKAGING:** Gallon-size (4 L) zip-top freezer bag

1 cup (235 ml) warm milk
2½ tablespoons (35 g) unsalted butter, melted
2 tablespoons (40 g) honey
1¼ cups (150 g) whole-wheat flour

1 cup (120 g) unbleached all-purpose flour
½ cup (60 g) oat flour
¼ cup (30 g) cornmeal
2¼ teaspoons active dry yeast
1 teaspoon salt

1. Combine all of the ingredients in your bread machine according to the manufacturer's instructions. Program the machine for the dough setting and start it.

If making the dough in a stand mixer, place the milk, honey, and yeast in the bowl of the mixer and stir. Allow to proof for 5 minutes. Add the butter, flours, cornmeal, and salt and mix with the dough hook. Knead for about 5 minutes until a smooth dough ball forms. Transfer the dough to a greased bowl and let rise until doubled in bulk, about 1 hour.

2. Grease a baking sheet or line it with parchment paper or a silicone baking mat. When the dough is ready, transfer it to a lightly floured surface. Divide it into eight equal parts. Form each piece of dough into a tight round and place on the prepared baking sheet to rise until doubled in bulk, about 1 hour.

3. Preheat the oven to 350°F (180°C or gas mark 4).

4. Bake the rolls for 20 minutes, or until golden brown. Cool completely.

FREEZING INSTRUCTIONS:

Place the cooled rolls into the freezer bag and seal, removing as much air as possible. Freeze.

TO THAW AND SERVE:

Thaw the rolls in their bag at room temperature before reheating in a low oven for about 5 minutes.

Garlic Focaccia

Freshly baked bread is a joy. But sometimes, even with handy gadgets and small kitchen appliances, there just aren't enough hours in the day to pull together a fresh loaf. That's when homemade breads prepared in advance and stashed in the freezer can save the day—or the dinner. Adapted from a recipe from cookbook author Beth Hensperger, this recipe is a family favorite. Bake it in 8-inch (20.3 cm) round cake pans for easy wrapping and freezing. I use a bread machine to speed things up. These rounds make delicious bases for Deep-Dish Focaccia Pizza Your Way (page 262).

// *Makes 3 focaccia rounds*

■ **PACKAGING:** Plastic wrap, three gallon-size (4 L) zip-top freezer bags

1¼ cups (295 ml) warm water
¼ cup (60 ml) plus 2 tablespoons (30 ml)
    olive oil, divided
2¼ cups (270 g) unbleached
    all-purpose flour
1 cup (120 g) whole-wheat flour

1½ teaspoons salt
1 teaspoon garlic powder
¼ teaspoon dried oregano
2½ teaspoons active dry yeast
Coarse salt

1. Combine the water, the 2 tablespoons (30 ml) olive oil, the flours, the 1½ teaspoons salt, garlic powder, oregano, and yeast in your bread machine according to the manufacturer's instructions. Program the machine for the dough setting and start it.

If making the dough in a stand mixer, place the water and yeast in the bowl of the mixer and stir. Allow to proof for 5 minutes. Add the 2 tablespoons (30 ml) oil, flours, salt, garlic powder, and oregano, and mix with the dough hook. Knead for about 5 minutes until a smooth dough ball forms. Transfer the dough to a greased bowl and let rise until doubled in bulk, about 1 hour.

2. Meanwhile, generously grease three 8-inch (20.3 cm) round cake pans with some of the remaining olive oil.

3. When the dough is ready, transfer it to a lightly greased surface and divide it into three portions. Press each portion into a prepared cake pan.

4. Flip each dough round over so that both sides are oiled. Spread the dough to the edges of the pans.

5. Cover the pans with plastic wrap and let the dough rise for at least 30 minutes, or longer if possible, until about doubled in bulk.

6. About 30 minutes before baking, preheat the oven to 450°F (230°C or gas mark 8). Remove the plastic wrap and drizzle the remaining olive oil over the bread rounds. Sprinkle the tops with coarse salt and bake the rounds for 15 minutes, or until golden brown.

FREEZING INSTRUCTIONS:

Cool the rounds completely on a wire rack. Remove from the pans, wrap securely in plastic wrap, and place each in a freezer bag. Freeze.

TO THAW AND SERVE:

Thaw the breads in their wrappings at room temperature. It thaws very quickly. Preheat the oven to 350°F (180°C or gas mark 4). Unwrap and warm the bread in the oven for about 5 minutes before serving.

▶ How Day-Old Bread and Your Freezer Can Work Together

I often buy marked-down artisan bread a day or two before the sell-by date. The grocery store or bakery wants to move it before the loaves are no longer saleable, so the price is marked down, sometimes to as little as 25 percent of the original price. Day-old bread becomes frozen bread cubes, to use later for egg dishes or homemade croutons. I cube all the bread and put the cubes back into the bread bags to freeze for a day when I want to make croutons or homemade bread crumbs or something like the Bacon-Cheddar Egg Bake (page 289).

Homemade Croutons

My toddler once ate an entire box of packaged croutons in one sitting. Not the most nutritious of snacks—packaged croutons are often full of additives. And don't ask me how he got hold of the box! Nowadays, I make croutons in minutes. Whether I've got a marked-down artisan bread or a loaf of home-baked bread that didn't turn out as light and fluffy as I'd hoped, homemade croutons make the most of bread that might otherwise go to waste. // *Makes 5 cups (250 g)*

5 cups (250 g) cubed bread   **2 tablespoons (30 ml) olive oil**

1. Preheat the oven to 375°F (190°C or gas mark 5).

2. In a large bowl, combine the bread cubes with the olive oil. Toss well to coat.

3. Pour the bread cubes onto a large rimmed baking sheet. Bake in the oven for 10 to 15 minutes, stirring every 5 minutes to prevent burning.

4. Cool completely before storing in an airtight container or zip-top bags.

Variation: Add ½ teaspoon garlic powder to the bread when you add the oil.

Bread Crumbs

Bread crumbs are an essential ingredient in meatloaves, meatballs, breaded chicken, and lots of other great dishes. Packaged bread crumbs are quite costly and often contain unwanted ingredients. Many people don't realize that bread crumbs are actually quite inexpensive and easy to make yourself. After all, they're just dried bread! Tear dry bread into chunks and place in the bowl of a food processor or blender. Pulse until you have the consistency you'd like. Store the bread crumbs in the freezer in an airtight container or zip-top freezer bag. Three regular slices of sandwich bread should make about 1 cup (50 g) of fresh bread crumbs.

Wholesome Energy Bars

Years ago, I worked in a Santa Barbara bakery and restaurant that sold delicious nut-and-fruit bars. They were extremely popular with the customers. Here, I've created my own version, full of flavor; they're delicious toasted for breakfast or a quick snack. They are a lot healthier than most of the so-called energy bars you can buy. // *Makes 12 bars*

- **PACKAGING:** Gallon-size (4 L) zip-top freezer bag

1 cup (235 ml) warm milk

3 tablespoons (45 ml) light olive oil
   or your favorite neutral oil

3 tablespoons (60 g) honey

1 teaspoon vanilla extract

1 cup (120 g) whole-wheat flour

2 cups (240 g) unbleached all-purpose flour

½ cup (60 g) oat flour

¼ cup (30 g) cornmeal

Grated zest of 1 orange

1 teaspoon ground cinnamon

2¼ teaspoons active dry yeast

1 teaspoon salt

¼ cup (35 g) dried cranberries

¼ cup (35 g) golden raisins

¼ cup (35 g) dark raisins

¼ cup (35 g) roasted sunflower seeds

1. Combine all of the ingredients in your bread machine according to the manufacturer's instructions. Program the machine for the dough setting and start it.

If making the dough in a stand mixer, place the milk, honey, and yeast in the bowl of the mixer and stir. Allow to proof for 5 minutes. Add the oil, vanilla, flours, cornmeal, orange zest, cinnamon, and salt, and mix with the dough hook. Once the dough starts to come together, add the cranberries, raisins, and sunflower seeds. Knead for about 5 minutes until a smooth dough ball forms. Transfer the dough to a greased bowl and let rise until doubled in bulk, about 1 hour.

2. Grease a baking sheet. When the dough is ready, transfer it to a lightly floured surface.

3. Press the dough into a 1-inch (2.5 cm)-thick rectangle. Cut into 12 rectangles and place them on the prepared baking sheet.

4. Preheat the oven to 350°F (180°C or gas mark 4). Allow the bars to rise for about 20 minutes.

5. Bake the bars for 20 minutes, or until golden brown. Cool the bars on a rack.

FREEZING INSTRUCTIONS:

Place the cooled bars in the freezer bag and seal, removing as much air as possible. Freeze.

TO THAW AND SERVE:

Thaw the desired number of bars at room temperature. Serve at room temperature, or cut the bars in half horizontally, toast, and serve with butter.

Easy Make-Ahead Garlic Bread

While preparing homemade garlic bread is inarguably easy, it does take a few minutes. And some-times you just want that garlic bread PRONTO. Win by keeping a few loaves stashed in the freezer, ready to throw on the grill or toss in the oven alongside the rest of the dinner. For a crispier top, unwrap the foil at the end of the baking time and broil the bread briefly. // ***Makes 1 large loaf***

■ **PACKAGING:** Heavy-duty aluminum foil

½ cup (112 g) (1 stick) unsalted butter,
  softened
2 cloves garlic, minced
1 tablespoon chopped fresh basil or oregano
  or 1 teaspoon dried basil or oregano
  (optional)

1½ teaspoons chopped fresh parsley
  or ½ teaspoon dried parsley flakes
1 large loaf French or Italian bread, halved
  lengthwise

1. In a small bowl, combine the butter, garlic, basil (if using), and parsley.

2. Spread the butter in a thick layer over the surface of each bread half.

FREEZING INSTRUCTIONS:

Put the two bread halves back together and wrap with foil. Freeze.

TO THAW AND SERVE:

Thaw the bread in the refrigerator. Bake, still wrapped in foil, at 375°F (190°C or gas mark 5) for 15 to 25 minutes, depending on the density of the bread. Or bake the frozen bread for 35 to 40 minutes.

10

DESSERTS WHEN YOU CRAVE THEM

‣ Sugar and Spice Cookies ▪ 337

‣ Cranberry-Oatmeal Cookies ▪ 338

‣ White Chocolate–Walnut Jumbles ▪ 339

‣ Lemon Whole-Wheat Spritz Cookies ▪ 341

‣ Gingerbread Crinkles ▪ 342

‣ Chocolate-Almond Biscotti ▪ 343

‣ Chocolate-Toffee Cookies ▪ 344

‣ Chocolate Minty Melts ▪ 345

‣ Cocoa Brownies ▪ 346

‣ Kahlúa Brownies ▪ 347

‣ Double Chocolate Magic Bars ▪ 348

‣ Caramel-Lime Bars ▪ 349

‣ Chocolate-Banana Marble Cake ▪ 350

‣ Chocolate-Zucchini Cake ▪ 351

‣ Mocha Hot Fudge Cake ▪ 354

‣ Pretzel Berry Cheesecake ▪ 356

‣ Spiced Pumpkin Custards ▪ 357

‣ Not Your Ice Cream Truck's Ice Cream Sandwiches ▪ 358

‣ Easy Chocolate Fudge Sundae Cups ▪ 360

‣ Mint Chocolate Fudge Ice Cream Pie ▪ 361

‣ Blueberry-Raspberry Croustades ▪ 362

‣ Nanna's Apple Pie ▪ 363

‣ Slab Apple Pie ▪ 364

‣ Lemon-Ginger Freezer Pie ▪ 365

‣ Coconut Crunch Pie ▪ 366

‣ Versatile Buttery Pie Crust ▪ 368

Sugar and Spice Cookies

These crispy Sugar and Spice Cookies are the result of the women in my family experimenting to create an "everything nice" kind of cookie. My sister and nieces tested them in their kitchen while my daughters and I tested in ours. The resulting cookie is sweet and comforting, what one child likened to a homemade animal cracker. Ten-year-old Cay gets props for discovering that flattening the cookie balls creates the best texture. // *Makes 2½ to 3 dozen cookies*

■ **PACKAGING:** Plastic containers with lids, waxed paper

1 cup (225 g) salted butter, softened
1 cup (200 g) sugar
1 egg, beaten
1 teaspoon vanilla extract
½ teaspoon almond extract
2½ cups (300 g) flour
1 teaspoon baking soda

½ teaspoon baking powder
½ teaspoon ground cinnamon
½ teaspoon ground ginger
½ teaspoon ground nutmeg
¼ teaspoon fine salt
Cinnamon sugar: 2 tablespoons (25 g) sugar
    mixed with 1 teaspoon ground cinnamon

1. Preheat the oven to 375°F (190°C or gas mark 5). Line baking sheets with parchment paper or silicone baking mats.

2. In a large bowl, cream together the butter and sugar until light and fluffy. Stir in the egg and vanilla and almond extracts.

3. Combine the flour, baking soda, baking powder, spices, and salt in another bowl. Add to the butter and sugar mixture and combine well. Shape the dough into 1-inch (2.5 cm) balls and roll in cinnamon sugar. Flatten each cookie with the palm of your hand. Bake on the prepared baking sheets for 8 to 9 minutes, or until set. Cool on racks.

FREEZING INSTRUCTIONS:

Layer the cookies in a plastic container between sheets of waxed paper. Cover and freeze.

TO THAW AND SERVE:

Remove as many cookies as desired from the freezer and thaw them at room temperature. They should thaw within 30 minutes.

Cranberry-Oatmeal Cookies

Oatmeal-raisin is a traditional cookie favorite. I've updated a vintage, egg-free recipe with dried cranberries for a tart and chewy sweet treat. Bake up several batches to keep in the freezer for spur-of-the-moment snacks, or freeze the dough balls to bake later. // **Makes about 2 dozen cookies**

■ **PACKAGING:** Plastic containers with lids, waxed paper

1½ cups (338 g) packed light
   or dark brown sugar
1 cup (225 g) (2 sticks) unsalted butter,
   softened
½ cup (120 ml) buttermilk
1 teaspoon vanilla extract
3½ cups (280 g) quick-cooking rolled oats
½ cup (40 g) old-fashioned rolled oats

1¾ cups (210 g) unbleached
   all-purpose flour
Grated zest of 1 lemon
1 teaspoon baking soda
1 teaspoon cinnamon
¾ teaspoon salt
2 cups (280 g) dried cranberries

1. Preheat the oven to 375°F (190°C or gas mark 5). Line baking sheets with parchment paper or silicone baking mats.

2. In a large bowl, cream together the sugar and butter. Add the buttermilk and vanilla. Blend well. Stir in both kinds of oats, the flour, lemon zest, baking soda, cinnamon, salt, and dried cranberries.

3. Drop the batter by rounded tablespoonfuls about 3 inches (7.6 cm) apart on the prepared baking sheets. Flatten each cookie with the bottom of a glass dipped in water.

4. Bake until set and lightly browned, about 10 minutes. Remove to racks to cool.

FREEZING INSTRUCTIONS:

Layer the cookies in a plastic container between sheets of waxed paper. Cover and freeze.

TO THAW AND SERVE:

Remove as many cookies as desired from the freezer and thaw them at room temperature. They should thaw within 30 minutes.

White Chocolate–Walnut Jumbles

My grandmother was famous for her baking, winning blue ribbons at the county fair every year. Family lore has it that when the time came for her to share her recipe on the radio, she would change some of the ingredients so that no one could duplicate her prize-winning baking. Even her daughters-in-law always wondered if they had "the real recipe." These white chocolate jumbles are based on Grandma's blue ribbon chocolate chip cookies. I've updated the recipe with whole-wheat flour, white chocolate chips, and Sucanat (a whole cane sugar), but it's still just as tasty. // ***Makes about 3 dozen cookies***

- **PACKAGING:** Plastic containers with lids, waxed paper

1 cup (225 g) Sucanat or light or dark brown sugar
1 cup (225 g) (2 sticks) unsalted butter, softened
2 large eggs
2 teaspoons (10 ml) vanilla extract
2 cups (240 g) unbleached all-purpose flour

2 cups (240 g) whole-wheat pastry flour
2 teaspoons (16 g) baking soda
1 teaspoon salt
One 12-ounce (340 g) bag white chocolate chips
1 cup (140 g) chopped walnuts

1. Preheat the oven to 350°F (180°C or gas mark 4). Line baking sheets with parchment paper or silicone baking mats.

2. In a large bowl, cream together the sugar and butter. Add the eggs and vanilla, mixing thoroughly.

3. Blend in the flours, baking soda, and salt until well combined. Stir in the white chocolate chips and walnuts.

4. Drop the batter onto the baking sheets by rounded tablespoonfuls. Bake for 8 to 10 minutes, or until set. Remove to racks to cool.

FREEZING INSTRUCTIONS:

Layer the cookies in plastic containers between sheets of waxed paper. Cover and freeze.

TO THAW AND SERVE:

Remove as many cookies as desired from the freezer and thaw them at room temperature. They should thaw within 30 minutes.

► Cookies and Bulk Cooking

I love the idea of serving a wide variety of Christmas cookies at one time. My goal is to bake a dozen kinds during the holiday season, but this can be a tricky feat. Who wants to spend three days baking? And who has the willpower to resist eating that "wide variety of Christmas cookies" before the holiday arrives?

This is where your freezer can make things a little easier for you at the holidays! There are several techniques that can help you during this hectic month. You can have 12 kinds of cookies and not go insane.

USE A FOOD PROCESSOR OR STAND MIXER

With a food processor or stand mixer, you can quickly prepare many batches of dough in quick succession. In fact, start with the plainest cookie dough and work your way up to the chocolate and the peppermint. Since these cookies most likely all start with butter, sugar, and flour, you don't need to wash the bowl between each batch.

Of course, if you'd rather wash the bowl in between batches, feel free to do so. You'll still save time by using a machine and by preparing many batches of dough in quick succession.

As each batch of dough is prepared, wrap it in plastic wrap or place it in an airtight container and stash it in the refrigerator. By performing all your like tasks together—mixing, forming, and baking—you'll save time and energy.

MAKE AND FREEZE BULK COOKIE DOUGH

Once you have your dough prepared, you can freeze the different varieties "as is" until you want freshly baked cookies. Wrap the dough well in plastic wrap and slip it into a zip-top freezer bag before storing it in the freezer. Thaw the dough overnight in the refrigerator, and it should be ready to roll and bake the next day. If you freeze the dough in logs, you don't even need the overnight thaw; the frozen dough will be ready to slice and bake in about an hour.

MAKE AND FREEZE INDIVIDUAL COOKIE DOUGH BALLS

Another option is to freeze the dough in ready-to-bake dough balls. Simply form your cookies and place them on baking sheets. Place the sheets in the freezer. Once the cookies are firm, transfer them to a zip-top freezer bag or plastic containers with lids and return them to the freezer for longer storage.

BAKE AND FREEZE THE COOKIES

This is probably the easiest—and my favorite—way to get a jump on holiday baking. I prepare the different dough varieties and then roll and bake several kinds of cookies in quick succession. I do three or four kinds at a time. Once the cookies are cooled, I layer them between sheets of waxed paper in airtight containers. Baked cookies should keep well in the freezer for at least a month if wrapped properly. When I want to assemble cookie

(continued)

trays, I pull my containers out of the freezer and place a few of each kind of cookie on each tray. The cookies thaw in a matter of minutes, and I have a great gift or dessert without a lot of last-minute prep work. This gives me a breather during the busy holiday season. I can also spend this "extra" time making my cookie presentation a little prettier.

TACKLE YOUR BAKING IN STAGES

Unless you want to bake all day, consider scheduling three or four baking sessions. One year, I just made a batch of cookies every day for a couple weeks. It didn't take more than an hour each day, and since I was stashing it all in the freezer right away, I built a sweet little stockpile very quickly.

INCLUDE THE FAMILY

It goes without saying that kids love to help bake cookies. I quiz my kids as the holidays approach to hear their cookie choices. They have so much fun helping me bake. While there's invariably a mess in the kitchen—and we have had some hilarious flops—it is always a great time. And our freezer holds enough cookies to last us at least a month.

For an easier holiday baking session, be sure to run the Holiday Baking Plan, page 48, through its paces. Its grocery and prep lists will have you organized and baking in no time!

Lemon Whole-Wheat Spritz Cookies

Spritz cookies are whimsical and fun. The cookie press makes quick work of preparing these elegant cookies to complement tea or coffee. Whole-wheat pastry flour gives them more substance and a nutty texture. // *Makes 5 to 6 dozen cookies*

- **PACKAGING:** Plastic containers with lids, waxed paper

1½ cups (338 g) (3 sticks) unsalted butter, softened	1 teaspoon vanilla extract
	Grated zest of 1 lemon
1 cup (200 g) granulated sugar	¼ teaspoon lemon extract
1 teaspoon baking powder	3½ cups (420 g) whole-wheat pastry flour
1 large egg	Turbinado sugar or candy sprinkles

1. Preheat the oven to 375°F (190°C or gas mark 5). Line baking sheets with parchment paper or silicone baking mats.

2. In a large bowl, beat the butter until light and fluffy. Add the granulated sugar and baking powder and blend until smooth.

3. Beat in the egg, vanilla, lemon zest, and lemon extract. Beat in the flour until smooth.

4. Put the dough into a cookie press fitted with a template and press cookies onto the prepared baking sheets, leaving about 2 inches (5 cm) of space between cookies. Sprinkle the tops of the cookies with turbinado sugar or candy sprinkles.

5. Bake the cookies for 8 minutes. Remove to racks to cool.

FREEZING INSTRUCTIONS:

Layer the cookies in plastic containers between sheets of waxed paper. Cover and freeze.

TO THAW AND SERVE:

Remove as many cookies as desired from the freezer and thaw them at room temperature. They should thaw within 30 minutes.

Gingerbread Crinkles

I've never really been successful at making beautiful gingerbread cutouts, but I love the flavor of gingerbread cookies. I get the best of both worlds—easy-to-prep, beautiful cookies and the luscious flavor of gingerbread—when I make these Gingerbread Crinkles. // *Makes about 18 cookies*

■ **PACKAGING:** Plastic containers with lids, waxed paper

½ cup (112 g) butter, softened
¾ cup (170 g) dark brown sugar
2 tablespoons (40 g) molasses
1 egg
1 teaspoon lemon zest
1½ cups (180 g) unbleached, all-purpose
    flour

1 teaspoon baking soda
1 teaspoon ground cinnamon
1 teaspoon ground cloves
1 teaspoon ground ginger
1 teaspoon ground nutmeg
Demerara or coarse sugar, for rolling

1. Preheat the oven to 350°F (180°C or gas mark 4). Line two baking sheets with parchment or silpat baking mats.

2. In a large bowl, cream together the butter and sugar until fluffy. Mix in the molasses, egg, and lemon zest until well combined.

3. In another bowl, stir together the flour, baking soda, and spices. Add to the butter and sugar mixture and blend well.

4. Roll the dough into 1-inch (2.5 cm) balls and roll in the demerara sugar.

5. Place 9 cookies on a sheet, spacing evenly. The cookies will spread while baking.

6. Bake the cookies for 10 minutes, or until set. Cool completely on a wire rack.

7. Place the baked and cooled cookies in layers separated by waxed paper in an airtight container; cover. Store at room temperature for 3 days or freeze for up to 3 months.

FREEZING INSTRUCTIONS:

Layer the cookies in plastic containers between sheets of waxed paper. Cover and freeze.

TO THAW AND SERVE:

Remove as many cookies as desired from the freezer and thaw them at room temperature. They should thaw within 30 minutes.

Chocolate-Almond Biscotti

This is my family's favorite biscotti recipe, and it fits well into the heart-healthier changes we're trying to make in our diet. Almonds and dark chocolate both are considered helpful in lowering cholesterol and blood pressure. And this relatively low-fat recipe does not call for butter or oil. // *Makes 2 dozen biscotti*

■ **PACKAGING:** Plastic containers with lids, waxed paper

3 large eggs
1 teaspoon vanilla extract
½ teaspoon almond extract
1 cup (225 g) dark brown sugar
1¾ cups (210 g) unbleached all-purpose
   flour
⅓ cup (40 g) unsweetened cocoa powder

½ teaspoon finely ground decaf coffee
1 teaspoon baking soda
¼ teaspoon salt
1 cup (140 g) whole almonds, toasted
¾ cup (130 g) mini or regular semisweet
   chocolate chips

1. Preheat the oven to 300°F (150°C or gas mark 2). Line a large baking sheet with parchment paper or a silicone baking mat.

2. In a large bowl, beat the eggs and extracts with a hand mixer. Blend in the sugar.

3. In another bowl, sift together the flour, cocoa, coffee, baking soda, and salt.

4. Add the dry ingredients to the wet ingredients, and mix. Stir in the almonds and chocolate chips.

5. Spoon the batter into one log, about 16 × 3 inches (40.6 × 7.6 cm), down the center of the parchment. Bake for 50 minutes. The dough will spread during baking.

6. Remove the pan from the oven and let cool for 5 to 10 minutes.

7. Slice the large cookie log crosswise into ½-inch (1.3 cm)-thick slices. Lay the cookie slices, with a cut side down, on one or two baking sheets, and bake 25 minutes. Turn the cookie slices over and bake 25 minutes more. Remove to racks to cool.

FREEZING INSTRUCTIONS:

Layer the baked cookies in plastic containers between sheets of waxed paper. Cover and freeze.

TO THAW AND SERVE:

Remove as many cookies as desired from the freezer and thaw them at room temperature. They should thaw within 30 minutes.

Chocolate-Toffee Cookies

These cookies will please chocolate lovers. Enriched with toffee bits, they are a perfect snack with a glass of milk or a cup of coffee. I love them with a little bit of sea salt sprinkled on at the end.
// *Makes 3 dozen cookies*

■ **PACKAGING:** Plastic containers with lids, waxed paper

2 cups (240 g) unbleached all-purpose flour
1½ teaspoons baking powder
¼ teaspoon salt
6 tablespoons (84 g) (¾ stick) unsalted butter, softened
1 cup (225 g) dark brown sugar
1 cup (175 g) semisweet chocolate chips

2 large eggs
1½ teaspoons vanilla extract
1 cup (175 g) toffee bits (such as Heath) or ½ cup (90 g) chocolate chips and ½ cup (90 g) toffee bits, plus additional for sprinkling
Coarse sea salt (optional)

1. Preheat the oven to 350°F (180°C or gas mark 4). Line baking sheets with parchment paper or silicone baking mats.

2. In a large bowl, whisk together the flour, baking powder, and salt.

3. In another large bowl, beat the butter until light and fluffy. Add the sugar and continue beating until incorporated. Heat the chocolate chips in a microwave-safe bowl in the microwave for 1 to 2 minutes at 50 percent power. Check after 1 minute. The chips will not lose their shape but will soften enough to stir together easily and smoothly. Beat the eggs, melted chocolate, and vanilla extract into the butter mixture. Beat until well combined.

4. Beat in the dry ingredients just until combined. Stir in the toffee bits.

5. Spoon the dough onto the prepared sheets by rounded tablespoonfuls. Bake for 10 to 12 minutes, or until set. About 5 minutes before the baking is complete, insert a few toffee bits into the tops of the soft cookies. Remove to racks to cool. Sprinkle with coarse sea salt.

FREEZING INSTRUCTIONS:
Layer the cookies in plastic containers between sheets of waxed paper. Cover and freeze.

TO THAW AND SERVE:
Remove as many cookies as desired from the freezer and thaw them at room temperature. They should thaw within 30 minutes.

Chocolate Minty Melts

These cookies, rich in chocolate and peppermint, are a family favorite come holiday time. I often bake double or triple batches so that there's no shortage of them. They are delicious eaten straight from the freezer! // *Makes about 42 cookies*

■ **PACKAGING:** Plastic containers with lids, waxed paper

1½ cups (180 g) unbleached
    all-purpose flour
1½ teaspoons baking powder
¼ teaspoon salt
½ cup (60 g) unsweetened cocoa powder
½ cup (112 g) (1 stick) unsalted butter,
    softened
1 cup (200 g) granulated sugar

6 tablespoons (75 g) light brown sugar
2 large eggs
1½ teaspoons vanilla extract
¼ teaspoon peppermint extract
Confectioners' sugar for rolling
About 42 mint-flavored Hershey's Kisses,
    unwrapped

1. Preheat the oven to 350°F (180°C or gas mark 4). Line baking sheets with parchment paper or silicone baking mats.

2. In a large bowl, combine the flour, baking powder, salt, and cocoa.

3. In another large bowl, cream the butter and sugars until well combined. Beat in the eggs, vanilla, and peppermint extract. Stir in the flour mixture until just combined.

4. Shape the dough into 1-inch (2.5 cm) balls and roll the balls in confectioners' sugar. Place the balls about 2 inches (5 cm) apart on the prepared sheets. Press a Hershey's Kiss into the center of each cookie ball.

5. Bake the cookies for 10 to 12 minutes, or until the tops are crackled. The kisses may look a little sunken.

6. Cool the cookies for 2 minutes on the baking sheets. Transfer them to racks. Smooth the tops of the chocolate kisses into flat disks with an offset spatula. Let cool completely.

FREEZING INSTRUCTIONS:

Layer the cookies in plastic containers between sheets of waxed paper. Cover and freeze.

TO THAW AND SERVE:

Remove as many cookies as desired from the freezer and thaw them at room temperature. They should thaw within 30 minutes.

Cocoa Brownies

I love brownies. But I consider the price of a box of brownie mix ridiculous. Instead of buying commercial versions, I make my own mixes, preparing several batches at once to stash in the pantry or freezer for later baking. You can customize each batch by adding any of the mix-ins listed below. Of course, you can also bake the brownies and freeze them as you would other cookies. If you package the recipe as a mix, be sure to label the bag of dry ingredients with the baking instructions and a list of wet ingredients to add right before baking. Bags of mix and mix-ins make great holiday and hostess gifts. // *Makes 16 brownies*

■ **PACKAGING:** Quart-size (1 L) zip-top freezer bag, plastic container with lid, waxed paper

DRY INGREDIENTS:
1 cup (200 g) sugar
⅔ cup (80 g) unbleached all-purpose flour
⅔ cup (80 g) unsweetened cocoa powder

½ teaspoon baking powder
½ teaspoon salt

WET INGREDIENTS:
½ cup (120 ml) vegetable oil
2 large eggs

1 teaspoon vanilla extract

OPTIONAL MIX-INS (CHOOSE ONE OR TWO):
¼ cup (35 g) chopped walnuts,
    chocolate chips, or M&Ms
2 teaspoons instant coffee crystals

¼ teaspoon ground cinnamon
1 teaspoon mint extract

TO PACKAGE AS A MIX:

Place all of the dry ingredients in the quart-size (1 L) freezer bag. Seal the bag and shake it gently to combine the ingredients. Store in the pantry or freezer.

BAKING INSTRUCTIONS:

1. Preheat the oven to 350°F (180°C or gas mark 4). Grease an 8-inch (20.3 cm) square pan, or line the pan with aluminum foil or parchment paper, letting the ends hang over the sides for easier removal.

2. In a large bowl, combine the wet ingredients and whisk to blend. Add the dry ingredients to the bowl. Stir gently to combine. Fold in the mix-ins, if using. Spoon the batter into the prepared baking pan. Bake for 20 to 25 minutes, or until a tester comes out with a few crumbs attached. Cool and cut into squares.

FREEZING INSTRUCTIONS:

Layer the brownies in a plastic container between sheets of waxed paper. Cover and freeze.

TO THAW AND SERVE:

Remove as many brownies as desired from the freezer and thaw them at room temperature. They should thaw within 30 minutes.

Kahlúa Brownies

These brownies were always a big hit with my mom and her friends when I was growing up. Could it have been the Kahlúa? Though the alcohol had obviously cooked out, Mom and the girls still perked up whenever these brownies were served. I've updated Mom's recipe with homemade brownie mix, dark chocolate chips, and unsweetened coconut. The result is a pan of chewy, chocolaty brownies that are rich without being overly sweet. // *Makes 16 brownies*

■ **PACKAGING:** Plastic container with lid, waxed paper

2 large eggs
¼ cup (60 ml) vegetable oil
¼ cup (60 ml) Kahlúa
1 batch Cocoa Brownies, dry ingredients only (opposite page)

½ cup (70 g) chopped pecans
½ cup (40 g) unsweetened shredded coconut
½ cup (90 g) dark chocolate chips

1. Preheat the oven to 350°F (180°C or gas mark 4). Line an 8-inch (20.3 cm) square pan with parchment paper or aluminum foil, letting the ends hang over the sides for easier removal.

2. In a large bowl, combine the eggs, oil, and Kahlúa. Blend in the dry brownie ingredients just until combined. Stir in the pecans, coconut, and chocolate chips.

3. Spoon the batter into the prepared pan and bake for 25 to 30 minutes, or until a tester comes out with a few crumbs attached. Cool completely on a wire rack.

4. Remove the brownies from the pan by lifting the edges of the parchment. Place on a flat surface and cut into squares.

FREEZING INSTRUCTIONS:

Layer the brownies in a plastic container between sheets of waxed paper. Cover and freeze.

TO THAW AND SERVE:

Remove as many brownies as desired from the freezer and thaw them at room temperature. They should thaw within 30 minutes.

Double Chocolate Magic Bars

Magic bars are an addictive, gooey, crunchy sweet treat. I've updated them by using Oreo cookie crumbs instead of graham crackers and unsweetened coconut instead of sweetened. The result is a rich and chocolaty dessert bar. They taste fantastic served cold from the freezer. // *Makes about 18 bars*

■ **PACKAGING:** Plastic container with lid

1½ cups (180 g) Oreo cookie crumbs
½ cup (112 g) (1 stick) unsalted butter, melted
1 cup (175 g) semisweet chocolate chips

1 cup (80 g) unsweetened flaked coconut
One 14-ounce (392 g) can sweetened condensed milk (the fat-free variety is fine)

1. Preheat the oven to 350°F (180°C or gas mark 4).

2. In a 9 × 13-inch (23 × 33 cm) baking dish, combine the cookie crumbs and the melted butter. Press the mixture lightly into the dish to form a crust.

3. Sprinkle the crumb layer with the chocolate chips, then the coconut.

4. Drizzle the sweetened condensed milk over all. Bake for 25 minutes, or until golden brown. Cool, then cut into bars.

FREEZING INSTRUCTIONS:

Layer the bars in a plastic container between sheets of waxed paper. Cover and freeze.

TO THAW AND SERVE:

Remove as many bars as desired from the freezer and thaw them at room temperature. They should thaw within 30 minutes.

Caramel-Lime Bars

Reminiscent of key lime pie, these sweet, tart bars are a refreshing dessert with a hint of caramel in the topping. Serve with a dollop of freshly whipped cream for an elegant presentation. // ***Makes about 18 bars***

■ **PACKAGING:** 9 × 13-inch (23 × 33 cm) baking dish with lid

2 cups (240 g) graham cracker crumbs
½ cup (112 g) (1 stick) unsalted butter, melted
4 egg yolks
One 14-ounce (392 g) can sweetened condensed milk

⅔ cup (160 ml) freshly squeezed lime juice
2 teaspoons grated lime zest
1 cup (225 g) sour cream
¼ cup (56 g) dark brown sugar
½ teaspoon vanilla extract

1. Preheat the oven to 350°F (180°C or gas mark 4).

2. In the baking dish, combine the graham cracker crumbs and the melted butter, pressing the mixture lightly into the dish to form a crust. Bake the crust for 8 minutes.

3. Meanwhile, in a large bowl, combine the egg yolks, sweetened condensed milk, lime juice, and lime zest. Blend well. Pour the filling over the crust and spread to cover. Bake for 8 minutes.

4. In another bowl, combine the sour cream, brown sugar, and vanilla. Spread this over the lime layer and bake for 5 minutes.

5. Cool the pan on a wire rack.

FREEZING INSTRUCTIONS:

Cover the cooled pan and freeze.

TO THAW AND SERVE:

Thaw at room temperature for 10 minutes, or until bars can be cut easily. Cut and serve semi-frozen.

Chocolate-Banana Marble Cake

Chocolate and bananas are a natural pairing; the flavors complement one another so well. And snack cakes are perfect for freezing. You can wrap the whole cake in plastic wrap or package individual slices to freeze, making for quick brown-bag desserts. If you can't find whole-wheat pastry flour, simply use unbleached all-purpose flour. // *Serves 12 to 16*

■ **PACKAGING:** Plastic wrap, gallon-size (4 L) zip-top freezer bag

1 cup (120 g) whole-wheat pastry flour
1 cup (120 g) unbleached all-purpose flour
2 teaspoons (16 g) baking powder
¼ teaspoon baking soda
¼ teaspoon salt
¾ cup (180 ml) vegetable oil

1¼ cups (295 g) dark brown sugar
3 ripe bananas, mashed
2 teaspoons (10 ml) vanilla extract
3 large eggs
⅓ cup (75 g) plain nonfat yogurt
½ cup (60 g) unsweetened cocoa powder

WHEN READY TO SERVE, YOU WILL NEED:
Confectioners' sugar for dusting

1. Preheat the oven to 350°F (180°C or gas mark 4). Spray a Bundt pan with nonstick cooking spray.

2. In a large bowl, whisk together the flours, baking powder, baking soda, and salt.

3. In another bowl, combine the oil, sugar, and bananas. Beat until smooth. Mix in the vanilla, eggs, and yogurt. Blend until smooth.

4. Add the wet ingredients to the dry ingredients, stirring just until blended.

5. Spoon half the batter into the prepared Bundt pan.

6. Add the cocoa to the remaining batter in the bowl and stir until just combined. Spoon the chocolate batter on top of the white batter in sections, leaving some non-chocolate spaces in between chocolate sections.

7. Use a knife to swirl the two batters together, taking care not to mix them too much.

8. Bake the cake for 35 to 40 minutes, or until a tester comes out with just a few crumbs attached.

9. Cool the cake in the pan on a wire rack for 15 minutes. Carefully run a rubber spatula around the edges of the pan to loosen the cake. Invert the cake onto a cooling rack and remove the pan. Cool the cake completely.

FREEZING INSTRUCTIONS:

Once the cake has cooled, wrap it securely in plastic wrap and place it in the freezer bag. Remove as much air from the bag as possible and freeze. Alternatively, you can wrap individual slices in plastic wrap and place them in the freezer bag. Remove as much air from the bag as possible and freeze.

TO THAW AND SERVE:

Thaw the cake, wrapped, at room temperature. Unwrap the thawed cake and place it on a serving platter. Sift the confectioners' sugar over the top of the cake before serving.

Chocolate-Zucchini Cake

The too-prolific squash that all your neighbors are apt to ditch on your front doorstep becomes something new and delicious when baked into this cake. It is moist and flavorful, best served simply with a dusting of confectioners' sugar and a glass of cold milk. I often freeze slices wrapped in pairs, making them easy to slip into lunches or grab for a snack on the go. If you can't find whole-wheat pastry flour, just substitute additional all-purpose flour. // *Serves 12 to 16*

■ **PACKAGING:** Plastic wrap, gallon-size (4 L) zip-top freezer bag

1 cup (120 g) unbleached all-purpose flour
1½ cups (180 g) whole-wheat pastry flour
½ cup (60 g) unsweetened cocoa powder
2½ teaspoons baking powder
1½ teaspoons baking soda
1 teaspoon salt
1 tablespoon ground cinnamon
¾ cup (180 ml) olive oil

1 cup (200 g) granulated sugar
1 cup (225 g) light or dark brown sugar
3 large eggs
2 teaspoons (10 ml) vanilla extract
2 cups (200 g) shredded zucchini
½ cup (120 ml) buttermilk
1 cup (140 g) chopped pecans or (175 g)
    chocolate chips (optional)

WHEN READY TO SERVE, YOU WILL NEED:
Confectioners' sugar for dusting

1. Preheat the oven to 350°F (180°C or gas mark 4). Spray a Bundt pan with nonstick cooking spray.

2. In a large bowl, combine the flours, cocoa, baking powder, baking soda, salt, and cinnamon.

3. In a second bowl, beat together the oil and sugars until smooth. Add the eggs, one at a time. Beat well. Stir in the vanilla and zucchini.

4. Alternately stir the dry ingredients and buttermilk into the wet ingredients. Fold in the nuts or chocolate chips, if using.

5. Pour the batter into the prepared pan. Bake for 1 hour, or until a tester comes out with just a few crumbs attached.

6. Cool the cake in the pan on a wire rack for 15 minutes. Carefully run a rubber spatula around the edges of the pan to loosen the cake. Invert the cake onto a cooling rack and remove the pan. Cool the cake completely.

FREEZING INSTRUCTIONS:

Once the cake has cooled, wrap it securely in plastic wrap and place it in the freezer bag. Remove as much air from the bag as possible and freeze. Alternatively, you can wrap individual slices in plastic wrap and place them in the freezer bag. Remove as much air from the bag as possible and freeze.

TO THAW AND SERVE:

Thaw the cake, wrapped, at room temperature. Unwrap the thawed cake and place it on a serving platter. Sift the confectioners' sugar over the top of the cake before serving.

▶ Other Ways to Put Your Freezer to Work

"I am not a glutton—I am an explorer of food." —Erma Bombeck

Lasagna? Check. Taco meat? Check. Pizza dough? Check.

Clearly the freezer can be a wonderful storehouse of meals and meal components. It's been known to hold a few quarts of ice cream and boxes of popsicles, too, and it does a great job with ice and ice packs. But there are even more ways that you can put your freezer to work, and they all make good eats.

HOMEMADE TV DINNERS

Repackage leftovers from a large holiday meal. Portion out cooled turkey, mashed potatoes, gravy, stuffing, and vegetables into aluminum pie plates. Wrap securely with heavy-duty aluminum foil and stash in the freezer for quick individual meals. Thaw in the refrigerator, and then reheat in the oven.

ROASTED GARLIC, PEPPERS, AND CHILES

These roasted vegetables add flavor to many dishes. I regularly roast big pans of fresh chiles to peel, seed, and chop. I store them in the freezer and add them as desired to egg

(continued)

scrambles, enchiladas, and other dishes that could benefit from an added punch. Roasted garlic and peppers complement salads, sandwiches, and pastas. Cook up bulk batches and package them in appropriately sized containers for adding to meals. Call on these rich flavors at any time for great taste without the wait.

SUMMER FRUITS AND VEGETABLES

Make use of your freezer to preserve fresh fruits and vegetables, so you can enjoy them throughout the year. Each type of produce has a different recommended method of freezing; some items need to be blanched first, whereas others should be treated with sugar and citric acid. Find a good book on food preservation to get the lowdown.

Many items, like bananas, berries, peppers, onions, and fresh herbs, can be frozen without blanching or pretreating. Chop or slice these items and freeze them on open trays in the freezer. Once the food is firm, place the items in a labeled freezer bag. This method of freezing allows you to uses small quantities at a time without having to thaw the entire bag. Zucchini can be shredded and stored in pint-size (470 ml) freezer bags. Be sure to thaw and drain the zucchini thoroughly before adding it to recipes. Citrus juices can be frozen in small plastic containers or in ice cube trays.

BULK PURCHASES

Make the most of your warehouse club purchases. Bulk packages of chicken or 5-pound (2270 g) bags of shredded cheese can be broken down into smaller packages and frozen. Even milk and buttermilk can go in the freezer. Just pour out a bit or transfer to other containers, if needed, before you freeze, to allow for expansion.

GOOD STUFF THAT DOESN'T COME IN SMALL PACKAGES

There are some pantry ingredients, like tomato paste and chipotle peppers in adobo sauce, that are usually used only in small quantities. When you don't use the whole package, divide the leftovers into small portions wrapped in squares of plastic wrap and freeze the lot in bags to pull out as needed.

SEASONAL SALES

Certain foods go on sale at certain seasons: hot dogs and sausages in the summer; butter, flour, and cranberries in the winter. Stock up and freeze them to enjoy all year long.

Mocha Hot Fudge Cake

When I was a kid, the local diner served a hot fudge cake to rave reviews. This one is reminiscent of that childhood cake but made a bit more sophisticated with coffee in both the cake and the ice cream. // *Serves 16*

■ **PACKAGING:** Plastic wrap

2 cups (400 g) sugar
2 cups (240 g) unbleached all-purpose flour
½ cup (60 g) unsweetened cocoa powder
1 teaspoon baking powder
1 teaspoon salt

1 cup (235 ml) vegetable oil
4 large eggs
1 teaspoon vanilla extract
1 teaspoon instant coffee crystals
1 pint (470 g) mocha ice cream

WHEN READY TO SERVE, YOU WILL NEED:
Hot fudge sauce
Whipped cream

Fresh or maraschino cherries (optional)

1. Preheat the oven to 350°F (180°C or gas mark 4). Line a 9 × 13-inch (23 × 33 cm) baking dish with parchment paper, letting the ends of the paper hang over the sides of the pan for easier removal.

2. In a large bowl, whisk together the sugar, flour, cocoa, baking powder, and salt. Add the oil, eggs, vanilla, and instant coffee crystals. Stir gently just until combined.

3. Spread the batter in the prepared baking dish and bake for 25 to 30 minutes, or until a tester comes out with just a few crumbs attached. Cool the cake in its pan on a rack.

4. Remove the ice cream from the freezer to soften slightly at room temperature.

5. Lift the cooled cake out of the pan by grasping each side of the parchment. Invert the cake on a flat surface and carefully loosen the parchment from the cake. Cut the cake in half horizontally.

6. Lay out a large length of plastic wrap on a flat surface. Place one half of the cake in the middle of the plastic wrap. Spread the softened ice cream evenly over the surface of the cake, working quickly.

7. Place the second half of the cake atop the ice cream layer. Wrap the ice cream cake securely with the plastic wrap and freeze immediately.

TO SERVE:

Allow the cake to soften for 5 minutes on the counter. Cut the cake into rectangular slices and place each piece on a serving plate, turning the slices on their sides. Top each portion with hot fudge sauce, whipped cream, and a cherry, if desired.

Pretzel Berry Cheesecake

A family favorite for our holiday get-togethers is a gelatin dessert featuring berries and cream cheese layered atop a pretzel crust. I've re-created that dessert in cheesecake form – but without the boxed gelatin. It's a delicious, contemporary version of a vintage favorite. Serve it topped with fresh berries.
// *Serves 8 to 12*

■ **PACKAGING:** Plastic wrap, gallon-size (4 L) zip-top freezer bag

2 cups (240 g) pretzel crumbs
¾ cup (150 g) plus 2 tablespoons (25 g)
    sugar, divided
¾ cup (170 g) (1½ sticks) unsalted butter,
    melted
Two 8-ounce (224 g) packages cream
    cheese, softened

3 large eggs
¾ cup (180 ml) whipping cream
1 teaspoon vanilla extract
½ cup (112 g) raspberry or other berry jam,
    warmed to liquid consistency

WHEN READY TO SERVE, YOU WILL NEED:
Fresh raspberries

1. Preheat the oven to 400°F (200°C or gas mark 6).

2. In a large bowl, combine the pretzel crumbs, 2 tablespoons (25 g) sugar, and the melted butter. Stir well to combine.

3. Press the crumb mixture into the bottom and up the sides of a 9-inch (23 cm) springform pan.

4. Bake the crust for 8 minutes. Remove the pan from the oven and set on a rack. Reduce the oven temperature to 325°F (170°C or gas mark 3).

5. In a large bowl, beat the cream cheese and remaining ¾ cup (150 g) sugar until smooth. Beat in the eggs, one at a time, scraping the sides of the bowl as needed. Beat in the whipping cream and vanilla.

6. Remove and reserve ½ cup (120 ml) of the batter. Pour the rest of the batter into the prepared crust.

7. Stir the jam and the reserved ½ cup (120 ml) of batter together. Drizzle this mixture gently over the top of the cheesecake. Swirl by running a knife in figure eights across the top of the cake.

8. Place a pan of water on the lower shelf of the oven. Place the cheesecake on the rack above it. Bake the cheesecake for 50 to 60 minutes, or until set in the center.

9. Cool the cheesecake for 15 minutes on a rack. Carefully run a knife around the edge of the cake. Remove the sides of the pan and allow the cake to cool to room temperature on the rack. Chill the cake for several hours in the refrigerator.

FREEZING INSTRUCTIONS:

Carefully remove the bottom of the springform pan, wrap the chilled cake in plastic wrap, and place it in the freezer bag. Remove as much air from the bag as possible and freeze.

TO THAW AND SERVE:

Thaw the cake, wrapped, in the refrigerator. Once thawed, unwrap the cake and place it on a serving platter. Cut into slices and serve with fresh raspberries.

Spiced Pumpkin Custards

This recipe is so easy— open a few cans, crack an egg, add some spices, and whisk away. It comes together in minutes. Served in individual ramekins with dollops of freshly whipped cream, it makes for an easy and elegant presentation. // *Serves 6*

■ **PACKAGING:** Six 5-ounce (140 g) ramekins, plastic wrap

One 15-ounce (420 g) can solid-pack pumpkin

One 14-ounce (392 g) can sweetened condensed milk

1 large egg

1 teaspoon ground cinnamon

½ teaspoon ground ginger

½ teaspoon salt

WHEN READY TO SERVE, YOU WILL NEED:

1 cup (235 ml) heavy whipping cream

1 tablespoon sugar

1. Preheat the oven to 350°F (180°C or gas mark 4). Grease six 5-ounce (140 g) ramekins.

2. In a large bowl, whisk together the pumpkin, sweetened condensed milk, egg, cinnamon, ginger, and salt.

3. Pour the mixture into the ramekins.

4. Place the ramekins in a 9 × 13-inch (23 × 33 cm) baking pan. Place the pan in the oven and fill it with hot water to a depth of about 1 inch (2.5 cm). Bake the custards for 20 to 30 minutes, or until set.

5. Remove the custards from the oven and cool on a rack.

FREEZING INSTRUCTIONS:

Cover each cooled ramekin with plastic wrap. Chill the custards in the refrigerator before freezing.

TO THAW AND SERVE:

Thaw the custards in the refrigerator. In a large bowl, combine the whipping cream and sugar. Beat with an electric mixer until soft peaks form. Serve each custard with a dollop of whipped cream.

Not Your Ice Cream Truck's Ice Cream Sandwiches

When you were a kid, you probably enjoyed those cheap ice cream sandwiches from the corner store or the ice cream truck. Two soggy chocolate cookies with ice cream sandwiched in the middle? The taste can take us back to third grade in an instant. These chewy, fudgy ice cream sandwiches update that frozen treat for today's palates. You're going to want to make several batches so as to keep your freezer well stocked. // *Makes 8 ice cream sandwiches*

■ **PACKAGING:** Plastic wrap, gallon-size (4 L) zip-top freezer bag

6 tablespoons (84 g) (¾ stick) unsalted butter, melted	½ cup (60 g) unbleached all-purpose flour
1 cup (200 g) sugar	1 teaspoon vanilla extract
¾ cup (90 g) unsweetened cocoa powder	½ teaspoon baking powder
3 large eggs	½ to 1 quart (470 to 940 g) ice cream of your choice

1. Preheat the oven to 350°F (180°C or gas mark 4). Line baking sheets with parchment paper.

2. In a large bowl, combine the butter, sugar, cocoa, eggs, flour, vanilla, and baking powder. Stir until well blended.

3. Drop rounded tablespoonfuls of the batter onto the prepared sheets, leaving at least 2 inches (5 cm) between them. You should have 16 cookies.

4. Bake for 8 to 10 minutes, or until set. Remove to racks to cool.

5. Remove the ice cream from the freezer to soften slightly at room temperature.

6. Place one cookie, flat side up, on a small sheet of plastic wrap. Place a scoop of ice cream on the cookie. Place a second cookie, flat side down, on top of the ice cream. Press the cookies together until the ice cream flattens and spreads to the edges of the cookies. Wrap the sandwich tightly in plastic wrap and place immediately in the freezer. Continue assembling the sandwiches and placing them in the freezer. Once all the sandwiches have been assembled and wrapped, place them all in the freezer bag and store in the freezer.

TO SERVE:
Serve frozen.

Easy Chocolate Fudge Sundae Cups

Sundae cups ready and waiting in the freezer are a treat for all ages. These sundaes feature a simple yet rich homemade fudge sauce that comes together quickly. The sauce can also be customized with a variety of flavorings. // *Serves 16*

■ **PACKAGING:** Sixteen 8-ounce (224 g) plastic containers with lids

⅓ cup (80 ml) evaporated milk,
    plus more for thinning if needed
2 cups (350 g) semisweet chocolate chips

Optional flavorings: ½ teaspoon ground
    cinnamon, 1 teaspoon mint extract,
    1 teaspoon vanilla extract, ½ teaspoon
    almond extract, or ¼ cup (60 ml) Kahlúa
1 gallon (4 L) ice cream of your choice

WHEN READY TO SERVE, YOU WILL NEED:
Whipped cream
Chopped nuts

Maraschino cherries (optional)

1. In a small saucepan, combine the evaporated milk and chocolate chips. Heat over low heat, stirring, until the chocolate is melted and the mixture is smooth. Thin with additional evaporated milk, if desired.

2. Add one of the optional flavorings, if desired. Remove the pan from the heat and let cool to room temperature.

3. Remove the ice cream from the freezer to soften slightly at room temperature.

4. Scoop enough ice cream into the plastic containers to fill them about halfway. Spoon some fudge sauce over the ice cream. Scoop more ice cream, filling the containers to within 1 inch (2.5 cm) of the top. Spoon more fudge sauce on top, leaving ½ inch (1.3 cm) headspace. Cover and freeze the sundaes immediately.

TO SERVE:

Let the sundaes soften briefly at room temperature. Top with whipped cream, chopped nuts, and a cherry, if desired, prior to serving.

Mint Chocolate Fudge Ice Cream Pie

Ice cream pies are an elegant way to dress up plain old ice cream. This version combines fudge and mint, a classic favorite. The whipped cream that tops the pie is unsweetened, helping to balance the sweetness of the pie. But if you prefer a sweeter topping, simply add 1 tablespoon of sugar to the cream before you whip it. // *Serves 8*

■ **PACKAGING:** 8-inch (20.3 cm) pie pan, heavy-duty aluminum foil, gallon-size (4 L) zip-top freezer bag

1½ cups (180 g) chocolate cookie crumbs
⅓ cup (75 g) unsalted butter, melted
One 5-ounce (140 g) can evaporated milk

2 cups (350 g) semisweet chocolate chips
1 teaspoon peppermint extract
1 pint (470 g) chocolate ice cream

WHEN READY TO SERVE, YOU WILL NEED:
1 cup (235 ml) heavy whipping cream

1. Preheat the oven to 350°F (180°C or gas mark 4).

2. In a medium bowl, combine the cookie crumbs and melted butter. Pat this crumb mixture into the bottom and up the sides of the pie pan. Bake for 8 minutes. Let cool on a rack.

3. In a small saucepan, combine the evaporated milk and chocolate chips. Heat over low heat, stirring, until the chocolate is melted and the mixture is smooth. Stir in the peppermint extract. Remove the pan from the heat and let the sauce cool to room temperature.

4. Pour ½ cup (120 ml) of the sauce into the bottom of the cooled cookie crust, spreading to cover the bottom of the crust. Chill in the freezer for 10 minutes.

5. Remove the ice cream from the freezer to soften slightly at room temperature.

6. Spoon the softened ice cream into the frozen pie shell, spreading to distribute it evenly.

7. Pour 1 cup (235 ml) of the remaining cooled sauce over the ice cream and place the pie in the freezer. Reserve any remaining sauce for another recipe.

FREEZING INSTRUCTIONS:
Wrap the frozen pie with aluminum foil, slip it into the freezer bag, and store it in the freezer for up to 1 month.

TO THAW AND SERVE:
Unwrap the pie. Let stand at room temperature for about 10 minutes. While the pie is softening, whip the cream until soft peaks are formed. Serve the sliced pie with dollops of whipped cream.

Blueberry-Raspberry Croustades

Having a stash of ready-to-bake homemade pies in the freezer brings me such joy. I don't have to do much prep work, but the rewards are huge: I can serve my family or guests a berry pie à la mode without breaking a sweat. These croustades are quick and simple, since they need no pie pan. Simply form the crust around the frozen berries and wrap carefully for freezing. Bake the frozen croustades for a delicious berry dessert. // **Makes 4 croustades**

■ **PACKAGING:** Plastic wrap, gallon-size (4 L) zip-top freezer bags

2 batches Versatile Buttery Pie Crust (page 368) or other favorite pie crust
2½ cups (400 g) frozen raspberries
2 cups (300 g) frozen blueberries

½ cup (60 g) unbleached all-purpose flour
1 cup (200 g) sugar
2 tablespoons (28 g) cold unsalted butter, cut into 8 cubes

1. Divide the pie crust into 4 disks and chill.

2. On a lightly floured surface, roll each disk into a ¼-inch (6 mm)-thick round, 6 to 8 inches (15.2 to 20.3 cm) in diameter. Place the disks on 1 or 2 parchment paper–lined baking sheets.

3. In a large bowl, combine the frozen berries, flour, and sugar. Spoon a quarter of the berry mixture into the center of each pie crust round, leaving a 1- to 2-inch (2.5 to 5 cm) border around the edges.

4. Fold the edges of the pie crust toward the center, overlapping as necessary and leaving the center uncovered. Place 2 cubes of butter on the filling of each croustade.

FREEZING INSTRUCTIONS:

Place the trays of croustades in the freezer and freeze until set. Once they are set, wrap each one in plastic wrap and place in a zip-top freezer bag. Store in the freezer.

TO SERVE:

Remove the desired number of croustades from the freezer. Preheat the oven to 425°F (220°C or gas mark 7). Line a rimmed baking sheet or sheets with parchment paper. Unwrap each croustade and place it on the parchment paper. Bake the frozen croustade(s) for 25 minutes. Reduce the oven temperature to 375°F (190°C or gas mark 5) and bake 25 minutes more, or until crust is brown and the filling bubbles. Remove the croustade(s) to a rack to cool to room temperature before serving.

DESSERTS WHEN YOU CRAVE THEM

Nanna's Apple Pie

Frozen fruit pies are ubiquitous in the grocery store, but their flavor is sadly lacking. Prepping several homemade pies and stashing them in the freezer is a wonderful way to have spur-of-the-moment desserts that burst with flavor. Set up an assembly line: Make four pie crusts, fill four pie crusts, top four pies with streusel mixed up in the food processor. Easy-peasy. This apple pie, a family favorite, comes together easily and quickly, and it bakes perfectly straight from the freezer. // *Serves 8*

■ **PACKAGING:** 9-inch (23 cm) deep-dish pie pan, heavy-duty aluminum foil

1 batch Versatile Buttery Pie Crust (page 368)
½ cup (60 g) unbleached all-purpose flour
½ cup (70 g) chopped walnuts
¼ cup (56 g) brown sugar
2 tablespoons (28 g) unsalted butter
1 tablespoon plus 1 teaspoon ground
  cinnamon, divided

½ teaspoon almond extract
6 tart apples (such Granny Smith,
  Gravenstein, or Braeburn), peeled, cored,
  and sliced
½ cup (100 g) granulated sugar
1 tablespoon freshly squeezed lemon juice

1. Line a 9-inch (23 cm) deep-dish pie pan with the pie crust. Chill the crust in the refrigerator while you make the filling and the topping.

2. In the bowl of a food processor, combine the flour, walnuts, brown sugar, butter, 1 teaspoon cinnamon, and almond extract. Pulse until coarse crumbs are formed. Alternatively, in a large bowl, combine the flour, brown sugar, and butter, cutting the butter into the sugar and flour with a pastry blender or two knives until coarse crumbs are formed. Stir in the walnuts, 1 teaspoon cinnamon, and almond extract.

Desserts When You Crave Them ■ 363

3. In a large bowl, combine the apples, granulated sugar, the remaining 1 tablespoon cinnamon, and the lemon juice. Pile this filling into the prepared pie shell.

4. Sprinkle the crumb mixture evenly over the apples.

FREEZING INSTRUCTIONS:

Wrap the pie securely with heavy-duty aluminum foil. Freeze.

TO SERVE:

Preheat the oven to 425°F (220°C or gas mark 7). Unwrap the pie and place it on a rimmed baking sheet to catch any drips. Bake the frozen pie for 15 minutes. Reduce the oven temperature to 375°F (190°C or gas mark 5) and bake 45 minutes to 1 hour more, or until the crust is browned and the filling bubbles. To prevent excessive browning, cover the pie with a sheet of aluminum foil. Allow the pie to cool before serving. Serve warm or at room temperature.

Slab Apple Pie

One day, I experimented with my usual apple pie recipe by baking it in a 9 × 13-inch (23 × 33 cm) baking dish. What I discovered was an even easier and equally delicious way to serve apple pie. This dessert has several things going for it: It's super easy to throw together, since you don't have to worry about fluting edges or getting the topping to form a perfect mound. There's a bigger crust-to-apple ratio. And it freezes just as well as a regular pie but has a shape that's more freezer-friendly. You can also slice smaller pieces when serving a crowd and no one will feel cheated. Maybe. // *Serves 8 to 12*

■ **PACKAGING:** 9 × 13-inch (23 × 33 cm) baking dish with lid

1 batch **Versatile Buttery Pie Crust** (page 368)
6 tart apples (such as Granny Smith, Gravenstein, or Braeburn), peeled, cored, and sliced
½ cup (100 g) granulated sugar
1 tablespoon (15 ml) freshly squeezed lemon juice

1 tablespoon ground cinnamon
1 cup (120 g) unbleached all-purpose flour
½ cup (112 g) (1 stick) unsalted butter
½ cup (112 g) brown sugar
½ cup (40 g) quick-cooking rolled oats

1. Line the bottom of the baking dish with the crust.

2. In a large bowl, combine the apple slices, granulated sugar, lemon juice, and cinnamon. Spread the apple mixture in an even layer over the crust.

3. In a food processor, combine the flour, butter, and brown sugar, pulsing until coarse crumbs are formed. Alternatively, combine these ingredients in a large bowl, cutting the butter into the sugar and flour with a pastry blender or two knives until coarse crumbs are formed.

4. Stir the oats into the crumb topping. Sprinkle the crumb topping over the apple layer.

FREEZING INSTRUCTIONS:
Cover the dish and label before freezing.

TO SERVE:
Preheat the oven to 425°F (220°C or gas mark 7). Uncover the frozen pie and bake it for 15 minutes. Reduce the oven temperature to 375°F (190°C or gas mark 5) and bake 45 minutes to 1 hour more, or until browned and bubbly.

Lemon-Ginger Freezer Pie

Creamy and lemony, with a little warmth from the ginger, this pie comes together easily and quickly. Stash it in the freezer for a "ready when you are" dessert. // *Serves 8*

▪ **PACKAGING:** 8-inch (20.3 cm) pie pan, plastic wrap, gallon-size (4 L) zip-top freezer bag

1½ cups (180 g) graham cracker crumbs
2 tablespoons (25 g) sugar
⅓ cup (75 g) unsalted butter, melted
½ cup (112 g) prepared lemon curd
8 ounces (224 g) cream cheese, softened

One 14-ounce (392 g) can sweetened
    condensed milk
½ teaspoon ground ginger
1 cup (235 ml) whipping cream

1. Preheat the oven to 350°F (180°C or gas mark 4).

2. In a medium bowl, combine the graham cracker crumbs, sugar, and melted butter. Pat this crumb mixture into an 8-inch (20.3 cm) pie pan. Bake for 8 minutes. Let cool on a rack.

3. In a large bowl, blend the lemon curd and cream cheese until light and fluffy. Blend in the sweetened condensed milk and ginger.

4. In a separate bowl, beat the whipped cream until stiff peaks form. Fold half of the whipped cream into the lemon mixture. Spoon this mixture into the cooled pie crust. Smooth the top.

5. Spread the remaining whipped cream over the top of the pie.

FREEZING INSTRUCTIONS:

Freeze the pie until firm. Wrap the pie securely with plastic wrap and place in the freezer bag. Store in the freezer for up to 1 month.

TO THAW AND SERVE:

Unwrap the pie. Let it stand at room temperature for about 10 minutes, until it can be cut easily. Serve cold.

Coconut Crunch Pie

This pie evokes the taste of a coconut cream pie—but you don't have to spend any time slaving over a hot stove to make it. It comes together in minutes and provides cool refreshment on a hot summer evening. // *Serves 8*

- **PACKAGING:** 8-inch (20.3 cm) pie pan, heavy-duty aluminum foil, gallon-size (4 L) zip-top freezer bag

½ cup (40 g) unsweetened shredded coconut
2 cups (240 g) shortbread cookie crumbs
¼ cup (56 g) (½ stick) unsalted butter, melted

1½ cups (355 ml) whipping cream
⅓ cup (40 g) confectioners' sugar
1 cup (120 g) coarsely crushed shortbread cookies

1. Preheat the oven to 350°F (180°C or gas mark 4). Spread the shredded coconut on a rimmed baking sheet and toast for 5 to 10 minutes, stirring frequently. Remove from the oven and let cool completely.

2. In a small bowl, combine the cookie crumbs and melted butter. Pat the crumb mixture into the pie plate. Chill in the freezer.

3. In a large bowl, whip the cream and the confectioners' sugar until soft peaks form. Fold in the crushed cookies and coconut.

4. Spoon the whipped cream mixture into the shortbread crust. Freeze until firm.

FREEZING INSTRUCTIONS:

Wrap the frozen pie with foil and place in the freezer bag. Store in the freezer for up to 1 month.

TO SERVE:

Unwrap the pie. Let it stand at room temperature for about 10 minutes before slicing and serving.

Versatile Buttery Pie Crust

Making this pie crust is as easy as, well, pie. Using a food processor makes quick work of it; the dough can be ready in less than five minutes. You can freeze the pie crust, tightly wrapped, in a disk and roll it out later or assemble your pies and freeze them prior to baking. This particular crust also works well as a "pat in the pan" crust. You don't need to roll it out if you don't want to—simply press it gently into the pan and up the sides. // *Makes enough for 1 single-crust pie*

■ **PACKAGING:** Plastic wrap, gallon-size (4 L) zip-top freezer bag

1 cup (120 g) unbleached all-purpose flour	**½ teaspoon salt**
½ cup (112 g) (1 stick) unsalted butter, cut into chunks	**1 to 2 tablespoons (15 to 30 ml) cold water**

1. In the bowl of a food processor, combine the flour, butter, and salt. Run the processor for 15 to 20 seconds, or until coarse crumbs are formed. Alternatively, in a medium bowl, combine the flour, butter, and salt with a pastry blender or two knives. Work these ingredients together until coarse crumbs are formed.

2. Quickly pulse or stir in the cold water and mix until a dough forms. Form into a ball.

FREEZING INSTRUCTIONS:

If using the dough in a recipe, proceed with the recipe. Otherwise, wrap the dough securely in plastic wrap, slip into a zip-top freezer bag, and store in the freezer.

TO THAW AND SERVE:

Thaw the dough in the refrigerator overnight. Let stand at room temperature for a few minutes to soften before rolling it out or patting it into a pie pan, pressing the dough across the bottom of the pie plate and up the sides. Use as is in recipes that call for an unbaked pie shell. For recipes that require a prebaked crust, preheat the oven to 350°F (180°C or gas mark 4) and prebake the crust for 10 to 15 minutes, until light golden brown. Cool completely before filling.

Acknowledgments

When I was just a little girl, I dreamt of writing a book—a cookbook, no less. It's amazing to me that so many years later that dream has come true—four times over. And not only that, but this book you hold in your hot little hands is a second edition. Imagine that! I could not have done it without the help of some wise and witty folk. Many thanks are due.

Thank you to the team at The Harvard Common Press, who embraced this project and patiently walked this rookie author through the paces: Bruce Shaw, for his enthusiasm for quality books; Adam Salomone, for the energy he brought to the project; Dan Rosenberg, for his encouragement and humor throughout the process; Valerie Cimino and Jane Dornbusch, who partnered with me to craft the best book possible; Pat Jalbert-Levine, for her amazing attention to detail and infectious enthusiasm; and the entire production crew for making it so spiffy and fun to look at.

Thanks to my agent, Alison Picard, for believing in the project and connecting me with such a great group of people.

Thank you to my wonderful readers at my blogs, Life as Mom and Good Cheap Eats. You make writing and cooking fun! Thanks to those friends who tested recipes or offered counsel for either edition, including but not limited to Aimee, Allison, Allie, Amy G., Amy McG., Amy N., Caroline, Cathy, Cristina, Crystal, Dawn, Erin, Jamie, Janel, JessieLeigh, Jessika, Joy, Jules, Lauren, Laurie, Lynn, Mandi, Marilyn, Michelle, Patti, Phoebe, Prerna, Shaina, Sheila, Tami, and Tsh. Thank you to Mom and Dad, Jace and John, and endless friends for your willingness to be my guinea pigs—er, taste testers.

Special thanks to my six sweet children, who willingly made my project theirs. The cookbooks have always been a group endeavor, and I'm so thankful for your excitement about them—and your willingness to eat batch after batch of ice cream sandwiches until the recipe was "just right." Your expertise is invaluable.

Deep gratitude goes to my precious husband, Bryan, who washed lots of dishes, flew solo on kid duty, cleaned up endless messes, orchestrated bedtimes, and cheered me on throughout it all. You are my rock. Thank you for encouraging me in all my wild dreams.

I give ultimate thanks to Jesus, who gave me all good things.

About the Author

Jessica Fisher is the creator of two popular blogs, *Life as Mom* and *Good Cheap Eats*; the author of four cookbooks; and a go-to source for fresh and clever ideas about how to live and eat well on a budget. The mother of six, she lives with her husband and family in the San Diego area.

Index

Alfredo Mac and Cheese, 210
Almonds
    Buttered French Toast Casserole
        with Almonds and Ginger, 284
    Chocolate-Almond Biscotti, 343–344
    Crumb-Topped Zucchini Muffins,
        311–312
    Mahi Mahi with Almond-Lime
        Butter, 152
    Maple Granola with Oats, Nuts, and
        Seeds, 267–268
    Sweet Almond Toasts, 282–283
Aluminum baking pans, 15
Apples
    Nanna's Apple Pie, 363–364
    Slab Apple Pie, 364–365
    Slow Cooker Applesauce, 295–296
Applesauce
    Raspberry Baked Oatmeal, 270
    Slow Cooker Applesauce, 295–296
Applesauce-Walnut Bread, 300–301
Asian Dipping Sauce
    Gingery Pork and Mushroom Let-
        tuce Wraps, 174
    recipe, 176
Asian Slaw
    Pulled Pork Sandwiches with
        Asian Slaw and Tangy Barbecue
        Sauce, 168–170
    recipe, 170
Asparagus
Spring Vegetable Soup, 231
Assembly line, kitchen, 23, 25
Avocado
Chili-Stuffed Sweet Potatoes, 99–100
Jalapeño Burn Pizza, 256
Mexican Beef Tortas, 77–78
Spicy Taco Lasagna, 142

Bacon
    Bacon and Spinach Quiche, 293
    Bacon-Cheddar Egg Bake, 289–290
    Bacon-Cheddar Egg Bake for a
        Crowd, 290
    Chicken-Bacon Subs, 140
    Make-Ahead Baked Bacon, 177–178
    Split Pea Soup with Bacon and
        Thyme, 227
Bacon and Spinach Quiche, 293
Bacon-Cheddar Egg Bake, 289–290
Bacon-Cheddar Egg Bake for a Crowd,
    57–60, 219
Baked Manicotti with Sun-Dried Toma-
    toes and Thyme, 212
Baking mixes. See also Muffins/muffin
    mixes; Pancakes/pancake mixes;
    Scones/scone mixes; Waffles/waffle
    mixes
    assembling your own, 10–11
    great recipes for, 308
    scones and biscuits, 312
Bananas
    Breakfast Smoothies, 287
    Chocolate-Banana Marble Cake,
        350–351
    Chocolate Chip Banana Bread with
        Oats, 301
    Cinnamon Banana Bread, 306
Barbecue Cheeseburger Pizza, 259
Barbecue sauce
    Pulled Pork Sandwiches with
        Asian Slaw and Tangy Barbecue
        Sauce, 168–170
    Tangy Asian Barbecue Sauce, 171
Barbecue Sauce for Meatballs, 106–107
    Barbecue Cheeseburger Pizza, 259
    recipe, 159

Barley
    Beef and Barley Soup with Dill, 233
    Mushroom Barley Soup, 232
Bars
    Caramel-Lime Bars, 349
    Double Chocolate Magic Bars,
        348–349
Basic Herb-Baked Chicken
    bones from, for Homemade Chick-
        en Stock, 114
    in menu plan, 57–60
    recipe, 111
Basic Pizza Dough. See also Pizzas
    in meal plan, 33–36
    Pepperoni Calzones, 263–264
    recipe, 249–250
    Spinach and Cheese Calzones,
        264–265
Basic pizza kits, 44–47
Basic Taco Seasoning Mix, 68
    Lawnmower Taco, 100, 102
    in meal plans, 42–47
    Not Your Convenience Store's
        Frozen Burritos, 96
    recipe, 97
    Southwest Seasoned Pork
        Chops, 162
Batch cooking, 7–8. See also Bulk
    cooking; Freezer cooking
    assembly-line approach to, 23, 25
    economical, 18–20
    instructions for, 7–8
    mixing and matching meal compo-
        nents for, 20, 22
    as a way to help others, 93
Bean and Cheese Nacho Bake, 57–60,
    117, 192, 219

Beans. *See also* Black beans; Kidney beans; Pinto beans; Refried beans
    Bean and Cheese Nacho Bake, 192
    precooked, 10
    Seasoned Versatile Pinto Beans, 189
    Smoky Multi-Bean Vegetarian Chili, 247
    Taco Soup with Hominy, 222
    White Bean Soup with Vegetables, 228
    Whole Wheat Black Bean and Pepper Wraps, 192–193
Beef. *See also* Chuck roast; Ground beef
Beef and Barley Soup with Dill, 233
freezing shredded, 10
Quick and Easy Pepper Steak, 85
Beef and Barley Soup with Dill, 117, 233
Beef Plans, 37–41
Beef Stew with Eggplant and Carrots, 242
Beefy Mushroom Gravy, 53–57, 68, 87
    Shepherd's Pie with Green Chile Mashed Potatoes, 92
    Swedish Meatballs with Dill, 94
Beer
    Chihuahua Chili, 244–245
Bell peppers. *See also* Green bell peppers; Red bell peppers
    Easy Sausage and Pepper Sandwiches, 179–180
    Fish Chowder with Red Potatoes and Corn, 236
    Gingery Vegetable Stir-Fry Kit, 202
    Penne with Italian Sausage and Tricolor Peppers, 184–185
    Quick and Spicy Marinara Sauce, 216
    Roasted Vegetable Quiche, 208
    Roasted Vegetable Soup, 224
    Shrimp and Vegetable Packets, 156–158
    Smoky Multi-Bean Vegetarian Chili, 247
    Spicy Shrimp and Tomatoes, 158–159
    Tortilla Soup with Shrimp, 235
    Whole Wheat Black Bean and Pepper Wraps, 192–193
Best-Ever Chicken Pot Pie, 16, 22, 127, 159, 219
gravy for, 115
Better Instant Oatmeal Packet, 26–28, 28–31, 31–33, 274
Big-batch cooking. *See* Batch cooking
Biscotti, Chocolate-Almond, 343–344
Biscuits
    Garlic-Parmesan Swirl Biscuits, 322–324
    Herb Biscuits, 323
    Make-Ahead Drop Biscuits, 322–323
    prepared ahead of time, 312

Black beans
    Black Bean Soup with Jalapeño, 234
    Burrito Pizza, 254
    Chihuahua Chili, 244–245
    Smoky Multi-Bean Vegetarian Chili, 247
    Taco Soup with Hominy, 222
    Tortilla Soup with Shrimp, 235
    Tres Chiles Chili Con Quinoa, 245–246
    Whole Wheat Black Bean and Pepper Wraps, 192–193
Black Bean Soup with Jalapeño, 36–39, 117, 234
Black olives
    Bean and Cheese Nacho Bake, 192
    Burrito Pizza, 254
    Italian-Spiced Cheesewiches, 201
    Jalapeño Burn Pizza, 256
    Lawnmower Taco, 100, 102
    Quick and Easy Cheese Enchiladas, 190
    Six-Layer Nachos, 195–196
Blueberries
    Blueberry-Raspberry Croustades, 362–363
    The Blue Maple smoothie, 288
    The Blue Pineapple smoothie, 289
    dried, Better Instant Oatmeal Packets, 274
    Fruit, Nut, and Oatmeal Bowls, 273
    Lemon-Blueberry Scones, 313–314
Blueberry-Raspberry Croustades, 362–363
Blue cheese
    Seasoned Steak with Gorgonzola-Herb Butter, 83–84
    Tarragon Turkey Burgers with Blue Cheese and Chipotle Mayo, 144–146
Bolillo rolls, 77, 78
Boules de Picolat (Catalan Meatballs), 108
Bowls, breakfast, 272
Bread(s). *See also* Rolls
    Applesauce-Walnut Bread, 300–301
    brioche, for Buttered French Toast Casserole with Almonds and Ginger, 284
    Buttermilk Cornbread, 299
    Chocolate Chip Banana Bread with Oats, 301
    Cinnamon Banana Bread, 306
    day-old, 332
    Easy Make-Ahead Garlic Bread, 335
    Italian-style, for Chicken-Bacon Subs, 140
    Nutty Zucchini Bread, 305
    Spiced Pumpkin Flax Bread, 303–304
    Sweet Almond Toasts, 282–283
    Vanilla Cranberry Bread, 307

Bread crumbs
    Broccoli Gratin with Tarragon and Buttered Bread Crumbs, 207
    Chicken Divan with Cheddar Crust, 131
    Crumb-Topped Cod Fillets, 154
    Garlic Butter Chicken Lemon Sauce, 133–134
    Garlicky Chicken Noodle Bake, 128
    Ham and Swiss Potato Gratin, 178
    Herbed Meatballs, 106
    homemade, 333
    Stuffed Chicken Parmesan, 132
    Swedish Meatballs with Dill, 94
    Sweet and Sour Turkey Meatballs, 148–149
    Tahini Vegetable Patties, 204
    Turkey Burgers with Scallions, 143
Bread cubes
    Bacon-Cheddar Egg Bake, 289–290
    Bacon-Cheddar Egg Bake for a Crowd, 290
    Individual Greek Egg Casseroles, 209
Bread machine, 22, 249
Breakfast Cookies, 31–33, 286
Breakfast Plans, 26–33
Breakfast Sliders, 296
Breakfast Smoothies, 117, 287
Broccoli
    Broccoli Gratin with Tarragon and Buttered Bread Crumbs, 207
    Cheddar Soup with Zucchini, Broccoli, and Carrots, 221
    Chicken Divan with Cheddar Crust, 131
    Gingery Vegetable Stir-Fry Kit, 202
    Roasted Vegetable Quiche, 208
Broccoli Gratin with Tarragon and Buttered Bread Crumbs, 36–39, 207
Brown, Alton, 4
Brownies
    Cocoa Brownies, 346–347
    Kahlúa Brownies, 347–348
Brown rice
Chicken and Wild Rice Bake, 134–136
Green Chile Rice Casserole, 197
Bulk-Batch Pancake Mix, 26–28, 31–33, 275–276, 308
Bulk cooking. *See also* Batch cooking
    cookies, 340
    forming a co-op for, 319–320
    quick tips for, 268
Bulk purchases, 10, 18, 353
Burgers
    Outside-In Cheeseburgers, 105
    Soy-Balsamic Burgers, 102–103
    Tarragon Turkey Burgers with Blue Cheese and Chipotle Mayo, 144–146
    Turkey Burgers with Scallions, 143

Burrito Pizza, 254
Burritos, 9
    Not Your Convenience Store's
        Frozen Burritos, 96
    Pepper Jack and Chile Burritos,
        197–198
Buttered French Toast Casserole with
    Almonds and Ginger, 28, 284
Buttermilk
    Bulk-Batch Pancakes, 275–276
    Buttermilk Cornbread, 299
    Chocolate Chip Banana Bread with
        Oats, 301–302
    Chocolate-Zucchini Cake, 351–352
    Cranberry-Oatmeal Cookies, 338
    Lemon-Blueberry Scones, 313–314
    Oatmeal-Chocolate Chip Pan-
        cakes, 276–277
Buttermilk Cornbread, 299, 308
Butternut squash
    Cheesy Butternut Squash Soup
        with Herbs, 226
Buttery Pie Crust. *See* Versatile Buttery
    Pie Crust

Cabbage, Grilled Tilapia or Shrimp
    Tacos, 155–156
Cake
    Chocolate-Banana Marble Cake,
        350–351
    Chocolate Zucchini Cake, 351–352
    Mocha Hot Fudge Cake, 354–356
Calzones
    Pepperoni Calzones, 263–264
    Spinach and Cheese Calzones,
        264–265
Caramel-Lime Bars, 349
Carne Asada, Easy, 82–83
Carnitas, 10
    Versatile Slow-Cooked Carnitas, 161
Carrots
    Beef and Barley Soup with Dill, 233
    Beef Stew with Eggplant and
        Carrots, 242
    Best-Ever Chicken Pot Pie, 127
    Cheddar Soup with Zucchini, Broc-
        coli, and Carrots, 221
    Cheesy Butternut Squash Soup
        with Herbs, 226
    Creamy Cauliflower Soup, 229
    Gingery Pork and Mushroom Let-
        tuce Wraps, 174
    Mushroom Barley Soup, 232
    Our Favorite Irish Stew, 240
    Pork Chile Verde with Hominy and
        Carrots, 162–163
    Quick and Spicy Marinara
        Sauce, 216
    Roasted Vegetable Soup, 224

Shrimp and Vegetable Packets,
    156–158
Split Pea Soup with Bacon and
    Thyme, 227
Spring Vegetable Soup, 231
Tortilla Soup with Shrimp, 235
Vegetable Bolognese, 90
Wild Boar Italian Sausage with
    Spicy Tomato Sauce, 186
Casseroles
    Broccoli Gratin with Tarragon and
        Buttered Bread Crumbs, 207
    Chicken Enchilada Bake with Green
        Chiles and Jalapeños, 126
    Chile Cheese Bake, 196
    Cozy Cheese and Potato Casse-
        role, 194–195
    Eggs Florentine Casserole, 292
    Garlicky Chicken Noodle Bake, 128
    Green Chile Rice Casserole, 197
    Individual Greek Egg Casseroles, 209
    Lawnmower Taco, 100, 102
Catalan Meatballs, 108
Cauliflower Soup, Creamy, 229
Cereal, preparing instant breakfast, 272
Cheddar cheese
    Bacon-Cheddar Egg Bake, 289–290
    Bacon-Cheddar Egg Bake for a
        Crowd, 290
    Barbecue Cheeseburger Pizza, 259
    Breakfast Sliders, 296
    Broccoli Gratin with Tarragon and
        Buttered Bread Crumbs, 207
    Burrito Pizza, 254
    Cheddar Coins, 323–324
    Cheddar Soup with Zucchini, Broc-
        coli, and Carrots, 221
    Cheesy Butternut Squash Soup
        with Herbs, 226
    Cheesy Overnight Casserole with
        Chicken or Turkey, 130
    Chicken Divan with Cheddar
        Crust, 131
    Chicken Enchilada Bake with Green
        Chiles and Jalapeños, 126
    Chile Cheese Bake, 196
    Cozy Cheese and Potato Casse-
        role, 194–195
    Green Chile Rice Casserole, 197
    Italian-Spiced Cheesewiches, 201
    Jalapeño Burn Pizza, 256
    Lawnmower Taco, 100, 102
    Mexican Beef Tortas, 78
    Not Your Convenience Store's
        Frozen Burritos, 96
    Outside-In Cheeseburgers, 105
    Quick and Easy Cheese
        Enchiladas, 190

Roasted Vegetable Quiche, 208
Shepherd's Pie with Green Chile
    Mashed Potatoes, 92
Six-Layer Nachos, 195–196
Sweet and Spicy Joes, 99
Cheddar Coins, 323–324
Cheddar Soup with Zucchini, Broccoli,
    and Carrots, 221
Cheese(s). *See also* individual types of
    cheeses
    Alfredo Mac and Cheese, 210
    Easy-Peasy Cheesy Pizza kit, 253
    freezing, 10, 11
    Hearty Shredded Beef Enchiladas,
        79–80
    Potatoes Stuffed with Caramelized
        Onions and Dubliner Cheese,
        206–207
    Salsa Verde Beef with, 75
Cheesecake, Pretzel Berry, 356–357
Cheesy Butternut Squash Soup with
    Herbs, 226
Cheesy Overnight Casserole with
    Chicken or Turkey, 130
Chest freezers, 303
Chicken. *See also* Chicken breasts;
    Chicken, cooked and chopped/
    shredded; Chicken tenders
    Chicken and Wild Rice Bake,
        134–136
    marinated, 122
    precut for stir-fries, 9–10
    roasting, Versatile Chicken from the
        Slow Cooker, 112
Chicken and Sun-Dried Tomato Pizza
    with Goat Cheese, 262–263
Chicken and Wild Rice Bake, 116,
    134–136
Chicken-Bacon Subs, 57–60, 140
Chicken breasts
    Basic Herb-Baked Chicken, 111
    Best-Ever Chicken Pot Pie, 127
    Chicken and Wild Rice Bake,
        134–136
    Chicken Cacciatore Stew, 239
    Garlic Butter Chicken Lemon
        Sauce, 133–134
    Garlicky Italian Chicken Breasts, 121
    Herb-Butter Chicken Tenders,
        122–123
    Sesame Chicken with Snow Peas
        and Mushrooms, 137
    Simply Poached Chicken, 113
    Spicy Dijon Chicken, 119
    Spicy Southwest Chicken, 118
    stuffed, 133
    Stuffed Chicken Parmesan, 132
    Versatile Chicken from the Slow
        Cooker, 112

Chicken Cacciatore Stew, 239
Chicken, cooked and chopped/
   shredded, 10
      as a building block for many
         meals, 113
      Cheesy Overnight Casserole with
         Chicken or Turkey, 130
      Chicken and Sun-Dried Toma-
         to Pizza with Goat Cheese,
         262–263
      Chicken-Bacon Subs, 140
      Chicken Divan with Cheddar
         Crust, 131
      Chicken Enchilada Bake with Green
         Chiles and Jalapeños, 126
      Chipotle Chicken and Onion
         Wraps, 138
      Creamy Chicken Enchiladas, 129
      Garlicky Chicken Noodle Bake, 128
      Green Chile Chicken Taquitos, 139
      Not Your Mother's Chicken Noodle
         Soup, 223
Chicken Divan with Cheddar Crust,
   131, 219
Chicken Enchilada Bake with Green
   Chiles and Jalapeños, 57–60, 219
Chicken gravy, 115
Chicken stock, 114
Chicken tenders
      Chicken Cacciatore Stew, 239
      Moo Shu-Style Chicken Wraps, 125
      Salsa Verde Chicken, 124
      Teriyaki Chicken Skewers, 123–124
Chihuahua Chili, 244–245
Chile and Sausage Oven Frittata,
   57–60, 219, 294–295
Chile Cheese Bake, 117, 196
Chili
      Chihuahua Chili, 244–245
      Quick and Easy Texas Chili, 244
      Smoky Multi-Bean Vegetarian
         Chili, 247
      Tres Chiles Chili Con Quinoa,
         245–246
Chili-Stuffed Sweet Potatoes,
   99–100, 116
Chipotle Chicken and Onion Wraps,
   138, 159
Chipotle peppers
      Chipotle Chicken and Onion
         Wraps, 138
      Tarragon Turkey Burgers with Blue
         Cheese and Chipotle Mayo,
         144–146
Chipotle-Rubbed Tri-Tip, 39–41, 80, 116
Chipotle Taco Seasoning Mix, 39–41, 68
      Creamy Chicken Enchiladas, 129
      recipe, 98

Chocolate-Almond Biscotti, 48–51,
   343–344
Chocolate-Banana Marble Cake,
   350–351
Chocolate Butterhorn Rolls, 329–330
Chocolate Chip Banana Bread with
   Oats, 301
Chocolate chips
      Breakfast Cookies, 286
      Chocolate-Almond Biscotti, 343–344
      Chocolate Butterhorn Rolls, 329–330
      Chocolate Chip Banana Bread with
         Oats, 301
      Chocolate-Toffee Cookies, 344–345
      Chocolate Zucchini Cake, 351–352
      Cocoa Brownies, 346–347
      Double Chocolate Magic Bars,
         348–349
      Easy Chocolate Fudge Sundae
         Cups, 360–361
      Kahlúa Brownies, 347–348
      Lime Chocolate Chip Scones,
         317–318
      Mint Chocolate Fudge Ice Cream
         Pie, 361–362
      Oatmeal-Chocolate Chip Pan-
         cakes, 276–277
      White Chocolate-Walnut Jumbles,
         339
Chocolate Minty Melts, 48–51,
   345–346
Chocolate-Toffee Cookies, 48–51,
   344–345
Chocolate Zucchini Cake, 351–352
Chuck roast
      Beef Stew with Eggplant and
         Carrots, 242
      Hearty Beef Stew with Olives, 241
      Hearty Shredded Beef Enchiladas,
         79–80
      Mexican Beef Tortas, 77–78
      Our Favorite Irish Stew, 240
      Salsa Verde Beef, 75
      Versatile Shredded Beef Filling,
         73–74
Cinnamon Banana Bread, 26–28, 306
Cinnamon French Toast Dippers,
   57–60, 281–282
Cinnamon Rolls, Whole-Grain, 324–326
Cinnamon Twist Loaves, 327–328
Clafouti, Savory Ham and Swiss,
   293–294
Cocoa Brownies, 308, 346–347
Coconut
      Coconut Crunch Pie, 366
      Double Chocolate Magic Bars,
         348–349
      Ginger-Coconut Scones, 316–317
Coconut Crunch Pie, 366

Coconut-Lime Muffins with Chocolate
   Chips, 308, 310–311
Coconut milk
      Coconut-Lime Muffins with Choco-
         late Chips, 310–311
      Ginger-Coconut Scones, 316–317
      Turkey Curry, 147
Cod fillets
      Crumb-Topped Cod Fillets, 154
      Fish Chowder with Red Potatoes
         and Corn, 236
Coffee
      Chocolate-Almond Biscotti, 343–344
      Cocoa Brownies, 346–347
      Mocha Hot Fudge Cake, 354–356
Coleslaw mix
      Asian Slaw, 170
      Moo Shu-Style Chicken Wraps, 125
Cookie dough, freezing, 340
Cookies
      bulk cooking, 340
      Chocolate Minty Melts, 345–346
      Chocolate-Toffee Cookies, 344–345
      Cranberry-Oatmeal Cookies, 338
      freezing made, 340–341
      Gingerbread Crinkles, 342–343
      Sugar and Spice Cookies, 337
      White Chocolate-Walnut Jumbles, 339
Co-op, bulk cooking, 319–320
Corn
      canned, Fish Chowder with Red
         Potatoes and Corn, 236
      Corn and Chile Tamales, 198–199
      Smoky Multi-Bean Vegetarian
         Chili, 247
Corn and Chile Tamales, 117
Cornbread, Buttermilk, 299
Corn husks
      Corn and Chile Tamales, 198–199
      Pork and Chile Tamales, 166–167
Cottage cheese, Eggs Florentine
   Casserole, 292
Couscous, Mediterranean Steak Salad,
   81–82
Cozy Cheese and Potato Casserole,
   57–60, 194–195, 219
Crackers, cheesy snack, 323–324
Cranberries
      dried
         Breakfast Cookies, 286
         Buttered French Toast Cas-
            serole with Almonds and
            Ginger, 284
         Cranberry-Oatmeal Cookies, 338
         Cranberry-Orange Granola,
            269–270
         Wholesome Energy Bars,
            333–334

fresh
Cranberry Pork Chops, 163–164
Vanilla Cranberry Bread, 307
Cranberry-Oatmeal Cookies, 338
Cranberry-Orange Granola, 28–31, 31–33, 269–270

Cranberry Pork Chops, 163–164
Cream cheese
Cream Cheese Mashed Potatoes, 86
Creamy Cauliflower Soup, 229
Creamy Chicken Enchiladas, 129
Lemon-Ginger Freezer Pie, 365–366
Pretzel Berry Cheesecake, 356–357
Spicy Taco Lasagna, 142
Cream Cheese Mashed Potatoes
Beef Stew with Eggplant and Carrots, 242
recipe, 86
Creamy Cauliflower Soup, 229
Creamy Chicken Enchiladas, 22, 116, 129, 219
Croutons, Homemade, 333
Crumb-Topped Cod Fillets, 53–57, 154
Crumb-Topped Zucchini Muffins, 308, 311–312
Crystal's Butterhorn Rolls, 326–327
Curry, Turkey, 147
Custards, Spiced Pumpkin, 357–358

Day-old bread, 332
Deep-Dish Focaccia Pizza Your Way, 159, 262
Deep freezers, 302–303
Dijon mustard
Chicken Divan with Cheddar Crust, 131
Ham and Swiss Potato Gratin, 178
Herb-Crusted Pork Roast, 176–177
Herbed Vinaigrette, 136
Spicy Dijon Chicken, 119
Dinner kits, 10
Double Chocolate Magic Bars, 48–51, 348–349
Doubling recipes, 11
Dubliner cheese, Potatoes Stuffed with Caramelized Onions and, 206–207

Easy Caesar Salad with Garlicky Italian Grilled Chicken, 120
Easy Carne Asada, 82–83, 116
Easy Chicken (or Turkey) Gravy, 68
Best-Ever Chicken Pot Pie, 127
Garlicky Chicken Noodle Bake, 128
recipe, 115
Easy Chocolate Fudge Sundae Cups, 360–361

Easy Homemade Salsa
Bean and Cheese Nacho Bake, 192
Burrito Pizza, 254
Chipotle-Rubbed Tri-Tip with, 80
Corn and Chile Tamales, 198–199
Green Chile Chicken Taquitos, 139

Grilled Tilapia or Shrimp Tacos, 155–156
Oven-Baked Beef Taquitos, 76
Pork and Chile Tamales, 166–167
Queso Fundido, 180–182
recipe, 77
Salsa Verde Beef, 75
Six-Layer Nachos, 195–196
Spicy Taco Lasagna, 142
Easy Make-Ahead Garlic Bread, 39–41, 57–60, 335
Easy-Peasy Cheesy Pizza kit, 33–36, 253
Easy Sausage and Pepper Sandwiches, 179–180, 219
Easy Slow Cooker Red Sauce, 68, 117, 159, 250
Baked Manicotti with Sun-Dried Tomatoes and Thyme, 212
with Italian Shredded Beef Filling, 74
in meal plans, 44–47
Pepperoni Calzones, 263–264
recipe, 217
Shells Stuffed with Pork, Mushrooms, and Onions, 173
Spicy Taco Lasagna, 142
Stuffed Chicken Parmesan, 132
Easy Stovetop Ratatouille, 33–36, 117, 200
Egg dishes
Bacon and Spinach Quiche, 293
Bacon-Cheddar Egg Bake, 289–290
Bacon-Cheddar Egg Bake for a Crowd, 290
breakfast, 272
Chile and Sausage Oven Frittata, 294–295
Eggs Florentine Casserole, 292
Egg noodles
Garlicky Chicken Noodle Bake, 128
Not Your Mother's Chicken Noodle Soup, 223
Eggplant
Beef Stew with Eggplant and Carrots, 242
Easy Stovetop Ratatouille, 200
Roasted Vegetable Soup, 224
Vegetable Bolognese, 90
Eggs Florentine Casserole, 44–47, 219, 292

Enchiladas
Creamy Chicken Enchiladas, 129
Hearty Shredded Beef Enchiladas, 79–80
Quick and Easy Cheese Enchiladas, 190

Enchilada sauce
Chihuahua Chili, 244–245
Corn and Chile Tamales, 198–199
Hearty Beef Stew with Olives, 241
Hearty Shredded Beef Enchiladas, 79–80
Not Your Convenience Store's Frozen Burritos, 96
Pork and Chile Tamales, 166–167
Quick and Easy Cheese Enchiladas, 190
Six-Layer Nachos, 195–196
Taco Soup with Hominy, 222
Energy Bars, Wholesome, 333–334
English muffins
Breakfast Sliders, 296
Everything (meal) Plans, 53–64

Feta cheese
Eggs Florentine Casserole, 292
Individual Greek Egg Casseroles, 209
Mediterranean Steak Salad, 81–82
Pesto Pizza with Shrimp, Feta, and Tomatoes, 258
Spinach and Feta Manicotti with Lemon and Oregano, 214
Tahini Vegetable Patties, 204
Fish and seafood. See also Shrimp
Crumb-Topped Cod Fillets, 154
Fish Chowder with Red Potatoes and Corn, 236
Hoisin-Glazed Salmon Fillets, 151
Mahi Mahi with Almond-Lime Butter, 152
Salmon Packets with Sun-Dried Tomato Pesto and Onions, 151
Spicy Shrimp and Tomatoes, 158–159
Tarragon and Lemon Rubbed Fish, 154–155
Fish Chowder with Red Potatoes and Corn, 61–64, 236
Flaxseed meal
Breakfast Cookies, 286
Spiced Pumpkin Flax Bread, 303–304
Flour, 26
Focaccia, Garlic
Deep-Dish Focaccia Pizza Your Way, 262–263
recipe, 331–332

Food processor, 23, 340
Freezer cooking. *See also* Batch
  cooking
    approaches to, 11, 13
    blog readers on benefits of, 21,
      187, 230
    case for, 4–6
    with children about, 163–164
    complete main dishes for, 9
    economics of, 18–20
    foods that can freeze for, 8–11
    foods you cannot freeze for, 11
    freezer space for, 16–17
    with friends, 291–292
    inventory of meals, 23
    keys to efficient, 20
    meal components for, 9–10
    packaging methods, 14–16
    planning pages, 65, 69–71
    for the road, 12
    saving money with, 18–20
    thawing techniques for, 17–18
    tools for, 22–23
Freezer Cooking Master Plan, 7, 67, 69
Freezer Cooking Planning Worksheet, 71
Freezer cooking plans, 25–26
    Beef Plans, 37–41
    Breakfast Plans, 26–33
    creating your own, 65–67
    Everything Plans, 53–64
    Holiday Baking Plan, 48–51
    Meatless Plans, 33–37
    Poultry and Seafood Plan, 42–44
    Protein Power Cooking Plan, 51–53
Freezers
    chest freezers, 303
    deep freezers, 302–303
    power failure and, 194
    upright freezers, 303
Freezing techniques, 13–14
French Bread Dippers, 159
French Bread Pizza Dippers, 260
Fresh Mango Salsa
    Grilled Caribbean Pork Tenderloin,
      171–172
    recipe, 172
Frittata, Chile and Sausage Oven,
  294–295
Fruit. *See also* individual fruits
    dried, Better Instant Oatmeal
      Packets, 274
    freezing, 353
    Fruit, Nut, and Oatmeal Bowls, 273
    Raspberry Baked Oatmeal, 270
Fruit, Nuts, and Oatmeal Bowls, 117, 273

Garbanzo beans
    Mediterranean Steak Salad, 81–82
    Tahini Vegetable Patties, 204

Garlic Bread, Easy Make-Ahead, 335
Garlic Butter
Chicken-Bacon Subs, 140
recipe, 140
Garlic Butter Chicken Lemon Sauce,
  53–57, 133–134
Garlic Focaccia, 331–332
    Deep-Dish Focaccia Pizza Your
      Way, 262
Garlicky Chicken Noodle Bake, 128, 219
Garlicky Italian Chicken Breasts,
  53–57, 116
    Easy Caesar Salad with, 120–121
    recipe, 121
Garlic-Parmesan Swirl Biscuits, 308,
  320–322
Gingerbread Crinkles, 48–51, 342–343
Ginger-Coconut Scones, 48–51, 308,
  316–317
Gingery Pork and Mushroom Lettuce
  Wraps, 117, 174
Gingery Vegetable Stir-Fry Kit, 117, 202
Glass baking dishes, 15
Gluten-free recipes, 116–117
Goat Cheese, Chicken and Sun-Dried
  Tomato Pizza with, 262–263
Gorgonzola-Herb Butter, Seasoned
  Steak with, 83–84
Graham cracker crumbs
    Caramel-Lime Bars, 349
    Lemon-Ginger Freezer Pie, 365–366
Granola
    Cranberry-Orange Granola, 269–270
    Maple Granola with Oats, Nuts, and
      Seeds, 267–268
    Milk and Honey Granola, 267
Gratin, Ham and Swiss Potato, 178
Gravies. *See* Beefy Mushroom Gravy;
    Easy Chicken (or Turkey) Gravy
Green beans
    Gingery Vegetable Stir-Fry Kit, 202
Green bell peppers. *See also* Bell
  peppers
    Easy Stovetop Ratatouille, 200
    Quick and Easy Pepper Steak, 85
    Savory Sausage and Quinoa
      Bowls, 297
    Sweet and Sour Turkey Meatballs,
      148–149
Green Chile Chicken Taquitos, 116,
  139, 159
Green Chile Rice Casserole, 36–39, 197
Green chiles
    Chicken Enchilada Bake with Green
      Chiles and Jalapeños, 126
    Chile and Sausage Oven Frittata,
      294–295
    Corn and Chile Tamales, 198–199
    Green Chile Chicken Taquitos, 139

Green Chile Rice Casserole, 197
    Hearty Shredded Beef Enchiladas,
      79–80
    Mexican Beef Tortas, 77–78
    Not Your Convenience Store's
      Frozen Burritos, 96
    Oven-Baked Beef Taquitos, 76
    Pepper Jack and Chile Burritos,
      197–198
    Pork Chile Verde with Hominy and
      Carrots, 162–163
    Shepherd's Pie with Green Chile
      Mashed Potatoes, 92
    Six-Layer Nachos, 195–196
    Smoky Multi-Bean Vegetarian Chili,
      247
    Tres Chiles Chili Con Quinoa,
      245–246
Grilled Caribbean Pork Tenderloin,
  61–64, 171–172
Grilled Tilapia or Shrimp Tacos, 51–53,
  116, 155–156
Grocery lists, making, 65
Ground beef
    Boules de Picolat (Catalan Meat-
      balls), 108
    Chihuahua Chili, 244–245
    Chili-Stuffed Sweet Potatoes,
      99–100
    Lawnmower Taco, 100, 102
    Not Your Convenience Store's
      Frozen Burritos, 96
    Outside-In Cheeseburgers, 105
    Quick and Easy Texas Chili, 244
    seasoned, 9
    Shepherd's Pie with Green Chile
      Mashed Potatoes, 92
    Soy-Balsamic Burgers, 102–103
    Swedish Meatballs with Dill, 94
    Sweet and Spicy Joes, 99
    Taco Soup with Hominy, 222
    Vegetable Bolognese, 90
Ground pork
    Boules de Picolat (Catalan Meat-
      balls), 108
    Gingery Pork and Mushroom Let-
      tuce Wraps, 174
    Herbed Pork Sausage Patties,
      182–183
    Shells Stuffed with Pork, Mush-
      rooms, and Onions, 173
    Swedish Meatballs with Dill, 94

Ground turkey
    Spicy Taco Lasagna, 142
    Sweet and Sour Turkey Meatballs,
      148–149
    Taco Soup with Hominy, 222

Tarragon Turkey Burgers with Blue
    Cheese and Chipotle Mayo,
    144–146
Turkey Burgers with Scallions,
    143–144
Turkey Curry, 147

Ham
    Ham and Swiss Potato Gratin, 178
    Savory Ham and Swiss Clafouti,
        293–294
    Zesty Italian Melts, 179
Ham and Swiss Potato Gratin, 61–64,
    178, 219
Hamburger buns
    Outside-In Cheeseburgers, 105
    Pulled Pork Sandwiches with
        Asian Slaw and Tangy Barbecue
        Sauce, 168–170
    Soy-Balsamic Burgers, 102–103
    Sweet and Spicy Joes, 99
    Tarragon Turkey Burgers with Blue
        Cheese and Chipotle Mayo,
        144–146
    Turkey Burgers with Scallions, 143
Hamburger patties, 9
Hamburgers
    Outside-In Cheeseburgers, 105
    prepping for the freezer, 103–104
    Soy-Balsamic Burgers, 102–103
Hearty Beef Stew with Olives, 241
Hearty Shredded Beef Enchiladas,
    79–80, 116, 219
Heavy cream
    Ham and Swiss Potato Gratin, 178
    Raspberry Baked Oatmeal, 270
Heavy whipping cream. See Whipping
    cream
Herb-Butter Chicken Tenders, 61–64,
    116, 122–123
Herb-Crusted Pork Roast, 61–64,
    176–177
Herbed Meatballs, 39–41, 44–47, 159
    Meatball Sub Kit, 88
    recipe, 106
Herbed Meatloaf, 107
Herbed Pork Sausage Patties, 51–53,
    117, 182–183
Herbed Vinaigrette
    Chicken and Wild Rice Bake,
        134–136
    recipe, 136
Hoisin-Glazed Salmon Fillets, 151–152

Hoisin sauce
    Hoisin-Glazed Salmon Fillets, 151–152
    Tangy Asian Barbecue Sauce, 171
Holiday Baking Plan, 48–51
Homemade Chicken Stock, 114

Homemade Cream of Celery Soup for
    Cooking, 68
    Broccoli Gratin with Tarragon and
        Buttered Bread Crumbs, 207
    Cheesy Overnight Casserole with
        Chicken or Turkey, 130
    Chicken Divan with Cheddar
        Crust, 131
    Chicken Enchilada Bake with Green
        Chiles and Jalapeños, 126
    Cozy Cheese and Potato Casse-
        role, 194–195
    Fish Chowder with Red Potatoes
        and Corn, 236
    Ham and Swiss Potato Gratin, 178
    in meal plans, 36–39, 56–64
    recipe, 238
Homemade Croutons, 333
    Easy Caesar Salad with Garlicky
        Italian Grilled Chicken, 120–121
Hominy
    Pork Chile Verde with Hominy and
        Carrots, 162–163
    Taco Soup with Hominy, 222
    Tortilla Soup with Shrimp, 235
Honey Butter, 299
Honey Multigrain Rolls, 330–331

Ice cream
    Easy Chocolate Fudge Sundae
        Cups, 360–361
    Mint Chocolate Fudge Ice Cream
        Pie, 361–362
    Not Your Ice Cream Truck's Ice
        Cream Sandwiches, 358–360
Ice crystals, freezing and, 13–14
Immersion blender, 23
Individual Greek Egg Casseroles,
    26–28, 209
Italian Shredded Beef Filling, 74
Italian-Spiced Cheesewiches, 201

Jalapeño Burn Pizza, 256
Jalapeño pepper
    Black Bean Soup with Jalapeño,
        234
    Burrito Pizza, 254
    Chicken Enchilada Bake with Green
        Chiles and Jalapeños, 126
    Easy Homemade Salsa, 77
    Green Chile Rice Casserole, 197
    Jalapeño Burn Pizza, 256
    Shepherd's Pie with Green Chile
        Mashed Potatoes, 92
    Spicy Southwest Chicken, 118
    Tahini Vegetable Patties, 204
    Tortilla Soup with Shrimp, 235
    White Bean Soup with
        Vegetables, 228

Jam
    Pretzel Berry Cheesecake, 356–357
    Raspberry Jam Cream Scones,
        314–316
    Sweet Almond Toasts, 282–283
Jamie's Spice Mix, 68
    Creamy Cauliflower Soup, 229
    in meal plans, 33–36, 53–57, 61–64
    Quick and Spicy Marinara Sauce, 216
    recipe, 98
    Spinach and Cheese Calzones,
        264–265
    Sweet and Spicy Joes, 99

Kahlúa Brownies, 48–51, 347–348
Kalamata Olives, Tomato Sauce with
    Oregano, 215, 265
Kale
    Chili-Stuffed Sweet Potatoes, 99–100
    Savory Sausage and Quinoa
        Bowls, 297
    Turkey Curry, 147
Kidney beans
    Taco Soup with Hominy, 222
    Tres Chiles Chili Con Quinoa, 245–256

Labeling packaged meals, 16, 17
Lasagna
    Spicy Taco Lasagna, 142
    Vegetable-Beef Lasagna, 91
Lawnmower Taco, 219
Leeks
    Mushroom Barley Soup, 232
    Spring Vegetable Soup, 231
Lemon-and-Honey Flax Waffle mix,
    28–31, 31–33, 278–280, 308
Lemon-Blueberry Scones, 28, 308
Lemon-Ginger Freezer Pie, 365–366
Lemon Whole-Wheat Spritz Cookies,
    48–51, 341–342
Lentils
    Red Lentil Dal, 203
    Smoky Multi-Bean Vegetarian
        Chili, 247
Lettuce
    Barbecue Cheeseburger Pizza, 259
    Burrito Pizza, 254
    Easy Caesar Salad with Garlicky
        Italian Grilled Chicken, 120–121
    Gingery Pork and Mushroom Let-
        tuce Wraps, 174
    Lawnmower Taco, 100, 102
    Mexican Beef Tortas, 77–78
    Outside-In Cheeseburgers, 105
    Soy-Balsamic Burgers, 102–103
    Tarragon Turkey Burgers with Blue
        Cheese and Chipotle Mayo,
        144–146
    Turkey Burgers with Scallions, 143

Life as Mom (blog), 21
Lime
Caramel-Lime Bars, 349
    Coconut-Lime Muffins with Choco-
        late Chips, 310–311
    Easy Homemade Salsa, 77
    Grilled Caribbean Pork Tenderloin,
        171–172
    Lime Chocolate Chip Scones,
        317–318
    Mahi Mahi with Almond-Lime
        Butter, 152
    Salsa Verde Chicken, 124
    Spicy Southwest Chicken, 118
Lime Chocolate Chip Scones, 308,
    317–318

Mahi Mahi with Almond-Lime Butter,
    42–44, 116, 152
Make-ahead and freeze meals. *See*
    Freezer cooking
Make-Ahead Baked Bacon, 57–60,
    177–178
Make-Ahead Drop Biscuits, 308,
    322–323
Make-Ahead Roast Turkey, 141
Malik, Prerna, 203
Manicotti
    Baked Manicotti with Sun-Dried
        Tomatoes and Thyme, 212
    Spinach and Feta Manicotti with
        Lemon and Oregano, 214
Maple Granola with Oats, Nuts, and
    Seeds, 267–268
Maple-Oat Waffles, 277–278, 308
Marinara sauce
    Meatball Sub Kit, 88
    Quick and Spicy Marinara Sauce,
        216
Marinated chicken pieces, 122
Masa harina
    Corn and Chile Tamales, 198–199
    Pork and Chile Tamales, 166–167
Mashed potatoes
    Beef Stew with Eggplant and Car-
        rots with, 242
    Cream Cheese Mashed Potatoes, 86
    Shepherd's Pie with Green Chile
        Mashed Potatoes, 92
Mayonnaise
    chipotle, 144
    not freezing recipes containing, 11
    Yogurt-Dill Dressing, 82
Meal planning, 20
Meat. *See also* Beef; Chicken; Pork
    marinated, 9
    precut for stir-fries, 9–10
Meat and Poultry Plan, 44–47

Meatballs, 9
    Barbecue Sauce for, 106–107
    Boules de Picolat (Catalan Meat-
        balls), 108
    Herbed Meatballs, 106
    Swedish Meatballs with Dill, 94
Meatball Sub Kit, 88
Meatless Plans, 33–37
Meatloaf, 9
    Herbed Meatloaf, 107
Mediterranean Steak Salad, 81–82
Mediterranean-Style Steak, 61–64,
    81–82
Metal baking dishes, 15
Mexican Beef Tortas, 61–64, 77–78
Milk and Honey Granola, 267
Mini cooking sessions, 11, 13
Mint Chocolate Fudge Ice Cream Pie,
    361–362
Minty Melts, Chocolate, 345–346
Mix-and-Match Muffin mix, 26–28,
    48–51
Mix-and-Match Muffins/mix, 308
    Coconut-Lime Muffins with Choco-
        late Chips, 310–311
    Crumb-Topped Zucchini Muffins,
        311–312
    recipe, 309–310
Mixes
    baking.*See* Baking mixes
    taco seasoning.*See* Basic Taco
        Seasoning Mix; Chipotle Taco
        Seasoning Mix
Mocha Hot Fudge Cake, 354–356
Monterey Jack cheese
    Chicken-Bacon Subs, 140
    Chicken Enchilada Bake with Green
        Chiles and Jalapeños, 126
    Chile and Sausage Oven Frittata,
        294–295
    Easy-Peasy Cheesy Pizza kit, 253
    Lawnmower Taco, 100, 102
    Pesto Penne and Cheese, 210
    Quick and Easy Cheese Enchila-
        das, 190
Month, cooking for a, 13
Moo Shu-Style Chicken Wraps, 125
Mozzarella cheese
    Alfredo Mac and Cheese, 210
    Baked Manicotti with Sun-Dried
        Tomatoes and Thyme, 212
    Barbecue Cheeseburger Pizza, 259
    Burrito Pizza, 254
    Chicken-Bacon Subs, 140
    Deep-Dish Focaccia Pizza Your
        Way, 252
    Easy-Peasy Cheesy Pizza kit, 253

French Bread Pizza Dippers, 260
Jalapeño Burn Pizza, 256
Meatball Sub Kit, 88
Pepperoni Calzones, 263–264
Pesto Penne and Cheese, 211
Shells Stuffed with Pork, Mush-
    rooms, and Onions, 173
Spinach and Feta Manicotti with
    Lemon and Oregano, 214
Stuffed Chicken Parmesan, 132
Vegetable-Beef Lasagna, 91
Muffins/muffin mixes, 272
    Coconut-Lime Muffins with Choco-
        late Chips, 310–311
    Crumb-Topped Zucchini Muffins,
        311–312
    Mix-and-Match Muffins, 309–310
Mushroom Barley Soup, 117, 232
Mushrooms
    Beef and Barley Soup with Dill, 233
    Beefy Mushroom Gravy, 87
    Boules de Picolat (Catalan Meat-
        balls), 108
    Chicken and Wild Rice Bake,
        134–136
    Chicken Cacciatore Stew, 239
    Easy Stovetop Ratatouille, 200
    Gingery Pork and Mushroom Let-
        tuce Wraps, 174
    Mushroom Barley Soup, 232
    Savory Sausage and Quinoa
        Bowls, 297
    Sesame Chicken with Snow Peas
        and Mushrooms, 137
    Shells Stuffed with Pork, Mush-
        rooms, and Onions, 173
    Turkey Curry, 147

Nanna's Apple Pie, 363–364
Neufchâtel cheese
    Chipotle Chicken and Onion
        Wraps, 138
    Vegetable-Beef Lasagna, 91
Not Your Convenience Store's Frozen
    Burritos, 44–47, 96, 159
Not Your Ice Cream Truck's Sandwich-
    es, 358–360
Not Your Mother's Chicken Noodle
    Soup, 22, 223
Nuts. *See also* individual types of nuts
    Cranberry-Orange Granola,
        269–270
    Crumb-Topped Zucchini Muffins, 311
    Maple Granola with Oats, Nuts, and
        Seeds, 267–268
    Sun-Dried Tomato Pesto, 218
Nutty Zucchini Bread, 305

Oatmeal
    Better Instant Oatmeal Packets, 274
    Fruit, Nut, and Oatmeal Bowls, 273
    Raspberry Baked, 270
Oatmeal-Chocolate Chip Pancakes/
    Mix, 36–39, 276–277, 308
Oats. See Old-fashioned rolled oats;
    Quick-cooking rolled oats
Oils, 26
Old-fashioned rolled oats
    Cranberry-Oatmeal Cookies, 338
    Cranberry-Orange Granola,
        269–270
    Maple Granola with Oats, Nuts, and
        Seeds, 267–268
    Milk and Honey Granola, 267
    Raspberry Baked Oatmeal, 270
Olives. See also Black olives
    Boules de Picolat (Catalan Meat-
        balls), 108
    Tomato Sauce with Oregano and
        Kalamata Olives, 215
Once a Month Cooking, 6
Open freezing, 15
Orange juice
    Easy Carne Asada, 82–83
    The Red Orange smoothie, 288
Oreo cookie crumbs
    Double Chocolate Magic Bars,
        348–349
Our Favorite Irish Stew, 51–53, 240
Outside-In Cheeseburgers, 44–47,
    105, 116
Oven-Baked Beef Taquitos, 16, 76,
    116, 159

Packaging foods for freezing, 14–16, 66
Pancakes/pancake mixes, 272
    Bulk-Batch Pancakes, 275–276
    Oatmeal-Chocolate Chip Pan-
        cakes, 276–277
Parmesan cheese
    Chicken Divan with Cheddar
        Crust, 131
    Easy Caesar Salad with Garlicky
        Italian Grilled Chicken, 120–121
    Garlicky Chicken Noodle Bake, 128
    Homemade Cream of Celery Soup
        for Cooking, 238
    Parmesan Herb Blend, 255
    Shells Stuffed with Pork, Mush-
        rooms, and Onions, 173
    Sun-Dried Tomato Pesto, 218
Parmesan Herb Blend, 68, 117
    Easy-Peasy Cheesy Pizza kit, 253
    in meal plan, 33–36
    recipe, 255

Pasta dishes
    Alfredo Mac and Cheese, 210
    Baked Manicotti with Sun-Dried
        Tomatoes and Thyme, 212
    Cheesy Overnight Casserole with
        Chicken or Turkey, 130
    Penne with Italian Sausage and
        Tricolor Peppers, 184–185
    Pesto Penne and Cheese, 211
    Red Sauce with Sausage, 183–184
    Shells Stuffed with Pork, Mush-
        rooms, and Onions, 173
    Spinach and Feta Manicotti with
        Lemon and Oregano, 214
Pasta sauce, 10
    Easy Slow Cooker Red Sauce, 217
    Quick and Spicy Marinara
        Sauce, 216
    Red Sauce with Sausage, 183–184
Patty pan squash, 224
Peas
    Best-Ever Chicken Pot Pie, 127
    Mushroom Barley Soup, 232
    Shepherd's Pie with Green Chile
        Mashed Potatoes, 92
Pecans
    Chocolate Zucchini Cake, 351–352
    Cranberry-Orange Granola, 269
    Crumb-Topped Zucchini Muffins,
        311–312
    Fruit, Nut, and Oatmeal Bowls, 273
    Kahlúa Brownies, 347–348
    Maple Granola with Oats, Nuts, and
        Seeds, 267–268
Penne with Italian Sausage and Tricolor
    Peppers, 184–185
Pepper Jack and Chile Burritos, 33–36,
    197–198
Pepper Jack cheese
    Bean and Cheese Nacho Bake, 192
    Corn and Chile Tamales, 198–199
    Creamy Chicken Enchiladas, 129
    Easy Sausage and Pepper Sand-
        wiches, 179–180
    Pepper Jack and Chile Burritos,
        197–198
    Queso Fundido, 180–182
    Spicy Taco Lasagna, 142
    Whole Wheat Black Bean and
        Pepper Wraps, 192–193
Pepperoni Calzones, 263–264
Pesto Penne and Cheese, 211, 219
Pesto Pizza with Shrimp, Feta, and
    Tomatoes, 258
Pesto, Sun-Dried Tomato. See Sun-
    Dried Tomato Pesto
Pie crust. See Versatile Buttery
    Pie Crust

Pies
    Blueberry-Raspberry Croustades,
        362–363
    Coconut Crunch Pie, 366
    Lemon-Ginger Freezer Pie,
        365–366
    Mint Chocolate Fudge Ice Cream
        Pie, 361–362
    Nanna's Apple Pie, 363–364
    Slab Apple Pie, 364–365
Pineapple
    The Blue Pineapple smoothie, 289
    Sweet and Sour Turkey Meatballs,
        148–149
Pinto beans. See also Seasoned Versa-
    tile Pinto Beans
    Chihuahua Chili, 244–245
    Taco Soup with Hominy, 222
    Tres Chiles Chili Con Quinoa,
        245–246
Pizza dough, 10. See also Basic Pizza
    Dough
Pizza kits, 252
Pizzas
    baking and grilling tips, 255
    Barbecue Cheeseburger Pizza, 259
    Burrito Pizza, 254
    Deep-Dish Focaccia Pizza Your
        Way, 262
    Easy-Peasy Cheesy Pizza, 253
    French Bread Pizza Dippers, 260
    Jalapeño Burn Pizza, 256
    Pesto Pizza with Shrimp, Feta, and
        Tomatoes, 258
Pizza sauce, 10, 250
    Tomato and Herb Pizza Sauce, 251
Plastic containers, freezing food in,
    15, 17
Poblano chiles, in Chile Cheese
    Bake, 196
Pork. See also Ground pork; Sausage
    Cranberry Pork Chops, 163–164
    freezing shredded, 10
    Grilled Caribbean Pork Tenderloin,
        171–172
    Herb-Crusted Pork Roast, 176–177
    Pulled Pork Sandwiches with
        Asian Slaw and Tangy Barbecue
        Sauce, 168–170
    Southwest Seasoned Pork
        Chops, 162
    Soy-Ginger Pork Tenderloin,
        167–168
    Versatile Slow-Cooked Carnitas, 161
Pork and Chile Tamales, 117, 166–167
Pork Chile Verde with Hominy and
    Carrots, 117, 162–163

Potatoes
    Best-Ever Chicken Pot Pie, 127
    Black Bean Soup with Jalapeño, 234
    Boules de Picolat (Catalan Meat-
      balls) with, 108
    Cheesy Butternut Squash Soup
      with Herbs, 226
    Cozy Cheese and Potato Casse-
      role, 194–195
    Cream Cheese Mashed Potatoes, 86
    Fish Chowder with Red Potatoes
      and Corn, 236
    freezing white, 11
    Ham and Swiss Potato Gratin, 178
    Our Favorite Irish Stew, 240
    Potatoes Stuffed with Caramelized
      Onions and Dubliner Cheese,
      206–207
    Shepherd's Pie with Green Chile
      Mashed Potatoes, 92
    Spring Vegetable Soup, 231
    Turkey Curry, 147
    White Bean Soup with
      Vegetables, 228
Potatoes Stuffed with Caramelized
    Onions and Dubliner Cheese, 53–57,
    206–207
Potluck-friendly main dishes, 219
Poultry and Seafood Plan, 42–44
Poultry, marinated, 9. See also Chick-
    en; Turkey
Prepackaged spice mixes, 97
Prep Chef List, 66, 67, 70
Prep chef list, 66
Preseasoned taco meat, 97
Pretzel Berry Cheesecake, 48–51,
    356–357
Processed foods, 18
Protein Power Cooking Plan, 51–53
Provençal Shredded Beef Filling, 74
Pulled Pork Sandwiches with Asian
    Slaw and Tangy Barbecue Sauce,
    168–170
Pumpkin
    Spiced Pumpkin Custards, 357–358
    Spiced Pumpkin Flax Bread,
      303–304
Pumpkin seeds
    Breakfast Cookies, 286
    Maple Granola with Oats, Nuts, and
      Seeds, 267–268

Queso Fundido, 57–60, 117, 180–182
Quiche
    Bacon and Spinach Quiche, 293
    Roasted Vegetable Quiche, 208, 219
Quick and Easy Cheese Enchiladas,
    36–39, 117, 219
Quick and Easy Marinara Sauce, 88

Quick and Easy Pepper Steak, 85
Quick and Easy Texas Chili, 51–53,
    117, 244
Quick and Spicy Marinara Sauce,
    61–64, 117, 216
Quick-cooking rolled oats
    Better Instant Oatmeal Packets, 274
    Breakfast Cookies, 286
    Chocolate Chip Banana Bread with
      Oats, 301
    Cranberry-Oatmeal Cookies, 338
    Maple-Oat Waffles, 277–278
    Slab Apple Pie, 364–365
    Spiced Whole-Grain Waffles,
      280–281
    Whole-Grain Cinnamon Rolls,
      324–326
Quick freezing, 15
Quinoa
    Savory Sausage and Quinoa
      Bowls, 297
    Tres Chiles Chili Con Quinoa,
      245–246

Raisins
    Better Instant Oatmeal Packets, 274
    Buttered French Toast Casserole
      with Almonds and Ginger, 284
    Wholesome Energy Bars, 333–334
Raspberries
    Blueberry-Raspberry Croustades,
      362–363
    Fruit, Nut, and Oatmeal Bowls, 273
    Raspberry Baked Oatmeal, 270
Raspberry Baked Oatmeal, 31–33,
    117, 270
Raspberry jam
    Pretzel Berry Cheesecake, 356–357
    Raspberry Jam Cream Scones,
      308, 314–316
Red bell peppers. See also Bell
    peppers
    Easy Stovetop Ratatouille, 200
    Quick and Easy Pepper Steak, 85
    Savory Sausage and Quinoa
      Bowls, 297
    Shepherd's Pie with Green Chile
      Mashed Potatoes, 92
    Sweet and Sour Turkey Meatballs,
      148–149
    Tahini Vegetable Patties, 204
    Vegetable Bolognese, 90
    White Bean Soup with
      Vegetables, 228
Red chile sauce
    Corn and Chile Tamales, 198–199
    Hearty Beef Stew with Olives, 241
    Pork and Chile Tamales, 166–167
Red Lentil Dal, 117, 203

Red Sauce with Sausage, 57–60,
    183–184
Red wine
    Provençal Shredded Beef Filling, 74
    Vegetable Bolognese, 90
Refried beans
    Bean and Cheese Nacho Bake, 192
    Not Your Convenience Store's
      Frozen Burritos, 96
    Pepper Jack and Chile Burritos,
      197–198
    Six-Layer Nachos, 195–196
Rice
    Boules de Picolat (Catalan Meat-
      balls) with, 108
    Chicken and Wild Rice Bake,
      134–136
    Gingery Vegetable Stir-Fry Kit
      with, 202
    Green Chile Rice Casserole, 197
    Quick and Easy Pepper Steak
      with, 85
    Salsa Verde Beef with, 75
    Sweet and Sour Turkey Meatballs
      with, 148
    Turkey Curry with, 147
Ricotta cheese
    Baked Manicotti with Sun-Dried
      Tomatoes and Thyme, 212
    Bean and Cheese Nacho Bake, 192
    Spinach and Cheese Calzones,
      264–265
    Spinach and Feta Manicotti with
      Lemon and Oregano, 214
Roasted chicken carcass, for Home-
    made Chicken Stock, 114
Roasted garlic, peppers, and chiles,
    352–353
Roasted Vegetable Quiche, 208, 219
Roasted Vegetable Soup, 117, 224
Rolls
    Chocolate Butterhorn Rolls, 329–330
    ciabatta, Easy Sausage and Pepper
      Sandwiches, 179–180
    Crystal's Butterhorn, 326–327
    French or sub, Cinnamon French
      Toast Dippers, 281–282
    Honey Multigrain Rolls, 330–331
    Italian, Zesty Italian Melts, 179
    kaiser
      Italian-Spiced Cheese-
        wiches, 201
      Pulled Pork Sandwiches with
        Asian Slaw and tangy Barbe-
        cue Sauce, 168–170
    submarine, for Meatball Sub Kit, 88
    Whole-Grain Cinnamon Rolls,
      324–326
Rump roast, Salsa Verde Beef, 75

Salads
  Easy Caesar Salad with Garlicky
    Italian Grilled Chicken, 120
  Mediterranean Steak, 81
Salami, in Zesty Italian Melts, 179
Salmon fillets
  Fish Chowder with Red Potatoes
    and Corn, 236
  Hoisin-Glazed Salmon Fillets,
    151–152
  Salmon Packets with Sun-Dried
    Tomato Pesto and Onions, 151
  Salmon Packets with Sun-Dried
    Tomato Pesto and Onions,
    116, 151
Salsa. *See also* Easy Homemade Salsa
  Chili-Stuffed Sweet Potatoes,
    99–100
  Easy Carne Asada, 82–83
Salsa verde
  Chile Cheese Bake, 196
  Creamy Chicken Enchiladas, 129
  Pork Chile Verde with Hominy and
    Carrots, 162–163
  Salsa Verde Beef, 75, 116
  Salsa Verde Chicken, 51–53,
    116, 124
Sandwiches. *See also* Burgers
  breakfast, 272, 296
  Chicken-Bacon Subs, 140
  Easy Sausage and Pepper Sand-
    wiches, 179–180
  Italian-Spiced Cheesewiches, 201
  Pulled Pork Sandwiches with
    Asian Slaw and Tangy Barbecue
    Sauce, 168–170
  Zesty Italian Melts, 179
Sauces, 68
Sausage
  Breakfast Sliders, 296
  Chile and Sausage Oven Frittata,
    294–295
  Easy Sausage and Pepper Sand-
    wiches, 179–180
  Penne with Italian Sausage and
    Tricolor Peppers, 184–185
  Queso Fundido, 180–182
  Red Sauce with, 183–184
  Savory Sausage and Quinoa
    Bowls, 297
  Wild Boar Italian Sausage with
    Spicy Tomato Sauce, 186
Savory Ham and Swiss Clafouti, 28,
  219, 293–294
Savory Sausage and Quinoa Bowls,
  117, 297
Scones/scone mixes
  Ginger-Coconut Scones, 316–317
  Lemon-Blueberry Scones, 313–314

Lime Chocolate Chip Scones,
  317–318
prepared ahead of time, 312
Raspberry Jam Cream Scones,
  313–316
Sealing machines, 15–16
Seasonal cooking, 19
Seasonal sales, 353
Seasoned Steak with Gorgonzola-Herb
  Butter, 61–64, 83–84, 116
Seasoned taco meat, 39–41, 116, 159
Seasoned turkey taco meat, 42–44
Seasoned Versatile Pinto Beans,
  117, 189
  Not Your Convenience Store's
    Frozen Burritos, 96
  Pepper Jack and Chile Burritos,
    197–198
Serrano chile, in Turkey Curry, 147
Sesame Chicken with Snow Peas and
  Mushrooms, 137
Shells Stuffed with Pork, Mushrooms,
  and Onions, 172
Shepherd's Pie with Green Chile
  Mashed Potatoes, 92, 219
Sherry
  Chicken Divan with Cheddar
    Crust, 131
  Garlicky Italian Chicken Breasts,
    121–122
  Gingery Pork and Mushroom Let-
    tuce Wraps, 174
  Gingery Vegetable Stir-Fry Kit, 202
  Herb-Butter Chicken Tenders,
    122–123
  Moo Shu-Style Chicken Wraps, 125
  Sesame Chicken with Snow Peas
    and Mushrooms, 137
Shortbread cookies, for Coconut
  Crunch Pie, 366
Shredded Beef Filling. *See* Versatile
  Shredded Beef Filling
Shrimp
  Grilled Tilapia or Shrimp Tacos,
    155–156
  Pesto Pizza with Shrimp, Feta, and
    Tomatoes, 258
  Shrimp and Vegetable Packets,
    156–158
  Shrimp Tacos, 155–156
  Spicy Shrimp and Tomatoes,
    158–159
  Tortilla Soup with Shrimp, 235
Shrimp and Vegetable Packets, 116,
  156–158
Simply Poached Chicken, 53–57, 113
Sirloin steak, Mediterranean-Style
  Steak, 81
Six-Layer Nachos, 117, 195–196

Slab Apple Pie, 364–365
Sloppy Joes, Sweet and Spicy, 99
Slow Cooker Applesauce, 117, 295–296
  Applesauce-Walnut Bread, 300–301
Slow cookers, 222
Smoky Multi-Bean Vegetarian Chili,
  117, 247
Smoothies
  The Blue Maple, 288
  The Blue Pineapple, 289
  The Red Banana, 287
  The Red Orange, 288
Snow peas, Sesame Chicken with
  Snow Peas and Mushrooms, 137
Southwest Seasoned Pork Chops,
  44–47, 117, 162
Soy-Balsamic Burgers, 39–41,
  102–103, 116
Soy-Ginger Pork Tenderloin, 61–64,
  167–168
Spice blends, 68. *See also* Basic Taco
  Seasoning Mix; Chipotle Taco Sea-
  soning Mix; Jamie's Spice Mix
Spiced Pumpkin Custards, 117,
  357–358
Spiced Pumpkin Flax Bread, 31–33,
  303–304
Spiced Whole-Grain Waffles,
  280–281, 308
Spice Whole-Grain Waffle mix, 36–39
Spicy Dijon Chicken, 53–57, 116
  recipe, 119
Spicy Shrimp and Tomatoes, 61–64,
  116, 158–159
Spicy Southwest Chicken, 51–57, 116
  recipe, 118
Spicy Taco Lasagna, 42–47, 142–143
Spinach
  Bacon and Spinach Quiche, 293
  Eggs Florentine Casserole, 292
  Individual Greek Egg Casseroles, 209
  Mediterranean Steak Salad, 81–82
  Spinach and Cheese Calzones,
    264–265
  Spinach and Feta Manicotti with
    Lemon and Oregano, 214
Spinach and Cheese Calzones, 159
Spinach and Feta Manicotti with Lem-
  on and Oregano, 214, 219
Split Pea Soup with Bacon and Thyme,
  117, 227
Spring Vegetable Soup, 117, 231
Spritz Cookies, Lemon Whole-Wheat,
  341–342
Squash. *See also* Zucchini
  Cheesy Butternut Squash Soup
    with Herbs, 226
  Easy Stovetop Ratatouille, 200
  Roasted Vegetable Soup, 224

Stand mixer, 23, 249, 340
Steel-cut oats, Fruit, Nut, and Oatmeal Bowls, 273
Stews
    Beef Stew with Eggplant and Carrots, 242
    Chicken Cacciatore Stew, 239
    Easy Stovetop Ratatouille, 200
    Hearty Beef Stew with Olives, 241
    Our Favorite Irish Stew, 240
Stockpots, 22
Strawberries
    Breakfast Smoothies, 287
    The Red Banana smoothie, 287
    The Red Orange smoothie, 288
Stuffed chicken breasts, 133
Stuffed Chicken Parmesan, 132
Sugar and Spice Cookies, 48–51
Sundae Cups, Easy Chocolate Fudge, 360–361
Sun-dried tomatoes
    Baked Manicotti with Sun-Dried Tomatoes and Thyme, 212
    Penne with Italian Sausage and Tricolor Peppers, 184–185
    Pesto Penne and Cheese, 211
    Sun-Dried Tomato Pesto, 218
Sun-Dried Tomato Pesto, 117
    Chicken and Sun-Dried Tomato Pizza with Goat Cheese, 262–263
    in meal plan, 33–36
    recipe, 218
    Salmon Packets with Sun-Dried Tomato Pesto and Onions, 151
Sunflower seeds
    Breakfast Cookies, 286
    Maple Granola with Oats, Nuts, and Seeds, 267–268
    Wholesome Energy Bars, 333–334
Super-Simple Guacamole
    Burrito Pizza, 254
    Green Chile Chicken Taquitos, 139
    Oven-Baked Beef Taquitos, 76
    recipe, 77
    Salsa Verde Beef, 75
    Six-Layer Nachos, 195–196
Swedish Meatballs with Dill, 53–57, 94, 159
Sweet Almond Toasts, 282–283
Sweet and Sour Turkey Meatballs, 116, 148–149, 219
Sweet and Spicy Joes, 53–57, 159, 219
Sweet Potatoes, Chili-Stuffed, 99–100
Swiss cheese
    Bacon and Spinach Quiche, 293
    Eggs Florentine Casserole, 292
    Ham and Swiss Potato Gratin, 178
    Savory Ham and Swiss Clafouti, 293–294

Taco kits, 97
Taco seasoning mixes. See Basic Taco Seasoning Mix; Chipotle Taco Seasoning Mix
Tacos, Grilled Tilapia or Shrimp, 155–156
Taco Soup with Hominy, 117
Tahini Vegetable Patties, 36–39, 204
Tamales, 9
    Corn and Chile Tamales, 198–199
    Pork and Chile Tamales, 166–167
Tandoori Chicken, 22, 42–44, 116
    recipe, 119–120
Tangy Asian Barbecue Sauce
    Pulled Pork Sandwiches with Asian Slaw and Tangy Barbecue Sauce, 168–170
    recipe, 171
Taquitos, 9
    Green Chile Chicken Taquitos, 139
    Oven-Baked Beef Taquitos, 76
Tarragon and Lemon Rubbed Fish, 51–57, 154–155
Tarragon Turkey Burgers with Blue Cheese and Chipotle Mayo, 144–146
Telera rolls, 77, 78
Teriyaki Chicken Skewers, 61–64, 116, 123–124
Thawing foods
    foods for quick, 159
    techniques, 17–18
The Blue Pineapple, 289
The Red Orange, 288
Tilapia or Shrimp Tacos, 155–156
Toffee bits, Chocolate-Toffee Cookies, 344–345
Tomato and Herb Pizza Sauce
    Deep-Dish Focaccia Pizza Your Way, 262
    Easy-Peasy Cheesy Pizza kit, 253
    French Bread Pizza Dippers, 260
    in menu plan, 33–36
    recipe, 251
Tomatoes
    Barbecue Cheeseburger Pizza, 259
    Burrito Pizza, 254
    canned crushed
        Boules de Picolat (Catalan Meatballs), 108
        Easy Slow Cooker Red Sauce, 217
        Quick and Spicy Marinara Sauce, 216
        Taco Soup with Hominy, 222
    canned diced
        Boules de Picolat (Catalan Meatballs), 108
        Chicken Cacciatore Stew, 239
        Easy Stovetop Ratatouille, 200

Red Lentil Dal, 203
Spicy Shrimp and Tomatoes, 158–159
Tomato and Herb Pizza Sauce, 251
Tomato Sauce with Oregano and Kalamata Olives, 215
Tortilla Soup with Shrimp, 235
Tres Chiles Chili Con Quinoa, 245–246
Turkey Curry, 147
Vegetable Bolognese, 90
Easy Homemade Salsa, 77
Mediterranean Steak Salad, 81–82
Outside-In Cheeseburgers, 105
Pesto Pizza with Shrimp, Feta, and Tomatoes, 258
Roasted Vegetable Soup, 224
Spicy Southwest Chicken, 118
Tarragon Turkey Burgers with Blue Cheese and Chipotle Mayo, 144–146
Turkey Burgers with Scallions, 143
Wild Boar Italian Sausage with Spicy Tomato Sauce, 186
Tomato paste
    Penne with Italian Sausage and Tricolor Peppers, 184–185
    Spicy Shrimp and Tomatoes, 158–159
    Tomato and Herb Pizza Sauce, 251
Tomato sauce
    Bean and Cheese Nacho Bake, 192
    Chicken Cacciatore Stew, 239
    Chihuahua Chili, 244–245
    Italian-Spiced Cheesewiches, 201
    Penne with Italian Sausage and Tricolor Peppers, 184–185
    Quick and Easy Texas Chili, 244
    Smoky Multi-Bean Vegetarian Chili, 247
    Spicy Shrimp and Tomatoes, 158–159
    Tangy Asian Barbecue Sauce, 171
    Tomato Sauce with Oregano and Kalamata Olives, 215
    Tres Chiles Chili Con Quinoa, 245–246
    Turkey Curry, 147
    Vegetable Bolognese, 90
    Wild Boar Italian Sausage with Spicy Tomato Sauce, 186
Tomato Sauce with Oregano and Kalamata Olives, 33–36, 117
    recipe, 215
    Spinach and Feta Manicotti with Lemon and Oregano, 214
Tortas, Mexican Beef, 77–78

Tortilla chips
    Bean and Cheese Nacho Bake, 192
    Lawnmower Taco, 100, 102
    Six-Layer Nachos, 195–196
    Tortilla Soup with Shrimp, 235
Tortillas
    corn
        Chicken Enchilada Bake with Green Chiles and Jalapeños, 126
        Chile Cheese Bake, 196
        Creamy Chicken Enchiladas, 129
        Easy Carne Asada, 82–83
        Green Chile Chicken Taquitos, 139
        Grilled Tilapia or Shrimp Tacos, 155–156
        Hearty Shredded Beef Enchiladas, 79–80
        Oven-Baked Beef Taquitos with, 76
        Queso Fundido, 180–182
        Quick and Easy Cheese Enchiladas, 190
    flour
        Chipotle Chicken and Onion Wraps, 138
        Moo Shu-Style Chicken Wraps, 125
        Not Your Convenience Store's Frozen Burritos, 96
        Pepper Jack and Chile Burritos, 197–198
        Salsa Verde Beef with, 75
    Whole Wheat Black Bean and Pepper Wraps, 192–193
Tortilla Soup with Shrimp, 61–64, 235
Tres Chiles Chili Con Quinoa, 117, 219, 245–246
Tripling recipes, 11
Tri-tip roast
    Chipotle-Rubbed Tri-Tip, 80
    Seasoned Steak with Gorgonzola-Herb Butter, 83–84
Turkey. *See also* Ground turkey
    Make-Ahead Roast Turkey, 141
    used in place of chicken, 146
Turkey Burgers with Scallions, 42–44
Turkey Curry, 116, 147
Turkey gravy, 115
TV dinners, homemade, 352

Upright freezers, 303

Vanilla Cranberry Bread, 48–51, 307
Vegetable-Beef Lasagna, 91, 219

Vegetable Bolognese
    in meal plan, 53–57
    as naturally gluten-free, 116
    recipe, 90
    Vegetable-Beef Lasagna, 91
Vegetables, freezing, 353. *See also* individual vegetables
Versatile Buttery Pie Crust
    Bacon and Spinach Quiche, 293
    Best-Ever Chicken Pot Pie, 127
    Blueberry-Raspberry Croustades, 362–363
    Nanna's Apple Pie, 363–364
    recipe, 368
Versatile Chicken from the Slow Cooker
    bones from, for Homemade Chicken Stock, 114
    recipe, 112
Versatile Shredded Beef Filling, 73–74, 76, 116
Versatile Slow-Cooked Carnitas, 117
    Pork and Chile Tamales, 166–167
    recipe, 161

Waffles/waffle mixes, 272
    Lemon-and-Honey Flax Waffle mix, 278–280
    Maple-Oat Waffles, 277–278
    Spiced Whole-Grain Waffles, 280–281
Walnuts
    Applesauce-Walnut Bread, 300–301
    Cocoa Brownies, 346–347
    Cranberry-Orange Granola, 269–270
    Crumb-Topped Zucchini Muffins, 311–312
    Maple Granola with Oats, Nuts, and Seeds, 267–268
    Nanna's Apple Pie, 363–364
    Sun-Dried Tomato Pesto, 218
    White Chocolate-Walnut Jumbles, 339
Water chestnuts
    Asian Slaw, 170
    Gingery Vegetable Stir-Fry Kit, 202
Whipping cream
    Coconut Crunch Pie, 366
    Lemon-Ginger Freezer Pie, 365–366
    Mint Chocolate Fudge Ice Cream Pie, 361–362
    Pretzel Berry Cheesecake, 356–357
    Spiced Pumpkin Custard, 357–358
    Spiced Pumpkin Custards, 357–358

White Bean Soup with Vegetables, 117, 228
White Chocolate-Walnut Jumbles, 48–51, 339
White wine
    Beef and Barley Soup with Dill, 233
    Garlicky Italian Chicken Breasts, 121–122
    Tomato Sauce with Oregano and Kalamata Olives, 215
Whole-Grain Cinnamon Rolls, 28, 48–51, 324–326
Wholesome Energy Bars, 31–33, 333–334
Whole Wheat Black Bean and Pepper Wraps, 192–193
Whole-wheat pastry flour, 26
Wild Rice Bake, Chicken and, 134–136

Yellow squash
    Easy Stovetop Ratatouille, 200
    Roasted Vegetable Soup, 224
Yogurt
    The Blue Maple smoothie, 288
    The Blue Pineapple smoothie, 289
    Chocolate-Banana Marble Cake, 350–351
    Coconut-Lime Muffins with Chocolate Chips, 310–311
    Crumb-Topped Zucchini Muffins, 311–312
    Green Chile Rice Casserole, 197–198
    Mix-and-Match Muffins, 309
    Raspberry Baked Oatmeal, 270
    Tahini Vegetable Patties, 204
    Tandoori Chicken, 119–120
    Turkey Curry, 147
    Vanilla Cranberry Bread, 307
Yogurt-Dill Dressing, 82
    Grilled Tilapia or Shrimp Tacos, 155–156

Zesty Italian Melts, 179
Zip-top freezer bags, 14–15, 17
Zucchini
    Cheddar Soup with Zucchini, Broccoli, and Carrots, 221
    Chocolate Zucchini Cake, 351–352
    Coconut-Lime Muffins with Chocolate Chips, 311–312
    Easy Stovetop Ratatouille, 200
    Nutty Zucchini Bread, 305
    Roasted Vegetable Quiche, 208
    Tahini Vegetable Patties, 204
    Vegetable Bolognese, 90

To my husband, Bryan, who has truly been my partner in all things. From kids to cookbooks (and everything in between), life has been such a joy to share with you.

Inspiring | Educating | Creating | Entertaining

Brimming with creative inspiration, how-to projects, and useful information to enrich your everyday life, Quarto Knows is a favorite destination for those pursuing their interests and passions. Visit our site and dig deeper with our books into your area of interest: Quarto Creates, Quarto Cooks, Quarto Homes, Quarto Lives, Quarto Drives, Quarto Explores, Quarto Gifts, or Quarto Kids.

© 2018 Quarto Publishing Group USA Inc.
Text © 2012, 2018 Jessica Getskow Fisher

First Published in 2017 by The Harvard Common Press, an imprint of The Quarto Group, 100 Cummings Center, Suite 265-D, Beverly, MA 01915, USA.
T (978) 282-9590 F (978) 283-2742 QuartoKnows.com

The Harvard Common Press titles are also available at discount for retail, wholesale, promotional, and bulk purchase. For details, contact the Special Sales Manager by email at specialsales@quarto.com or by mail at The Quarto Group, Attn: Special Sales Manager, 401 Second Avenue North, Suite 310, Minneapolis, MN 55401, USA.

22 21 20 19 18   2 3 4 5

Digital edition published 2018

ISBN: 978-1-55832-890-7

Library of Congress Cataloging-in-Publication Data available

Design and Page Layout: Megan Jones Design
Photography: Maria Siriano
Author photo by Sharon Leppellere

Printed in China